# ARMS

### AND THE

# STATE

A VOLUME IN THE *Twentieth Century Fund's* PROJECT ON *Civil-Military Relations;* HAROLD STEIN, RESEARCH DIRECTOR

# ARMS
## AND THE
# STATE

## CIVIL-MILITARY ELEMENTS IN
## NATIONAL POLICY

BY WALTER MILLIS

WITH HARVEY C. MANSFIELD AND HAROLD STEIN

THE TWENTIETH CENTURY FUND

NEW YORK 1958

# FOREWORD

●●●●●●●●●●●●●●●●●●●●●●●●●●●●●●●●●●●●●●●●●●●●●●●●●●●●●●●●●●●●●●●●●●●●●●●●●●●●●●●●●●●●●●●●●●●●●●●●●●

$S$ince its founding in 1919 the main emphasis of the Twentieth Century Fund has been on economic research. In 1951, however, the Trustees began exploring the possibilities of using other disciplines in their search for the keys to major contemporary problems. The area then chosen for investigation was civil-military relations. The disciplines were to be political science and history, with use in this particular instance of the technique of the case study.

The broad proposal was given extended consideration by a committee of the Trustees and by two advisory committees. In 1953 Harold Stein was appointed Research Director for the project, with the responsibility of working out its precise scope and defining the methods of research.

A two-part scheme for the project was developed. One part of the work was to consist of detailed case studies, following the pattern developed by Mr. Stein as Staff Director of the Inter-University Case Program. The interplay of military, diplomatic and economic factors in the shaping of national decisions — as well as the interrelationships of civilian and military personnel — were to be explored. This part of the work has gone forward, with a dozen case studies having been undertaken on the events of the quarter-century since 1930 where research was feasible and where it seemed likely that various aspects of civil-military relations could be illuminated. These case studies will in due time be published.

The present volume represents a second part of the work. It consists of a historical survey of United States civil-military relations in the period beginning with 1930 but with special emphasis on the decade between 1945 and 1955. Mr. Stein had originally intended to write the greater part of this volume, but a serious illness in 1955

# Foreword

resulted in changes in authorship as well as in focus. What began largely as a study of the relations of civilian officials with officers of the armed services has turned primarily into a consideration of the confluence of civil and military factors in the development and application of national policy. Particularly in Part II emphasis has been placed on large substantive issues of national policy in which the military element has been of critical importance.

The enormous impact of atomic and hydrogen weapons, growing steadily more evident since the study was planned, has altered and blurred many of the older issues of civil-military relations. This book is an effort to sketch the new synthesis and to indicate the form of inner balance which a democracy must attain in the light of unprecedented conditions.

AUGUST HECKSCHER, *Director*
*The Twentieth Century Fund*

41 East 70th Street, New York
August 1958

# *ACKNOWLEDGMENTS*

•••••••••••••••••••••••••••••••••••••••••••••••••••••••••••••••••••••••••••••••••••••••••••••

When illness interrupted my work on this project in 1955 I was fortunate in being able to count on the assistance of my collaborator, Harvey C. Mansfield, who agreed to carry a larger share of the burden than he had expected to undertake. Walter Millis subsequently consented to join the work, drawing upon his wide knowledge of the field to cover that portion of the historical survey which I had originally planned to write. My own responsibility became chiefly an editorial one, and my name appears on the title page as co-author only because Mr. Mansfield made use of certain preliminary materials which I had written before the onset of illness.

Inevitably, and not undesirably, the mode of presentation used by the two authors is quite different from what mine would have been, and each differs from the other. The authors and the editor are also not in total concord in judgments and emphases, though these differences are minor, partly because all three share many of the same ideas and attitudes, and partly because both authors have been exceedingly tolerant of my editorial pleadings. Some differences — both technical and substantive — remain, but there is, I think, a significant unity underlying the two parts of this volume. I have tried to indicate what this is in the Introduction.

As in most highly condensed works dealing with the contemporary world, the authors of this one have relied primarily on published government documents, on newspapers, on biographies and memoirs, to some extent (especially in Part I) on scholarly studies, on interviews, and on discerning criticisms. References to this indebtedness are included in the Notes on Sources.

The authors have also made free use of the case studies prepared or in preparation for the study. Those that were particularly useful

# Acknowledgments

for their purposes are cited in the Notes on Sources. (Titles of the case studies are tentative.) But all the case study authors have made contributions and they will, of course, be given their due credit when the cases are published. Mention must, however, be made here of the devoted research assistance rendered by Dr. Francis Loewenheim.

HAROLD STEIN

# *CONTENTS*

Introduction BY HAROLD STEIN

## Part One
BY HARVEY C. MANSFIELD WITH HAROLD STEIN

1   The Pre-war Decade: Collapse and Reversal
of a Policy   13

2   The War: Domestic Organization and the Military
Impact at Home   61

3   The War: Looking Abroad   91

## Part Two BY WALTER MILLIS

4   Reorganization   139

5   Cold War   187

6   New Men and New Methods   231

7   Truman and MacArthur   259

8   The Global Problem   333

9   The New Look   375

NOTES ON SOURCES   415

INDEX   421

# Introduction BY HAROLD STEIN

# INTRODUCTION

SANTAYANA'S FAMOUS PHRASE "Those who cannot remember the past are condemned to repeat it" is sound advice for statesmen concerned with arms and the state — those who must constantly endeavor to maintain balance in those mysterious scales that weigh the imponderable civil-military elements in national policy. The largest figure in the American quarter-century after 1930 is Roosevelt, who never forgot the past. His last years were almost dominated by his vivid memories of Wilson's travail. The spectacular success with which he and Truman and Eisenhower secured and maintained Congressional and wide public acceptance of the United Nations and of our membership therein is eloquent testimony to the practical utility of Santayana's warning.

Yet remembrance of the past is not enough. Keynes, writing in 1919, spoke of the dreadful unconsciousness in England and America of the fact that an era had ended and that the world faced "the fearful convulsions of a dying civilization." In such an environment, the Congress of Vienna could not serve as the model for the Peace Conference of 1919. So too today.

The Second World War showed, for example, that the English Channel no longer was an inviolable shield, for the Channel is no one-way street. Even though the severe but limited danger of submarine attack on an island's lifelines was once again defeated, survival under aerial bombardment executed with old-fashioned planes using old-fashioned bombs was barely achieved — and even old-fashioned explosives became a deadlier menace with the arrival of the V-2's.

Disturbing as these events were, greatly though they presaged the evanescence of America's effective physical isolation, we might per-

3

haps have re-entered the cocoon of unconsciousness of the world about us (as we did after 1918) had it not been for two successive developments: Hiroshima and Nagasaki, for one; and, for the other, the stark emergence of the Soviet Union not only as a disliked and even hated nation, but clearly also as a great world power. Our painful awareness and acceptance of our active global involvement was coincident with our realization of the fact that the United States is itself a great world power, and for the immediate future, a great power in a world in which only one other nation also possesses great power.

Here is a fate for the United States never clearly foreseen. Some foreshadowings can be found in the writings of Henry Adams and others. Yet the combination of a shrunken globe and new explosives of enormous destructive power presents problems of national policy in which the changes in magnitude are so great that the difference between the world in which we actually live, and our images of it, and the world of 1930, or of 1941, or even of 1945 is too impressive to be judged in quantitative terms. "Disengagement" may be a meaningful term in the Middle East, perhaps by a narrow definition of its meaning, in Europe — but hardly for the Soviet Union and the United States. Five thousand, ten thousand miles of neutral zones do not avert the danger of sudden attack, by design or even by accident, and the resultant possibility of fateful war. Whether major atomic war would indeed be "total war" for mankind is a matter for speculation, but that it would be vastly destructive seems obvious.

The foregoing observations, assuming they are sound as well as currently widely accepted, imply necessarily a dramatic change in ends and means in the making of national policy. No one has seriously questioned the wisdom and democratic propriety of Churchill's deliberate secretiveness in regard to the invention and construction of tanks in the First World War, nor, for that matter, of Hitler's endorsement of the V-2 rocket program in the Second. These were wartime decisions, comparable in kind, though not in degree, to the decision to drop the A-bomb at Hiroshima. The bomb had a far more appalling and decisive immediate effect; but all three altered, though in strikingly varying degrees, the future strategies of nations, and all three were the result of executive actions in wartime secrecy. Yet Truman's later decision — inevitable, I think — to proceed with the H-bomb in circumstances of cold war, not hot, roused again all the questionings that had been foreclosed, but not silenced, by the *fait accompli* at Hiroshima. Facing the hard dilemmas of secrecy in a democracy, he sought as best he could for public approval of this decision after it was made. But his critics were not content to accept it either as a mere technical matter, of interest and concern only to the scientists and the military, or as a question for the President alone to decide. The hard dilemmas remain to plague us.

This dramatic and profound shift in the nature of man's world presents painful problems for statesmen. Yet the ivory tower is also affected. Both political scientists and historians find difficulties in applying their arts in unaltered fashion to two different eras. Arms are no longer the sole concern of the warriors: the whole state is involved, and not merely in the diversion of limited resources to military needs. The demarcation line between "civil" and "military" in assessing the elements of national policy has become blurred. Counter-intelligence, formerly a technical task of the military, now spreads throughout government and through much of society. The adoption of elaborate loyalty-security programs has been popularly applauded, insisted on by Congress, actively pursued by successive chiefs of state: it has never been a response to the demands of the "military." Do we live in a garrison state, as some say? If we do, it is not a garrison administered by the soldiers.

The blurring of the demarcation line is most apparent at the upper levels of government, but even there the line, however blurred, still exists. At the bottom it is much more clear and sharp. A young man entering military service finds himself in a new world, an enclave, a sizable microcosm with its own societal rules and customs. It is American, but it is America with a difference. The new entrant's acceptance of this new world and self-identification with it may be great or small, permanent or merely passing. The degree and permanence of acceptance and identification will inevitably be far greater for the man who plans a military career than for the draftee, the temporary enlistee, the national guardsman or the reserve officer. And the sense of belonging to a world unlike other worlds is necessarily most striking and significant in the combat forces, where ultimate objectives and needs impose a larger reliance on command than is appropriate or customary in American civilian hierarchies, governmental and private. (Hierarchy is no specialty of the military: all organizations in modern society have a formal hierarchical structure.) Finally, within the combat forces, the officers, notably the career officers, constitute what might be described as an enclave within an enclave; here a pride in special gratifications and special responsibilities is very deep and very conscious.

Yet the identifiable impact of military specialization is not felt exclusively by the career officers immediately concerned with combat forces and actual or potential combat missions on the air, at sea, on the land. The impact is felt throughout the officer corps. Military officers form ". . . a conscious and coherent group operating within but largely apart from the larger governmental structure. Such a group . . . has its own distinctive entrance and tenure procedures, its own salary system, its own traditions and group attitudes, its own sensitivity and code of privacy. It constitutes as it were a guild." These words were written some years ago and were intended to be descriptive of the Foreign Service, yet clearly they apply to the Army, to the Navy and to the Air Force, and, with less coherence, to the services as a whole. What I, the author of the remarks, went on to say still seems valid:

> Other guilds, with common traditions, interests and codes of conduct, exist elsewhere in the government, the armed services constituting merely the largest and most widely recognized example. Wherever guilds exist, they and their titular — or real — superiors must find an accommodation that takes into account guild loyalties and convictions, along with broader interests and the need for political responsiveness in the widest sense.

The great changes in the world and in our own government that have been crystallizing in the last decade have not led to the disappearance of the governmental guilds, nor of that great semi-guild group, the career civil service, nor of the various titular and real superiors. Rather there has been a vast enhancement in the number and importance of the problems that cannot be decided in isolation, that must be dealt with jointly by men whose habits of work, whose traditional orders of priority, are quite different. To seat around a conference table a group, for example, that includes officers of the three services, of the Foreign Service, a scientist or two, a budget specialist, two or three assistant secretaries whose careers have been shaped in the world of big business, and maybe a congressman and senator as well, is no great oddity today: between the wars it was so rare as to be almost unthinkable.

What has led to this kind of activity is the wide acceptance of the concept that accelerated technological progress, the stirring of new forces in the great underdeveloped areas, the emergence of new modes of diplomacy (for better or for worse — irresistibly, none the less) piled on top of the startling shift in the world balance of power and the arrival of the atomic and missile age require a pooling of our human resources. Thus, to use the academic phrase, our government today deals with its great issues by inter-disciplinary means.

This is new, but not entirely new. Our president under the ineluctable responsibilities imposed by the Constitution itself, has always had what might be described as inseparable inter-disciplinary roles: commander in chief, sole organ of foreign policy, adviser on the state of the union — to name but three of many. The post-war development consists of a shift from merely inter-departmental to inter-disciplinary teamwork, to use the term once more. This development has proceeded with an almost infinite series of major problems, has become institutionalized — and normal. The doctrine of completed staff work, as the military call it, has been so sanctified that at times it has even been touted in effect as a substitute for political decision. Major crises like Korea and Dienbienphu are grim illustrations of the inherent necessity of decision by those ultimately responsible rather than by the experts and specialists.

Nevertheless, the fact that there are visible limits on the values of governmental expertise and technology is no sign that this professional interpenetration of bureaucrats in and out of uniform is not a great gain. Another, therefore, of the major developments of the post-war period is the dramatic improvement in communications between the civilian officers in the State Department and the officers, military, and civilian too, in the Department of Defense. This is but one crucially important example; parallel developments have proceeded between the men in the Pentagon (and their associates in the field, at home and abroad) and scientists; there have been stirrings of mutual confidence and understanding between the military and labor leaders and even leaders of groups like the NAACP — pariahs in the days of officially segregated forces. Finally, the nexus of interrelationships with business, especially big business, and with Congress, always close and always complex, has been intensified in both depth and breadth so that the traditional separations of powers and responsibilities between the branches of the government and between the public and private sectors of our society are far less sharp today than they used to be. The advantages are real, but the difficulties and dangers are very real too, as is made apparent by the painful island of secrecy that surrounds the members of the Joint Committee on Atomic Energy, and the exceedingly broad extension of the personnel security program in industry.

These observations, however sketchy, should make clear the diversity of problems of presentation that political scientists and historians must face when they attempt to convey in a single volume some sense of the present dimensions and directions of the old-new problems of arms and the state. The perspectives, the forms of analysis that seemed so appropriate for the days of Stimson as Secretary of State, even as Secretary of War for the second time, seem old-fashioned today. Yet Santayana's warning still survives.

There was no absolute break between the thirties and early forties and our current post-war years. Naturally the decade and a half that began in 1930 had roots in the past, but the signs and portents of the new era were more apparent and came far closer to practical expression in the fifteen years before VJ-Day than in any earlier epoch. The linking of the years between the Far Eastern crisis and VJ-Day with the presidencies of Truman and Eisenhower thus has its own justification. Yet an attempt to fit both periods into the same model would have more artistic than intellectual value.

What follows in this volume is therefore, in Part I, essentially an extensive introductory or background piece, while the main subject of inquiry — arms and the state in the atomic age — is treated in Part II. Part I makes available to the reader a partly historical, partly analytical account, couched in conventional categorical terms, which reveals in highly summarized form the developments and experiences of the fifteen years that seem to have laid the main groundwork for what has followed. The approach is pragmatic; in large part the perspective is that of the administrative analyst. In Part II the sights are raised, and the sense of immediacy and urgency is ever present. An understanding of the problems and solutions of Roosevelt, Stimson, Knox, and the Joint Chiefs of 1942 is helpful in understanding the problems and solutions of Truman and Forrestal, of Eisenhower and Wilson and their respective Joint Chiefs; for Truman and Eisenhower have faced many of the same kinds of issues that Roosevelt could not avoid. But Truman and Eisenhower, and all of us alive today, also live with the new problems of that terrifying new world we never made, or at least never meant to make.

# Part One

BY HARVEY C. MANSFIELD WITH HAROLD STEIN

# The Pre-war Decade:

## COLLAPSE AND REVERSAL

## OF A POLICY

Until the unlikely day when social scientists so far reduce human behavior to laws as to eliminate from practical calculation the effects of chance and purpose, the data of history — and analogies and inferences based on them — will supply the main guides to policy choices. The data must ordinarily be drawn, for want of better, from the unordered redundancy of known events: at his peril the historian may now and then glance speculatively at the greater obscurities of the unrecorded, especially if they are recent; or at hypothetical might-have-beens. He has some advantages of hindsight, to compensate for its risks, and in this — in the perspective of a later day — he generally finds his sense of relevance, his criteria of deliberate exclusion. He looks for recurrent problems and for emergent solutions that promise to add to the accumulated stock of later wisdom. It is as arbitrary to select a time period as it is to ignore most happenings within a given space, for all events have antecedents as well as repercussions. But choice is the price of action, even in writing.

The purpose in this and the next two chapters, then, is to array some events of the 1930's and 1940's, in order to shed light on a major governmental concern of our time: the impingement and interaction of civilian and military elements and considerations in American policy-making. In somewhat different form, and in more detail, the same concern will be reviewed in the light of the events of the post-war decade, in the succeeding chapters.

The dogmas of civil-military relations inherited from earlier times and focussing on the doctrine of civilian control are today not so much belied in practice — no one questions the President's prerogatives of command, or the power of Congress to declare war or raise armies, or the continuing need for citizen-soldiers — as they are beside the points on which hard thinking needs to be done. The realities have changed abruptly, and are changing; their proper future course, in the national interest, is deeply perplexing. For civil-military relations, though they evoke traditional symbols for traditional values, are nothing intrinsic — rather, they are an aspect of the interplay of a set of ideas and attitudes, institutions and processes, interests and individuals; and so necessarily a function of the changing times. No more ambitious conceptual framework than this informs the array that follows; freedom and strength, with all their ambiguities and latent conflicts, are still the nation's goals.

In retrospect time marks the grand divisions. For present purposes a watershed of sorts divides the 1930's from the years before: in 1931 the Japanese turned to force to improve their position in Manchuria, while in Europe the precarious structure of reparations and war debts collapsed; and allied creditors conceded to Von Papen what they had refused to Bruening and Stresemann. With these events and the deepening depression, the settlement of World War I, and the hopes attending it, began to crumble openly: American policy confronted new needs. The culmination of the policy that emerged — in the events from Munich to Pearl Harbor — sets off the 1930's still more sharply from the years of war and reconstruction. Even the 1940's look remote, now that almost any country may be a potential brandisher of nuclear power. Yet the evolving policy and machinery in all these years looked ahead, some of it shaping adjustments in the durable institutions of government, some of it anticipating new needs more clearly seen, if still not satisfied, today.

## THE DOMINATION OF IDEAS, 1931-37

Some historical developments are dominated by men; others are controlled by ideas which impose a constrictive framework of beliefs on the decisions of policy-makers. At home in the 1930's, President Roosevelt broke through just such a paralyzing set of economic beliefs, and vigorously directed the course of domestic policy. But not so in foreign affairs. Here, from the outbreak of the Far Eastern crisis in 1931 to the end of 1937, American policy was dominated — willingly in Hoover's case, and willingly too, until the latter part of the period, in Roosevelt's, except that he never much relished having his hands tied — by certain ideas widely disseminated and accepted throughout the United States. Norman Davis, chairman of the American delegation, put these in a speech on May 29, 1934 to the General Disarmament Conference at Geneva:

> We are prepared to cooperate in every practicable way in efforts to secure a general disarmament agreement and thus to help promote the general peace and progress of the world. We are furthermore willing, in connection with a general disarmament convention, to negotiate a universal pact of non-aggression and to join with other nations in conferring on international problems growing out of any treaties to which we are a party. The United States will not, however, participate in European political negotiations and settlements and will not make any commitment whatever to use its armed forces for the settlement of any dispute anywhere. In effect, the policy of the United States is to keep out of war, but to help in every possible way to discourage war.

Three ideas stand out here: trust that limitation of armaments would help prevent war; faith in the renunciation of war by treaty; rejection of American participation in collective-security arrangements. To these might be added the belief that cut-throat nationalist trade policies were a major source of war. Hull derived this from Adam Smith and thought it might be abated by the sense of interdependence that would result from universal adoption of his reciprocal trade agreements approach. The Navy, accepting Mahan's neo-mercantilist formulation of the doctrine, also thought war stemmed from economic causes, but drew a very different moral: that England, as our principal trade rival, was therefore our likeliest enemy in another war. On that supposition, our military planners, even after World War I, accordingly spent much effort in planning to meet a RED (as the code designated the English) attack. Presumably both were innocent of the Marxian doctrine that the roots of war are economic. By that time, professional historians were deep in study and controversy over the actual causes of World War I; and the main point to note here is that there seems to have been no enlightened discussion, between the principal civil and military departments, of the likely causes of another war, to inform the military planners.

## ISOLATION

Along with the concern about trade policies went a revulsion against traffic in arms and war matériel as an evil *per se;* and the fervid conviction, which united Hoover and the midwest Progressives, that we could isolate ourselves from war by refusing to become involved. There were ardent advocates of "collective security," to be sure — Walter Lippmann and the *Nation* among them, as well as many more active supporters of the League of Nations — but they did not mean military action when they used the term. Most of them shied away from "economic sanctions" too. No responsible American commentator or public figure advocated military intervention in the Far East when the Japanese began their expansion in 1931, though Secretary Stimson drew applause for his announcement that we would not "recognize" territorial gains made by conquest.[1] After the Japanese moved from Manchuria to Shanghai in January 1932, Stimson thought of a bluff, and to that end held the fleet in Hawaii, where it happened to be engaged in maneuvers. But Hoover's policy forbade any public intimation of sanctions, and presently, in May, required an explicit statement from the department opposing them. That disposed of any bluff. Somewhat simi-

[1] Michael D. Reagan's case study, "The Far Eastern Crisis of 1931-32: Hoover, Stimson and the Services," Twentieth Century Fund, mimeo., p. 11; see also Henry L. Stimson, *The Far Eastern Crisis,* Harper, New York, 1936.

larly, even verbal "collective security" never mustered a majority in Congress. On the other hand, Congress also balked at adopting Bernard Baruch's reiterated proposals to use the taxing power punitively and preventively, to "take the profits out of war."

These popular ideas found formal expression of one sort or another in official policy. The Kellogg-Briand Pact remained on the books, a symbol and a snare. In the aftermath of the Nye Committee hearings on the "merchants of death," President Roosevelt's effort to secure a selectively discretionary authority for the application of economic sanctions was defeated by the terms of the Neutrality Act of 1935. The extension of that act in 1936, and especially the application of its principle in the Spanish arms embargo of 1937, gave the fullest expression both to the opposition to any arms traffic and to the faith that an act of Congress could keep us from involvement in a foreign war. The President's plea in his famous "quarantine" speech in Chicago on October 5, 1937 for, presumably, concerted economic sanctions against aggressors, was rejected. The peak of isolationist sentiment in Congress perhaps came on January 10, 1938 when the full force of Administration opposition was barely sufficient to defeat, 209 to 188, the Ludlow resolution stipulating that, except in case of invasion, the United States could never again go to war without the prior approval of a popular majority in a national referendum. Some remembrance of such proposals may have lingered, to emerge in SCAP headquarters in Tokyo early in 1946, when General MacArthur directed the inclusion of a prohibition against going to war in the present Japanese constitution.[1]

These ideas, and the policies they enforced on the legislative and executive branches, it might be argued, kept the United States out of war during the 1930's; and in a world of men of good will they might conceivably have done so indefinitely — though their premise was the contrary, that other countries were full of bad people whom we could not trust or control, and had best stay away from.

This is another way of saying that in the world as it was, our dominant ideas made bystanders of the American people and gov-

[1] Robert E. Ward, "Origins of the Present Japanese Constitution," *American Political Science Review*, December 1956, pp. 980-1010.

ernment, who watched helplessly while events abroad took a more and more unwelcome, disturbing course. For however ambivalently our policy was compounded of high-mindedness and prudence, of hope, indifference and suspicion, the rest of the world took us to be speaking very plainly. We would never use force except to beat off an attack on our own territory; we would not go beyond diplomacy to defend our foreign trade or investments; we would not consider any agreement with potential allies looking toward a condition of war; we would not risk involvement by using our economic power to support any nation against aggression; and our moral opposition to aggression included opposition to the existence of aggressive weapons. In a world where "bad" men were in power and were bold, this was an invitation to make hay while their sun shone. The Manchurian invasion spread southward, Hitler rearmed Germany, Mussolini moved on Ethiopia, Franco rose in Spain, Hitler browbeat Czechoslovakia; and England and France acquiesced, hailing "peace in our time" too. These events so harshly confirmed the American ideological premise about human nature abroad that it should not be surprising that their first tendency was to reinforce isolationist sentiment. And indeed, though the America Firsters ultimately declined in numbers after 1939, they grew progressively more shrill in their convictions, and sensed a conspiracy when the tides of national sentiment finally turned against them.

BUT NOT IN THE WESTERN HEMISPHERE

The one great exception to all this was in our relations with the rest of the Western Hemisphere. Here the second premise of our dominant ideology — that we could not control events abroad anyhow — did not hold. The isolationists did not assail the Monroe Doctrine. The rule of abstention from commitments and concerted action overseas did not apply to Latin America. Ironically, when the tide turned, the defense of the Western Hemisphere was the means of reversing isolationist policy, for "much of what passed for hemisphere defense planning was in reality a planning for defense against the Axis." [1]

[1] Mark S. Watson, *Chief of Staff: Prewar Plans and Preparations,* Historical Division, Department of the Army, Washington, 1950, p. 96.

The beginning of that turn can be dated from the fall of 1937, the time of the "quarantine" speech, early in Roosevelt's second term. Until then our policy in Latin America had concentrated on disentanglement, to erase the memories of previous interventions, to show that we had become a "good neighbor." Now State Department observers in some Latin American countries with sizable German and Italian immigrant colonies were alarmed to see unmistakable signs of Nazi and Fascist infiltrations — local party organizations forming, overt expressions of approval for the rising European dictators, secret agents at work, and German military missions being sent in to help train the local armed forces. Reports of these activities led the State Department to arrange a series of conferences with War and Navy early in 1938, and these presently brought a proposal from Hull to the President in April for the establishment of a Standing Liaison Committee — in Hull's formulation to be composed of the second-ranking officers of State, War and Navy — to meet regularly to work out joint policies and coordinate official activities abroad. Roosevelt "heartily" approved, but substituted the Chief of Staff and the Chief of Naval Operations for the civilian Assistant Secretaries of War and Navy, whose other duties had more to do with domestic than foreign policy. With Sumner Welles taking the lead, and partly because of the accident of his special interest in that area, SLC gave most of its attention to Latin American affairs. Although its specific recommendations for action were of minor consequence, its deliberations, especially after Marshall and Stark became its military members in 1939, encouraged a major shift in military thinking, away from the purely passive posture of repelling an invader at our coast lines to the more active anticipatory policy of securing bases and taking other measures in cooperation with friendly Latin American nations to deny to the Axis powers footholds in the Western Hemisphere from which they might further their ambitions. So the notion of hemisphere defense was born. SLC was the first formal mechanism since the old and moribund Council of National Defense, established in 1916, to provide for high-level civil-military collaboration on national policy. It proved to be a temporary and limited arrangement, but responded to a real need and pointed ahead to broader and more elaborate institutions later.

## THE ROLE OF THE MILITARY

The *a priori* rejection of the use of force resulted in an almost complete exclusion of the military departments, their civilian and uniformed heads alike, from the formulation of national policy during the 1930's. Secretary Stimson handled the Far Eastern crisis, in consultation with President Hoover, of course; and Hoover dealt directly with General MacArthur, then Army Chief of Staff, and Admiral Pratt, Chief of Naval Operations, when he thought it necessary — when troops and marines were moved into Shanghai, for instance. But when Stimson announced the policy of non-recognition, Admiral Pratt was not consulted until afterward about any possible naval implications of what had just been done, like a Japanese blockade of the China coast. Presumably to obtain professional concurrence in his own decision that inaction was strategically wise as well as morally correct, Hoover checked with Pratt and MacArthur, who assured him we were not in any state of readiness to fight. Stimson's policy was brought up in a Cabinet meeting and ridiculed there by Patrick Hurley, the Secretary of War, who thought we should not move at all unless we were prepared to go on and fight; but Hurley was not advocating fighting.[1] On the other hand, neither Stimson nor any other top authority seems to have considered the strategic aspects of Japanese expansion, nor was there any interdepartmental staff work, or consultation at operating levels, devoted to study of the inherent military risks of the situation, whether we acted or not. It was not the potential danger to us, or even to the Philippines, that alarmed Stimson, so much as the damage to the principle of the renunciation of force.

It was easy to overlook the armed services. Their civilian chiefs were appointed with no thought of special competence or interest in their activities. Their career chiefs were professionals who had worked their way up through the tiny bureaucracy of officers who

[1] Henry L. Stimson and McGeorge Bundy, *On Active Service in Peace and War*, Harper, New York, 1948, pp. 243-45.

had survived the demobilization after World War I and the parings of the Coolidge budgets. The entire outlay on the military establishment, land, sea and air, amounted to no more than $700 million out of total expenditures of just under $4 billion for the fiscal year 1930. Apart from a handful of specialized industries, and localities that thrived on proximity to camps and bases, military spending had no appreciable influence on the economy. Because of the geography of Congressional politics, the Army was better deployed to fight Indians than to repel invaders, and military budgets were worked out within ceilings determined by civilian authorities whose primary criteria were the tax revenues. The uniformed spokesmen for military appropriations were long since tamed, in their testimony before Congressional committees, to talk in figures the committee members would think realistic. Hoover had had his fill of military officers in World War I, and as President he did not seek out their company. Career officers, for their part, were a fairly closed group. They were brought up to think of themselves as apolitical and seldom voted or qualified themselves to vote, even in the relatively few states with practicable absentee voting laws, or gave much attention to local civic affairs. It was common for the sons of officers to secure appointments to West Point or the Naval Academy, to follow their fathers' careers. Service codes inculcated a slight distaste for the money-making goals of businessmen — which did not extend, however, to the top levels of finance and industry — and service traditions took a generally aristocratic view of society and a conservative view of domestic political and social issues, though the officers themselves held no elite status in civil society. Service careers were simply outside the main currents of American life.

For another reason the services were becoming more inconspicuous. The Army, and especially the Corps of Engineers, had a long record of civil functions, as in rivers and harbors work and the Panama Canal, that contributed to the building of the nation. But the Hoover Administration marked the end of the long era in which a dispatch of troops, a landing of marines, or a show of naval force made occasional sensational headlines, in the traditional business of protecting American lives and property abroad. The Good Neighbor policy, begun then, has been an article of faith ever since. The Mexican oil expropriations, the sinking of the *Panay,* the mistreatment of American citizens in Axis countries, were all handled by diplomatic notes, not by force or the threat of it. Possibly the most significant use of troops during the Hoover Administration was a domestic, not a foreign, police action, ordered by the President. On the afternoon and night of July 28, 1932 General MacArthur personally led — and made an elaborate military exercise of — a descent, first on some government-owned buildings about to be razed along Pennsylvania Avenue, and then on the ramshackle squattings of the defiant bonus marchers encamped on the Anacostia flats, across the river from Washington, to break up their settlement and drive them out of the capital.[1] (It is perhaps significant to note that Tugwell records Roosevelt as having remarked, shortly after this incident and during the 1932 campaign, that he regarded MacArthur and Huey Long as the two most "dangerous" men in America, because of their authoritarian tendencies.[2]) Especially in the years since then, though still used on rare occasions as a peacetime instrument of force in civilian affairs, as at Little Rock, the National Guard and the regular forces, at home and at stations abroad, have cultivated a very different reputation as benevolent rescue squads in all sorts of emergencies: sheltering evacuees from floods, flying hay to snowbound cattle, coal to beleaguered Berlin, or pilgrims to Mecca, as well as in more prosaic tasks.

In contrast to Hoover, President Roosevelt dealt easily and readily with Army and Navy officers, and, to the irritation of many of his New Deal supporters, used them frequently in civilian assignments, sometimes to neutralize partisan suspicions, or to handle emergency operations. So the Army flew the airmail routes for a time after Postmaster General Farley cancelled the airline contracts, until mounting accidents hastened the renegotiations with the carriers.[3] Less spectacularly, admirals were appointed as ambassadors and

---

[1] The event pre-empted front-page headlines as well as editorial attention for several days; see the *New York Times* for the last week of July 1932.

[2] Rexford G. Tugwell, *The Democratic Roosevelt,* Doubleday, Garden City, 1957, p. 349.

[3] Paul Tillett, *The Army Flies the Mails,* Inter-University Case Program Series: No. 24, University of Alabama Press, 1954.

army engineers were brought into WPA posts; the Army ran the CCC camps. These were broadening experiences for the individuals involved — for Leahy, Somervell and Clay among the officers, and for Harry Hopkins, who later was to bridge so many civil-military gulfs. But they led to no institutional modifications or interpenetrations. They did not help the Army to get larger funds for its own purposes, or noticeably abate the mutual suspicion that prevailed between New Dealers and the military. Ickes opposed Roosevelt's allocation of PWA funds for naval construction about as vehemently — though not as successfully — as he did the release of helium from the government's monopoly store to the Nazis for their big new zeppelin.[1] General Marshall later lamented that the Army had been too disapproving to avail itself fully of the opportunity to get WPA help in strengthening its posts and facilities scattered around the country. Perhaps most significantly, the Army mobilization planners turned to big business and the Treasury but not to the rest of the government — e.g., to Miss Perkins' Department of Labor — for outside consultation and advice on the successive versions of their industrial mobilization plans during the 1930's. By shutting themselves off from the main sources of energy, policy and influence within the Administration they made it almost inevitable that, when the time came, their plans would be both unrealistic and suspect.

In this general atmosphere, and rather against the advice of his strongest New Deal supporters, the President pushed steadily though cautiously for larger annual appropriations for the services. The Navy benefited most from this — a consequence that was popularly laid to Roosevelt's past ties with naval affairs and his obvious enthusiasm for sailing, but was equally compatible with the traditional American belief that control of the seas was our best assurance of security at home. It was not a rejection of the concepts underlying the neutrality legislation, but rather a reflection of his growing appreciation, amid the crowding concerns of domestic politics, that the aggressive policies of Germany and Japan might sooner or later provoke a new general war which the United States could not ulti-

[1] Michael D. Reagan's case study, "The Helium Controversy," Twentieth Century Fund, mimeo.

mately ignore; and a navy takes a long time to build. In the event, the cautions imposed on this policy by the prevailing sentiments in the country made the pace of achievement too small to be of any decisive moment.

## ARMY AND NAVY PLANNING

Until the end of 1937 at least, Army and Navy planning proceeded mostly, and necessarily, in a vacuum. No one here had any designs for aggressive war, nor any clear and persuasive answer to President Coolidge's question: "Who're we going to fight?" Defensive war, to all concerned, meant strictly a reaction to attack on our own territory, with an ill-defined exception for possible attacks on Latin America. The implied commitments of the Monroe Doctrine, and the successive inter-American treaties of the 1930's that were largely designed to turn that doctrine into a multilateral defense responsibility, represented our nearest approach to a system of alliances. The "color" plans of the period, worked up for the Joint Board, therefore took up possible "enemy" countries one by one, and consisted mainly of theoretical plans for largely non-existent forces to cope with attacks from each.

Army planners, as usual, had the least tangible possibilities to reckon with. They could decide firmly to protect our shores against invasion — our shores for this purpose including Alaska, Hawaii and the Panama Canal. An attack on the Philippines might be an automatic cause for war, but our forces there were so small and so far away from reinforcements that in case of a strong assault the most that could be expected of them was a stubborn retreat to capitulation. Strengthening the fortifications of Manila and Guam was prohibited under the treaties of 1922 and politically unsalable after 1936; but, equally, any Army proposal to withdraw our forces was likewise sternly rejected. The timing of ultimate Philippine liberation would therefore depend chiefly on naval initiative and capacity. These premises and purposes were reflected in the various versions of the Protective Mobilization Plan, based on the National Defense Act of 1920. It was a manpower plan, divided among Regular Army, National Guard and Reserves, that envisaged an immediate shore defense and a contingent expeditionary force — destination unknown. Coupled with it were sketchy paper plans for economic mobilization and logistic support. Actually, since all realistic expectations of fighting England disappeared, at least after the 1922 naval treaties, and Germany did not emerge as a seriously conceivable enemy until after Hitler announced his intention to rearm it, the only concrete possibility on the horizon for most of the period was Japan; and there, presumably, the Army, aside from mobilization preparations, could be involved on a major scale only in the late stages of a naval war.

Army planning of a practical nature, until 1938, was therefore almost entirely tactical: how to better the anti-aircraft defenses of the Canal Zone and Oahu, how to deal with invaders who slipped past the Navy to a landing, how to retake the Philippines. This kind of planning put stress on the coast artillery, and, more usefully, on ground combat training and mobilization. It depended on no Army theory of the causes of war; it attempted no solutions of the problems of coalition warfare, or of an invasion of the European continent, or of island-hopping and amphibious operations in the Pacific (though the Navy and Marine Corps did concern themselves with capture of the Japanese mandates) — these became the main concerns of World War II; and it considered the possibility of holding bases in the Caribbean only as an adjunct to the defense of the Canal. As late as May 1938 its influence was still strong enough to lead the Deputy Chief of Staff, Major General Stanley D. Embick (Wedemeyer's father-in-law), to deny an Air Corps budgetary request for funds for the construction of the B-17 bomber, not because of Army jealousy toward the Air Corps, but on the ground that it would encroach on the Navy's jurisdiction over planes capable of flying over water, and also because a long-range bomber was an aggressive weapon. "Our national policy contemplates preparation for defense, not aggression."

Navy planning through the 1930's was more pointed: after 1922, when the British, partly at our request and Canada's, had abandoned their twenty-year-old Japanese alliance, the Navy had practically ceased to reckon on a war with England as one of its concerns — a conclusion the British authorities had themselves reached a decade earlier, before World War I. The tradition of rivalry lingered on among some older officers, and contributed to the Navy's failure to realize — until the danger of losing it became more than an abstract possibility — that the British fleet, in time of trouble, would likely be a positive asset added to ours; our navy counted on no outside help except in the Far East. Nevertheless, eliminating the British from hostile consideration left only Japan to worry about. No other Atlantic power could get past the Royal Navy. In a Pacific war, by contrast, the British were too far away to be a decisive factor, and our island possessions were obviously exposed and vulnerable. Not only the capabilities of the Japanese, moreover, but also their intent, was a cause for anxiety. No doubt suspicion was fed by traces of chauvinism, racial prejudice and other factors outside stated official policy. But at bottom it rested on evidences of Japanese expansionist policies, traceable at least as far back as 1915 and clearly renewed after 1931. Official rationalizations of the going policy put in such traditional terms as the need to protect American trade with China — though that argument was heard often enough — persuaded very few. We would not fight for the Open Door, for Standard Oil or for the missionaries, not even for our "honor," as the *Panay* incident in 1937 showed; and it was not until 1940 or 1941 that people began to say we could not let Chiang Kai-shek go under. But the Philippines were another matter. The promise of independence in 1946, given them in 1934 (from whatever mixture of motives), did not entitle us to wash our hands of them, whatever the technical military prudence of such action. The Joint Army-Navy Basic War Plan ORANGE of 1928, which called for "an offensive war, primarily naval," in case of a Japanese attack, set the focus of professional concern for the next decade on the western Pacific.

Apprehensions over Japanese designs consequently monopolized Navy planning until early 1939, and drew the support of the President, Secretary Hull and Carl Vinson, the energetic chairman of the House Naval Affairs Committee, for a gradual expansion of strength, which finally eventuated in authorization of a two-ocean navy. Meanwhile, by a somewhat circular if eventually useful logic, the Navy, whose chief historic reason for being (apart from defense against actual invasion) was the protection of American shipping, led the campaign for the passage of the Merchant Marine Act of 1936, which it justified on the ground that a large merchant fleet would strengthen the Navy in time of war. Even in 1939, after Munich and after the revised ORANGE plan was superseded by the RAINBOW series that were realistically designed for the contingency of fighting a coalition of the Axis powers, the Navy continued to look first to the dangers in the Far East. Navy planners here parted company with the Army and brought out a latent disagreement of long standing. Following the acquisition of the Philippines, and until the Russo-Japanese War in 1905, the two services had agreed that our main Pacific base should be in the Philippines, with Manila representing for us what Port Arthur had been for the Russians. Ever since that war the Army had been convinced that we could not hold the Philippines against a determined Japanese attack. From this premise the Army concluded that the Alaska-Oahu-Panama line was our forward reliance for Pacific defense; the Philippines would be lost. The Navy, on the contrary, clung to the Asiatic base; conceding the possibility of an initial loss there, it concluded that we would have to defeat Japan to retake the Philippines, and planned accordingly. The Army thought this would require Army participation on a far larger scale than the Navy contemplated, and opposed it on the ground that the game would not be worth the candle. This issue, which had bothered Theodore Roosevelt and President Taft, now arose in the new setting of the Axis threats.

In view of this quite natural concern over the fate of our Pacific possessions, it was in a sense quite true, as recurrently charged, that the Navy was preparing for war with Japan, but also quite misleading, for there was no thought of *starting* such a war. The Navy would fight if Japan attacked the Philippines or any other American territory; it would expect to fight alone, without much help from the Army; and it would fight offensively against Japan proper, if need be, in order to liberate any initially captured territory. This was all quite consistent with prevailing national policies and popular attitudes.

THE DEPARTMENT OF STATE

Between 1931 and 1937 the Secretaries of State, Stimson and Hull, bent their energies to the maintenance of peace — world peace if possible, and if not, then peace for the United States at any rate, or almost any rate. The dominant faith in isolation, however, limited them to means — moral exhortation and diplomacy — that ordinarily neither required nor permitted joint action by the State and military departments. The diplomatic notes and official speeches took moral positions with no evident military implications. The reciprocal trade agreements legislation was no concern of the military. The long debates over the neutrality acts had indirect military significance, but the military departments had, and apparently sought, no formal voice in them.

The crux of these debates, so far as the Administration was concerned, lay in the repeated efforts, and unvarying failures, of Roosevelt and Hull to secure from Congress some tempering of the automatic and mandatory character of the prohibitions in the legislation: some discretionary authority to discriminate between aggressor and victim in applying them, some selective choice among war materials to be embargoed. This would have put the possibility of economic sanctions behind our moral stands, and opened the way to diplomatic conversations looking toward concerted sanctions that might have been more effective. Precisely for this reason, Congressional antagonists succeeded in blocking any moves toward statutory flexibility with the argument that the President would try to coordinate embargoes "with a League of Nations sanctions list and thus lead the nation into war."

The neutrality acts contained export controls of a limited and rigid sort, but unlike the Helium Act of 1937 or later export control legislation, they were not addressed to the conservation of strategic materials for our own defense, or the denial to potential enemies of stockpiles built from our supplies. Until these became active military concerns, the services showed only a passive interest in export controls.

The Army and Navy were actively concerned and consulted in

some phases of State Department policy, to be sure, as in connection with China, Panama and the independence of the Philippines. But the principal exception to the general rule of going their separate ways, the field of foreign policy that most obviously called for the full cooperation of the Army and Navy with State, was the negotiations looking toward armaments limitation. The long interdepartmental discussions, culminating in the Geneva conference in 1932 [1] and continued for the London conference of 1935-36, had some lasting institutional benefits in spite of the public disappointments with the outcome of the conferences. They furnished an arena for threshing out some inter-service disputes, e.g., over poison gas, and bombing planes for coastal defense, and intra-Navy and Anglo-American quarrels over cruiser parity and sizes, and paved the way for the first continuing Anglo-American exchanges of defense information. They did not, apparently, lead to any reconsideration of the desirability of disarmament as a policy, based on its effects on the relative strengths of potential friends and enemies, either in Europe or in the Far East. The demise of the disarmament treaties themselves brought an end to the restrictions they had imposed on further fortification of the Philippines and Guam, but this had little immediate practical effect. It also stimulated the Navy, through the medium of the report of the Hepburn Board late in 1938, to review its posture in the Pacific and advocate a substantial development of naval bases. The Board's recommendations were but a minute precursor of the post-war program of great naval and air bases in the Pacific; but in 1939 the House of Representatives flatly refused to allow the fortification of Guam, or even the dredging of a harbor there.

The 1936 disarmament conference had at least one forward-looking by-product. After the Japanese had walked out, and announced their unwillingness to extend the earlier agreements that were to expire that year, the United States, Great Britain and France reached an understanding to continue their own limitations, subject to an escape clause if a non-signatory power ignored them, and with a stipulation in that case that the three powers would give each other advance

---

[1] Arthur S. Olick's case study, "Conference for the Reduction and Limitation of Armaments — Geneva, 1932," Twentieth Century Fund, mimeo.

notice of their construction programs. An exchange of letters between Norman Davis and Anthony Eden afterwards reinforced this last stipulation, and disclosed, what in fact had been British policy for a long time, that "in estimating our [British] naval requirements we have never taken the strength of the U. S. Navy into account." Publication of these letters, after a news leak, put the Congress effectively on notice of the prospect of future Anglo-American naval conversations. They were not long in coming.

## THE TRANSITION, 1938-41

The dominating American faith in the policy of isolation began to break up, in reaction to the increasing scale and tempo of aggression abroad, in 1936 and 1937. The price of the policy began to emerge: helpless moral indignation as events moved in ways we profoundly disapproved of, toward situations still less to our liking, unhindered by our influence. The rewards of the policy were no more encouraging: the prospects of world peace, and of American ability to remain uninvolved — if not of our actual safety from attack at home — grew dimmer rather than brighter. Only actual indifference to the outcome — not the sort of fear that might constrain a small nearby power — would ultimately sustain public support for a policy of do-nothing neutrality, let alone a policy of positive self-restraint like the embargo on arms shipments and the prohibition on loans to previous "defaulters" regardless of their current circumstances. Indifference began to give way to anxiety or outrage; and the intermediate props for continuing faith, either a conviction of futility because of our impotence to control the unwelcome developments anyway, or a prudent shrinking from a plunge into unpredictable consequences, began to crumble.

This transition was spread over the five years leading to Pearl Harbor. It came sooner to some than to others, and in varying degrees, as one was stirred by reports of Hitler's activities, or another by Japan's adherence to the Anti-Comintern Pact. A few were never persuaded. In Roosevelt's case, the general shift in his thinking seems to have coincided with second thoughts on the Spanish civil war. He and the Congress had won wide popular acclaim by the immediate imposition of the arms embargo there — which paralleled British and French policy toward that tragic contest — and the embargo was still in effect at the end. But as the war went on a deep split developed within the Administration over aid to the Spanish Republic, and Roosevelt's attitude wavered; he apparently had a desire to help the Republic but felt restrained, perhaps by apprehensions over the reaction of his Catholic supporters. When Hitler emerged from the Munich settlement, although isolationists might construe this to be a formal vindication of American policy — after all, we were still uninvolved and uncontaminated, and the British and French did not think it worth fighting about — both Roosevelt and Hull and many other Americans, as well as Europeans, knew Hitler had won a great and ominous victory. We got what we thought we wanted, peace, only to find it unsavory to the taste.

The unsettling of faith in the rightness and wisdom of our course brought not only splits within the Administration in the appraisal of events and proposals, but also for the first time in several years a divergence between popular and official reactions to foreign events. This heightened the political stakes on the issues as they came to be decided. A confident change in foreign policy, moreover, could not be rested, in spite of the 1936 election results, on a secure base of consensus respecting domestic affairs. Nineteen thirty-seven was the year of the President's major political setback in the Court-packing controversy, of continuing conflict over the rights of organized labor, and of the year-end recession. Nineteen thirty-eight was another year of domestic struggle, over the executive reorganization proposal, the Hatch Act, the wages-and-hours act (which found little favor in the South, where Hull's support was strongest) and Congressional elections which for the first time went against the New Deal. In foreign affairs, therefore, though Roosevelt was increasingly persuaded of the need to take preparatory actions, he was equally cautious — not to say secretive — about avowing publicly their full grounds and implications. Within the government, nevertheless, he found scope for movement along three directions prior to the outbreak of war in Europe in 1939: naval expansion linked both to the danger from Japan and to possible future cooperation with the British; hemisphere defense linked to military cooperation with Latin American countries; and a greatly enlarged aircraft construction program linked to the Nazi threat. The evolution of civil-military relations during the transition period can be traced along these innovating steps.

### NAVAL EXPANSION AND THE INGERSOLL MISSION

Before the end of 1937, Roosevelt decided to meet the growing Japanese threat in the Far East with a very substantial increase in naval building, and the Navy was set to work developing a much larger budgetary request to be presented early in 1938, for the fiscal year 1939. It was a 20 per cent step-up, that clearly foreshadowed a two-ocean navy as our counter to Japan's refusal to renew beyond 1936 the armament limitations of previous years. This prospect in turn made it necessary, under our recent agreement with the British, to inform them of our building program, and highly desirable to learn about theirs.

The upshot was the dispatch of Captain Royal E. Ingersoll, then director of the Navy War Plans Division, during the Christmas holidays of 1937 for a fortnight's visit to London. The President gave him his final instructions and received his report after his return. The conversations were informal and exploratory, and involved no commitments on either side. They covered the required exchanges of information, and a good deal of other ground in addition: to both sides a Pacific war seemed not unlikely, and it might involve all the European powers with Far Eastern possessions if Japan moved southward after digesting the China coast; and perhaps the Soviet Union as well, over Manchuria. The British were especially concerned — in view of the Anti-Comintern Pact — about the problems they would face in the event of a war with Germany, for then they would have to reduce their strength in the Far East. So the talk turned on the needs and means and possibilities of concerted action; and from this may be dated the beginnings of Anglo-American strategic and tactical naval cooperation, a major break with isolationist policy and a precedent to be repeated. With Ingersoll's report in hand General Embick and Admiral Richardson made a fresh start on the revision of the ORANGE Plan then under way, which was approved by the end of February. It assumed British cooperation if an ultimate offensive against Japan became necessary; and it took account of the possibility that Germany might then be hostile too. The possibility of a two-ocean war had already been clearly implied in the President's message of January 28; and some realization of the danger was reflected in Congressional approval in May 1938 of the President's request for a 20 per cent naval increase.

News of Ingersoll's mission leaking to the Hill a little later, and following on the heels of the defeat of the Ludlow resolution in the House of Representatives, led to some pointed questions from isolationists in Congress, directed to Secretary Hull, though he had had nothing to do with the mission. He stood them off; but the experience of hostile criticism in Congress, connected to the suspicion of military commitments abroad, reinforced his personal distastes. From that time on he made it a working rule to avoid participation in, and hence first-hand knowledge of — and hence influence on — military planning, however important its bearing on foreign policy. This too affected the shape of things to come and taught a later lesson. When the National Security Council was established a decade later, its first object was to bring the Secretary of State and the Secretary of Defense into a regular working relationship.

HEMISPHERE DEFENSE AND THE
STANDING LIAISON COMMITTEE

In contrast to his sensitive attitude about military plans that involved "foreign entanglements" with Europe, and especially Britain, Secretary Hull felt safe in dealing with the affairs of the Western Hemisphere, still universally regarded as "our" business. There was need for a policy here, and for machinery by which a policy could be formulated, since the Pan American Union had historically kept strictly to innocuous topics like cultural exchanges. The means chosen was the establishment of a Standing Liaison Committee, already mentioned, in April 1938.

Whether Hull's suggested civilian composition of the SLC was naive or knowing is hard to tell at this distance. Hull was well aware that the Assistant Secretary of War, Louis Johnson, was deeply involved in the statutory duties vested in his office for industrial mobilization, and was also feuding with his official superior, Secretary Woodring, whom he hoped to succeed; while at the Navy Department, Secretary Swanson was in failing health and Assistant Secretary Edison was afflicted with deafness and other ailments. Roosevelt may have been thinking of his own role as Commander in Chief in wanting to foster closer personal ties with the military commanders. At any rate, the combination of the service chiefs and the Under Secretary of State worked well for the next couple of years. Hemispheric defense — an impeccable objective — took a place alongside the ORANGE Plan. Army planners moved from purely passive to preventive concepts of defense, and began to think of offshore bases; the strategic utility of distant places like Natal and Dakar came into view. The SLC worked actively, and Welles' initiative foreshadowed the one area where the State Department maintained its responsibility. The President or the military members decided on the facilities needed in Latin American territories and the department proceeded to negotiate for them. In addition the department pushed the concept of hemispheric solidarity, culminating in the Declaration of Lima in December 1938. The President not only supported these moves but also in one of his characteristically bold and expansive strokes swept Canada in under the Monroe Doctrine too. In a speech at Kingston, Ontario, on August 18, 1938, going beyond the State Department's draft text, he said: ". . . the Dominion of Canada is part of the sisterhood of the British Empire. I give to you assurance that the people of the United States will not stand idly by if domination of Canadian soil is threatened by any other Empire." Two years later the Permanent Joint Board on Defense Canada–United States put on an institutional footing the systematic cooperation to the north that in a later era would produce the Distant Early Warning network, directed to dangers not remotely thought of in 1940.

AIR POWER

The Spanish civil war gave the general public perhaps its first vivid impression of the terrifying and dramatic offensive potentialities of modern air power used against ground troops and civilian populations. Colonel Charles A. Lindbergh, still a gallant figure in American eyes and a recurrent guest — from whatever motives — of Hitler's air force builder and chief, Hermann Goering, had a closer and more technical basis for judgment. He was impressed too, and told first his professional acquaintances and then general audiences at home so; it may have helped form his more and more ardent political conviction that we should stay out of Germany's way. At the same time England began to suffer from the same apprehension — but was spurred into some action by it. In the summer of 1938 British procurement officials launched a commercial purchasing program to augment their own resources, and Secretary Morgenthau helped them along. President Roosevelt got his own confirmation of danger in October 1938, when our Ambassador to France, William Bullitt, returned to Washington to report that the main source of German confidence, and of British and French fear, was the overwhelmingly superior strength of Goering's *Luftwaffe*.

The next day after hearing Bullitt's report, Roosevelt told his press conference that he was going to "reorganize the whole national defense picture." A fortnight later, in mid-November, at a large interdepartmental conference at the White House — attended by, among others, Harry Hopkins, who had already become the President's closest adviser, and Treasury and Justice as well as Army and Navy chiefs but not, notably, by any State Department representative — he announced plans for a major expansion of aircraft plant construction and production. In spite of the urgent pleas of the service chiefs for a balanced military force, embracing ground troops, bases, training and supplies, he put the whole emphasis on aircraft.[1] It was at least a recognition of the new role of air power in a balanced force. It was probably also part of an unspoken plan even then to prepare for the need and desirability at some later date to furnish large num-

[1] Watson, *Chief of Staff*, pp. 126-38.

bers of planes to England and France, if not to wage coalition warfare. If planes were transferred, the British could be expected to
supply the bases and the rest of the balance. This momentous conference seems a clear indication of Roosevelt's prescience, an antici-
pation of lend-lease and the time when the United States might
become the main source of global supply.

In sum, by 1939 the doctrine and premises of isolationism were no
longer gospel, and each successive event made them less so. Controversy over them split the Administration as it did the country, and
the split deepened as the 1940 elections came into view; but the
earlier faith no longer dominated policy. The Navy and Air Corps
had begun to expand, the first conversations with the British had
been held, and in Latin America the State Department and the
services were working cooperatively to substitute a hemispheric
and preventive for a strictly continental and passive concept of
defense.

Yet it would be easy, from these indicators, to exaggerate in retrospect the pace of popular and official conversion, and to forget how
many, even to the last, clung to what, in the event, proved wishful
thinking. To lose faith in isolation was one thing; to advocate
intervention quite another, and most people looked for a stand in
between. Even after Germany invaded Poland in September a
Roper poll showed three out of ten still uncompromisingly isolationist. Only half as many were ready to say we should ultimately
go to war if necessary to prevent Britain and France from losing,
and meanwhile limit ourselves to material aid. A mere 2.5 per cent
were for outright intervention. The largest proportion, 37.5 per cent,
found their middle ground in a non-committal cash-and-carry position. In this broken field, and beset with divided counsels, the
President had to run.

Hitler's absorption of Czechoslovakia in March 1939 and the conclusion of the Nazi-Soviet Pact in late August were major turning
points. They gave the lie to any hopes from the Munich settlement.
They forced a revision in the estimate, reflected in the new RAIN-
BOW 5 Plan of 1939, that war in Europe would be longer in material-
izing than in the Far East. And they underscored the melancholy

fact that the initiative lay in the most unpredictable and the most un-scrupulous hands. The invasion of Poland settled the question whether there would be a war, but not what would become of the major belligerents if they were left to themselves; the "phony war" period of seven months was the most confusing of all. Hitler's whirl-wind campaigns in Norway, the Low Countries and France in the spring of 1940 settled very swiftly what would become of the Conti-nent, but not what the British would do if left alone. Churchill's rally of the British people after Dunkirk evidently resolved that question to Roosevelt's satisfaction, as his Charlottesville speech showed. But it was not until the onset of the Battle of Britain in the summer that the United States, people and government alike, could be said to have reached the stage of implicit moral commitment to prevent Britain's going under, if indeed that could still be prevented. The preponderance of professional and official opinion in this country was probably in the negative. If it could be, that left the question of how and under what circumstances the commitment would be con-verted into an actual declaration of war — a question that was put off by the success of the RAF in the air battle over the Channel, and postponed again by Hitler's switch to the Russian invasion in June 1941. It was open and dangling until the Japanese settled it in December 1941. Over the two-and-one-half-year interval before Pearl Harbor there was only hope, and no longer confidence, that the United States could avoid war, whatever its policy, and a grow-ing and reluctant conviction that a right and necessary policy probably required war.

During that interval the significant developments in civil-military relations can be traced along three lines: the emergence of the President as the personal and public leader, and of the Executive Office as the center of decision, in the new direction of policy away from isolation; the progress of military and diplomatic preparations; and the start toward economic mobilization.

## THE PRESIDENT'S APPROACH

Some governing considerations in Roosevelt's approach are worth noting. First, though he saw sooner and farther than most the implications of events and worked steadily for preparations and moves that would, for a change, enable the United States to influence their course, he shared the hopes of nearly all Americans that somehow Hitler would fail without our having to go to war. This dictated a step-by-step involvement rather than an all-out plunge, and so kept him short of the position of Stimson, among others, who argued for immediate intervention or at least for faster strides toward intervention; or of Admiral Stark, who thought we could do more good in the war than on the edge of it. Until Pearl Harbor he could always have retreated and called off his efforts without much embarrassment if some miracle abroad made them no longer necessary.

Second, like Hull he was acutely sensitive to the power of Congressional opposition, though less respectful of Congress as an institution. Therefore he would take no step that Congress could and would block, and so not only leave him committed and repudiated, but also cause despair and perhaps surrender on the part of those abroad, facing Hitler, who looked to us for sustenance and salvation. In the spring of 1939 Hull failed, in spite of Roosevelt's support, to induce Congress to amend the Neutrality Act. Again in July, at an evening conference in the White House, Roosevelt and Hull tried to persuade Garner and some senators, among them Borah, that immediate amendment of the act might avert war. Borah brushed Hull aside — the last time Borah had to be taken seriously — with the assertion that his private sources of information, more trustworthy than Hull's, assured him there would be no war. Garner ended the meeting by telling the President: "Well, Captain, we may as well face the facts. You haven't got the votes . . ."[1] Rather than be so rebuffed Roosevelt preferred, until Pearl Harbor, to work within existing legislation, however inadequate, if possible; though he was quite willing to see it stretched by interpretation. When he had to go to Congress, he waited until he felt confident he would have "the votes," and he avoided complicating the prospects of one crucial measure by introducing another before the first was safely assured. So he appeared reluctant and let others push

---

[1] Robert E. Sherwood, *Roosevelt and Hopkins*, Harper, New York, 1948, p. 133.

the Selective Service bill until it was near enactment in 1940; and he held up introduction of the price control bill for months in 1941.

Third, he did not mean to move in vain, to suffer the chagrin of acting too late and then finding the action futile, or worse. For instance, near the end of Hitler's invasion of France, some 150 American planes, under cover of "subtle and possibly questionable legal shenanigans worked out by Henry Morgenthau's lawyers in the Treasury," as Sherwood relates, were flown to Canada and there put aboard the French aircraft carrier *Béarn*. The planes spent the war idly on the Caribbean island of Martinique, however, for France surrendered while the carrier was at sea. Roosevelt did not want to repeat that sort of mistake. By contrast, at about the same time he watched Churchill, acting against his inclination but on the insistence of his military advisers, receive bitter recriminations from the French for refusing Reynaud's desperate appeal for the dispatch of more RAF fighter squadrons to France. As the event proved, the British needed their planes equally desperately a few weeks later, to turn back Goering's assaults. Congress listened to this kind of argument more eagerly, and before June was out tacked a rider on a current naval appropriation bill, prohibiting the transfer of military matériel to a foreign government unless the service chief concerned — *not* the President — would certify that it was not needed for the defense of the United States. (So too in 1941 and 1942, when there was doubt about how long the Soviets could hold out, the argument was often heard in military and other quarters opposing Russian lend-lease, that it was foolish to send critically needed equipment in short supply in a probably futile effort to sustain an ally whom they expected to go down anyway. But then and later the risk was sometimes taken. The decisions were hard and the long-term results were, alas, sometimes painful: the Chinese Communists used to advantage, first against Chiang Kai-shek, and finally against Americans in Korea, weapons we had managed to send to shore up the Nationalist government.)

In 1940, at any rate, it was crucial for Roosevelt's plans to know how far the British could be relied on to continue to resist, no matter what. He was not fully reassured on that score until Churchill made his "fight them on the beaches . . . [and] in the streets" speech on June 4; or perhaps until Churchill responded to his anxious suggestion, that in the event of a successful German invasion the British fleet be dispersed to Canada and other safe ports for a later liberation return, by saying in effect that the condition Roosevelt envisaged presupposed the total destruction of that fleet in the defense of the British Isles. After that, Roosevelt felt safe in sending all that he could, and as fast as he dared. On June 10, in the Charlottesville speech, best remembered for its "hand that held the dagger" reference to Italy's entrance that same day into the war, he made his first public pledge of aid to the "opponents of force." This was a major turning point in our policy. The President was leading rather than following both public and military opinion; months later the planners still expected Britain to go down.

The timing of this decision was tied up with a fourth consideration, his own renomination for an unprecedented third term. From the 1938 elections onward, his intentions on that point were a topic of the liveliest domestic speculation, and were enveloped in the most complete mystery and silence. He was ambivalent about it himself. Even when his decision was made — so far as appears, it was Hitler's actions on the one hand, and Churchill's reaction on the other, that decided him — he would not lift a finger to get the nomination, nor answer a question nor say a word (unless to Hopkins) about it even to his most ardent supporters. To have done otherwise would probably have paralyzed the government from the time his intentions were known until the campaign was over. Willkie's surprising nomination from the Republican convention in June, as it turned out, largely removed the foreign policy issues from the party contest. But Roosevelt's pledge of aid to Britain in his Charlottesville speech was made before Willkie was chosen, when Taft seemed the likeliest candidate, and while the passions and uncertainties in his own party, which convened in mid-July, were at their height. He made it before the appointments of Stimson and Knox to War and Navy were announced on the eve of the Republican convention, at a time when his political power to get his way on foreign policy, though on the rise from its 1939 ebb, was still very low.

These considerations in retrospect make all the more remarkable the emergence of the President and the Executive Office as the initiating and directing center in foreign and military policy — the role Roosevelt had long played in domestic affairs under the New Deal — now that the constricting effects of isolationist ideas were losing their force. Throughout the three years from Munich to Pearl Harbor the accelerating change of American policy was chiefly the work of the President. Reacting to events abroad, gauging domestic sentiment, his decisions on important matters were always his own. His readiness to take up innovating suggestions, to grasp their potentialities, and to find ways of turning them into working programs of decisive effect, was characteristic. So also was his determination to keep himself firmly in the driver's seat, abdicating no constitutional responsibility of his office. Policy innovation was therefore closely bound up with the development of administrative structures, working relationships and lines of access to the President.

Examples are familiar. The raising of Army, Navy and Air Corps sights he accomplished through ordinary channels. But in the initiation and expansion of cash-and-carry sales of military equipment, following the finally successful effort to amend the Neutrality Act in the fall of 1939, the Treasury was given the leading role; Roosevelt counted on Morgenthau's zeal, and by-passed Secretary Woodring. Until Lend-Lease took over, Treasury lawyers and Colonel, soon General, James H. Burns, executive officer to the Assistant Secretary of War, worked out the arrangements between industrial suppliers, the military and the British and French purchasing commissions.

A conversation with Alexander Sachs of Lehman Brothers, armed with a letter from Albert Einstein, led Roosevelt to appoint the first Uranium Committee in the fall of 1939. Refugee physicists had a crucial share in solving the scientific problems of the A-bomb, while Secretary Stimson gave the whole project continuing top-level support and energy. Meanwhile Vannevar Bush of the Carnegie Institution got access to the President through Harry Hopkins, and with President Conant of Harvard readily secured the establishment of the National Defense Research Committee in June 1940. The NDRC, and its successor, the Office of Scientific Research and Development (OSRD), created in 1941 and headed by Bush, dealt directly with the Chiefs of Staff and the President, and achieved spectacular successes in the development and use of radar, anti-submarine devices and other military applications of scientific research.[1]

The dramatic step toward bipartisanship in the appointments of Knox and Stimson in June 1940 was Roosevelt's own inspiration. On the other hand the request to Congress shortly afterward for a peacetime Selective Service Act was pushed by a group of energetic New Yorkers headed by Grenville Clark. The combination of previous negotiations for offshore bases and Churchill's urgent appeal for fighting ships in the English Channel into the destroyers-for-bases deal that circumvented Congressional limitations was promoted by Secretary of the Interior Ickes, and by William Allen White and his committee, in the summer of 1940. The idea of lend-lease Roosevelt conceived on a vacation cruise that fall, as a means of extending aid to Britain while avoiding the post-World War I recriminations he remembered so vividly. He decided on its extension to Russia after the Nazi invasion in June 1941, over the protests of the military. His decision against returning the Pacific fleet from its Hawaiian base to California in 1940 and 1941, by contrast, was the anxious weighing of protracted arguments and competing considerations urged by the diplomatic and military advisers.[2] The secret ARGENTIA rendezvous in August 1941 with Churchill in Newfoundland where the Atlantic Charter was agreed upon, and the decision to relieve the British fleet by moving units of our Atlantic fleet into anti-submarine patrols between our ports and Newfoundland, and later to Iceland, and also along the southern Atlantic route, were on his initiative. Throughout the 1938-41 period the military, so far from pushing the country toward war, rather lagged behind the changing trend of public opinion. Except for the beginning of naval staff conversations with the British, all of the major policy moves that marked the successive stages in the shift appear to have

[1] James P. Baxter 3d, *Scientists Against Time,* Little, Brown, Boston, 1946.
[2] Robert J. Quinlan's case study, "Home Base for the Fleet: Diplomacy, Strategy and the Allocation of Ships," Twentieth Century Fund, mimeo.

had a civilian origin; and all except selective service depended on Roosevelt's active approval and support, or even on his initiative.

## THE EXECUTIVE OFFICE

The institutional arrangements had characteristic features that bore the mark of the President's hand: a certain looseness at the joints of formal coordination, a proliferation of new agencies, often with euphemistic circumlocutions for names, a direct line to the military, and an easy, informal aptitude (system would be too orderly a word) for lateral communications that disregarded formal boundaries, and stimulated inter-agency feuding as well as cooperation.

In July 1939 the Reorganization Act, the small but ultimately significant remnant salvaged from the more ambitious proposals of the President's Committee on Administrative Management two years earlier, took effect, and with it a Reorganization Plan that established the Executive Office of the President, or, more precisely, gave formal recognition to an emerging fact. The staff help so assembled proved invaluable. The Budget Bureau was the main operating component, and, with some prescience, a paper place for an Office for Emergency Management was included; this became the legal launching site for many war agencies. The sponsors of the scheme hoped it would help bring a new tidiness to the center of the Administration, and so for a time it did, under the guidance of the new Budget Director, Harold Smith, a quiet, orderly and perceptive man. But once defense began to take precedence over economy, and war materials, plants and equipment and trained men became scarcer than money, the budget lost its controlling importance. The Bureau of the Budget, devoted to orderliness, correspondingly lost most of its leverage for influence on the development of policy. The Cabinet was at best a discussion group, not a place to get things done. The Standing Liaison Committee was an interdepartmental group but without corporate contact with the President, and it was displaced early in 1941 when Stimson, Knox and Hull agreed informally to meet weekly. The old War Council, consisting of the Secretaries of State, War and Navy and the service chiefs, had, like the Cabinet, no staff or procedure of its own and had fallen into disuse; its functions had been partly taken over by the statutory Joint Board, which, however, left out both State and the Air Corps. The Council of National Defense existed only in the statute books. The Executive Office therefore had somehow to provide the center for top-level staff work and coordination.

During the "defense" period three interdepartmental agencies were given a direct and formal relationship to the President. In July 1939, at the time of the Reorganization Plan, he issued a Military Order directing the Joint Board and the Army-Navy Munitions Board (ANMB) to report directly to him, rather than through the civilian Secretaries, then Swanson and Woodring. In May 1940 he revived the Advisory Commission to the Council of National Defense (NDAC) and ordered it also to report directly to him. The latter two agencies, however, shortly became involved in lower-level operations and drifted away from his cognizance. He remained in close touch with the Joint Board, on the other hand, and even more closely with its effectual successor, the Joint Chiefs of Staff. In contrast to the civilian side of things, his actions in the field of military strategy and tactics were made far more orderly by the inescapable need for relating them to the increasingly well organized, carefully recorded and amply staffed activities of the service chiefs, whether sitting as the Joint Board or as the Joint Chiefs.

Roosevelt was acutely aware of the perennial danger that confronts every president, of becoming a prisoner of his intimates and of the very machinery of government. His main defense was a policy of "divide and rule," to which he added a considerable measure of secretiveness and an occasional dash of talkativeness, and a readiness to reach directly into operating agencies below the level of their chiefs. He was apt to give similar assignments to more than one agency, and he freely established new agencies to pick up and push activities that might be (and frequently were) thought to fall more properly in the jurisdiction of existing agencies. These working habits opened up to him more lines of access, more points of view and interest, than presidents ordinarily allow — or enjoy. They balanced off rivals who competed for his support, and they kept him exceptionally well informed. They compensated for his physical handicap in getting around. They provided unexampled scope for the activities of government lawyers and economists, two highly creative professional groups. They gave a premium to "operators" in and out of government who moved easily across jurisdictional boundaries on the strength of their talents and knowledgeability — to General Burns for instance, who, among many other important activities, expedited lend-lease to Russia; or to Jean Monnet, who shifted from the Franco-British Economic Commission to the British Supply Council after the fall of France and did so much to inform and galvanize the processes of industrial mobilization in 1940-41; or to Leon Henderson, who left the Securities and Exchange Commission for a roving commission across the problems of supply and price stabilization from an initial base in the NDAC; or, to take the supreme example, to Harry Hopkins, the "man who came to dinner" at the White House on the evening of Hitler's march into the Low Countries, May 10, 1940, and stayed for nearly three and a half years as the President's *alter ego* in every sort of matter, domestic and foreign. But the President's working habits had a danger of their own, when there was so little to match them, outside the military establishment, in the form of established machinery for orderly procedure; and so long as Roosevelt was President there was little such machinery. His unique relationship with the Joint Chiefs tended to by-pass the Secretaries of War and Navy, much as he admired and respected Stimson and Knox. Similarly, Hopkins had a close triangular relation with him and the Joint Chiefs, and so, when operating in diplomatic or economic fields, tended sometimes to stand in the way of direct relations between the diplomats or agency heads on the one hand and the military on the other.

ROLE OF THE STATE DEPARTMENT

Some of the difficulties the State Department was to encounter after Pearl Harbor were foreshadowed in the years immediately preceding, but on the whole the department between 1938 and 1941 — and between Hull and Welles — was still close to the center of action and policy. For example, it continued its rewarding efforts toward Latin American solidarity, symbolized by the Declaration of Panama and the Act of Havana, and translated more specifically into economic agreements. It undertook the protracted task of negotiating for military bases, working here in a congenial field, on projects that appealed to Congress. The long wrangle over American bases in the British Caribbean possessions illustrates the complexities of that task. State, characteristically concerned to show its support of the principle of equal sovereignty throughout the hemisphere, wanted the bases to be nominally available for use by all the American republics, but not, for fear of Congress, by the British navy; while the War and Navy Departments, just as characteristically, were demanding far-reaching American rights and exclusive jurisdiction for themselves. The British, beset on their side by complaints from the Admiralty and the colonies, objected to both plans. Nevertheless, with a flourish of favorable publicity for the destroyers-for-bases deal, compromise arrangements were successfully carried through and satisfactory interdepartmental relationships maintained.

Similarly, the department's conduct of diplomatic relations with Vichy France, though bitterly attacked at the time, seems to have achieved the military and intelligence objectives in view. After the fall of France, and with the leverage of limited shipments of food and other civilian supplies carefully doled out, Hull and Admiral Leahy, who was appointed Ambassador to Vichy in January 1941, tried to maintain steady pressure to hold Pétain to the line of keeping the French fleet out of German hands, and German controls out of French North Africa. Naturally Pétain shared these aims, and whether American pressure made a real difference is, of course, unknowable. Parallel negotiations with Finland and some Balkan states, aimed at keeping them out of the Axis camp, failed. To lay the groundwork for eventual landings in Africa, Hull arranged for the introduction of military intelligence agents as soon as the American consulates in Algeria and Morocco were reopened. These agents were ostensibly to supervise the use of American supplies of oil and food. Their preparations for groups to aid our later military landings were helpful; but their intelligence results were mixed. More generally, it can be said that both in the Standing Liaison Committee and later in the weekly meetings of the three Secretaries set up soon after Stimson and Knox took office in June 1940, the three departments succeeded ordinarily in keeping each other informed of their actions, without, however, formulating policy jointly.

Against Germany the State Department could do little directly. Hitler brushed aside Roosevelt's peace proposal of 1939 with sarcastic scorn, and the Welles mission to Europe early in 1940 came to nothing. But the department continued to be consulted about German reactions to the steady enlargement of American aid to Britain and the extension of the undeclared war in the Atlantic.

In the negotiations with the Japanese, on the other hand, Hull had the leading role, and played it with extraordinary skill. He incurred a good deal of public criticism for his restraining influence on various proposals for coercive measures such as embargoes, and he was frequently at odds tactically with Stimson and Knox for his refusal to use pressure instead of persuasion; they were more impatient. But fundamentally all three were responding to the desire of the military professionals to avoid a Japanese war, for which, in the consensus of informed opinion, we were not prepared, and which, if it came, could only detract from our support of Britain against Germany. Regarded as a delaying action, therefore, Hull's conduct of the negotiations was remarkably successful, though in the light of what we now know it may have been unnecessary. The Japanese were playing for time too. They attacked when they were ready, at a time of their own choosing, yet a mishandling of the negotiations might have precipitated action.

The department was also active on matters of economic aid and economic warfare. It carried the battle for the cash-and-carry amendment to the Neutrality Act that was put through at the special session of Congress in the fall of 1939. It spoke for the Administration in the enactment of the Export Embargo Act in July 1940, about which the military were uneasy. It had a major share in the preparation and passage of the Lend-Lease Act in March 1941.

STATE'S HANDICAPS

Despite this record, three kinds of trouble for the department emerged during this period, and grew worse as time went on. The first is chronic in our form of government and was accentuated in this case by some of Roosevelt's most characteristic traits of behavior: it was the falling out between Hull and his Under Secretary, Sumner Welles, and the strains of divided loyalties and independent lines of communication below, and of lessened confidence above and outside, that ensued. Career people in the department, habituated to the knowledge that Congressional masters usually last longer than Executive superiors, adjusted only slowly and gingerly to the new trends in dominant opinion, and were the more cautious because of the visible break above them.

Another symptom related to the same basic malady, also chronic and also accentuated now, was less obvious to outsiders but probably no less of a handicap at operating levels, particularly in the department's overseas posts: this was the distrust, and consequent inadequacy and avoidance, of State's official channels of communication. At a time when so much depended on keeping major diplomatic and military messages secret, the increased tendency to resort to other channels had unfortunate results. Roosevelt and Hopkins regularly used the Navy's communication lines. The embassies and the Foreign Service were kept in the dark about much that otherwise would have come to them in the ordinary course of operations.

A second sort of difficulty stemmed from the size and traditions of the department when the new policies of defense called for a greatly increased volume of administrative operations. The entire staff of the department in Washington in 1939 numbered something of the order of 800 people — tiny in comparison with the other civilian departments with domestic programs to conduct, let alone with the War and Navy Departments — and their previous experience had given them, by and large, practically no contact or familiarity with the business community in this country, its ways, its leaders and its infinite complexities of location and behavior. When it came to the administration of export controls, of the procurement and forwarding of lend-lease supplies, of the stockpiling and pre-clusive buying of foreign materials, of the financing of new facilties, and the like, the department was helpless to operate the activities for which it had been so helpful in securing legislative authority.

The decision to administer these various activities initially through new independent agencies — independent of the Army and Navy too — was inevitable, for Hull had no desire to change the depart-ment's general character; but it had far-reaching consequences for the later development of civil-military relations. The State Depart-ment reserved to itself the right to negotiate the master lend-lease agreements, which were essentially statements of post-war economic policy, and neither guided nor restricted the operations of the in-nocuously named Division of Defense Aid Reports and its successor, the Lend-Lease Administration. The President himself in 1941 set lend-lease policy and priorities toward Britain, Russia and China. In consequence the State Department thereafter could do little but plead for driblets of aid to the American republics and other small nations whose importance, in the eyes either of the military or of the agencies controlling exports and imports, did not warrant much attention. In the many heated arguments over the allocation of munitions and supplies, which the Army and Navy wanted to use for training purposes and to equip our growing forces, but which lend-lease countries could put to immediate use in combat, State was on the sidelines. Seven years later, when the Marshall Plan was en-acted in 1948, it was again argued and decided that a new independ-ent agency, ECA, and not State, should administer foreign economic aid.

A third element of weakness in the department's role was Hull's unwillingness to inform himself about, much less to participate in, discussions and decisions which he regarded, or thought might be regarded, as military planning, particularly if they touched the North Atlantic, and especially Britain. He was a man of peace and in part this was perhaps personal distaste for the subject; in part, with an eye on Congress, he thought ignorance on such topics a political necessity, or at least the course of prudence. Whatever the motive, what began as abnegation later became exclusion from most of the war councils of the nation.

This tendency emerged early in 1941. In the preceding fall Marshall and Stark and their staffs had started to lay out a "national objective," as Stark put it, for the President's consideration. In its final version, dated November 12, 1940, Stark's memorandum set forth various plans for action in case of war. The fourth of these, Plan DOG as it was called, providing for "a strong offensive in the Atlantic and a defensive in the Pacific," [1] embodied — not for the first time — what became the basic American military strategy during the war. With the third-term election out of the way, Roosevelt responded vigorously to this memorandum and called for a joint estimate of the over-all military situation by the three departments. The machinery of government, however, was not geared to such a production. To save time, Stark and Marshall prepared an estimate for submission to the President after the concurrence of the three Secretaries was obtained; and it was ready a little before Christmas. In summary, it concluded: "Our interests in the Far East are very important. It would, however, be incorrect to consider that they are as important to us as is the integrity of the Western Hemisphere, or as important as preventing the defeat of the British Commonwealth. The issues in the Orient will largely be decided in Europe." It recommended, therefore, rapid rearmament and abstention from steps that would provoke attack by any other power — specifically, Japan; and in case of attack by Japan, restriction of Pacific operations so as to permit a major offensive in the Atlantic. This last was coupled with a reservation, however, against the acceptance of allied commitments without a clear prior understanding as to objectives, forces to be provided, operations planned, command arrangements, etc. When this was shown to Hull, he "felt that the recommendations were of a technical military nature outside the proper field of his Department. He listened to the argument that the purpose of the recommendations was to set up a policy approved by all three De-

[1] Watson, *Chief of Staff*, pp. 118 ff.; Maurice Matloff and Edwin M. Snell, *Strategic Planning for Coalition Warfare, 1941-1942,* Office of the Chief of Military History, Department of the Army, Washington, 1953, pp. 25-28.

partments rather than by the military alone. He did not commit himself, . . ." [1] It is only fair to say that he followed broadly the implications of the policy recommended; he was not out of step, only aloof.

Hull's attitude was reasserted more emphatically that spring when the most important of the pre-war Anglo-American military and naval staff conferences, begun in Washington in January 1941, were concluded in March with the preparation of two agreed papers, ABC-1 dealing with joint strategy and strategic cooperation, and ABC-2 dealing with air power. They were military documents, to be sure, with no acknowledged political standing, and were treated gingerly by all concerned. But when they were circulated, Hull refused even to look at them.[2]

An episode illustrating the converse occurred in April, when the need for taking over from the British the protection and garrisoning of Iceland, as envisaged in ABC-1, suddenly became urgent. The President demanded prompt action on an agreement with the Icelandic authorities. Whether from fear of the risk of disclosing the existence or contents of ABC-1 or for other reasons, he assigned the task of reopening negotiations with the Icelandic Consul-General to Hopkins and the Navy; Hopkins was assisted by Welles, but apparently Hull learned of it only later. The incident was both symptomatic and prophetic.

Although in 1941, for the first time in some years, our diplomatic and military policies were actually in fair alignment, deficiencies in the State Department's machinery of coordination with the rest of the government — as distinguished from circumstances attributable to the personality of its incumbent chief — began to show in the fall months. As the Japanese negotiations ground on to their impasse, the department was receiving a great deal of pertinent information from abroad, east, west and south, nearly all of it alarming in varying degrees, and was dutifully passing it along to the other appropriate authorities. It pointed to the probability of an attack upon us.

[1] Watson, *Chief of Staff*, p. 123.
[2] William L. Langer and S. Everett Gleason, *The Undeclared War: 1940-1941*, Harper, New York, 1953, p. 288.

But in contrast to the military, who by that time had at least some plans for what they thought they should do in that event, State had no regular organization for preparing and clearing foreign policy plans that took the collapse of the Japanese negotiations as their point of departure.

## ECONOMIC MOBILIZATION

As in other areas of organized and intensive civil-military relations, the wartime evolution of economic mobilization was foreshadowed in pre-war beginnings. These started even more nearly from scratch than the military preparations, and the mature stage—never quite as "total" as the commonly used phrase implied—re-required at least as complete a revolution in previously dominant ideas and habits. But in contrast to the development and prosecution of grand strategy, the course of economic mobilization was a zigzag which remained far more subject to the influences of domestic politics. The theory, the problems and the techniques of managing an economy in full-scale war, which the British had to master between 1939 and 1941, were little appreciated on this side of the water, and the understanding of correlative organizational needs was nebulous. Although Bernard Baruch had preached the need to a select audience for years, no one in this country had given it perceptive study.

Government planning for economic mobilization, vested by the National Defense Act of 1920 as a specific responsibility of the Assistant Secretary of War, was centered on the procurement of industrial materials and products. Its chief feature, and the only one worked out in any detail, was a priority system designed to assure the fulfillment of military needs. Industrial mobilization plans contemplated the priority-granting agency as the central agency for over-all economic policy as well as for its own operations. The industrial mobilization plans were worked out in cooperation with businessmen and the planners anticipated that businessmen would occupy all the major positions in time of war, as in World War I. During any transition to war, officers of the ANMB would lead the way. IMP assumed the existence of a state of war before it came into effect.

Roosevelt had already begun to pay attention to the subject in 1937 when he appointed Louis Johnson as Assistant Secretary of War. Johnson would give vigor to any program, and Roosevelt wanted defense preparations speeded up, but he did not accept the existing organizational proposals as Johnson did. Roosevelt objected to complete centralization over such diverse matters as priorities, selective service and propaganda; he did not intend to turn over the whole machinery of government to businessmen; and he wanted civilian, not military, control at all stages, including any transition period. His own suggestion for organizing economic mobilization, at least initially, was to use the Advisory Commission to the Council of National Defense (NDAC), still legally in existence though dormant since World War I. This would have the great advantage of flexibility. It would minimize the risks of premature commitments to untried appointees, their agencies and policies. It would not necessitate new legislation immediately, which might be difficult to get. It would avoid the undesirable features Roosevelt saw in the Industrial Mobilization Plan.

Johnson mistook the depths of the President's convictions on the subject, sidestepped any immediate issue, and proceeded by 1939 to complete a revised IMP. It was modified in numerous minor respects to take account of New Deal sensibilities but it adhered to the pattern of earlier plans. Finally in 1939 Johnson proposed to the President a public unveiling of the plan by way of the establishment of a board to review and report on it. Roosevelt agreed and suggested that Edward R. Stettinius, Jr., the youthful head of U. S. Steel and scion of a Morgan partner, be made chairman. Johnson, Edison and the military planners named the other members of the board, to which they gave the name of War Resources Board — a name for which the country was not yet ready. Aside from the presidents of MIT and Brookings the members were drawn exclusively from finance and big business. In due course this fact, and the real or supposed connections of several members with J. P. Morgan and Company, also drew unfavorable comment. To cap these maladroit moves, Johnson and Edison announced, just as the war in Europe was breaking out, that in an emergency this board would become the proposed War Resources Administration.

All this was hardly calculated to win Roosevelt's support, and the WRB compounded its difficulties by disregarding his instructions to prepare a scheme of organization along the lines of the NDAC. When the board finally realized that the President meant what he said, it was too late. The board's report was impounded and the board itself disbanded. By that time the Nazi conquest of Poland was over, the "phony war" stage had set in, the immediate need for action was less apparent, and any plan to initiate economic mobilization was set aside. A lull of several months followed this false start.[1]

The only other positive move in this area in 1939, the transfer of the Army-Navy Munitions Board (ANMB) to Roosevelt's supervision on July 5, also proved abortive. Unlike the Joint Board, covered in the same Military Order, ANMB had too technical and restricted a sphere of competence to warrant the President's attention. The coordination and prosecution of Army and Navy requirements and procurement, ANMB's prime function, was an important but specialized part of the over-all task of economic mobilization.

Roosevelt's failure to establish a mobilization agency in 1939 has been very widely criticized, yet it is hard to see what such an agency could have accomplished in the prevailing temper of the time. In retrospect the urgent preparatory need was for a vast expansion of raw materials capacity, of machine tool production and of shipbuilding, aircraft and other industrial plant facilities, together with large-scale imports and stockpiling of tropical and other overseas-source raw materials like rubber and tin. These all became critically scarce in another two or three years, and it took time to enlarge or replace supplies then, or to develop synthetic substitutes. Earlier expansion would have relieved later inflationary problems, too. But our recent experience with Civil Defense should be reminder enough

[1] An account of the whole episode from 1936 to 1939 is given in Albert A. Blum's case study, "The Birth and Death of the M-Day Plan," Twentieth Century Fund, mimeo.

how futile such proposals would have been in 1939. The steel industry's operating rate averaged just under 65 per cent for that year. The copper industry languished with a 9-cents-a-pound price. Military orders, foreign and domestic, were still small. There were millions of unemployed.

The necessary galvanizing stimulus for initial organizing steps at least — stern actual measures were still months away — came with the disasters of the spring of 1940; and then Roosevelt moved swiftly. On May 31 he re-established the NDAC, and economic mobilization was under way. The commission had seven members: Edward R. Stettinius, Jr., for industrial materials; William S. Knudsen, from General Motors, for industrial production; Sidney Hillman, from the Amalgamated Clothing Workers, for labor problems; Ralph Budd, from the Burlington railroad, for transportation; Chester Davis, with Federal Reserve and Farm Credit experience, for agriculture; Leon Henderson, from the Russell Sage Foundation and SEC, for price stabilization and civilian supply; and Harriet Elliott, from the Women's College of the University of North Carolina, for consumer problems. The commission had no designated chairman. Aside from formal meetings, its members individually had to find their own tasks. Though in form advisory to the Council of National Defense, the NDAC was in fact advisory to the President, if indeed advisory is the proper term. Much of its "advice" soon took the shape of directives to the procurement authorities and to businessmen.

The NDAC has not had many admirers, and it was not adapted to cope with mobilization problems as the economy finally began to respond to the incentives and demands put up to it. Yet during the eight months of its existence it served many essential purposes. It enlisted the participation of business, agriculture, labor, academic people and the world of civilian government in mobilization. It was educational and energizing. It ensured the active use of two indispensable professional groups, the economists and lawyers. It was a first testing and training ground for what were to become the key mobilization and stabilization agencies — agencies that would have had no nucleus in WRB or WRA — and for leadership talent.

NDAC attained no great popularity with the War and Navy Departments. The civilian heads were accustomed to men like Stettinius and Knudsen, but Henderson, Davis and Hillman were outside their ken as working partners. The reactions of uniformed officers in the two departments tended to be even more emphatic. Some of them stood in unreserved awe of executives of companies like U. S. Steel and General Motors; but there was far less community, on both sides, between the military and the representatives of other segments of the economy that were included in NDAC.

In February 1941, responding to prodding and criticism from all sides, and to demands, especially from the military, for a production chief, Roosevelt by Executive Order created instead, within the legal framework provided by the Office for Emergency Management, the Office of Production Management to deal more effectively with the growing problems of industrial supply. At intervals afterward other agencies were hived off from NDAC to handle labor disputes, price control and civilian supply, scientific development, petroleum supply, foreign intelligence and other special functions.

In time, OPM too proved inadequate to its task. Still resisting proposals for concentrated authority in one man — proposals that inevitably sharpened the controversy over whether a businessman with a business outlook should be allowed to run the economy (and so, it was charged, reverse the social gains since 1933) — Roosevelt appointed Knudsen and Hillman as Director-General and Associate Director-General to head OPM; with the Secretaries of War and Navy they also composed its policy council. Pressed at a news conference, the President explained the new arrangement with the unconvincing analogy of a law partnership.

The compromise of interests in this dual headship served his political purpose for the time being, but it plainly bewildered Knudsen and it complicated some growing administrative difficulties. Hillman's Labor Division was not easily linked with the Production, Purchases and Priorities Divisions of OPM, which in turn were in process of being reorganized into groupings along commodity lines in order to reduce the number of points of industry contact and make industrial programs more coherent. OPM's formal powers were in the main to supervise, to review, to question and to coordinate, leaving the letting of contracts and the assignment of specific priorities to the Army and Navy, the Maritime Commission and Treasury Procurement. But increasingly it was drawn into operations, in the management of priorities, arrangements for plant expansion and the like, to the detriment of its role as a central agency for policy guidance. For that role its council was also too restricted in membership to comprehend the needs and viewpoints of other agencies with different orientations. Henderson's Office of Price Administration and Civilian Supply, for instance, with no powers but brains and the right of free speech, was energetically trying to restrain domestic price increases. Lend-Lease, meanwhile, was trying to secure for Britain and Russia a share of the inadequate flow of finished munitions which military authorities felt were desperately needed to improve our own defenses. Neither OPACS nor OLLA had a formal place in OPM councils.

Complaints mounted as the rate of industrial mobilization seemed discouragingly slow. In August 1941 Roosevelt superimposed on OPM the Supply Priorities and Allocations Board (SPAB) as a top policy council. Vice President Wallace was its chairman; its other members were all operating agency heads in their own right, except for Hopkins. SPAB too had an unhappy life, though the inclusion of Hopkins, Wallace and Henderson in its membership stepped up the pace of defense activities noticeably, and brought their direction closer to the President's way of thinking. It was ironic that through 1941 the Henderson New Deal wing, charged with concern for the civilian economy, consistently pressed for a faster and more drastic change-over to defense purposes than the Army programming and procurement officials who dealt with OPM, or than many OPM officials at operating levels. But SPAB's lines of authority were confusing, and neither the Army nor the Navy fully understood the usefulness of separating the coordinating function of SPAB from the operating functions that were swamping OPM.

One clearly constructive development in military-civilian cooperation in economic mobilization emerged in the latter part of 1941. No complaint of OPM and SPAB against the military was oftener repeated than the inability or refusal of the Army and Navy to supply a firm program of requirements — a deficiency the services in turn laid to the uncertainties of their targets. Pressure to meet this lack came from many sources: from Knudsen, Henderson and others in SPAB and OPM; from Hopkins; from Stimson and his Assistant Secretaries Robert P. Patterson and John J. McCloy in the War Department; from Marshall and several of his assistants, most notably General James H. Burns who was working with Hopkins on lend-lease; from Arthur B. Purvis and Jean Monnet of the British Supply Council, who because of Britain's earlier involvement understood better than most Americans the general theory of mobilization and were versed in its techniques as well; and, in decisive fashion, from the President himself.

Out of the apparent confusion three documents were drawn up in the fall. One was the first Anglo-American-Canadian "balance sheet" showing the existing stocks and currently projected production of major military items; this statement was drafted, with much assistance from others, of course, by Stacy May, chief economist for OPM. Another, prepared by the military and shown only to the President, was a strategic estimate of how we could win the war if we entered it. The third, also prepared by the military, was the Victory Program of material needs to carry out the proposed strategy; and this served as a basis for production planning in OPM. However imperfect these documents by later standards, they represented a tremendous advance in programming and were of inestimable value when full-scale mobilization began after Pearl Harbor.

The nature of the cooperative effort that produced these papers is significant, for it was based on personal relationships, more than on the formal cooperation of SPAB or OPM with the War Department or the Joint Board. Monnet, for example, was an old friend of McCloy, and cultivated Hopkins' friendship. Whole paragraphs from a Patterson memorandum designed only for use inside the War Department turned up a few weeks later in a letter from Roosevelt that provided the initiative for the formulation of the Victory Program.[1] General Burns shuttled back and forth between the War

[1] Watson, *Chief of Staff*, Chapter 11.

Department and Hopkins' office in the White House, dealing with friends, whether or not his formal superiors, in both places. The habits and organization of the military establishment afford opportunities for concerted action across jurisdictional lines, based on personal confidence. As in business or diplomacy, negotiations entirely dependent on formally organized intercorporate or international or interdepartmental relations are apt to find the going rougher, more protracted, and less productive of satisfactory results.

••••••••••••••••••••••••••••••••••••••••••••••••••••••••••••••••••••••••••••••••••••••••••

# CHAPTER 2

# The War:

## DOMESTIC ORGANIZATION
## AND THE MILITARY IMPACT
## AT HOME

The attack on Pearl Harbor was a shock and a surprise to all Americans; the coming of war was not. For months the growing probability of war had been sensed, if vaguely, by most of those who paid attention to public affairs, and it was quite definitely foreseen by the President and his advisers. The unexpected manner of its coming was in a way a relief, for it spared our government from two decisions the President had dreaded: what to do in the Far East if the Japanese should proceed into Southeast Asia against the Dutch, French and British possessions while carefully refraining from attacking the Philippines; and what to do in Europe if Japan attacked us and Hitler made no move. Hitler's declaration of war, on the heels of the Pearl Harbor assault, tied together at once both the Atlantic and the Pacific wars, before the disastrous extent and devastating power of the Japanese sweep through the South Pacific could be felt. The basic foreign policy arguments of the previous two years were over. Coming full circle around from its faith in isolation and self-sufficiency, the country was now united on the uncomplicated propositions that Germany and Japan must be defeated, and that the help of all available hands, here and abroad, would be welcomed as well as needed to that end.

Other and controversial goals, near-term and long-term, foreign and domestic, emerged later to divide the interests and sentiments of the country, divisions that persisted into the post-war years. But for the time being and for the agreed goals the need was for the largest and strongest military forces possible, in the shortest possible time. The processes of getting them and the later fact of having them brought profound changes in civil-military relations in the domestic scene, though the adjustments were less drastic for us than for any other major power.

The shock of actual war dissolved many official inhibitions grounded in the uncertainties of approaching crisis, and released barriers to more decisive steps along lines already at least partially indicated, and tentatively or ardently discussed, or taken for granted. But overt hostilities also entailed some obvious shifts in the centers of public attention and official power, and corresponding though subtler changes in the relative weights and influence of established institutions, as significant as the formal reorganizations. The quiet abolition of the WPA in the spring of 1942, by Executive Order and with the full approval of Harry Hopkins, was in a small way symbolic. More important illustrations are to be seen in Executive-Congressional relationships and in the temporary eclipse of the judiciary.


## THE CONSTITUTIONAL BALANCE

No inhibition had operated more inexorably to limit the pace and nature of Roosevelt's moves to stop Hitler in 1940 and 1941 than his estimate of what the Congress would stand for, or would muster the votes to support if legislation was required. During that period "the Congress" often meant, concretely, the attitudes of such members as Andrew J. May, chairman of the House Military Affairs Committee, or David I. Walsh, chairman of the Senate Naval Affairs Committee, who were not to be persuaded by the logic of appeals to the national interest. The one-vote margin in the House for the renewal of Selective Service in September 1941 was an achievement that carried its own warning: the President could not afford to lose in such a try.

## THE ROLE OF CONGRESS

After Pearl Harbor the legislative situation was transformed. No member wanted to be accused of delaying or getting in the way of the military. Officers in uniform suddenly became effective witnesses before Congressional committees. Word that the War Department favored a bill was likely to be decisive testimony, and civilian agencies maneuvered to get that support if possible for bills they were interested in.

In the first few weeks and months debate was shortened and votes were overwhelmingly given for bills the President requested. The declaration of war against Japan, an easy decision now, went through both houses in less than half an hour. The declarations against Germany and Italy, on December 11, went through all stages in a day. A week later, on the 18th, the First War Powers Act became law, giving the President the power, among others, to create, abolish and reorganize executive agencies as he thought fit. Two days afterward, on the 20th, the draft age limits were widened to 18 and 64. Military appropriations virtually unlimited in language or amount were voted one after another without demur; within six months nearly $100 billion was appropriated, and another $60 billion was added in the next four months.[1] Before the end of January 1942 the Senate, after insisting on concessions to agricultural interests, passed the Emergency Price Control Act, which the House had passed in November only after four months' reluctant consideration. While the Senate voted, the newspapers echoed with news of Rommel's capture of Bengasi and of the Japanese siege of Singapore and landings in the Solomons and New Guinea. On March 27, two

[1] U. S. Bureau of the Budget, *The United States at War*, G.P.O., Washington, 1946, p. 112.

weeks after MacArthur's evacuation from Corregidor to Australia, the Second War Powers Act went through, though not without debate and some changes in the draft bill proposed. It expanded the President's authority to requisition, enforce priorities, and allocate materials and facilities in short supply. For civilian consumers, "allocate" was a statutory euphemism for "ration"; tires and sugar were already on the list, and, for the eastern seaboard, gasoline was shortly to follow.

Taken altogether, and in combination with previous legislation, these acts were still considerably less sweeping than the one-sentence endowment the House of Commons gave Churchill in a single day's work in May 1940: that all persons in the realm might be called upon to place "themselves, their services and their property" at His Majesty's disposal, in accordance with regulations and directions to be formulated later. Nevertheless, outside the area of domestic economic stabilization, and perhaps the ticklish field of censorship, a sufficient statutory base for the prosecution of the war was on the books.

The time would come — it began even before the Congressional elections of 1942, in fact — when legislative influences would be strongly felt again in the domestic aspects of wartime economic policies, on price controls and rationing, on draft deferments, on agricultural and labor policies, on the abortive attempt to limit upper-bracket salaries, on taxes, on OWI's domestic information program, on administrative problems brought under the scrutiny of the Truman Committee, and later, on reconversion policies. Congressional standing and investigating committees heard a great deal of testimony, much of it in secret, and picked away at particular points and issues. The Truman Committee's activities were unusually noteworthy and constructive.[1] It avoided the Civil War precedent of legislative interference; it helped and supported the armed services; and it reassured the public by its functioning. The quite different Pearl Harbor investigating committee was probably either too early or too late for its purpose. Some others — the Smith and

---

[1] See the voluminous *Hearings* and *Reports* of the Senate Special Committee Investigating the National Defense Program, 76th and 77th Congresses.

the Dondero Committees, for example — fell short of the standards of these, and kept up their anti-New Deal vendettas. Generally speaking, the tendency of Congressional influences on wartime regulations was to prevent the executive agencies from pushing too dogmatically their policy concepts.

Later on, anxiety over Congressional support for a post-war organization of nations became a major factor in the President's calculations. But for the time being, Congress was rather in the position of a sidewalk superintendent, watching the immense construction program in the executive branch go forward in all its apparent confusion and haste.

## THE JUDICIARY

The judiciary as an institution affecting civil-military relations in wartime can be dismissed briefly. Individual Supreme Court justices performed some notable individual services in other capacities. Roberts headed the Pearl Harbor investigation, Frankfurter was a confidential adviser to many former students and other officials in the executive branch on their particular perplexities. Byrnes resigned to become Director of the Office of Economic Stabilization, and at the end of the war Jackson took leave to prosecute the Nuremberg trials. But the Supreme Court as a corporate body, already in a temporary "twilight" since its conversion in 1937, retired even further to the sidelines. It swiftly refused to review the military trials of the Nazi saboteurs who were caught slipping ashore on Long Island and on the Florida coast. It declined to intervene in the shameful Japanese-American relocation center cases until after that damage was done, and then acted only feebly.[1] It sustained the constitutionality of price and rent controls and rationing.[2] It denied any jurisdiction to hear appeals from the post-war international trials of war criminals.

It would not be fair to conclude from these instances simply that

[1] Clinton Rossiter, *The Supreme Court and the Commander in Chief,* Cornell University Press, Ithaca, 1951.

[2] *Yakus* v. *United States,* 321 U. S. 414 (1944); *L. P. Steuart & Bro.* v. *Bowles,* 322 U. S. 398 (1944).

*inter arma silent leges;* for, to the contrary, an immense volume of regulations poured from the government agencies into the *Federal Register,* drawn by lawyers who gave meticulous attention to their legal authorities and limits. But the breadth of statutory delegations and the marked absence of constitutional issues, beyond those just noted, left the judiciary with more enforcement than interpretative work to do; and enforcement was always auxiliary. OPA violation cases alone came to outnumber all other types of cases put together on federal court dockets.

## CIVILIAN IMPACTS

A large standing army, so the framers of our Constitution supposed, was *ipso facto* a menace to liberty. Yet the experience of World War II in this country (however it may sometimes have been in the immediate wake of our invading troops in Europe), including the behavior of soldiers on leave and more or less free to travel about the country, furnished remarkably little to justify the apprehensions of eighteenth-century libertarians. The services maintained their military police and shore patrol; extended their patrol to railway and bus terminals, the streets and gathering places of civilian population centers; operated their disciplinary systems; resorted to "off limits" designations at local trouble spots; cooperated with civil authorities; and generally minimized friction in the direct contacts of troops with the citizenry at large. The draftees, after all, were a cross-section of the population in their age bracket; out of uniform, they were indistinguishable.

The significant domestic impingements of the wartime military establishment, the adjustments and potential conflicts between civilian and military activities and interests, instead were felt indirectly through the intermediary instruments of government agencies, business firms, trade unions and other organized groups. No single formula of organization or policy emerged to govern these adjustments.

In some cases it was possible to draw fairly clear jurisdictional lines that gave the military all the leeway they wanted and eliminated inter-agency friction. This method, for example, disposed of most fiscal matters. The supply of money into the Treasury from tax revenues and borrowing was ample throughout the war; the services did not have to worry about that. Their spending from the Treasury they handled themselves. The Army and Navy were exempt from the Executive Order of June 10, 1933 that had centralized civilian disbursements in the Treasury; and they kept their historic autonomy in the operation of their own accounting systems. The volume of their transactions overwhelmed the auditing facilities of the General Accounting Office. Military fiscal administration, accordingly, was a headache chiefly for the services, though the Treasury played an important part in determining pay arrangements, exchange rates, and other financial policies in liberated and occupied areas.

So it was with postal service, too. For security reasons as well as convenience, the Army and Navy operated their own postal system, interchanging with the Post Office Department at a few designated domestic offices, and using a series of APO numbers to cloak destinations as well as to facilitate military mail distribution. This permitted a military censorship of incoming and outgoing military mail, and of civilian mail to and from the war zones.

In the field of transportation, the airlines were perhaps most sharply affected. About two thirds of the planes owned by the companies were requisitioned by the military, and the pilots and other operating personnel were taken over either as soldiers or as uniformed civilians. All or virtually all overseas flights were operated by the Air Transport Command and the Naval Air Transport Service. At home, the airlines operated their very limited stock of planes under a governmental priority system, which meant that the seats were allocated to civilians who seemed important enough, or whose business seemed important enough for the war effort, subject to being "bumped" by higher-priority passengers. The services requisitioned rolling stock for freight, and some Pullman space was preempted for military use on the railroads; the rest was handled by priorities doled out by the Office of Defense Transportation (ODT).[1]

---

[1] *The United States at War*, pp. 155-72; U. S. Office of Defense Transportation, *Civilian War Transport . . . 1941-1946*, G.P.O., Washington, 1948.

But soldiers and civilians alike could stand in the aisles of coach trains and inter-city buses and local transit facilities. Taxis went unrationed.

Official price controls over suppliers' charges to the military establishments, although legally vested in OPA by the sweeping terms of the Emergency Price Control Act, were waived as to combat items and components, and were otherwise drastically modified in accordance with an agreement first worked out in the fall of 1942 between Henderson for OPA and Patterson for the Army, and then extended by Forrestal for the Navy. In essence it preserved OPA price controls over the procurement of goods that were sold in civilian markets, but recognized the need for more speed and freedom in pricing munitions and other special items than OPA procedures allowed. Contract renegotiation, administered by the military contracting authorities, was the substitute for price controls over military goods, and the excess profits tax was a second line of protection for the government's interest.

## CENSORSHIP AND PUBLIC INFORMATION

Censorship over the publication of news in the interests of military security was exercised on a basis of voluntary cooperation by the newspapers, wire services and other media, through an Office of Censorship. Presumably any statute on the subject would have been unconstitutional. To secure cooperation, the President called on Byron Price, general manager of the Associated Press, to head the Office; and this worked well enough except in the case of the *Chicago Tribune,* which refused to go along on one or two critical occasions. Censorship over publication, however, was a second line of defense: the primary control was at the source, and the sources of most of the war news were inevitably in government hands to begin with. The practical questions were therefore what and how much to give out to whom and when, and in what form. The Army and Navy with commendable intent allowed accredited war correspondents to enter the combat theaters, and generally helped them to travel about, while maintaining a censorship over their dispatches through control of the lines of communication. But in addition the armed services as well as all civilian war agencies, in Washington and in the field, built up publicity staffs which ground out reams of press releases and other informational materials. Most of it was factual; some of it, necessarily or intentionally, was a conscious instrument of the policy of the issuing agency, and as such might have ramifications beyond that agency and its immediate audience.

To exert some central policy guidance in this field, to eliminate contradictions and control inter-agency conflicts, as well as to accent the positive notes in our war aims, the President in the late spring of 1942 established the Office of War Information. OWI was an amalgamation, and enlargement, of several previously established independent agencies headed by distinguished writers like Archibald MacLeish, then Librarian of Congress, and Lowell Mellett, reporter and editor. OWI was given coordinating authority over releases affecting more than one agency. To head it Roosevelt chose Elmer Davis, the most respected of political commentators and a devoted defender of civil liberties; the head of the Overseas Branch was Robert Sherwood, playwright and ghost writer for Roosevelt. This link with the White House led, eventually, to his writing of *Roosevelt and Hopkins* — a major contribution to our knowledge of the decade. The Domestic Branch of OWI quickly ran into conservative Congressional trouble over its impulses toward candor and greater social equality. The Overseas Branch survived uncertainly into the post-war years. OWI proved no match for the autonomous tendencies, whether predatory or self-laudatory, of some of the more assertive agencies, civil as well as military. But so far as its influences were felt they were wholesome.

Along with these there were many more minor matters, relatively speaking. The big domestic issues had to do with manpower and labor problems, food supply, and above all, industrial production.

## MANPOWER PROBLEMS

The special problems of recruiting various highly professional skills and adapting them to military needs must be put outside the scope of this account. Two professional groups may be mentioned in passing, however, as illustrating contrasts in adjustment: the medical profession and the physical scientists, especially those in the new fields of electronics and nuclear fission. The doctors were needed where the troops were, and so were spread around and assigned to every sizable military and naval unit wherever located, at home or abroad. Being habituated to a measure of organized political activity through the medical associations which could speak for their occupational interests in Washington, and having a secure and historic organizational base in the military and naval establishments in the Surgeon Generals' offices, they assimilated readily to military patterns. If some of them came away disgruntled in the end, it was because their skills rusted from disuse in what turned out to be quiet sectors of the war. Those who drew the most active assignments contributed to great advances in certain branches of medical science and technology.

The scientists on the other hand were clustered at a relatively few laboratories and development installations. Their traditions were open and apolitical. They chafed at the secrecy and nearly every other aspect of their work for the military. Nevertheless, by the consummate skill of Vannevar Bush and his associates in the Office of Scientific Research and Development, their talents were enlisted and mobilized with striking effect.[1] OSRD was both an innovator and a buffer in military-scientific relations. Bush's early and continuing connection with Marshall, and Stimson's consistently active support, were largely responsible for the fruitfulness of scientific contributions to the development of new weapons. The great development of university contacts with government was a lasting by-product. Still, many scientists emerged from their wartime experience, in spite of their achievements, with a strong anti-military bias. Their feelings about secrecy were only temporarily mollified by the issuance of the Smyth report on atomic energy in 1945. Their

[1] James P. Baxter 3d, *Scientists Against Time*, Little, Brown, Boston, 1946; see also Vannevar Bush's subsequent reflections, *Modern Arms and Free Men*, Simon and Schuster, New York, 1949; Henry L. Stimson and McGeorge Bundy, *On Active Service in Peace and War*, Harper, New York, 1948, pp. 464-69; and Don K. Price, *Government and Science*, New York University Press, New York, 1954.

feelings about national policy found a partial outlet in the formation of a new scientific society and the publication of a new journal, the *Bulletin of the Atomic Scientists*. The long-run problem of articulating organized scientific endeavor with the military establishment, to the mutual advantage and satisfaction of all parties, loomed among the major post-war issues, during the controversies over unification and over H-bomb development, and down into post-sputnik days.

The recruitment of professional and executive personnel constituted a group of critically important specialized problems. More generally, manpower policy during the war hinged on the resolution of the three-way tugs of the draft, of war industries and the service occupations associated with them, and of agriculture.[1] In part, these needs were met by successful efforts to draw new workers, mainly women, into the labor force, and to break down racial and other discriminations against the full utilization of available skills. World War II, like World War I and the Civil War before it, had permanently relaxing effects in opening occupations previously barred to various groups, most notably women and Negroes. The wartime Committee on Fair Employment Practices became the model and stimulus for post-war activities, national and state, along similar lines. Furthermore, to an unprecedented degree, the wartime labor force was mobile. Millions of citizens, men and women, soldiers and civilians, moved to places and into occupations they had never known before. The conflicts of interest remained, however, and sharpened by increasing military needs, were reflected in the behavior of local boards and millions of citizens in the presence of the threat of induction and the incentives of high wages, among other factors influencing personal decisions.

SELECTIVE SERVICE

The Selective Service System, as established in 1940, had and kept a close military tie at its national headquarters. But its field network of state directors and local boards of citizens, nominated by the

---

[1] *The United States at War*, Chs. 7, 14.

governors, had a distinctly less military and more grass-roots character than the War Department's previous plans had called for. The
early abundance of men available for induction meant that until
the summer of 1943 the local boards, in responding to their monthly
numerical quotas, were largely free to decide for themselves the
hard questions of priorities in deferment on occupational, depend-
ency, age and other grounds. The habits of local autonomy so developed proved beyond the power of national headquarters to control.
They also attracted strong Congressional support. When the War
Manpower Commission, created by Executive Order in April 1942,
was reorganized and strengthened in December, the Selective Service was made a part of it. WMC never succeeded in assimilating
this major component. Local boards typically deferred farmers
and fathers, even young ones, in spite of WMC's continued endeavors
to direct men into war industries, and of the Army's growing insistence on getting the younger age groups. The boards were suspicious of claims of "essentiality" in either industrial or government
service. By the Tydings amendment in November 1942, Congress
sustained the boards' tendency to approve agricultural deferments,
which made up four sevenths of the 3.6 million occupational deferments extant on September 1, 1943. While the Wheeler "father-draft
bill" was being considered in the fall of 1943, local boards simply
failed to meet their monthly quotas, still running then at about
400,000. The watered-down version that finally passed on December
5, 1943 reinforced local board attitudes on the immediate subject and
restored Selective Service a few days later to its previously independent position, outside WMC. Except as local arrangements were
worked out with state directors and war plant managers in some
areas, therefore, selective service was never operated as an implement
of a comprehensive manpower policy.

LABOR SUPPLY

The rest of WMC consisted chiefly of parts of the Federal Security Agency (of which Paul McNutt remained the Administrator),
especially the recently federalized United States Employment Service, which operated a job referral system and was a potentially

useful, though badly handicapped, instrument for a more stringent labor allocation policy; and of the Labor Division of WPB, till then under Sidney Hillman, and now given to Wendell Lund, former head of the Michigan Unemployment Compensation Commission. In these components the voices of professional personnel management people, social workers and organized labor were influential. Meanwhile, outside WMC control, the Army and especially the Navy continued to recruit directly, both men and women into uniform, and civilian workers into government-operated arsenals, shipyards and other establishments (their civilian force reached a peak of 2 million); the Civil Service Commission recruited government workers and to some extent influenced federal personnel policies; the Department of Agriculture and its county war boards recruited farm labor; and the War Shipping Administration supervised the manning of the merchant marine. Until the end of 1942 WMC had no significant field establishment of its own. With manpower even more than with food supply, the ingrained memories of pre-war unemployment and the attitudes accompanying them postponed, and in the end prevented, the general acceptance of any coordinated scheme and machinery of control.

So throughout the war WMC sought to maintain that, as the agency with primary responsibility for labor supply, it should be able to investigate and control civilian labor utilization. High turnover rates, negotiated cost-plus contracts and common observation around war plants gave point to its claim. But despite Chairman McNutt's paper powers to issue directives, WMC lacked the prestige to make good its position. It could not carry labor leaders' support unless the unions were to become the vehicles of its proposed controls. Employers resolutely opposed this as an interference with their right to hire and fire. WMC was brushed aside by the WPB and the contracting officers of the Army and Navy procurement agencies and their field representatives who controlled the practical shape of the problem by their choice of the plants and locations for the award of contracts. Against such opposition, and even with War and Navy Department support, McNutt was unable to get Presidential, let alone Congressional, support in 1942 for a national service bill along British lines, with USES as the proposed operating agency. On the other hand, when the Austin-Wadsworth "work-or-fight" bill revived the national service issue in 1944, with the blessing of the President's annual message (given on the recommendation of the War and Navy Departments and without consultation with McNutt), and in a sterner form that contemplated using Selective Service as the operating agent, WMC found labor and management this time allied with it in opposition. That bill failed, too.

In the meantime, labor supply problems had become sufficiently acute to require some sort of action. In 1943, for the first time since 1918, full employment was reached. Since the summer of 1940 the ranks of the unemployed had dropped by more than 8 million; over 5 million additional women and many young people under 18 had entered the labor force; and the average work week had increased about 8 hours. The most disturbing facts were that the average monthly turnover rate of separations in industrial employment had run up to a fraction above 8 per cent — about 100 per cent a year — and that a stable total meant a shrinking civilian component, for the draft boards still inexorably drew their 400,000 men monthly toward the military goal of 10.8 million in uniform. The goal itself was a compromise figure, below the military request. JCS refused to recede from it when WMC questioned whether the civilian economy could feasibly sustain it; and the President backed the JCS stand, reaffirming the compromise.

The steps taken in the fall of 1943 recognized the essentially local nature of most labor supply problems, in spite of the extraordinary mobility of the American labor force. With prodding from Director Byrnes of the Office of War Mobilization, and the prestige support of a Baruch-Hancock report, Area Production Urgency Committees and Area Manpower Priorities Committees were established, beginning on the west coast. They brought together field representatives of all the procurement agencies in each area under WPB and WMC chairmanship, respectively, and introduced a healthy note of realism into inter-agency discussions of local measures to mitigate the difficulties. But their results depended on consent, and mainly on the attitudes taken by employers and the contracting officers. In the one test case early in 1945 where WMC drove for compulsory measures to shift textile workers from low- to high-priority plants, in New Bedford, Massachusetts, the effort was a complete failure.[1] It is hazardous to speculate on the steps that might have been taken had the war lasted considerably longer, as war planners for the final campaign in the Far East anticipated. But it is clear that in this war, the military authorities, though they could readily create labor shortages, had not the political support necessary to introduce compulsory labor controls to deal with them. And it is equally clear that WMC lacked the political strength to alter substantially the procurement and industrial policies that produced the shortages. It is not at all clear that compulsory controls would have solved more problems than they raised.

## LABOR DISPUTES

Labor disputes concerned the military only as they threatened interruptions in essential production. Roosevelt resisted compulsory legislation for dealing with these, and instead relied on the uneasy balancing of interests in the tri-partite machinery of the War Labor Board and its predecessors. These agencies began as mediatory bodies and only slowly assumed regulatory functions that finally included what in practical effect amounted to compulsory arbitration. But the sanctions for WLB decisions — and also its calculated inactions — ultimately rested, on the one hand, on labor's "no-strike" pledge, given to Roosevelt just after Pearl Harbor; and on the other hand, on the President's statutory power to take over the plants of recalcitrant employers. When the latter expedient was resorted to, a government agency, the Secretary of Commerce, or Interior, or War, was designated as the titular operator, and management and labor were directed to continue or resume work under an American flag and the nominal supervision of a government official, on WLB or Presidential terms. The Army had no relish for this type of duty even when the plant affected was working directly on military orders.

[1] Kathryn S. Arnow, *The New Bedford Manpower Incident*, Inter-University Case Program Series: No. 38, University of Alabama Press, 1957.

When ultimately the principle and prestige of WLB control were at stake in April 1944 in the case of Montgomery Ward, which could only be linked most indirectly to the war effort, it became a painful necessity for the Army to remove Sewell Avery physically from his board chairman's office in the firm's headquarters in Chicago, and land him in the street outside. In this partly grim, almost comic operation, in which both parties pursued their principles uncharacteristically to a logical conclusion, the soldiers who actually hoisted the embattled old champion of free enterprise in his chair behaved with the most gingerly circumspection. *Molliter manus imposuerunt.* It was a symbolic precedent for the peaceable handling of strikers.

## FOOD SUPPLY

The impact of Army, Navy and lend-lease needs on the food production and distribution resources of the country raised immense operating problems for the procurement authorities, but its effect on civil-military relations was only indirect and tangential. The basic issues were domestic, political and administrative. They involved civilian agencies, organized farm and food trade interests and, inevitably, Congress, its members and committees.

The impact on the civilian economy was felt in three principal ways. First, the purchasing agencies bought from the major food processors in huge, but varying and often unpredictable quantities, to feed some 10 million people in uniform more and better food than they had ordinarily eaten in peacetime, to stock supply depots strung east and west across two oceans, and to support allied armies and peoples. To insure themselves of adequate supplies, the military procurement agencies issued "set aside" orders stipulating generously calculated percentages of the suppliers' output, to be reserved for filling military purchase orders. This was usually a sufficient measure for their purposes, though on at least one occasion when poultry producers in the Del-Mar production centers showed a preference for black market outlets in New York City in 1943, soldiers stopped loaded poultry trucks on the highways and requisitioned their cargoes on the spot. Civilian consumers, with growing purchasing power, competed for what remained after military orders were met. Second, farm and food processing labor, and food handlers and distributors, moved away into uniform or into better paying war industry jobs, even after agricultural draft deferments became almost automatic. Third, the military spokesmen in WPB, in their concern for steel and munitions production, insisted on drastic curtailment of the manufacture of farm machinery that might have made the dwindling farm labor force more productive.

Repercussions of these influences were delayed by the existence and use of large pre-war accumulations of surplus stocks of the major farm commodities that could be stored. The war bailed out the government's investment in previous price support operations, and the initial shortages were chiefly among the imported tropical agricultural products — coffee, vegetable fats and oils, sugar, chocolate, bananas and the like — that were cut off by interruptions to shipping. Aggregate domestic farm production, notwithstanding its handicaps, nevertheless belied some gloomy predictions by rising to the astonishing degree of something like 25 per cent by 1944 in comparison with the 1939-40 average.[1] Aggregate per capita consumption consequently increased over those years, despite the huge overseas shipments. No decline in the real standard of living occurred. But relative demand grew even faster, inventories were depleted, and by the spring of 1943 food rationing and price controls were in general force.[2] Normal distribution patterns were turned upside down as consumers, handlers and processors reached back to bid at the sources of supply, instead of letting producers come bidding to them in the central markets. Rationing (except for sugar, which lingered longer) lasted somewhat over a year, and price controls — with diminishing effectiveness — until shortly after the end of hostilities. Food distribution troubles agitated domestic politics from 1943 down into the post-war period, but they did not threaten Americans with malnutrition, nor directly involve the military. It was otherwise with the liberated areas at the end of the war, with

---

[1] W. W. Wilcox, *The Farmer in the Second World War,* Iowa State College Press, Ames, 1947.

[2] H. C. Mansfield *et al., A Short History of OPA,* G.P.O., Washington, 1948.

peoples exhausted and undernourished and dependent on American supplies.[1] The troubles in meeting their needs stemmed partly from the improvidence of our food policy, and more from what were apparently undue military claims on shipping.

At home, huge stocks of grain and favorable price ratios led to an unprecedented surge in livestock production in 1943, and so to abundant supplies of meat, especially pork, in 1944; that was a good growing year for other crops too. But instead of husbanding this bounty, official policy and private inclination converged in the opposite direction, in a splurge of domestic consumption. General Eisenhower's rallying message to the public from London on New Year's Day, 1944, intimating that the war in Europe might be won before that year was over, had consequences he did not intend or foresee. The food trades saw a specter of surfeit in the markets once military buying ceased, and pushed for a "bare shelf" policy of clearing out inventories. A shortsighted and premature civilian drive for the abolition of food controls was precipitated, and officials who should have known better fell into line. OWMR chief Byrnes hastened it along as the fall elections of 1944 drew near. The trend was too strong to be reversed when military success was postponed by the German counter-attack in December. So when VE-Day came, American food supplies, while perhaps barely adequate to cover overseas relief needs, were under continuing domestic pressures and left little margin to spare.

Meanwhile the Army's main supply concern in 1945 was over the drain on shipping occasioned by the redeployment and build-up across the immense distances of the Pacific. Commanders in that theater reacted to the inadequacies of local harbor facilities and the uncertainties of their next movements by treating the supply ships they received as floating warehouses, instead of turning them around as quickly as possible. The War Shipping Administration and military authorities at home ultimately diagnosed what was happening and took measures to regain control of the freighters and tankers; but critical months in 1945 and 1946 went by before the situation

---

[1] George Woodbridge (staff director), *UNRRA: The History of the United Nations Relief and Rehabilitation Administration,* Columbia University Press, New York, 1950, 3 vols.

eased, and plans and commitments of UNRRA — the United Nations Relief and Rehabilitation Administration — for relief shipments eastward across the Atlantic and beyond were frustrated or disrupted. The transport and supply job was handled generously and in good spirit by the military when they got around to it, though poor crops abroad in 1946 and one of the coldest European winters in modern history in 1946-47 put off until 1948 the time when civilian living standards abroad began to approach pre-war peacetime levels. This was a critical factor in post-war policies for both occupied and liberated areas.

## ECONOMIC MOBILIZATION

In England during the 1930's there was much debate among planners within the government over "the concept of a great war." In the end the accepted definition was "one in which the whole resources of the nation would be engaged." In that concept, the mobilization and direction of national resources, public and private, would resemble a gigantic budgeting operation, encompassing the entire economy and matching and allocating available resources against the most urgent needs according to priorities determined in the top councils of government, in the light of approved strategic plans. Only, the budgeting would be reckoned not in pounds sterling, but in units of the ultimately scarce and decisive resources; these might be foreign exchange, shipping, imported raw materials and supplies, food, manpower, etc., depending on how the war fared. Refined, dependable and current statistics of the supply and use of these resources, as well as the newly developing techniques of national income analysis, were basic to these calculations. Not until this mobilization concept was accepted could effective economic and organizational planning for war get a realistic start. The goal was a balanced effort toward maximum strength such that all contributing elements would be fully used, and hence equally scarce.[1]

The realization of such a concept was slower in the United States. Our own World War I experience was brief; by later standards the

[1] W. K. Hancock and M. M. Gowing, *British War Economy*, H.M.S.O., London, 1949.

mobilization of our economy in 1918 was partial and imperfect. Sophisticated economic analysis of the problem was practically nonexistent. So General MacArthur, for instance, was merely expressing a common lay opinion when he testified in 1931 as Chief of Staff that "the maximum force we are capable of supporting greatly exceeds any we would conceivably mobilize." Actually, at the 1943-44 peak it required nearly half the total resources of the United States in materials and labor to support the forces we did mobilize (and help our allies). This relative degree of engagement closely approached the level of national effort achieved by the British, who appear to have surpassed the Axis powers in this respect. What we might have supported under conditions of invasion at home is pure speculation.

Pearl Harbor had an immediate and powerful effect on the thinking of the military and of most civilians, some of whom were more sensitive and sophisticated about the scope and depth of the economic drain of a great war. It also led promptly to important organizational changes and to the emergence of new leaders. In the nature of things, once the War Department was assured of its manpower needs, its main concern on the logistic side was with industrial production; and by the same token the primary governmental relationships of any production control agency were with the War Department.

WPB AND THE SUPPLY SERVICES

The ARCADIA conference and the President's 1942 New Year announcement of his victory production program — 60,000 planes,[1] 45,000 tanks, 20,000 AA guns and 8 million tons of shipping *in that year* — spurred a major reorganization of OPM and SPAB. The establishment of the War Production Board on January 16, 1942 appeared to mark, for the first time, the delegation in the most

[1] *The United States at War*, p. 103. Robert E. Sherwood, *Roosevelt and Hopkins* (Harper, New York, 1948), p. 474, gives the figure as 45,000 "operational aircraft," in a table showing how the procurement sights were lifted after Pearl Harbor; the other 15,000 were trainers. These were among the figures regarded as unrealistic in March. *Minutes of the WPB Planning Committee*, Historical Reports on War Administration, WPB Doc. Pub. No. 5, G.P.O., Washington, 1946, p. 130.

sweeping terms of all the President's powers in this field in the hands of one man, Chairman Donald M. Nelson, the former head of Sears, Roebuck. Sherwood records Harry Hopkins as having pressed the decision, urged the selection, and consummated the arrangements, all within two or three days,[1] though the general problem and various alternative moves had been under discussion for months. In December the Secretaries of War and Navy and the two military chiefs had strongly but unsuccessfully urged the President to create a new top-priorities committee under military control.

As events showed, the delegation to Nelson was all too sweeping. He was supposed to be simultaneously the director of general mobilization policy and active head of a large, complex operating agency. The combination was not a happy one. Furthermore, Nelson was no empire-builder, and in his position he confronted some others who were, notably General Brehon B. Somervell, who shortly became chief of the Army Services of Supply (SOS, in 1943 renamed Army Service Forces, ASF) in the March 1942 reorganization of the Army. Under Secretary of War Patterson was also an extraordinarily vigorous and decisive man. Judicious and tolerant himself, and disposed to operate by processes of negotiation and consent, Nelson faced men and circumstances demanding more aggressive driving methods. For a complex of reasons, therefore, the President's apparent gift of concentrated authority to him proved vain, and the relations of WPB with the services, as well as with the civilian war agencies, always left a good deal to be desired. At the same time, the lines of civil-military division of labor and of power were continually blurred and were, perhaps inevitably, controversial at each of the main stages in the acceleration and control of industrial production — in the determination of total requirements and of the priorities among major programs; in the allocation of materials and components; in the business of procurement; and in the more detailed scheduling and expediting of production and construction. Between partial and zealous views of what was going on and of

---

[1] *Roosevelt and Hopkins,* pp. 474-77; cf. James W. Fesler *et al., Industrial Mobilization for War,* Civilian Production Administration, G.P.O., Washington, 1947, pp. 207-26; James F. Byrnes, *Speaking Frankly,* Harper, New York, 1947; Donald M. Nelson, *Arsenal of Democracy,* Harcourt, Brace, New York, 1946.

what was needed, a general touchiness among businessmen as much as among soldiers about prestige and jurisdiction in a novel and fluid situation, the gossip that pervaded all conversation and the press, and the needlings of the Truman Committee, it was hard to stabilize any relationships.

The March reorganization brought together under Somervell the Army supply services, engineers, ordnance, medical, chemical warfare, signal, quartermaster, and shortly afterwards transportation, together with a rapidly developed headquarters staff called the Resources Division.[1] This put an energetic central military authority over (though it was still a long way from coordinating) all the main Army procurement agencies except the Air Force, which pursued an autonomous course. It gave Somervell, too, virtual control over the ANMB, then headed by Baruch's protégé Ferdinand Eberstadt — an investment banker generally regarded as a strong partisan of the Army — who, since December 7, had administered military priorities and other supply functions of joint concern to the two services as a representative of the Under Secretaries of War and Navy. Vice Admiral S. M. Robinson, who under King's reorganization of the Navy on January 30, 1942 had charge of, or at least some coordinative responsibility for, the Navy supply bureaus, held aloof from most ANMB operations, and, like the Air Force, followed an independent path; unlike the Air Force, the Navy played its supply cards close to the vest. Almost immediately, on March 12, Nelson negotiated with Under Secretary Patterson an agreement purporting to spell out WPB-Army functions and relationships, which Nelson called his Magna Carta. A similar agreement with Under Secretary Forrestal followed on April 22; but neither of these covered ANMB.

It soon became clear that the generalities in these agreements meant little specifically. In theory Nelson had the legal power to take over the procurement function directly, but he quickly disclaimed any such intent: Baruch had warned him that businessmen letting contracts would be suspect; he had no adequate staff for the purpose, and he thought civilians would not be competent for the

[1] Richard M. Leighton and Robert W. Coakley, *Global Logistics and Strategy, 1940-1943,* Department of the Army, Washington, 1955, Ch. 9.

responsibility of inspecting and accepting finished goods for military use. Instead he asserted a right of policy control, while encouraging WPB officials and others with purchasing or production experience to join Somervell's staff.

For their part, the procurement agencies, now in a great hurry, proceeded in the spring of 1942 to place a mass of contracts with industrial firms, each agency looking after its own needs with little regard to others. The contracts, amounting to about $100 billion in the first six months of 1942, soon aggregated far more than the productive facilities and raw materials in prospect could possibly yield in the coming year. They also entailed a good deal of wasteful commitment of scarce steel and copper to the conversion and construction of plant facilities that could not be used. But the services paid little attention to all this. Instead they built up a huge field force of hastily uniformed ex-civilians as "expediters" assigned to every contractor and plant, to follow through on the contracts, to press all concerned to hurry, to locate bottlenecks, report delays and secure information. This thwarted WPB's policy of channelling all industry contacts through its own industry branches. The Army and Navy also "infiltrated" WPB by designating officers as liaison representatives in the operating units of WPB and as members of its clearance committees. Meanwhile ANMB awarded priorities to contractors, who extended them freely to their suppliers, in quantities again far beyond available supplies, so that inflated priorities became only hunting licenses. On February 21 Eberstadt secured from the President independently an enlarged charter for ANMB, further overlapping WPB's province, though nominally he was to report through Nelson. A sort of chaos in production ensued, in which balance and control temporarily disappeared. With far more contracts and priorities outstanding than could be fulfilled, the race for production would go to the easiest-to-produce items and to contractors with inside tracks to their suppliers.

## THE FEASIBILITY DISPUTE

This was the general background of the so-called "feasibility" dispute, the major issue between WPB and the armed services through the spring and summer months of 1942, over WPB's insistence that military production programs be cut back to limits within the nation's feasible capacity, lest all semblance of central direction over the effort be lost.[1] Somervell, refusing to reduce Army requirements (which came to him with JCS or Marshall's authority), denied WPB's right to determine them. Robert R. Nathan, chairman of WPB's Planning Committee, argued on Nelson's behalf that without requirements figures that were both firm (something WPB had been unable to get) and realistically related to resources, no priority system could work; and that without a knowledge of approved strategic plans no criteria for judging program priorities could be developed. It followed, Nathan argued, that Nelson should participate in JCS deliberations in some fashion; and such a proposal in fact was discussed with the President, Harry Hopkins and JCS in the autumn, with little concrete result. It was no solution to this need that Patterson and Forrestal sat in WPB board meetings representing their departments, for their concerns were with supply, not military strategy. And Somervell, or ANMB when he chose to use it, was firmly interposed between WPB and JCS.

Both sets of arguments, in the event, were wide of the mark. Somervell's intransigeance in early 1942 contributed importantly to the head-on inter-service collision late in that year over the competing claims of the escort vessel, aircraft, synthetic rubber and high-octane gasoline programs, as the consequences of previous over-contracting came to light. Yet it was Somervell, in a compromise with OPD (Marshall's command post) and JCS over their respective roles, who ultimately suggested the cut-backs in military supply programs that were needed to bring current goals within the limits of capacities.

Meanwhile, following a reorganization of WPB in July 1942, Nelson brought Eberstadt over into WPB in September as program vice chairman, and with him the administration of priorities. In WPB Eberstadt proceeded to institute the controlled materials plan (CMP) covering steel, aluminum and copper, and got it into tolerable working order before he was fired, in February 1943, in the

[1] John Brigante, "The Feasibility Dispute," Committee on Public Administration Cases, Washington, 1950.

backlash of a fresh effort on the part of the services, this time seemingly on the point of success, to persuade the President to "dump" Nelson. Before this, in September 1942, Charles E. Wilson, president of General Electric, had come into WPB as production vice chairman. From that vantage point, and with an increasing measure of control over the industry and materials branches that formed the core of WPB operations, he installed and developed a system of detailed WPB supervision over production scheduling and the use of "critical common components" — motors, gears, bearings, valves, pumps and the like — which were needed in large quantities for all the top-priority programs for which the services competed. These two devices, controls over materials and controls over scheduling, emerged as indispensable civilian contributions to effective industrial mobilization. After they worked, the services became reconciled to them.

STRATEGY AND LOGISTICS

On the other side of the coin, the WPB demand for firm military requirements figures and strategic plans as a basis for mobilizing the economy was, in retrospect, an impossible stipulation in 1942. And, because of the "lead time" required, it was in 1942 that contracts had to be let, production programs established, and facilities converted or built, if finished munitions in quantities sufficient for offensive fighting in 1943 were to be forthcoming. In 1942 other reasons in addition to the normal and necessary military fears about security prevented the disclosure of strategic plans to a civilian agency. For practical purposes no firm strategic plans *existed* until the autumn, too late for WPB's needs that year; and this for simple and painful reasons beyond even JCS control, or the President's. The basic decision, confirmed at ARCADIA, still held, that victory over Germany would be sought ahead of Japan; otherwise the unfavorable tide of the fighting through the spring upset military plans as fast as they were formed, and put new strains on the British, Russians and Chinese. The naval battles at Midway and in the Coral Sea in May and June 1942 for the first time contained the Japanese advance. The North African landing in November 1942 was not decided upon until late July, a fact first publicly disclosed three years later in General Marshall's comprehensive report on the war in 1945. The Guadalcanal invasion was agreed upon in the same month. It was not until May 1943 that the cross-Channel invasion became a firm commitment. Until then, therefore, and apart from lend-lease and our own limited operations in the Solomons and in North Africa, the production build-up was for inventory, for raising and equipping armies and squadrons for destinations still unspecified.[1] The only goal the supply services could define in the spring and summer of 1942 was to get all they possibly could of everything that might be needed.

Luckily, the dangers in this delay in strategic decisions while logistic preparations were proceeding were alleviated by the fact that most munitions were more or less interchangeably usable from one theater to another: tanks, trucks, planes and guns. Trouble arose when tanks designed for the temperate climates of Europe had to be adapted for operations in the desert heat of North Africa. Much worse trouble — perhaps the most serious and chronic of all military equipment shortages — arose from the ignorance of civilian officials about the extent and urgency of the need for specialized landing craft, and from disagreements among the military about how to get them. Churchill has remarked that some American planners seemed to suppose in the earlier phases of discussion that troops and materials carried across the ocean to Britain could cross the Channel on their own momentum. Nelson, the top civilian in charge of production, first stumbled belatedly on information about this shortage and its implications while on a trip to London. On his return, his proposal for an expanded and accelerated construction program for landing craft won Roosevelt's immediate and vigorous support. By the time production got rolling, however, the Navy's growing appreciation of the utility of the craft for its greatly expanding operations in the Pacific led to demands on such a scale as to leave Army requirements for the cross-Channel invasion still unsatisfied — a factor in the delay of the Normandy landings. This was perhaps an exceptional case, showing forcefully that the more spe-

---

[1] Leighton and Coakley, *Global Logistics and Strategy*, Ch. 8.

cialized a military operation was to be, the more important it was to unite the strategic and logistic planning for it. The failure to let civilian agencies in on miltary planning seldom had more damaging consequences.

## LOGISTICS IN THE HIERARCHY OF PRESTIGE

For present purposes, two points are worth noting. The first is suggested by an irony which might have comforted Nelson's partisans if they had realized it: the JCS did not take Somervell into their strategic councils sufficiently to suit him either. The official Army historians have noted that the influence of ASF inside the Army grew steadily as the scale of the war increased. Somervell spoke with great authority on what could be accomplished logistically, and he had to cope with the confusions that occurred when strategic decisions took too little account of logistic imperatives. He had personal access to Marshall, and attended international conferences at which Roosevelt and Churchill met. But he was not on JCS nor represented in the joint strategic committees. JCS, through Marshall, dealt with OPD, and OPD furnished the Army components of the staff planners, JPS and JWPC. The planners got information and advice from ASF, but "they saw little to be gained by undertaking to convince the logisticians, while strategy was in the planning stage, that contemplated operations actually could be carried out." [1] So OPD was a buffer between Somervell and JCS. A long and bitter quarrel developed as Somervell tried to improve his position and was rebuffed. After 1942 an uneasy compromise lasted through most of the war. Somervell cherished the same grievance in principle that Nathan in the feasibility dispute was urging on Nelson's behalf: the gulf between strategy and logistics in the top councils.

On the Navy side, Admiral Robinson, chief of the Office of Procurement and Material, fared no better.[2] Admiral King sent his

---

[1] Ray S. Cline, *Washington Command Post: The Operations Division,* Department of the Army, Washington, 1951, p. 259.

[2] Robert H. Connery, *The Navy and the Industrial Mobilization in World War II,* Princeton University Press, Princeton, 1951, p. 151; cf. Ernest J. King and Walter M. Whitehill, *Fleet Admiral King,* Norton, New York, 1952.

requirements to the Bureaus, and Robinson's O P & M had to collect them back from Bureau sources. JCS paid far more attention to Hopkins, but he was chiefly concerned with lend-lease supply.

In this course the service chiefs were only emulating their chief, the President. For Roosevelt too, though he was ready enough to proclaim bold production goals in big round numbers, had little patience to follow through the details and problems of their achievement. He is recorded as once telling Marshall that "planners were always conservative and saw all the difficulties, and that more could usually be done than they were willing to admit." [1] Military strategists, in turn, called supply problems logistics and relegated them to others to solve. Top strategists, in uniform or not, regarded production and supply as a lower order of activity except when shortfalls or mistakes directly jeopardized specific operations.

The second point is a corollary. The key names, the processes and organizations chiefly involved in the domestic production effort were, in the main, separate and distinct from those involved in the military effort proper, both in the War and Navy Departments and elsewhere. This held true even at the top levels of the war agencies. For WPB it furnished an added reason why the old maxim of administration was proved again, that operations drive out staff work. WPB was never able to fill the broad role its charter envisaged. As has been suggested above, machinery of coordination and adjudication to bridge the policy gulfs between WPB and the other agencies, civilian and military, had to be divorced from WPB operations and constructed later elsewhere, much closer to the White House.

OES AND OWM

Even before Pearl Harbor the different agencies controlling various aspects of the domestic stabilization efforts were often at loggerheads. By the summer of 1942, following the April announcement of the President's seven-point stabilization program, which called for a halt to further price and wage increases, rent control, restrictions on installment buying, etc., these disputes were boiling over. Only the

[1] Cline, *Washington Command Post*, p. 259.

President was in a position to resolve them authoritatively, and by that time his attention was engrossed elsewhere. But he was determined to keep the economy on an even keel, and when in early October he secured from Congress the Stabilization Act of 1942, he also established the Office of Economic Stabilization, to set policy standards for the contending agencies and settle disputes among them. To head OES he appointed Mr. Justice Byrnes, who resigned from the Supreme Court to accept the assignment.

The formula proved successful. OES kept out of small disputes, had no operational entanglements, and maintained its White House tie with assiduous care. Byrnes had an office in the White House from which he could see who else came calling on the President, and he told Hopkins, with a smile, "to keep the hell out of my business." [1]

Seeing what had been accomplished, Roosevelt applied the same formula on a larger scale in 1943 when the full strains on the economy were felt. On May 27 he established the Office of War Mobilization with very broad powers, extending to the military departments and WPB, and with Byrnes as its head.[2] OES, now directed by Judge Fred M. Vinson from the District of Columbia Court of Appeals, became a subsidiary of OWM. Significantly, both Byrnes and Vinson had had long experience in Congress.

OWM kept to the OES pattern of operations, and it too attained a considerable measure of success. Byrnes built up a very personal relationship with the military. His pressure on them was based on his prestige, on his use of individuals whom they trusted, and on his own very considerable powers of persuasion and negotiation. He had not been the frequent floor manager of Administration bills in the Senate for nothing. He timed his pressures carefully to the progress of the war, and so was sometimes able to win where WPB had lost. In 1944, for instance, he pushed and persuaded the Navy into cutting back its battleship construction program. But he avoided issues of principle over the right to review service requirements that plagued others before and since.

[1] Sherwood, *Roosevelt and Hopkins*, p. 634.
[2] H. M. Somers, *Presidential Agency: OWMR*, Harvard University Press, Cambridge, 1952.

FEUDING BY PROPAGANDA

One painful aspect of WPB-Army feuding, which finally led to Nelson's displacement, was the abuse of public relations techniques on both sides. The techniques were different but equally deplorable. WPB resorted to planted stories about military domination over civilian authorities, the Army to dire tales of a production collapse and its demoralizing effects on our fighting men. Army chiefs were convinced that people at home, particularly after the initial victories in the summer of 1944, lacked a "sense of urgency." Not without some blessing from Byrnes, Army spokesmen proceeded to try to scare the American people. The propaganda was largely based on unverifiable statistics, and much of it had an anti-labor slant. In the course of this campaign, under the tensions created by the Battle of the Bulge, the Army for a few months did dominate the economic mobilization machinery. In August 1944, at the climax of the feud and as the election campaign was about to start, the President had sent Nelson away on a mission to China. J. A. Krug, who succeeded him at WPB, could not make up the ground that Nelson had lost, and from the Battle of the Bulge that winter to the crossing of the Rhine in the early spring of 1945, WPB was little more than a service agency for the military.[1] The War Manpower Commission and other agencies were also swept along on the tide. This was, of course, the period of the Army's most extended effort. After VE-Day the military were in a position to turn their attention to other concerns, and government control of the economy was no longer subject to strong military influence except in some special fields. The official propaganda techniques and effects were not forgotten, however. In the post-war years they reappeared to becloud such issues as the control of atomic energy and the unification of the armed services. The constitutional separation of powers enables military as well as civilian officials and agencies to conduct their battles of policy and ambition outside as well as within the confines of the executive branch. In wartime it is even harder than usual to sort out the wheat and chaff in official press leaks and propaganda.

[1] Jack W. Peltason, *The Reconversion Controversy,* Committee on Public Administration Cases, Washington, 1950; also in Harold Stein, ed., *Public Administration and Policy Development,* Harcourt, Brace, New York, 1952.

••••••••••••••••••••••••••••••••••••••••••••••••••••••••••••••••••••••••••••••••••••••••••••

# CHAPTER 3

# The War:

## LOOKING ABROAD

The United States entered the war fully, at last, because it was attacked from one quarter, and had war declared upon it from another. It entered with moral indignation at what had happened, and idealistic aspirations for a better post-war world to come, but with the simple immediate purpose of self-defense, and next beyond that, of crushing the Axis regimes, and their supporting domestic systems, utterly. To that end, and in company with other parties at interest who shared at least that common denominator of purpose, it mobilized its own people and resources to an unprecedented degree, it sustained its allies with material aid on a scale never before matched, and it marshalled against the common enemies military forces beyond any previous example in our history. In less than four years from Pearl Harbor this effort was enough to accomplish the original American goal, the only clearly defined goal that all the "united nations" had in common, thoroughly and conclusively. The immediate goal of destroying the Axis forces being essentially negative, its very accomplishment left the United States at the end of the war a global power, fully committed to participation in world affairs in pursuit of longer-range aims, and badly in need of operational definitions of the new, positive and often conflicting purposes that by then had come to animate it and its allies. Only the Russians seemed to know consistently and specifically what they wanted. The United States needed to transform its attitudes and traditions about war and foreign affairs to correspond to its new role. It needed means of meeting or reconciling national purposes where they clashed. Especially, it needed not only education but also the means for knowing its own mind politically and administratively, that is, machinery for formulating its own purposes and policies.

The emergence of the military establishment, the temporary subordination of the State Department, the organization of coalition warfare, the confrontation of new problems for which neither traditional military doctrine nor the original war goals furnished guidance, the limits of the Presidency as a source of direction and coordination for the solution of these problems, and the groping for new organs for policy planning and review — these are accordingly the main themes to be noted in civil-military relations during the war period.

## ROLES OF THE STATE AND WAR DEPARTMENTS

For over a year before Pearl Harbor there had been undeclared war in the Atlantic, economic mobilization on a growing scale, selective service, and export controls. The President was familiar with Joint Board strategic plans; the close triangular relation of the Joint Board with Roosevelt and with Hopkins was well established; and consultations with the British were frequent and cordial. The State Department and the economic control agencies were shifting away from the center of the President's attention. Roosevelt had shown his penchant for handling some military and diplomatic matters himself, and for disregarding official channels occasionally in doing so. For his own reasons he had readily supported the military chiefs most of the time, but he had proved quite capable of standing up to them, and of supporting other civilian officials when they did so too. The war accentuated these tendencies that Roosevelt had already displayed.

## FRONT AND CENTER FOR WAR

On November 27, 1941 Hull finally "washed his hands" of the Japanese negotiations and turned the problem over to Stimson and Knox. In his *Memoirs* he summarized the shift in institutional roles:

During peacetime the State Department had been responsible, under the President, for the conduct of our international relations and also for making recommendations regarding movements of our military forces abroad, as, for instance, whether our troops in China should be increased or decreased. When war came the Department was no longer connected with military operations abroad, which became subject only to the command of the appropriate military authorities.

Almost immediately after Pearl Harbor I said to my associates that the role of the State Department from now on was to contribute to the war effort, and I wanted everyone in the Department to cooperate to the full with the War and Navy Departments and all war agencies, and to place at their disposal all our facilities.[1]

Later Stimson in his memoirs put the matter more fully, with less reserve. (It should be noted that his description of the peacetime role of the Secretary of War is, of course, no longer correct.)

The existence of a state of war radically revises the functions of a Secretary of War. In time of peace he is ordinarily one of the most independent and least noticed of Cabinet officers; once or twice a year he takes the stage to make his plea for funds; occasionally the public will be somewhat surprised to discover that he has other than military functions. In a time of approaching crisis he becomes somewhat more important; he must tell what his Department needs, always in terms of defense, and his counsel will have weight in diplomatic problems. In wartime all this changes; suddenly his branch of the Government becomes central. This shift will please some and annoy others of his colleagues, but it is inevitable. He finds himself in constant contact with the President, whose function as Commander in Chief takes precedence over all his other responsibilities; the nature of this relationship depends entirely on the individuals concerned, for it has no constitutional rule, and no set tradition. Only a part of the Secretary's duties concerns directly military questions, for in wartime the demands of the Army enter into every aspect of national life. Furthermore

[1] *The Memoirs of Cordell Hull,* Macmillan, New York, 1948, Vol. II, p. 1109.

the enhanced prestige of the War Department will often operate to draw its officials into activities which even in wartime are no central part of their business, and frequently the men who mutter most about "military dominance" will be among the first to seek military support when they think they can get it; others, reluctant to accept the responsibility for unpopular decisions, will secure War Department approval for their action and then let it be understood that they have acted only under military pressure.[1]

### HULL AND STATE BY-PASSED

Stimson could take care of himself with the President as with the military professionals, but Hull's personality rather aggravated than counterbalanced the institutional tendencies they both noted here. Hull had none of Harry Hopkins' knack for sensing what Roosevelt wanted, or the relative importance of things in Roosevelt's general scheme of thought and action. He clung tenaciously to points that did not impress the President, whether with their merit or their timeliness. Roosevelt responded by frequently ignoring him. At the same time the President was fully aware (and later was to receive renewed proofs) of the value and strength of Hull's support on foreign policy measures in Congress. Moreover, the President's characteristic reluctance to dismiss anyone he had appointed operated with special force in the case of the remaining trio of his original Cabinet members. So in the upshot, Roosevelt would not listen to Hull's repeated suggestions of resignation, but neither would he listen to much of his advice, nor even take pains to see that he was informed of what went on.

Finding itself on the sidelines, the State Department had difficulty in recruiting new talent at headquarters, for newcomers in Washington were attracted chiefly into the temporary agencies and the military establishment, where the main excitement was. The professional staff, and especially the middle ranks of division chiefs in the department, could not readily be augmented or replaced. Even after the reorganization ordered by Stettinius, who succeeded Welles as Under Secretary in 1943, they remained the same.

Weakness at the center inevitably embarrassed the department's

---

[1] Henry L. Stimson and McGeorge Bundy, *On Active Service in Peace and War*, Harper, New York, 1948, p. 408.

agents abroad also, and especially in its principal outpost, the Embassy in London. Roosevelt had found in John G. Winant (who succeeded Kennedy there in June 1941) an ambassador exceptionally devoted and sympathetic to his policies. Nevertheless, he did not on that account give up the personal correspondence with Churchill, begun a year earlier and expanded in 1941 through Hopkins as an intermediary, which by-passed both Hull and Winant. By the time Winant arrived, systematic military staff liaison in London was provided by Army and Navy observer groups using their own lines of communication. The Harriman lend-lease mission was housed in the Embassy in Grosvenor Square, but operated autonomously and reported to Hopkins through Navy channels. Winant and Harriman were good friends, but by October 1943 Winant was cabling Hopkins:

> During the past six months a situation has developed which has cut down my usefulness. I have had no business delegated to me as Ambassador that could not have been done by an efficient Foreign Service officer. I have been by-passed continuously. I have had no contacts with the Prime Minister except on two occasions . . . Nine-tenths of the information I receive comes from British sources. . . . they are quick to appreciate when one in my position has been deprived of his authority.[1]

When Harriman a little later became Ambassador in Moscow he too began to complain in cables to Hopkins that no one was telling him anything. Probably the worst case was in China, where Gauss and the other "old China hands" of the Foreign Service lived in a world apart from everything else our government was doing. Among places that mattered it was perhaps chiefly in Vichy, where until June 1942 Admiral Leahy was Ambassador, where lend-lease was not involved, and where military attachés had little other business than to collect intelligence, that the State Department managed to maintain its normal role abroad.

## WAR DEPARTMENT: OPD AND CAD

Until late in the war, therefore, State and the two military departments moved in separate worlds, with a minimum of working

---

[1] Robert E. Sherwood, *Roosevelt and Hopkins,* Harper, New York, 1948, p. 754.

contacts between them.[1] The War Department characteristically groped toward self-sufficiency, to fill the vacuum. OPD collected copies of the Roosevelt-Churchill correspondence which Sir John Dill, representing the British Chiefs of Staff in Washington, occasionally let them see "on a strictly personal basis,"[2] and used the military aide who helped maintain the White House map room to pick up copies of Roosevelt memoranda that might not otherwise have come its way. After June 1942 the Joint Chiefs could turn to their chairman, Admiral Leahy, who in his capacity as the President's personal Chief of Staff had his office in the White House, for closer liaison there, supplementing the guidance they got from Hopkins and from the President direct. After the Army's taste of inexperience in the handling of civil affairs following the North African landings, Assistant Secretary John J. McCloy made a tour there which led not only to a tightening of Eisenhower's control over civilian agencies operating in his theater, but also to the establishment of a new Civil Affairs Division, under Major General John H. Hilldring, in the department at Washington; of which more later.

STATE AND WAR: SWNCC

The principal wartime development toward organized collaboration between State and the military departments was an outgrowth of the foreign ministers' conference in Moscow in the fall of 1943, at which it was decided to set up a European Advisory Commission to deal with post-war questions. The machinery devised by State to instruct our delegate on the EAC, the Working Security Committee, will be noticed at a later point. The wheels of inter-agency concert turned slowly, and when the JCS, at the time of the Normandy landings in June 1944, set up its own Joint Post-war Committee, this machinery became more complicated. A more authoritative interdepartmental arrangement was needed. The old State-War-Navy Committee composed of the three Secretaries, was revitalized. Fur-

[1] Ray S. Cline, *Washington Command Post: The Operations Division*, Department of the Army, Washington, 1951, Ch. 16.
[2] *Ibid.*, p. 316.

thermore, on the proposal of Stettinius, now Secretary of State, the State-War-Navy Coordinating Committee was constituted in November, consisting of an Assistant Secretary from each department, McCloy for War and Will Clayton for State. Area subcommittees for Europe, Latin America, the Middle East and the Far East were set up to assist SWNCC; and OPD (whose Policy Section included no less than four former Rhodes scholars) furnished the staff work for McCloy's share in its deliberations. SWNCC marked an advance both in organization and significance over the pre-war SLC, though in contrast to that earlier trio it confronted a situation in the closing months of the war in which the practical shape of its subject matter was largely determined by the military commanders in the field, Eisenhower in Europe and MacArthur in the Far East.

## THE ARCADIA CONFERENCE: COALITION WARFARE

On the night of Pearl Harbor, Churchill "went to bed and slept the sleep of the saved and thankful." When he awoke he "decided to go over at once to see President Roosevelt." [1] Five days later he sailed, and during the voyage composed and circulated among his staff three documents, dealing with the Atlantic Front, the Pacific Front, and the War in 1942. On his arrival he laid these before the President, and they became the main basis for the ARCADIA conference discussions which extended, with interruptions, over the next three weeks. ARCADIA and these working papers set a pattern for the succession of summit meetings held at intervals through the war to settle the course of the coalition, its ends and its means. In this first of the wartime conferences, Churchill was Roosevelt's guest at the White House, and the conferees took full advantage of the opportunities for informal talk. With Hopkins and sometimes Hull, Stimson and Knox, as well as Marshall, Stark and Arnold, in attendance generally on the American side at the regular sessions, strategic plans were developed and approved along the lines agreed on in ABC-1 and ABC-2 for Atlantic operations; a North African landing

[1] Winston S. Churchill, *The Grand Alliance,* Houghton Mifflin, Boston, 1950, p. 608.

(GYMNAST, later called TORCH) was optimistically approved for launching perhaps as soon as March 1942 if circumstances permitted or required — as in the event they did neither; and plans for holding operations in the Pacific were also agreed to, which were likewise almost immediately made futile — for the time being — by the sweep of the Japanese advances.

## POLITICAL OBJECTIVES

Ahead of these military decisions, however, the President and the Prime Minister characteristically determined — as they had at AR- GENTIA the previous August — to issue a rallying statement as the first order of business. It was to form the political and propaganda basis for a grand coalition, an array before the world of the powers large and small committed to the defeat of the Axis. The upshot was the announcement on January 2 of the Declaration of the United Na- tions — the first use of that term — which included a flourish of principles, an agreement to cooperate in the fighting, and a pledge not to conclude a separate peace. Hull had been working on the draft of this for the preceding fortnight, and he notes that Roosevelt's only serious hesitation was over his constitutional authority to sign a pledge of no separate peace unless it were in the form of a treaty to be ratified by the Senate.

Along with this declaration Hull also presented the conferees with a draft proposal for the creation of a Supreme War Council, com- prising members from the United States, Britain, Russia and China, with *ad hoc* representation of other governments when appropriate, and to include subsidiary councils on military, naval, aviation, ship- ping and economic affairs. This proposal was rejected as promising to bring too many touchy sovereign authorities into too much urgent business. Subsequent attempts by the State Department to introduce other governments (except for Canada) into the Anglo-American agencies later established were never seriously considered.

## COMBINED CHIEFS AND UNIFIED COMMANDS

Since Roosevelt and Churchill could not sit together in continuous session for the rest of the war, the remaining major task of the conference was to settle on the future machinery of command and coordination — "post-ARCADIA collaboration," as the staff papers called it. Toward this end the most significant steps of the conference were taken. At Marshall's urging, strongly seconded by Hopkins, the principle of combined forces and unified commands (first put into operation, abortively, in the Far East) in all combat theaters was soon accepted, despite Churchill's initial objections. Though it never was applied to the Russians and was intended as little more than a conciliatory fiction so far as the Chinese were concerned, it developed into a working reality in Anglo-American operations to a degree unmatched in the history of coalition warfare. Inter-service as well as international rivalries had to be faced in giving effect to the principle, and the staffs in unified commands had to be apportioned with due regard to the relative national contributions of forces in the several theaters in order to assuage national sensitivities; but the principle stuck.

Unified theater commands meant unified machinery for giving them directions. That question, at first glossed over with the ambiguous phrase "an appropriate joint body," was faced too. Adopting a British suggestion for terminological usage, the conference created the Combined Chiefs of Staff (CCS), to be located in Washington. A resident British delegation headed by Sir John Dill was appointed to make up the British component of it except when the British chiefs were able to attend in person. Staffs were assigned to serve it from the staffs of the chiefs on both sides. Subject only to the direction of the President and the Prime Minister, it was to settle strategy, establish unified commands in the theaters, and issue strategic directions to the theater commanders.

Next in importance to the CCS was the Munitions Assignments Board, which was to allocate finished munitions to the different theaters and fighting nations. For this the British proposal, drawn in apprehension of American military control of so vital a subject, was a division of the world into two spheres of British and American influence and responsibility, with Hopkins to become a supreme commander for supplies and to coordinate the allocation of production and raw materials among the United States, Britain and Canada.

Roosevelt, knowing that Hopkins' domestic unpopularity made such an arrangement politically impossible to announce at home — especially since he had himself for two years refused to name an American production "czar" — proposed instead two coordinate boards, in London and Washington, to be headed by Beaverbrook and Hopkins, and to report directly to the Prime Minister and the President — in a status equal to CCS. But Marshall would have none of this dilution of unity in command over what he deemed a military essential, and Hopkins supported him: MAB must be subordinate to CCS. Besides, all the American conferees objected to an arrangement that would have given the British control over the disposition of American-made munitions in the Mediterranean and Middle East theaters. Roosevelt therefore acquiesced, and so ultimately did the British, in a temporary compromise trial — good, as it turned out, for the duration of the war — of an MAB established in Washington as a "subcommittee" of CCS, but headed by Hopkins.[1] It worked well except when Hopkins was in the hospital. Foreshadowing the preponderant strength the United States was to contribute, the establishment of CCS and MAB, and their location, meant broadly that the last word in strategic direction of the war — the Russian and perhaps the Chinese fronts apart — would in the end rest with Roosevelt.

COMBINED BOARDS

Two other combined agencies were set up during the ARCADIA meetings. The Combined Raw Materials Board, in which William L. Batt was the leading figure, never achieved anything like the dominant position of CCS in its field. It was not an operating or directing agency, but depended on the domestic production authorities in the United States and the United Kingdom to give effect to its recommendation. It "had greater effect when dealing with other peoples' raw materials." [2] Nevertheless it worked usefully throughout the war in identifying and solving particular shortage problems,

---

[1] Sherwood, *Roosevelt and Hopkins*, pp. 470-73.
[2] S. McKee Rosen, *The Combined Boards of the Second World War*, Columbia University Press, New York, 1951, p. 27.

and in promoting measures to increase resources and to make the available supplies, especially from overseas sources, go around.

The Combined Shipping Adjustment Board was an unhappy experience for all concerned. In 1942 the board was supposed to deal with the most desperately critical shortage of the war. The United States was committed to maintain (and replace losses in) a pool of 8 million tons operating in the Atlantic under direction from Washington, while the British were to maintain 20 million tons, directed by the Ministry of Shipping. The British were much further advanced than we in measures for conservation and for centralized control of the available tonnage; they were also more alarmed than we had yet become over our failure to control losses or to restrict nonessential uses sufficiently. The newly created War Shipping Administration was not yet on top of its job and Lewis Douglas, its chief, was at loggerheads with the Army over both policy and jurisdiction. In these circumstances the poverty of resources seemed to induce, at the operating levels, attitudes of grabbing and hoarding rather than sharing. The elaborate plans of Sir Arthur Salter, head of the British Merchant Shipping Mission, for a combined control, were dropped. By mid-1943 when Sir Arthur left and Douglas had made WSA's controls stick, the submarine menace was abated and the record of recriminations too long to undo. By then the Navy was becoming the target of British complaints for its expansively possessive attitude in behalf of its Pacific operations. All in all, the lot of CSAB was to provide a forum for unseemly wrangles until it fell into disuse.

Two more combined boards were created in June 1942, both with Canadian as well as British and American membership: the Combined Production and Resources Board and the Combined Food Board. Both foundered on the inability of their American counterparts, WPB and the Department of Agriculture (replaced later by the War Food Administration), to master their domestic jurisdictions as effectively as the armed service chiefs did. This appears, indeed, more generally stated, to be a first condition of successful coalition operations.

## COALITION WARFARE: RUSSIA AND CHINA

A second condition, mutual trust and disclosure, explains in
large part why the Russians were not coalition partners in the same
way. There was never, of course, unless in the final weeks of the
Nazi collapse, any practicable possibility of large-scale combined
operations, for obstinate geographical reasons. But even opportunities for tactical cooperation — for instance, the use of Russian air
bases as turn-around points for American bombers over Germany,
which at the time, it was thought, would have greatly increased our
effective bombing range from Britain — were lost in endless negotiations that revealed an underlying Soviet unwillingness to let American military forces get into a position to observe Russian operations
in the field. And Roosevelt had to decide at a very early stage that
lend-lease allocations and shipments to Russia would be made, within
our capabilities and in the light of our other needs, on the basis of
stated Soviet requests and without the detailed supporting information and screening of requirements that we insisted on in the case of
the British and other applicants. Top-level conferences were held,
and staff conversations took place in Moscow and Washington; but
field operations touched gingerly without merging at the points of
contact.

The Soviets made known their basic demands very bluntly in the
spring of 1942, at the time of Molotov's visit to London and Washington: a second front in Europe immediately, and post-war recognition of the territorial gains Russia had made in Eastern Europe
between 1939 and the Nazi invasion in June 1941. We could not
comply with the first, and would not with the second. Instead, the
clash in objectives was put off. Thereafter, and almost to the end,
Roosevelt and the Joint Chiefs continued to regard the Russian fighting contribution as essential to the defeat of Germany, and of Japan
later also; they continued to be apprehensive until after the Russian
victory at Stalingrad in the winter of 1942-43 that Russia might be
forced to a separate peace; and they continued accordingly their firm
support of Russian lend-lease. To the end of his life, in spite of re-
buffs that grew increasingly exasperating, and probably because he

thought it the necessary price of getting the USSR into the UN, Roosevelt kept on hoping for the best from Russian post-war policy on the basis of demonstrated American good faith. And what he wanted for political reasons the Joint Chiefs wanted for military reasons.

Outside the lend-lease operation, however, a good deal of military opinion, as in some civilian war agencies too, was doubting and grumbling. After the war, and even before the peaks of McCarthyism were reached, some officials who had been active in Russian lend-lease affairs were rewarded for their zeal by finding their future careers in government blocked. The Russian connection was an alliance that fell short of a coalition.

CHINA

In the case of China both of the coalition requisites already mentioned were absent, and other complications entered in addition. China was at the furthest end of our supply lines. What could be, or was, sent was always less than what was asked, less than what was needed, and less than what was promised. China was in a civil war and had been under invasion for a decade. It was no more than a gesture of good will, therefore, when Roosevelt and Churchill, at the ARCADIA conference, designated Chiang Kai-shek as the allied theater commander for China. Until the success of the island-hopping campaign in the Pacific appeared in 1944, they expected after the defeat of Germany to need China as a base against Japan, and to give her massive help then. But while supplies were tight, British and Russian needs had priority, and when supplies became plentiful, Chinese help was no longer needed for the conquest of Japan. After that, Chiang Kai-shek's China was past American help — though much was poured in during the next two years — unless by a massive military intervention that was politically inconceivable.

In February 1942, long before the tide of victory in the Pacific had begun, Roosevelt sent out General Stilwell, the only American general officer fluent in Chinese, and a fighting soldier, to be Chief of Staff to Chiang Kai-shek (and in command of any Chinese troops that might be assigned to him), field commander of the meager American forces there (though not as it turned out in fact, of General Chennault's air forces), and the subordinate of the British theater commander for Burma and India. In that ambiguous position, with inadequate supplies, and with every move conditioned by the political affairs of the Chinese government, he was supposed as time moved along to live as best he could with the Communists and the Nationalist government, to open a land route to Burma, conduct a strategic bombing offensive against Japan, create and train a strong Chinese army, and maintain pressure against the Japanese forces in China. This was a one-man coalition with a vengeance, if it could be brought off; it could not. Chiang Kai-shek needed what no ally could then spare or deliver to him, while Stilwell asked him for authority no sovereign government could give an alien. Confusion and recriminations persisted even after Stilwell was finally replaced. Wedemeyer, his successor, attempted less and came off better, but still could not prevent the emergence of the insoluble problem that post-war China presented. Many valiant individual efforts went into the ill-starred, ill-coordinated attempt, along with everything else, to sustain China and help it become a free, strong, democratic and united nation. But Chiang was never accorded a place in the top councils, except at the first Cairo conference in 1943; and the decision there to mount a full-scale offensive through Burma was reversed ten days later in his absence, on Roosevelt's return to Cairo from Teheran. Later in the war the United States and Britain, at Yalta, made commitments regarding China without Chiang's knowledge, though with a provision that his consent was to be secured, as indeed it afterwards was.

All in all, the unity of the coalition was sufficient, as Herbert Feis has observed,[1] to free American military planners to proceed, as their inclinations already dictated, on "three constant premises: that all members of the coalition were fighting the same war, not separate ones with different purposes; that decisions about military actions could be based on military grounds, and need not reckon with their

[1] Herbert Feis, *Churchill, Roosevelt, Stalin,* Princeton University Press, Princeton, 1957, p. 37.

political bearings; and that the war was to end only on complete surrender of the enemies." These premises suited Roosevelt's political purposes too, which goes far to explain why he so seldom disagreed with the Joint Chiefs on strategy. But they carried a corresponding danger, as Feis hastens to add. The postponement of political decisions until after the war exposed the results of victory to the hazards of the fighting and left room for suspicion and maneuver within the coalition. For to the extent that post-war goals were in fact not the same, the partners were tempted in varying degrees to pursue their separate political aims through their military strategies — the Russians in Eastern Europe, the British in the Mediterranean, and the Americans in the Pacific.

## EMERGENCE OF JCS

Growing out of the ARCADIA conference, though not a part of it, were various organizational developments in the American government.[1] The establishment of the War Production Board to supersede OPM and SPAB has already been mentioned. The appointment of Joseph Eastman to head the Office of Defense Transportation, long under discussion, was announced on January 2. The President also presently set up a War Shipping Administration, of which Lewis Douglas shortly became the effective chief, and later, in the spring, the Office of War Information, also noted earlier. The War Manpower Commission, again after lengthy discussion, was set up in May, among other more specialized agencies. Of much greater and more lasting significance, however, was the creation of the Joint Chiefs of Staff, shortly after the conference, as a permanent corporate body. JCS came into being without any formal charter or executive order of any sort, not even a letter; indeed, when an executive order was later proposed to legitimize it and define its work, the President rejected the idea as unnecessary and cramping.

JCS was a working necessity if CCS was to function. As so often in the history of the formation of federal structures, the efficient

[1] *The United States at War* (U. S. Bureau of the Budget, G.P.O., Washington, 1946) covers the organizational development of all the civilian war agencies.

unifying impulse was an external threat to the self-sufficiency of the rival components. More specifically, Marshall and Stark and their assistants were both impressed and acutely embarrassed at the vastly superior preparation of the British Chiefs of Staff for the ARCADIA talks, and at their ability to reach concerted decisions rapidly and maintain them in the presence of their opposite numbers. The demonstration was enough to convince Marshall and Stark of the need for more effective concerted American action in future conferences and in the continuing work of CCS, if American viewpoints were to prevail. They were also both fresh from their efforts to explain to the Roberts Commission why the traditional Army-Navy liaison arrangements, either in Washington or between Admiral Kimmel and General Short in Honolulu, had failed to mitigate the damage at Pearl Harbor.

JCS was historically a lineal descendant of the Joint Board (which actually remained in existence for a time), but it attained a far greater stature. It differed in three major respects.

### JCS CHARACTERISTICS

First, it was for practical purposes a command organization — in that agreement within it was promptly followed by commands from the appropriate services — and not merely a planning body or liaison committee or council of ambassadors. It assigned operating missions to its members in their individual capacities as service chiefs, to carry out its collective decisions. As executive agents of joint policies they were individually answerable to JCS for their performance.

Second, JCS had more highly developed subcommittee, staff and secretariat structures and procedures. These served as the American component of the CCS machinery, and became more comprehensive and specialized as the war went on. Marshall drew on the War Plans Division of the War Department General Staff — soon to become his Washington command post, the Operations Division — and so secured the services of men of the caliber of Gerow, Eisenhower and Handy. Committees were set up to deal with logistics, intelligence, transportation (including shipping allocations), communications, munitions allocation, meteorology and civil affairs (occupation and military government). A group known as the Joint Staff Planners (JPS, the American side of the Combined Staff Planners, CPS), a Joint Strategic Survey Committee (JSSC) of senior officers, and a working subcommittee later called the Joint War Plans Committee (JWPC) furnished a central coordinating channel for all sorts of policy papers reaching JCS and CCS, and for directives from these bodies.

Third, JCS from the outset, and at least partly because the RAF was always so represented on the British side, included in its membership the Chief, presently the Commanding General, of the Army Air Forces, General H. H. Arnold. This brought the Air Force in principle to within a couple of steps of its long-time goal of coordinate status with the Army and Navy. Admiral King, however, continued to appeal from Arnold to Marshall in the long controversy over the strategy and control of air operations in the Atlantic antisubmarine campaign.

At first Admiral King, then newly made Commander in Chief U. S. Fleet, was included along with Admiral Stark, the Chief of Naval Operations. When Stark was sent to London early in February (in what King thought an unjust and discriminatory demotion consequent on the Roberts Commission report), King took over both places and JCS membership dropped to three. This made a difference. The driving force of King's personality was exerted not only in favor of Navy interests generally, but more particularly in favor of Pacific operations; it was Stark who, with Marshall, had emphasized the priority of concentrating first on defeating Germany. A further change occurred later, when Admiral Leahy returned from Vichy in June 1942 and was named Chief of Staff to the President — against the recommendation of King, who wanted no single military chief between the President and the Navy. He presided over JCS meetings, though without a vote; his office was in the White House, he saw the President daily, and he strengthened the link between the President and JCS.

BY-PRODUCTS

The establishment of JCS had many by-products. It was good for inter-service cooperation. Though it by no means eliminated feuds and rivalries, it minimized them at the top, where the example was most needed. It hastened and shaped reorganizations already under way in both the War and Navy Departments, though these involved other factors of scale, tempo and specialization as well. Marshall had tried during the preceding months to establish a command post (GHQ) in Washington, headed by General Lesley McNair and located on the site of the War College, to give a firmer, prompter, better integrated direction to the growing military establishment, over the heads of the combat and supply arms and services, and without altering the role of the General Staff. The attempt had not worked out. General McNair found himself in an eddy apart from the main flow of policy and papers in the channels of the War Department; and the War Plans Division of the General Staff, in particular, was unable to draw a practical line of jurisdiction or division of labor between its work and General McNair's.[1] Now Marshall gave up this scheme. Instead, shortly after ARCADIA, and taking advantage of the President's new authority under the First War Powers Act, he put through a general reorganization of the military components of the War Department. WPD, renamed the Operations Division (OPD), at first under General Gerow, who was succeeded in February 1942 by General Eisenhower, became Marshall's Washington command post. It drew strategic plans, issued operating directives to theater commanders and Army service chiefs, and followed up on performance. It maintained direct top-level communications and centralized outgoing commands. It developed a weekly statistical inventory of force deployments, and otherwise tried to keep track of the status and progress of the Army from an over-all viewpoint. The rest of the General Staff, except for G-2 (Intelligence) and some parts of G-1 (Personnel), was largely liquidated, its functions combined with those of the operating bureaus, and these parcelled out among a high command comprising three grand groupings:

[1] Cline, *Washington Command Post*, pp. 61-83.

the Army Ground Forces (mainly training) under General McNair, the Army Air Forces under General Arnold, and the Services of Supply (later named the Army Service Forces) under General Somervell. The results greatly strengthened Marshall's hand, and by assembling so much of supply operations under Somervell, inevitably diminished the influence of Assistant (now Under) Secretary Patterson and his civilian aides in that field.

The Navy reorganization was less extensive. While King was Commander in Chief Atlantic Fleet, before Pearl Harbor and at a time when most naval operations were in the Atlantic, he set up a headquarters staff whose functions were difficult to distinguish in practice from those of the Chief of Naval Operations. When he became Commander in Chief U. S. Fleet, these jurisdictional difficulties were aggravated. But after Stark's departure for London, King became Chief of Naval Operations too. His two headquarters staffs were consolidated, the lines of communications tightened and his control over the Navy bureaus strengthened. The Navy for the first time had a single professional chief in fact as well as in name, and King was a suitable name for him.[1]

Other more subtle consequences flowed from the operation of JCS as an executive committee. It increased the already existing tendency of the President to by-pass the Secretaries of War and Navy. Yet it would be a mistake to suppose that Stimson or Knox lost all influence with him after Pearl Harbor, and Stimson's memoir is at some pains to dispel that notion; the devoted loyalty and the immense influence of their principal civilian lieutenants, Patterson, Forrestal and the rest, on the conduct of their departments is sufficient testimony to that. But it is true that the Secretaries saw him less frequently than before, and the Joint Chiefs saw him more; and operations were so gigantic and complex that the direct line to the military inevitably entailed some degree of isolation for the Secretaries from happenings in their departments.

JCS gained strength from its corporate character. What one service did, it did as the executive agent carrying out a joint decision.

[1] Ernest J. King and Walter M. Whitehill, *Fleet Admiral King,* Norton, New York, 1952.

Objections, or requests for changes in plans, from another service or from a civilian department could be met, and were, with the reply that the agent could not overturn an inter-service decision.

Finally, JCS enjoyed the advantages of the military controls over communications to all major theaters of the war. The services operated the main facilities themselves. They could refuse clearance, on security grounds, to dispatches containing information they deemed classified. Other channels of communication were not easily available, and in the Pacific there were no other channels. Civilian representatives of other agencies in the field, until they came home and could talk, or until their guarded letters reached home, were largely confined to messages that passed through Army or Navy centers and censors. Naturally the priorities, when lines were congested, ran in favor of the military traffic. Except for a few civilian VIP's, this was of course true of the movement of people as well as of messages. Through these controls of overseas communications, JCS was in a position to be informed, forewarned, and therefore forearmed, to a degree no civilian agency could match.

### ROOSEVELT AND JCS

Roosevelt rarely overruled JCS, apparently only two or three times on the record, as, for example, when he decided to go ahead with the North African invasion (which they opposed) as the only practicable way of getting American troops into combat with Germans in 1942. He sided with Churchill and Lewis Douglas of WSA against them at Cairo late in 1943, in abandoning, for lack of shipping and resources, the large-scale Burma offensive and related amphibious operations in the Indian Ocean, which had been pledged to Chiang Kai-shek only a few days before. Earlier, in the summer of 1942, he had also rejected the recommendation from Marshall and King for a showdown with the British over basic strategy: that if they were unwilling to concentrate on the earliest possible invasion of northwest Europe, we should turn our major efforts against Japan at once. From Hyde Park on July 14 he sent Marshall a curt message that he did not approve the Pacific alternative, as too much like threatening to "take up your dishes and go home."[1] The long record of agreement otherwise between the President and JCS is no evidence of weakness on either side; on the contrary, all parties to the relationship were quite evidently capable of thinking and speaking independently. Roosevelt's regard for Marshall was perhaps best expressed in Cairo, at the time Eisenhower was selected for the supreme command in Europe against the known preference of Churchill and Stalin and the strong recommendations of Stimson and Hopkins, very simply in the President's words as Marshall recalled them: "I feel I could not sleep at night with you out of the country."[2] King and Arnold also wanted Marshall kept in Washington as a key member of a winning combination. Considering the President's hold on the country and the civil administration, and this testimony of Marshall's standing among the military, the mutual confidence and agreement between these two leaders could not but make JCS an influence of enormous importance.

Emphasis on the importance of the JCS should not, however, obscure Roosevelt's readiness to put and support civilians in key positions directly affecting military capabilities and operations. This was true particularly in matters of supply, where the three services and lend-lease, and the several theaters of the war and their commanders, were in competition. Hopkins' appointment as chairman of MAB was an outstanding case in point. After the decision to invade North Africa, which to the service chiefs seemed a compromise of the basic strategy of concentrating on the main chance against Germany, the growing involvements of that campaign, and its later extension into Italy, made a tremendous drain on resources. Meanwhile the tide had begun to turn in the Pacific, and great pressures came from King and MacArthur to support increasing operations there. While Hopkins arbitrated among the services and protected lend-lease commitments, by the end of 1942 not only the bulk of the Navy but also half the Army and a third of the Air Force's planes

---

[1] Sherwood, *Roosevelt and Hopkins*, pp. 594, 600-01, and footnotes to pp. 600-01, 612 in the revised (1951) edition; Maurice Matloff and Edwin M. Snell, *Strategic Planning for Coalition Warfare, 1941-1942*, Office of the Chief of Military History, Department of the Army, Washington, 1953, pp. 272-78; Stimson, *On Active Service*, p. 425.

[2] Sherwood, *Roosevelt and Hopkins*, p. 803.

outside the United States were engaged in the Pacific. During 1943 the implicit principle of allocation appeared to be that increases in the resources committed to the Mediterranean would be roughly matched by additions in the Pacific. The build-up in the British Isles looking to the cross-Channel attack was correspondingly slowed, and the flow to the China-Burma-India theater kept to a trickle. By June 1944, Pacific operations absorbed more landing craft than were available for the landings in Normandy and in southern France.[1] But by that time Hopkins was out of the picture. As Feis points out,[2] "the Allies waited for shipyards to build more rather than deplete the great assembly in the Pacific."

A more dramatic case was the control of non-combatant shipping. Here military supply objectives — "the right item, in the right amount, at the right time, at the right place" — collided with the canons of economy in the use of ships, i.e., full cargoes balancing bulk and weight, loading at a single port, mixed loads of military and civilian goods to the same destination, rerouting to shorten distances, quick unloading and turn-around, etc. The Army and Navy, in their transport services, owned or controlled sizable (but inadequate) numbers of ships, and sought block allocations of enough more to meet their expanding requirements. WSA on the other hand had a broad charter of authority and was committed to the principle of pooling all available resources, which meant assigning ships on a single one-way voyage basis. An initial *modus vivendi* was reached in May and June 1942, while ship losses rose. But in the fall, during the hasty improvisations for the North African campaign, WSA became increasingly critical of military practice. Early in December General Gross, chief of the Military Transport Service, precipitated a showdown by stopping the mixed loadings at New York without warning.

Douglas with the encouragement of Hopkins ("these fellows will not be persuaded") went immediately and directly to the President and came away with a signed directive which was a sweeping

[1] Chester Wilmot, *The Struggle for Europe* (Collins, London, 1952), makes this a major ground of criticism of American policy.

[2] *Churchill, Roosevelt, Stalin*, pp. 44-45.

reaffirmation of WSA authority over merchant ship "operations, including loading." Roosevelt signed, on Douglas' insistence, without consulting the Army or Navy; he only said, "If this doesn't work you will catch hell." In the ensuing explosion Stimson at first refused to put this order into effect until it had been studied, and Somervell demanded its revocation as a condition of further discussions. But Douglas construed his directive moderately in a proposal calling for inter-agency working-level consultations over specific cases, and stood his ground in a stormy session he and Land had with the Joint Chiefs, Somervell and Admiral Griffin, chief of naval transport, on December 28. He took pains too, through Hopkins, Oscar Cox of Lend-Lease, Budget Director Harold Smith and Wayne Coy of the White House staff, to make sure there was no weakening in the President's support. In the War Department, McCloy took his side. So within about a fortnight Somervell backed down, Gross cooperated and Griffin's official head rolled.[1] Thereafter there was more pooling of cargo, though it is only fair to add that by January 1943 shipping losses were down, new ship deliveries were up, and logistic operations lent themselves more readily than in 1942 to more systematic scheduling.

## MILITARY DOCTRINE ABOUT WAR

Because the State Department was so effectively sidetracked, because the military establishment had such a dominant institutional position, and because American experience furnished so little in the way of precedents for guidance, the inherited and ingrained American military doctrines about war and the functions of force in national policy became unusually important.

### THE PURE DOCTRINE

The senior officers of the military services, perhaps of the Army more than of the Navy, were brought up to believe that the sole function of military force in a war is to secure victory. As MacArthur

[1] R. M. Leighton and R. W. Coakley, *Global Logistics and Strategy, 1940-1943*, Department of the Army, Washington, 1955, pp. 618-23.

told the senators in 1951, "the concept I have is that when you go into war you have exhausted all other potentialities of bringing the disagreements to an end . . ." Long before, as Chief of Staff in 1931, he had told another Congressional audience that "the objective of any warring nation is victory, immediate and complete." On both occasions, if military opinion had been polled, he was presumably asserting only common sense premises. When he went on to claim in his 1931 testimony that "decisive victory on the field of battle invariably results in the attainment of the national purpose for which the appeal to arms was made," he was taking an extreme view.

So flatly stated, the doctrine provides no place for politics and precludes the use of armed force during the war for secondary "political" purposes: military planners are dedicated to the proposition that a straight line is the shortest distance between two points, subject of course to qualifications about terrain, supply lines and the like, and taking into account, in practice, the enemy's "will to resist" and the state of morale among our own people at home. The doctrine of pure war also leaves no room for military moves dictated by political considerations of post-war advantage: if victory assures the attainment of national objectives it makes no difference, when the surrender occurs, what armies are where, what cities are occupied and what areas are still in enemy possession, or in the hands of which allies. The management of the victory is a problem for the politicians, not for the soldiers; and by the same token, modification of the straight-line route to victory in order to further post-war objectives is improper.

This quasi-moral dogma has deep roots in American beliefs — beliefs long held, and reinforced by revisionist teachings about the conduct and settlement of World War I: our belief in civilian supremacy that would exclude the military from making political judgments; our physical self-containment that left us nearly without geographical ambitions for more territory; and our distrust of spheres of influence and other aspects of what Americans, civilian and military alike, tended to regard distastefully as power politics for commercial and financial advantage. Like the pre-war faith in isolation, this military doctrine of war proved inadequate to the occasion.

## QUALIFICATIONS

Actually, of course, our military leaders were already well acquainted with the domestic politics of military appropriations, inter-service rivalries, the status of the National Guard, and the like; and they took for granted certain foreign policies that had obvious military implications, as the Monroe Doctrine had for the Panama Canal. Then, as the war progressed they were exposed to an intensive political education, with varying individual effects, and they met and in some fashion dealt with essentially political problems, with mixed results. Basically they had a good military case for the kind of war they wanted to fight, and generally Roosevelt had good political reasons for seeing eye to eye with them on their strategy. A good example of the effects of education was Eisenhower's attitude in France and Germany, after his tempering experience in North Africa. "If you have political considerations in view let me know them," he told his superiors in effect, hoping not to hear of any, and disregarding them unless he did. The difficulties — of the semi-avoidable kind, that is — arose from the constrictive effects of the doctrine and from civilian failures to provide the military with timely political guidance in effective form. Of these, Stilwell's course in China provided a classic illustration.

Sometimes, of course, the admixture of political considerations was overt and made no problem. To take a small domestic instance, there could be no quarrel with, but only a faint surprise at the source of, a telegram Marshall sent to Hopkins at Hyde Park in July 1942, when Rommel seemed about to overwhelm the British forces in Egypt:

In the event of a disaster in the Middle East it is believed to be important to the future conduct of the war that the United Nations present to the world a solid front. To this end it is suggested that the President guide public comment so as to indicate that the United Nations stand together in adversity as they ultimately will in victory.[1]

[1] Sherwood, *Roosevelt and Hopkins*, p. 598.

Sometimes, too, the Administration respected the doctrine in spite of an obvious and partisan domestic political disadvantage. So when Eisenhower, for logistic reasons, postponed the date of the North African landings to November 8, 1942, five days after the Congressional elections of that year, Roosevelt made no move to intervene or complain, although all the military planning had assumed a target date in October. The Democratic candidates fared badly, and blamed Leon Henderson's price controls; the Administration unquestionably would have derived a welcome benefit in votes from news a few days earlier that our troops at last were fighting.[1] On the other hand, the means if not the end were open to serious question when Somervell in 1944 ignored the doctrine by involving the War Department, as already mentioned, in a propaganda campaign to instill a greater "sense of urgency" on the home front by the use of misleading statistics.

More significant problems in the juncture of war and politics emerged when questions of strategic policy, especially of coalition policy, had to be settled, and again as issues of occupation policy and military government were confronted. By the time the war was over two very different images of the post-war world were taking shape in outline; blurred as they were they counselled sharply contrasting courses of action by the military toward our allies as well as toward our defeated enemies. To the clarification of these choices, the traditional military doctrine contributed chiefly confusion. In the post-war years, when the unification of the services, foreign aid and the Korean War were issues, a new doctrine and new educational goals for military leaders were needed.

## STRATEGIC AND COALITION POLICY

Both the Army and the Navy were familiar enough before the war with the use of armed forces as deterrents, as in the stationing of troops at Shanghai, or in the retention of the fleet in the Pacific, however they disagreed on the wisdom of particular moves or differed in their reading of events.

[1] Sherwood, *Roosevelt and Hopkins*, p. 630.

IN THE FAR EAST

In actual practice during the war it proved easier to hew to the accepted line where British interests — or what were taken to be British interests — were at stake than where our own concerns, practical or sentimental, were involved. We showed no enthusiasm for supporting or retaking Hong Kong, Singapore or Malaya; but the Philippines were a very different matter, both in the losing and in the regaining. This was evident very early, when MacArthur's endorsement of President Quezon's proposal for the evacuation and neutralization of the islands was emphatically turned down. Stimson and Marshall were as determined as the President in rejecting it, and equally conscious that the political consideration, i.e., the moral effect of such a move, was the decisive factor. It was evident again, later in the war, during the protracted debate over the course of the advance toward Japan. MacArthur advanced cogent strategic reasons for retaking the Philippines on the island-hopping route, and his personal feelings of obligation were well known, but the political significance of the move was not glossed over.

In China too both the Army and the Navy accepted political involvement as normal and necessary, for both had long traditions of service and friendship there. Even after JCS interests in China as a base for American operations against Japan began to fade, no question was raised about the propriety of diverting to China what military supplies could be spared, and of furnishing her other aid. Nevertheless, the assumption of political responsibility in China was grudging on Stilwell's part and inept all around. His mission was probably foredoomed, but the bitterness of his failure might have been alleviated if he and his superiors had shown more sophistication about the limits of action that were open to him. As it was, he lost his usefulness by resisting Chinese "political interference" with military operations and by his unconcealed contempt for the Chinese government to which he was attached; Marshall and Stimson insisted on keeping him there after his usefulness had plainly ended; and the Chinese, playing off factions among divided American counsels, were able on occasion to participate in making American policy.

IN EUROPE

The main evidences of the limitations of traditional doctrine appeared, however, in the long arguments with the British, and especially with Churchill, over Mediterranean strategy and its relation to BOLERO, the build-up for the cross-Channel invasion through France. These lasted from early 1942 through most of 1944, and once or twice jeopardized the unity of the coalition. Roosevelt was as much involved as our military leaders, for he had sound political reasons for being as anxious as they were to win the war quickly, avoiding side diversions. Without going into the merits of the opposing views, or speculation on how different the post-war world might have been if a different course had been followed, it is pertinent here to note the actual differences in the two approaches to the common aim of defeating Hitler.

Even after Churchill accepted in principle the need and plans for a French coast invasion — and in fact gave it wholehearted support when it occurred — he kept hoping that some other way to win the war would be found, some way that depended more on wits and time and less on the massive costs and corresponding risks of a frontal assault; he repeatedly said that the only way the war could be *lost* was by the failure of such an assault. He visualized the direct invasion as a necessary final clincher, to be applied only after all doubt of success and risk of heavy loss of life had been removed by other measures in other places. Beyond this basic appraisal, he wanted to vindicate in some fashion his Dardanelles strategy of World War I; he put great faith in the effects on Hitler of a collapse in the Balkans, of an Italian surrender, or of the capture of Vienna; he had a special aversion to the plans for landing in southern France; and he was extremely anxious, after disappointments in the Far East and in Egypt, for notable victories by the predominantly British armies in Italy, led by a British general. (Parenthetically, it may be noted that Eisenhower, while he was there, and Mark Clark too, when he was in charge, sometimes wanted more aggressive action in Italy than his superiors were prepared for.) In 1944 Churchill became increasingly concerned about Russia's evident intention to dominate Eastern

Europe. Throughout, he was concerned to preserve the British Empire, as he preferred to call it. Animated by all these sentiments, he was therefore continually advancing, or reverting to, schemes for action in the eastern Mediterranean, from Italy and the Adriatic to Turkey or Hungary. They were arguable and argued on military grounds; they also opened up endless vistas of political and military involvements for which the Americans had no relish. Roosevelt at one point cabled Churchill that he could never face the American people if it became known that he had sent American troops to "the Balkans."

With some wavering on Roosevelt's part, for he was little inhibited by doctrine and always intrigued with Churchill's conversation, the Americans were convinced and remained convinced that Churchill's plans could only weaken the assault through France, which they thought was the only sure way of winning. They accepted Roosevelt's decision for the North African landings in 1942 on Roosevelt's grounds, i.e., that in the existing state of readiness North Africa was the only site where Americans could fight in force in 1942, and that Americans *had* to fight somewhere in 1942, for political and psychological reasons; but they accepted it reluctantly — Marshall especially opposed it — because it would delay the finish fight. They were sure that Churchill was not wholehearted in his support of the cross-Channel invasion, and suspected him of some sort of devious desire to extend British influence in the Balkans. They wanted as much as Roosevelt to keep American troops out of Eastern Europe. What they thought of Churchill's later desire, in the fall of 1944, to forestall Russian advances in that area is not known; presumably, by that stage the Russians were in any case too far along to be deflected by any flanking move from Italy or the Adriatic.

## LIBERATION AND OCCUPATION POLICY

American military doctrine provided rules for behavior in enemy countries and in the lands of allies, like England or Australia, where soldiers were guests with as much of a temporary freehold as could be wangled. But there were no rules for North Africa, where we had the task of creating an ally; or for Italy, neither friend nor foe; or for France, obviously friendly, but with a government that we did not fully accept. Military doctrine also contemplated the negotiation of a field surrender of opposing troops, or the delivery of surrender terms on behalf of a higher political authority. What was not contemplated and had to be faced was a "military" surrender, as of the French in North Africa, on terms involving important political elements, or a "political" surrender subject to military considerations as in Japan.

IN NORTH AFRICA

So in North Africa the "deal with Darlan" made sense: Eisenhower and General Mark Clark, finding that "existing French sentiment in North Africa does not even remotely resemble prior calculations," believed and had reason to believe that Darlan alone — unexpectedly on the ground at the time of the landings — could and would bring about a cease-fire from the colonial governors who were loyal to constituted authority, i.e., to Vichy, and who were in possession. But when Robert D. Murphy, the State Department's political adviser in Algiers who had arranged to import Giraud by submarine to assume French leadership, found that his hopes for Giraud were vain — as Darlan said, "He is not your man, for politically he is a child" — Murphy withdrew from the problem. Eisenhower, on his own, had his first lesson in politics, and put his "neck in the noose" by putting Darlan in charge of French civil affairs. As he later explained, "I believe in a theater commander doing these things without referring them back to his home Government and then waiting for approval. If a mere General makes a mistake, he can be repudiated and kicked out and disgraced. But a Government cannot repudiate and kick out and disgrace itself — not, at any rate, in wartime." [1] Perhaps this put the best face on his improvisation. But liberal opinion at home was outraged, criticism turned on the State Department because of Hull's unfortunate and premature press conference hailing the Giraud arrangement, and Roosevelt, equally

[1] Sherwood, *Roosevelt and Hopkins,* pp. 648-55.

distressed, made it plain publicly that the Darlan deal was a temporary expedient — as indeed Darlan's assassination a few weeks afterward literally made it. Yet the subsequent situation remained unsatisfactory after Giraud took his place in January 1943. Murphy caught on, but slowly. Our military authorities, for example, preoccupied with the frustrations of the campaign eastward, failed to push the French civil administration to release those Frenchmen who had ventured to aid the American landings, and had been jailed for their reward. Eisenhower would doubtless have made the French turn loose these Free French prisoners if Murphy had told him to. But Murphy had been turned down when he cabled for the recognition of de Gaulle, and did not venture further. So the failure to insist on simple justice to Free French friends was excused on grounds of "military necessity." And in justice to Hull it should be said that when he finally changed his mind and recommended de Gaulle's recognition, Roosevelt still would not have it.

IN ITALY

In Italy, by contrast, Eisenhower had no such free hand in the armistice negotiations with the Badoglio regime that started shortly after Mussolini's downfall in July 1943.[1] He had anticipated some such opportunity soon after the invasion of the Italian mainland was decided on, and sought a directive that would empower him to snatch any fleeting favorable chance to eliminate Italy from the Axis without fighting and before the Germans could prevent it. But Roosevelt at Casablanca in January had announced the controversial "unconditional surrender" formula which might preclude political negotiations. Although he and Churchill foresaw an armistice possibility too, they preferred to keep the terms of it in their own hands; Eisenhower's request for plenary powers was rebuffed. Protracted negotiations ensued around the "long terms," including unconditional surrender and political clauses developed in Washington and London, and the "short terms," principally military stipulations, prepared at Eisenhower's headquarters in Algiers. These were

[1] Robert J. Quinlan's case study, "The Italian Armistice," Twentieth Century Fund, mimeo.

eventually resolved in alternative documents that fixed the conditions Eisenhower might offer. After the contacts with the Badoglio government were made in Lisbon in August, and as the time for the mainland Italian landings in September approached, it became evident that the success of any armistice agreement might depend more on the time and manner of its publication than on its contents; for the troop limitations placed on the Italian campaign in favor of the continued build-up in Britain for what was now named OVER-LORD, made it Eisenhower's principal anxiety to get Italian help in driving the Germans from Italy if possible. The Germans were already strengthening their forces there. If the armistice was broadcast simultaneously with the landings, in Eisenhower's reckoning, no Italian government could refuse or deny it and stay in office; but unless the announcement were delayed until *after* the landings, so Badoglio's representatives argued, the Germans would at once seize control and make any Italian agreement futile. In the event, Eisenhower held to his calculation and Badoglio's prediction proved correct: the German reaction was so prompt and vigorous that, apart from the surrender of the Italian fleet and the absence of Italian resistance at the Salerno beachhead, the net effect of the armistice was only to substitute German troops for Italian in the defense of Italy — a limited effect, but an important one. The long previous inter-allied and civil-military negotiations were wide of the mark, for the real problem turned out to be, not how to compel Italian surrender, but how to permit it.

One sidelight is pertinent: throughout the July-to-September negotiations with Washington, Eisenhower's political adviser was no American at all but Harold Macmillan, the British Foreign Office's spokesman at AFHQ in Algiers. For after the North African fiasco the War Department had set up its own Civil Affairs Division and vetoed any State Department appointment to Eisenhower's staff of an adviser on Italian military government matters. Murphy's jurisdiction remained for a period limited to French questions, and Eisenhower, no chauvinist, took his political advice where he found it.

IN FRANCE

In France the next year Eisenhower was still cheerful but wiser: he pushed for an acceptance of de Gaulle's government — over de Gaulle's past record of intransigeance and over Roosevelt's previous opposition — on "military" grounds, i.e., that de Gaulle was the only one in sight who could lead Frenchmen into fighting Germans. But Roosevelt for other reasons then thought a military government was needed in France; he expected a civil war there when troops were withdrawn, and wanted no provisional government in office and making reprisals until conditions permitted free and orderly elections. Eisenhower continued to urge recognition. He was also quick to see the "military" advantages in letting French forces be the ones to liberate Paris. Again, for genuinely military reasons at the time of the Battle of the Bulge he wanted to let Strasbourg go; the French, mindful of this symbol of German conquest since 1870, objected. Eisenhower finally decided they were right and found a "military" reason — that a resentful French population might endanger his lines of communication.

One other aspect of liberation — and presently occupation — policy that became entangled in military doctrine deserves mention here: the amount and types of supplies to be distributed to the civil populations in the wake of the advancing armies. UNRRA did not come into full operation until after VE-Day, and its efforts were mainly directed to eastern and southeastern European areas. Obviously our national interests as well as our humanitarian sentiments dictated that French, Dutch, Belgian, even Italian and other civilians should not be left to their own resources. After years of Nazi occupation more than the elements of food, fuel, clothing and shelter were needed to restore their self-sufficiency. Just as obviously, the United States, and more particularly the Army, was the only adequate source of immediate supply in sight. But military doctrine taught that military appropriations were for the supply of troops, and the sustenance of civilians was no Army concern. Eventually the War Department's Civil Affairs Division devised the formula of furnishing sufficient supplies to "prevent disease and unrest," backed up by the sternly military requirement that there be "repose among the indigenous population." After the end of the war, to continue to meet this formula, the Army secured appropriations under a special heading, General Appropriation for Relief in Occupied Areas (GARIOA), which ultimately ran to over $1.5 billion.

## MILITARY GOVERNMENT

Both Army and Navy were familiar with the concept of military government; in fact, in 1941 both were still engaged in it, in the Canal Zone and Guam. Stimson had had a good deal of experience with it in his earlier years and assumed that the Army would have to take responsibility for the control of civil affairs in any occupied country that lacked an effective and friendly central government. With this in mind, he established a school at Charlottesville in May 1942 to train officers for that purpose.

To many Americans on the other hand, notably Roosevelt and many members of his Administration, military government was at first a repulsive notion, associated in their minds with imperialism, dollar diplomacy and other aspects of our behavior that we had abandoned in favor of the Good Neighbor policy and the Philippine Independence Act. The practical problems of maintaining society in a war zone were ignored, or, when dimly seen, were classed as something to be handled by civilians.

### IN NORTH AFRICA

The North African expedition was hastily put together and the Army was unprepared to take over civil functions. The situation of the French was confused enough, and the confusion was increased by the arrival in Algiers of a flow of civilians eager to deal with French affairs and unimpeded by any strict respect for jurisdictions; they represented a diversity of agencies — State, Lend-Lease, the Board of Economic Warfare, Treasury, and the Office of Foreign Relief and Rehabilitation Operations, among others. Conflicting instructions from Washington were common. The supervisory authority of Robert Murphy was uncertain in any of his three assigned roles, as political adviser to Eisenhower, personal representative of the President, and officer of the Foreign Service.

The confusion was the harder to resolve because this was a combined operation and the British too were represented by a political and economic mission. And for a time the confusion seemed hopelessly confounded when Roosevelt at Casablanca made a variety of unrecorded promises, about imports of civilian supplies, the franc exchange rate and other matters, to Giraud and other French leaders. The confusion plagued Eisenhower, and he finally appealed for help.

Eventually Stimson secured Roosevelt's permission to send the Assistant Secretary of War, John J. McCloy, to Algiers to untangle the strands and make a rope. McCloy's visit was successful: the civilians were brought together in a loose economic mission and put under the supervision of Murphy as head of a Civil Affairs Section, AFHQ, reporting to Eisenhower. The mission was brought together with the British in an organization called the North African Economic Board. Thereafter, the operation was reasonably well coordinated and effective. One basic problem remained unsolved: what to do about policy guidance from a civilian agency when it conflicted with military judgments of military necessity.

Coherent administration in Algiers required coherent administration in Washington. At first the burden fell on the State Department, which established a committee of interested agencies; this committee, acting with British representatives, constituted CCNA, the Combined Committee for North Africa. CCNA was hardly an ideal instrument: as many as forty or fifty Americans, and a handful of British, would attend its meetings, and the chairman, a Special Assistant to the Secretary of State, was a moderator without powers of decision. Messages from the committee were transmitted by the Army to Eisenhower, so that the Army representatives had an effective veto power, mitigated, however, by the flow of uncensored letters from other constituent agencies to their representatives in Algiers, and by tales brought back by returning civilian travellers.

All this was distasteful to Stimson and he moved to prevent a repetition elsewhere. In May 1943 he arranged for the establishment of a Civil Affairs Division, soon headed by Major General John H. Hilldring, as a branch of the War Department Special Staff, and for a Combined Civil Affairs Committee, as a subcommittee of the Combined Chiefs of Staff. McCloy was chairman of CCAC, and an Assistant Secretary of State was a member. In due course the CCAC spawned subcommittees, most notably a Supply Subcommittee, labelled in the military manner CCAC(S); and the American "side" on each level also constituted a committee. Other agencies were brought in as needed. Since military government and other civil affairs in liberated and occupied areas were entrusted to the military commanders and their subordinate officers, the prospects for orderly administration were improved.

Difficulties remained. CAD was a newcomer in the War Department with uncertain authority. Its jurisdiction overlapped the jurisdictions of two other powerful units: the International Division, which dealt with lend-lease and similar problems, a part of the Army Service Forces and hence backed by Generals Clay and Somervell; and OPD, the Operations Division of the General Staff, that largely supplied the membership for the most important subcommittees of JCS and the American side of CCS. There was thus the possibility, and sometimes the actuality, of divergence within the War Department.

More important, while the administration of civil affairs became more orderly, it became still less responsive to policy views of the State Department and other civilian agencies. JCS was in the saddle and Army members of JCS subcommittees held the whip hand. A single example will illustrate.

In CCAC(S) American membership included a representative of the Foreign Economic Administration, successor (after the Henry Wallace–Jesse Jones blow-up) to the Board of Economic Warfare and Lend-Lease. For months in 1943 and 1944 CCAC(S) debated about civilian supplies that would be needed in France and the Low

Countries after D-Day. The Army proposed to buy supplies out of its own appropriated funds. It took the position that it could purchase only those items clearly necessary to prevent "disease and unrest," such as food, clothing and medicines. It admitted the desirability of sending materials to rehabilitate industry and agriculture too, but insisted that FEA purchase those materials — on speculation, for there was no promise of shipping. The Army also insisted for no very clear reason that its supplies would be sold to the French and other governments for cash. FEA and the State Department protested all three decisions long, loudly and vainly. In the end, at the time of the post-war lend-lease settlement, the cost of the Army supplies was charged off to the lend-lease account, where, under long-established and well-known policies, it had always belonged. None of these matters in dispute, be it noted, except the question of shipping space, had any connection whatever with military operations; shipping was vital for the Army and in this forum (if not in WSA) the Army's judgment on its own needs was usually unchallengeable.

Although combat troops were cleared out of the former enemy countries not long after hostilities were over, the continuance of military government and its location in the War Department gave that department a leading role in the reorientation and administration of our diplomatic and overseas economic policies in the most critical areas for years afterward. One incidental consequence flowed from the geographical nature of the layers in War Department organization. In 1943 and 1944 plans for military government in Germany were considered and formulated in Washington, both in CAD and in State. State's plans never penetrated the iron curtain of CAD, and CAD's plans seem not to have gotten beyond that agency's files. In the early months of 1944, before D-Day, Eisenhower's staff at SHAEF in London also included a team that planned diligently on the same subject without knowledge of what had been or was being done on it in Washington; but after D-Day Eisenhower's headquarters were moved to the Continent and these plans too found their destination in the files. When the practical tasks were finally tackled by General Clay's staff in Berlin, they started afresh, hardly aware that anyone else had ever looked at their problems before.[1]

## GERMAN ZONAL BOUNDARIES

A final topic to illustrate the influence of military doctrine and military institutions on our wartime foreign policy is the determination of the German zonal boundaries and the Berlin corridor, which became crucial matters in later crises. In the normal procedure the question of boundaries for allied occupation zones in Germany and Austria would have been an appropriate item on the agenda for CCAC; it was a politico-military problem like the Italian armistice terms and other subjects handled by CCAC. It was not referred to CCAC, however, for reasons to be made clear presently.

What to do with Germany and Italy after victory, both immediately and for the long term, were questions first raised by Hopkins in 1942. Roosevelt asked Hull to study them and initiate discussions with the British and the Russians. In 1943, proposals were developed in the State Department and presented by Hull at the Moscow conference of foreign ministers. The three foreign ministers were not ready to make any final decisions and instead referred these and other questions of the management of victory to a new body to be set up in London, the European Advisory Commission mentioned earlier. They promptly named their representatives to EAC; ours was John G. Winant, our Ambassador in London.

### EAC'S HANDICAPS

The first EAC meeting was held in December 1943, and it immediately became necessary to provide a focus in Washington for the formulation of Winant's instructions. The American side of CCAC could not do this because its instructions to the field were

---

[1] The stages and details of the formation of American policy for post-war Germany, starting from issues raised by Hopkins in 1942, are set forth in the case study by Paul Y. Hammond, "Directives for the Occupation of Germany: The Washington Controversy," Twentieth Century Fund, mimeo.

inevitably transmitted through military channels, normally JCS, to military commanders. Instructions for Winant must obviously be forwarded by the State Department. Recognizing this, and recognizing also the valid military interest in the problems before EAC, the State Department set up a special interdepartmental committee, the Working Security Committee previously noted, with representation from State, Army and Navy; the Army representative was an officer of the Civil Affairs Division.[1] State provided the chairman and the channels of communication to Winant, but WSC operated under the rule of unanimity; the Army therefore had an effective veto over State Department proposals.

WSC's inauspicious beginnings have been described by Philip E. Mosely, then in the State Department:

> For a fortnight the representative of the [Civil Affairs] Division maintained that the surrender and occupation of Germany were purely a military matter which would have to be decided "at the military level"; and that therefore there was no need for the WSC, or, for that matter, for a European Advisory Commission. In rejoinder, it was pointed out that the President, who was also commander-in-chief, had joined with the heads of two other governments in creating the EAC and in expressing the intention to work out Allied agreements on postwar Germany. According to the Civil Affairs Division, military government was a purely military matter; when the time came, the necessary orders would be issued by the Combined Chiefs of Staff, and that was all. This view ignored the fact that the Combined Chiefs of Staff would probably not be allowed to determine American *postwar* policy, that there was no Soviet representation on it, that the President was committed to seeking postwar agreement on Germany with both the Soviet and British Governments, and that meanwhile the American representative on the EAC was completely without instructions.[2]

This struggle for WSC's mere existence was settled, by intervention from above, before December was out; in the meantime State Department officers were preparing proposals on three German problems: the zonal boundaries, the allied control machinery, and the surrender instrument. Prompt agreement on these was needed if Winant was to get instructions in time to take the initiative in EAC.

Progress on the last of these problems, the surrender instrument,

---

[1] Cline, *Washington Command Post*, pp. 320-26.
[2] "The Occupation of Germany," *Foreign Affairs*, July 1950, at p. 585.

was not rapid, but there was progress. Winant was able to circulate a draft in EAC in March that became the basis for the final document. Progress on the zonal boundaries was nil; this, said CAD, was a purely military problem. The argument dragged on to the extent that CAD even vetoed draft messages to Winant telling him not to expect an early reply to his agitated inquiries.

ROOSEVELT'S ROLE

What the State Department officials did not know was that they were latecomers in the warfare of the zones. For in the summer of 1943 Sir Frederick Morgan, a British lieutenant general and chief of advance combined planning for OVERLORD, had hurriedly prepared a zonal map to be used if there was a sudden collapse of Germany. Morgan proposed the establishment of three approximately equal zones with Berlin as a special enclave. For sound and practical military reasons Morgan assigned the East to Russia, the Northwest to Great Britain and the Southwest to the United States — representing the directions from which the three armies would converge.[1] The plan was accepted at the Quebec conference in August 1943, apparently for use whether victory was gained by German collapse or by hard fighting. Hull and his aides were neither consulted nor informed.

In the months that followed Roosevelt changed his mind about the zonal assignments. Wishing to avoid entanglement in Austria, fearful of future troubles in France, and also eager to facilitate redeployment to the Pacific, he decided to demand the Northwest zone and so informed JCS on the way to Cairo and Teheran in November 1943. The State Department officials were not informed of this either, nor of the further fact that early in December Roosevelt debated the matter with Churchill at Cairo. Roosevelt's reasons, as already noted, were primarily political, though there was a logistic excuse as well; the British wanted the same area, with logistic con-

---

[1] Lt. Gen. Sir Frederick Morgan, *Overture to Overlord*, Doubleday, Garden City, 1950, pp. 112-22; Forrest C. Pogue, *European Theater of Operations: The Supreme Command*, Department of the Army, Washington, 1954, pp. 348-49; Hammond, "Directives for the Occupation of Germany," Pt. I.

siderations immediately in mind, but for economic reasons in addition, since German industrial and commercial centers were heavily concentrated there. The disputed zone included the Ruhr and the ports of Hamburg and Bremen. Roosevelt and Churchill were both stubborn and were still haggling when WSC was born.

Whether CAD ever learned of the Roosevelt-Churchill dispute seems doubtful; apparently their representatives in WSC were merely instructed to prevent WSC action and were certainly not instructed to explain why delay was necessary — a matter that they probably did not understand themselves. The State Department officers were thus frustrated by ignorance as well as by the roadblock. In the outcome, WSC could never send Winant any instructions on the zones. A State Department proposal that would have provided a definitely specified corridor to Berlin was thereby lost. WSC was at a standstill.

EAC was also at a standstill. Finally the British would wait no longer, and presented EAC with a plan for occupation zones in January 1944 — the same plan that had been presented by General Morgan the previous August. The Russians followed with another in February. In the Soviet plan, the Eastern zone and the Greater Berlin enclave were the same as in the British plan, and the Soviet delegate announced that the allotment of the Western zones was a matter of indifference to his government.

NO BERLIN CORRIDOR

The argument between the American military, under instructions from the President, and the British over possession of the Northwest zone — the other one was mostly Bavaria, and more agricultural — continued, and finally EAC approved a protocol establishing the three zones but leaving blank the allocation of the western two. In May, Winant, on a trip to Washington, again proposed a stipulation for a corridor to Berlin; but CAD refused, reiterating that this was a "military" matter to be settled on the "military" level, and stating that it would be *unwise for the Army to commit itself in advance to any particular route.*

In sharp contrast to this easy assumption that we could always count on passing through the Soviet zone anywhere at will, or at least could count on stipulating any convenient route later, was the Army's attitude toward the British when the President finally accorded them the Northwest zone at the Quebec conference in September 1944. Although we obviously could always count on British cooperation in transit arrangements, the military nevertheless insisted on control of ports and access through the British zone. The British readily agreed in principle, but it took months to work out, in what was in effect a lengthy and detailed treaty negotiated at arms' length, a formula on ports and access that both the British and the Army would sign. A similar impasse developed when the French were given a zone; military logistics again demanded the fullest measure of control. So when the Berlin blockade made a major postwar issue hinge on these arrangements we had nothing specific in writing to rest on in our contest with the Russians.

Admission of the French created another problem, for coordinate status required giving them also a sector in Berlin. Both American and British military authorities insisted that the Russians give up one *Bezirk* (a city district), while each of them gave up one, for that purpose; the Russians refused. A month later, when it dawned on the Americans that they, and not the Russians, would be supplying the food for the French and British sectors as well as their own, they hastily withdrew their request for the cession of a Russian *Bezirk,* not appreciating that in such circumstances added responsibilities are apt to bring added power. In all this, the State Department was unable to play a significant role. The views its staff developed were never presented — or never effectively presented — to the President, and went unheeded by the Army.


## LIMITS OF THE PRESIDENCY

The wartime disruption, illustrated in these pages, of the normal balance of agency and Congressional influences on the formulation of national policy led, by the time hostilities ceased, to something of a crisis in the adequacy of the coordinating and directing elements of our government, where civil-military affairs were concerned. Before VE-Day the UN was brought into being as a permanent organization to prevent or help resolve conflicts of national interests. But the progress of world organization does not yet warrant relying on it as a substitute for a consistent national policy of our own. Before VE-Day too, some further progress was achieved in the development of interdepartmental coordinating committees in our government, most notably in the work of SWNCC, the State-War-Navy Coordinating Committee. But barring miracles from above or below, the Presidency remained, and remains yet, the focal point for coordination. And despite the institutionalization of JCS and the Bureau of the Budget, the wartime Presidency was to the end a highly personal affair, as Sherwood's account of it amply shows. In Roosevelt the country had an extraordinarily knowledgeable, vigorous and versatile President. The strain of office took his life. The personal tragedy perhaps underlines some limits of the office as well.

Some aspects of the Yalta conference in February 1945 will serve for illustration. At the time, the occasion seemed to mark the peak of the President's influence on his partners in the wartime coalition. The conference led to agreements — on China in Chiang Kai-shek's absence, on Soviet participation in the war against Japan, on recognition of Soviet claims in the Far East and in Eastern Europe, on voting memberships in the UN General Assembly, among other matters — that have since been widely criticized. The principals, on the other hand, came away feeling tolerably content that they had done their best with some intractable problems and had won agreements on objects they prized most.[1] Without arguing the merits of these, it is worth noting some of the circumstances under which they were reached. First, it was a conference of principals in which the three chiefs of state dealt with each other directly. In part, at least, this converted the negotiations from bureaucratic maneuvering to discussions in which personality and the willingness to assume personal responsibility had some bearing on the outcome. This kind of conference, dear to the hearts of both Roosevelt and Churchill,

---

[1] Sherwood, *Roosevelt and Hopkins*, pp. 869-70; Feis, *Churchill, Roosevelt, Stalin*, p. 557.

has its legitimate uses, particularly in war; and also its dangers. In this one, as in many previous, Roosevelt, aware that in our form of government the more who are privy to such a conference the harder it will be to keep the results secret, confined his accompanying staff to a minimum. Churchill, more confident of maintaining privacy and discretion with his staff, felt able, and preferred, to have more of them around and available. Roosevelt also, and only partly because he had travelled so far, was under the greatest pressure of time to keep the conference short. This was a disadvantage in bargaining toward the end of it. So personal an office could not stand vacant at home for long.

Second, if there is to be a conference of principals, prudence requires that they be adequately prepared. Here the American arrangements were seriously defective. Roosevelt was for many major purposes — China policy, most notably — his own Secretary of State, and Hopkins his deputy. Stettinius, by then the holder of the Secretary's title, was himself uninformed and played a minor part — a boy on a man's errand.[1] The President, weary and impatient at the end — there is dispute on how sick he was — relied on his military advisers, on Hopkins who was ill, on Byrnes and on Harriman. They were all exceptionally knowledgeable and the military part of the discussions went smoothly. But in spite of State's briefings, management of the political topics was uneven and rough. For the European problems, the State Department officers had tended to ignore the President's stated preferences in their preparatory work, and the President therefore negotiated without the advantage of a solid, fully prepared position. In the case of China, the President simply excluded the State Department representatives from the negotiations. Thus he lacked the full benefit of a solid underpinning of staff work of a sort not possible within the White House itself, and not then forthcoming elsewhere, that would have presented an informed and consolidated government-wide position.

Third, the secrecy surrounding the agreements, some of it quite essential for the time being, was unnecessarily extended in time and scope, to the detriment of our relations with China, of executive rela-

[1] E. R. Stettinius, *Roosevelt and the Russians,* Doubleday, Garden City, 1949.

tions with the Congress and the public, and of the morale of the State Department, which was itself kept in ignorance of some of the agreements made — most conspicuously and deplorably, of Roosevelt's promise to support Stalin's request at the forthcoming San Francisco sessions on the UN Charter for seats in the General Assembly for the Ukraine and Byelorussia. Acting in ignorance, the department later acted in error. The demoralization that resulted from working in a vacuum, whether from being by-passed or from having information withheld, was not limited to the Yalta conference and crippled the department for a long time afterward.

The Yalta example argues for a greater institutionalization of an office so dependent on the strength and personality of its tenant, even one of the stature of Roosevelt. The lesson was scarcely unfolded when a fresh example was presented. Before VE-Day the country had another and far less prepared President in Harry S. Truman, who had everything to learn about the problems he immediately confronted, and very different habits of work. Without peering ahead into his post-war record it can be said of his first few weeks and months that in his anxiety to accept responsibility and avoid being a bottleneck he was all too ready to decide, sometimes prematurely, the issues put up to him, and to sign what was laid on his desk with a favorable recommendation. It took him time to learn the need for staff work and coordination.[1]

The war ended, leaving more politico-military problems pressing for action or attention than anyone had thought of when it began. The end of hostilities discharged in full the simple defensive purpose for which the country took up arms, to beat Italy, Germany and Japan. But the march of events to 1945 and beyond belied a basic premise of wartime strategy, that "the issues in the Far East will be decided in Europe," for the issues in the Far East turned out to hinge on China as well as on Japan. As a military strategy it was correct; as a political strategy it proved to be wrong. Churchill was wrong in supposing that China did not matter, and Roosevelt in

[1] Harry S. Truman, *Memoirs*, Vol. 1, *Year of Decisions*, Doubleday, Garden City, 1955, p. 228.

thinking he could keep it under control. Events also belied, alas, the basic premise of our wartime political strategy, that with Germany and Japan beaten the three victorious powers could work out the remaining problems harmoniously through the instrument of a universal international organization. (The premise, it should be noted, was probably inescapable.) In our domestic government they left as a legacy an urgent need for a reconsideration of the machinery of government to equip the President to integrate more effectively the diverse civil and military influences in American institutions, to match more consciously the resources and responsibilities of America's position in the world, to anticipate and respond to new opportunities and challenges in the formation of our national policies.

Part Two BY WALTER MILLIS

•••••••••••••••••••••••••••••••••••••••••••••••••••••••••••••••••••••••••••••••••••••••••••••••

# CHAPTER 4

# Reorganization

## END OF AN ERA

As the Second World War reached its end, it was apparent that drastic revision of our pre-war institutions of civil-military policy-making and direction had become imperative. What was not apparent was the direction which the revisions should take. The old principles, the old shibboleths, which had for so long ruled in this field, were wearing thin, even before the shattering revelation of the atomic bomb. New principles, adequate to the problems before the nation, were not easily discernible.

The greatest and most enduring of the old principles was "civilian control" of the armed forces; and in the reorganization of our politico-military institutions after 1945 there was to be much concern with the maintenance of this supposed absolute. Few noticed that it was not, in fact, of much relevance to the practical issues which confronted the country. It had been born in the eighteenth-century fear and loathing of a standing army as a menace to the liberties of the people. But by 1945 our liberties seemed safe enough from military subversion. The danger of a military dictator using the bayonets of his troops to turn the Congress into the streets or overthrow the

Constitution had lost what little shred of reality it ever had in the United States.

But if the fear of the military dictator had faded, the fear of militarism had lived on. By the end of the nineteenth century the principle of civilian control had become a bulwark, not so much against the military as against militarism. It was no longer the standing armies of King George III which the country detested, but the "overgrown," "strutitudinous," "saber-rattling" and "crushingly" expensive military systems of continental Europe. The authority of the civil power had to be maintained, it seemed, not to prevent military subversion, but to prevent a military caste or military interest from asserting excessive claims upon the civilian economy, or using its influence to distort national policy into unduly aggressive, chauvinistic or dangerous paths. Admirals and generals were disliked and frequently distrusted, not as potential threats to liberty, but as menaces to the taxpayer and unsound guides to foreign policy. Yet at the end of two great wars in which we had been compelled to imitate so many of the features of the Continental military systems we had abhorred, this concept also had lost much of its relevance.

Even the old and seemingly clear-cut division between the civilian and the military was itself fading into insubstantiality. The Second World War, to a far greater extent even than the First, had inextricably intermingled the civilian and the military components on all the higher levels of policy-making; and the difficult future into which we were gazing as the war ended seemed to offer little hope that they could ever be fully separated. In 1945 the stage was filled with civilians more militaristic than the military, and with military men — like Marshall, Eisenhower, Bradley and a host of others — with a breadth of view on national and world problems which often made them seem more "civilistic" than the civilians. It was no longer clear that the substitution of a politician or businessman for a professional soldier at any given post of command would necessarily affect the course of policy.

### THE NEW ROLE OF THE MILITARY

The "military mind," supposedly inculcated at West Point and Annapolis and hardened thereafter in the narrow routines of services which "never had to meet a payroll," did not seem, when it reached the highest levels of responsibility and authority, to be markedly different from the diplomatic or legal or business mind. Indeed, the number of top officers of the Second War period who were to be readily received, on their retirement, into the top echelons of industry is a comment not only on the military mind but also, perhaps, on the nature of modern industrial management. The best of the soldiers had been made acutely aware, during the war, of their dependence in their every strategic move upon industrial production, scientific effort, the civilian labor force, as well as upon diplomacy, public opinion and political support. Conversely, the shrewdest of the civilians had been made acutely aware of their dependence upon the soldiers, not only for the conduct of actual war, but in arriving at the many decisions at once political and military in character which the successful conduct of the prospective peace seemed likely to demand.

It was beginning to appear, as Masland and Radway have put it,[1] that "To attain national security objectives without resort to war requires a national strategy in which the disposition of military forces is integrated with political bargaining, policy statements, alliances, foreign economic policy, propaganda, and any and all measures that may foster the growth of friendly factions within foreign governments." Though the fact was less plain than it has since become, many even in 1945 were realizing that "the role of the military officer of tomorrow" would be "even less conventional than the role he has played in the recent past." Though the problem was to be repeatedly and exhaustively argued thereafter as one in restoring "civilian control" over the military, this was seldom in fact central to the issues. In those controversies which turned, or seemed to turn, upon the locus of power within the state there were usually not two but three major interests significantly involved — the uniformed military bureaucracy, the appointed civilian bureaucracy[2] and the elected political representatives in Congress. Each of these,

[1] John W. Masland and Laurence I. Radway, *Soldiers and Scholars: Military Education and National Policy,* Princeton University Press, Princeton, 1957, p. 26.

[2] "Bureaucracy" is often used as a technical term distinguishing the career civil service from the political appointees. Since there seems to be no good word including both, the term is made to do double duty throughout this book, referring to both classes.

moreover, was much divided within itself along lines which in no way corresponded to the supposed dichotomy of civilian and military. The Air Force was to find, on more than one occasion, more powerful allies in Congress than in the Joint Chiefs of Staff; the civilian bureaucrats in Defense were frequently at outs with their civilian colleagues in the State Department or the Budget Bureau and might have to call up military support for their supposedly civilian determinations. In these contests both of policy and of power, the issue of civilian control was frequently available as a club with which to best the opposition, but it had little objective reality. When in 1951 General MacArthur presented what to many seemed one of the clearest challenges in our history by military high command to civilian supremacy, the resultant issues were debated with little reference to this supposed fundamental of our constitutional system. They were argued violently as questions of policy, politics and personality, but hardly at all as a question of military as against civilian power in the state.

CIVIL-MILITARY INTEGRATION

The basic problem confronting the nation in 1945 was not that of restoring a civilian control over the military establishment; it was the problem of integration — of how military factors, military forces and military plans were to be integrated with the civil diplomacy and civil domestic policy, of how their respective exponents were to learn to talk a common language to common ends. Neither civil nor military policy could exist and prosper in isolation. They were now deeply interlinked, not only in theory but in human fact, by a host of already existing joint boards, committees, policy-forming groups, in which professional soldiers, civilians temporarily in uniform and civilians still in their gray-flannel suits combined to make policy decisions both great and small. The basic issues of civil-military relations over the ensuing decade were not to lie in the promotion of one group or class into power over another; they were to lie in the proper combination of the skills and outlooks of all into an integrated national strategy which would, so far as might be possible, provide adequately for the very difficult future that more and more plainly appeared to lie ahead.

## THREE URGENT ISSUES

Already, in the closing months of 1945, this future was presenting three major and urgent issues, each of them demanding a sound resolution of civil-military relationships. The most immediate (if probably least critical) was the problem of administration of the occupied territories. We had conquering armies or supporting forces scattered all around the periphery of Eurasia; their commanding generals were final sources of civil authority in such great areas as Japan, Korea, much of the Southwest Pacific, the American zones of Germany and Austria. And in much larger areas, notably China and Italy, American military commanders were exercising, as the principal representatives of American power on the spot, a large influence in the civil affairs of the people with whom they were working. They were supported by State Department and other civilian advisers, but the lines of responsibility were ill-defined. In the closing days of the war the relation between the military command and the political direction had been unclear and at times uneasy, and this had led to some unfortunate results. In the dawn of peace it seemed desirable to get the War and Navy Departments out of the governing business and the State Department or some other civilian agency back into it; but the military commitments and military problems in these areas rendered this difficult.

The second major problem was far more ominous. The atomic bombing of Hiroshima and Nagasaki had left an enormous question mark upon the international skies. How were we both to regulate the use and control of atomic energy as a military weapon, and also to exploit its enormous potentialities for the benefit of mankind? The atomic bombs had been produced by a remarkable collaboration of political, scientific, industrial and military skills; it was obvious that in the future management of this appalling new force, political and military considerations must be closely integrated. But there was absolutely no existing pattern to indicate how this might be accomplished.

The third problem was obvious, though its solution was not. Once more, as after most of our previous wars, we would have to reorganize the military establishment. The war had, of course, effected reorganizations of the most drastic kind. Most of the wartime expedients had worked at least well enough under the dire pressures of necessity. They had included such innovations as the Joint Chiefs of Staff, working as a corporate command directly under the constitutional Commander in Chief, and thus largely by-passing the civilian Secretaries, who were reduced mainly to providing the industrial support. They had included a virtually complete autonomy for the Army Air Force as a third service. They had provided some centralization for intelligence operations and analysis. And they had included the many civilian agencies in control of war production, prices, manpower, shipping, propaganda and scientific research. In the final result, these expedients had been proved successful. But it was patently necessary to transfer the lessons of this experience to a peacetime organization, to adapt and institutionalize them into a permanent structure of peacetime policy.

These three inescapable and practical issues — of occupation policy and operation, of atomic energy and of military reorganization — had a common denominator: each of them deeply concerned the relationship between the civil and the military factors in modern governance. None raised a valid question of the locus of power, of civilian control in the old sense; each raised a question of proportion between the strategic and the non-strategic factors in the formulation of national policy. The fundamental problem in each was whether the technical, military advice as to force levels, weapon systems, expenditures, could be combined with the political, civilian advice as to diplomacy, budget and tax policy and popular acceptance into a coherent and adequate national strategy on the world stage. The real issue was not between the civilian and the military. It was how to balance a proper combination of the non-strategic or non-violent with the strategic or violent components of national policy. It was with this issue, seldom clearly seen, that the history of the ensuing decade was to be concerned.

## REORGANIZATION PLANS

On June 19, 1945 the Secretary of the Navy, James Forrestal, addressed a letter to his old friend and associate, Ferdinand Eberstadt. It was hardly more than a month since Germany's collapse; the bloody battle for Okinawa was at its height; it would be another month before the first test shot of an atomic bomb would be fired in New Mexico. A Japanese surrender seemed many months and many tens of thousands of American lives away. At this juncture, the Secretary asked his friend to study and report on three questions: Would unification of the War and Navy Departments under a single head contribute to the national security? if not, what changes in the military structure had war experience indicated to be desirable? and what form of post-war organization of the military and other government departments would "most effectively provide for and protect our national security?"

The post-war history of civil-military relations thus began in what seemed a rather simple problem of military reorganization. Actually, it was a problem neither simple nor even new; its roots ran far back into the unresolved controversies of the inter-war years over the proper place and employment of military aviation, which since 1918 had been the great apple of discord in all issues of military policy. The Second World War had allayed these controversies. The initial defeats and the extremity of the peril had enforced upon all the service factions a degree of unity which had been unobtainable in peace; while the extraordinary outpouring of war production had provided enough, or almost enough, resources for all. The familiar peacetime competition for tax dollars had been swamped in the floods of war appropriations. At the same time, war experience had given rise to a widespread conviction, within the services as well as among the public, that the two-service system was an anomaly. There had been duplication of effort. There had been failures of coordination and cooperation traceable to service rivalry and particularism. It had been found necessary (and practicable) to institute unity of command in almost all the combat theaters, with all forces under a single responsible commander, regardless of the hat he wore.

In the summer of 1945 it seemed both logical and relatively easy to extend these unifying tendencies to the departmental structure in Washington.

As far back as March 1944 the House had established a select committee under Representative Clifton A. Woodrum of Virginia, to consider "postwar military policy." Its first hearings, in late April and May, well before the launching of the Normandy invasion, had been devoted to the question of "a single department of the armed services." The Secretary of War, Henry L. Stimson, was already convinced that unification should be "the primary objective of the postwar period." [1] While the committee recognized that nothing could be done at the time, it had found nearly all its witnesses favorable to unification after the war's end. But there was one significant dissent. The new Secretary of the Navy, Forrestal, announced that he was "not prepared to say that the Navy believes that the consolidation into one department is desirable."

The pre-war issues had been allayed; they had not been resolved. While the Woodrum Committee hearings were in progress, the Joint Chiefs of Staff set up a special committee of two Army and two Navy officers to study the problem of post-war reorganization. Under a retired admiral — the redoubtable J. O. Richardson, who as commander of the Pacific Fleet in 1940 had tangled with Franklin Roosevelt — this committee spent the rest of the year touring the headquarters in Europe and the Pacific and taking the views of the leading commanders. In April 1945 it reported that, except for its senior naval member (Richardson), it was "unanimously in favor of a single department system of organization of the armed forces of the United States. This view is supported by Generals of the Army MacArthur and Eisenhower, Fleet Admiral Nimitz, Admiral Halsey, a substantial number of other commanders in the field and many officers in Washington. . . . The great majority of Army officers and almost exactly half of the Navy officers whose views were heard favored the single department." But "Jo" Richardson was in dissent, and it was to prove a powerful one.

[1] Henry L. Stimson and McGeorge Bundy, *On Active Service in Peace and War*, Harper, New York, 1948, p. 518.

Richardson had perceived the approaching peacetime issues which in 1944 were obscure to many of the combat commanders. The war was drawing toward a close; its unifying pressures would soon relax and its flood of appropriations would certainly dry up. The problems of peacetime military policy and administration would in fact be quite different from those of conducting a major war. Richardson clothed his dissent in various cogent arguments, but its core was quite obviously his fear that the single department, involving equal status for the Air Force as a third service, would "inevitably" end with the Air Force absorbing the Navy's aviation and possibly with the Army absorbing its Fleet Marine Force as well.

## DEMOBILIZATION PLANS

Just as the civilians had begun very early to argue and plan the post-war international structure (already, by 1945, being shaped at Bretton Woods, Dumbarton Oaks and San Francisco), the military services had been busy at least since 1943 on planning against the outbreak of peace. Their plans, unfortunately, had proceeded in a large measure of isolation, although by early 1945 they had hardened, as Fleet Admiral Ernest J. King put it, into "very definite ideas." The ground Army, engulfed in the problems of the approaching demobilization and the supposedly temporary duties of occupation, was less specific as to its permanent needs than the other two. Its planners had taken as their goal a regular and reserve structure capable of mobilizing 4.5 million men within a year of an outbreak of hostilities; but while Marshall, its Chief of Staff, had "figures in his mind" as to the permanent regular establishment that would be required, "only studies were made," and the general put all his public efforts into securing a system of universal military training. The Navy, on the other hand, developed a quite concrete program, calling for the retention in active service of some 600,000 men, 371 combat ships, about 5,000 auxiliaries, landing craft and similar smaller types, and about 8,000 operating aircraft.

The Army Air Force was, if anything, even more specific. By early 1945 it had designed its post-war program: a separate service, to maintain seventy regular air groups (with numerous National Guard and reserve formations in addition), a complete structure of technical and supporting services, the whole to be manned by 400,-000 regular officers and men. This was presented as the irreducible minimum requisite to meet the new demands of "air power." Like the Navy, the Air Force never explained the strategic calculations on which its requested force levels were based.[1] It certainly never submitted them for coordination by the Joint Chiefs of Staff. As General Carl H. ("Tooey") Spaatz was soon to testify: "In the Joint Chiefs of Staff there is a general interchange of ideas as to numbers and forces involved. But as to the specific items, there is no detailed interchange of ideas in the preparation of the Army and Navy requirements for the air forces." Neither he nor his representatives had ever "sat around a table" with the Navy to decide upon the best employment of the two air arms.

But whatever its strategic foundation, the "seventy-group program" soon passed beyond the realm of strategy. It became the "package" which symbolized the Army Air Force's claim to independence and to dominance over the military policy of the nation. On August 21, 1945, with the Japanese war virtually at its end, Truman expressed a nascent alarm over these disparate developments. The services were all pressing him for permanent peacetime legislation fixing their strengths; he felt that "the time had come to put an end to piecemeal legislation and separate planning." He wrote the Joint Chiefs, asking for a review of the Navy's post-war plan under a consideration of the "combined" requirements which the future might present.[2] This was not very productive. JCS referred the President's letter to its Joint Planning Staff. The problem was what the roles and missions of the several armed services were to be. The Army felt that in the absence of any firm political guidance and any

[1] They would seem to have been based mainly on a calculation of what the traffic would bear. Some years later an Air Force spokesman, Major General Frederic Harrison Smith, Jr., told a Congressional committee that the object had been to design a "balanced" establishment capable of meeting military requirements, but also capable of "providing a proper mobilization potential in the form of a sound and adequate aircraft industry, but one which would still remain within reasonable budget limitations."

[2] Harry S. Truman, *Memoirs*, Vol. 2, *Years of Trial and Hope*, Doubleday, Garden City, 1956, p. 48.

decision as to how the services were to be unified, it was impossible to come to any conclusions on force levels or what the specific roles and missions should be; the Navy felt that in the absence of any firm decision as to force levels and roles and missions, it was impossible to proceed to unification. It was a chicken-and-egg problem.

## UNIFICATION PROPOSALS AND FEARS

As both Richardson and Forrestal appeared to realize, the really driving pressure for unification did not come from the wartime experience with inter-service inefficiencies and wastes (though this contributed); it came from the unanswered claim of the pre-war Army aviators, dating back to 1920, for a commanding position in American military planning. Unification was in fact the Army aviators' one practicable avenue to independence and authority. In the debates of the time, few voices were ever seriously raised for "merger" — one service wearing one uniform. Most of the various plans proposed began with three services, to be unified only at the top under some kind of single command. A single service, aside from being impossibly unwieldy, might have left the Army aviators no better off than before. Three wholly separate and uncoordinated services would have produced a military and administrative monstrosity. But an independent, co-equal status "at the bottom" under a structure unified "at the top" provided the opportunity for independent development to begin with, together with the chance to secure increasing authority over general policy by securing increasing control of the top machinery.

This last the Air Force was very likely to do under any system of tri-partite autonomy at the bottom with single and centralized control over all. It had public opinion overwhelmingly behind it. Few questioned its dubious thesis that "air power" (always meaning, by implication, Army air power, or the power of the Army Air Force) had been the decisive factor in the war. There was, moreover, a compelling simplicity about the notion of a tri-partite system under a single command. The creation of three services, to wage, respectively, land, sea and air war, seemed to carry an obvious logic —

though it was a logic which overlooked the critical fact that "air war" was inextricably involved with both land and sea war as well. In the summer of 1945, unification was being accepted on all sides as the obvious lesson of war experience. Some of the high civilian officials who, like Stimson, advocated unification may also have seen it as a method of reinserting a civilian authority between the Joint Chiefs and the President. The Congressional committees were getting ready to grind out the bills; and while the problems of how to organize the central direction of the three services presented some difficulties, they were not regarded as serious. It was at this point that Secretary Forrestal addressed his three questions to Mr. Eberstadt.

Admiral Richardson had dissented from the report to JCS, and had since been actively proselytizing in the Navy; he had converted Admirals Nimitz and Halsey and many of the lesser naval officers who had supported the "one uniform" idea to a clearer realization of the menaces which lurked for the Navy in unification. Forrestal was impressed; and perhaps his deepest motivation at the time was, as with Richardson, a simple desire to preserve the Navy as an institution. "The Navy Department," he had written to Senator David I. Walsh (a Massachusetts Democrat and long-time chairman of the Senate Naval Affairs Committee) on May 27, "cannot be in the position of merely taking the negative in this discussion, but must come up with positive and constructive recommendations." [1] It hints at a man looking for "good" reasons to support his real reasons for the position he was taking. But Forrestal was aware that larger issues were involved. He had long been deeply concerned with the problems of national policy and policy-formation. In his letter of June 19 he was asking Eberstadt not simply to defeat the Army's pressure for unification, but for genuinely "positive and constructive recommendations" in the whole field of security policy. A little over three months later, Eberstadt and his assistants provided them.

---

[1] *The Forrestal Diaries*, Walter Millis (ed.), Viking, New York, 1951, p. 61.

## THE EBERSTADT PLAN

By that time, the atomic bombs had exploded; Japan had surrendered; the face of the world had changed. But in October 1945 the Senate Military Affairs Committee opened its hearings on the several unification plans dating from what was now a past era. The initial proceedings were fairly routine. Robert P. Patterson, who had just replaced the large figure of Henry L. Stimson as Secretary of War, declared that "the unification of the armed forces is an essential step." Senator Lister Hill (Democrat of Alabama) read a statement just issued by MacArthur in Tokyo: "The victory was a triumph for the concept of the three dimensions of war — ground, sea and air." General Marshall endorsed Patterson. General of the Army H. H. ("Hap") Arnold, Commanding General of the Army Air Forces, repeated the familiar theses of Air Force dogma. But the routine was interrupted when on October 22 Forrestal appeared, bearing the Eberstadt report.

Mr. Chairman: I do not appear here simply in opposition to the unification of the War and Navy Departments. I prefer here to present a comprehensive and dynamic program to save and strengthen our national security. I do not feel that unification of the services meets these requirements. . . . Current proposals . . . fail to give adequate attention to an effective coordination of all the departments concerned with national security. . . . The immediate integration necessary is that of the War, Navy and State Departments. Beyond that, however, . . . there will be required . . . the creation of a mechanism within the government which will guarantee that this Nation shall be able to act as a unit in terms of its diplomacy, its military policy, its use of scientific knowledge, and finally, of course in its moral and political leadership of the world.

Forrestal presented the proposed Eberstadt organization chart. This provided for three services (a conclusion, Forrestal noted, "with which I am not yet prepared to agree") but no single department; in its place there was provision for a National Security Council which would link the State Department to the three military arms and correlate all four. Other joint agencies were proposed to interlock military with economic, intelligence and production planning. Of the quotation from MacArthur, Forrestal drily observed that the general was "referring to the victory which has just been achieved by the system which now exists. . . . Certainly it doesn't mean that a glorious victory was achieved by a system which doesn't yet exist." Finally:

> Civilian control over the military establishment is exercised through the President, through the civilian Secretaries and through Congress. The influence of each of them would be severely diluted by unification of the services. The plan advanced by certain proponents of unification in effect amounts to an isolation and derogation of civil authority.

As the Secretary concluded, Senator Edwin C. Johnson (Democrat of Colorado) seemed to draw a long breath: "Prior to your testimony, everything had been sweetness and accord with respect to these bills, and now we are glad to hear from the other side."

Forrestal had established that there was another side; the Navy was not simply (as it was caricatured at the time by the cartoonist Jay Darling) the one recalcitrant steed in what should be a docile three-horse defense team. He had established the principle that military reorganization must include a higher organization of the political, diplomatic, industrial and economic factors in defense and foreign policy as well. This was not, of course, an original idea. There had been pre-war plans of this sort. And the war had produced numerous tentative (and sometimes only temporary) integrations of State with War and Navy; at home, the economic impact of war had induced successive integrations of the military services with the civilian economy and civilian manpower and production resources. In the spring, the Richardson Committee had added to its unification proposals a rather vague recommendation for a "council, to be composed of representatives of the Department of the Armed Forces and Department of State . . . to correlate national policies and military preparedness." Other proposals for integrating scientific research or civilian production with military policy were in the air. When, eight days after Forrestal's appearance, the War Department presented the "Collins Plan" it contained a gesture toward correlating the military with State and other civil agencies, but did not seek to spell this out, on the ground that its plan dealt only with the military factor.

THE COLLINS PLAN

Forrestal and Eberstadt, building on such foundations, had pretty well made good their case for a higher organization; they had been less successful in establishing their argument that within the military departments themselves the unification proposals had failed to "deal with the vital problems" actually before the uniformed services. The Collins Plan, so called because it was presented by Lieutenant General J. Lawton Collins, a distinguished corps commander then serving as Deputy Commander and Chief of Staff to the Army Ground Forces, was both sketchy and, for the Navy, ominous. It proposed a single department, a single Secretary, and a single Chief of Staff of the Armed Forces, who would be not only adviser to but "executive" for the Secretary. The Air Force would become a separate and co-equal service, under which "we would have all land-based combat aviation, other than that which is assigned to the Navy [surely an infelicitous phrase] or to the Army for reconnaissance purposes or for the spotting of gunfire and for messenger service." Not unnaturally, the Navy tended to see the War Department plan as essentially one for depriving it of control over its own (now vitally important) air arm and promoting the Army Air Force into a dominant position in all future military policy. "Hap" Arnold was at this time completing his final report as Commanding General of the Army Air Forces (dated November 12, 1945), carrying his advice to posterity. His recommendation for "one integrated, balanced United States military organization that will establish, develop, maintain and direct at the minimum expense the forces, including the mobile striking forces, required for peace enforcement and for national security . . . in case of all-out war," had a presumptuous ring to a sister service which also had large air components and considered itself a mobile striking force of great value and power in the national defense. But when General Arnold continued to advocate a "ruthless elimination of all arms, branches, services, weapons, equipment or ideas whose retention might be indicated only by tradition, sentiment or sheer inertia," naval officers had real reason for alarm. They not only valued their sentiments and traditions; they also questioned, and not without logic, whether all military wisdom resided in the

Army's theorists of independent air power — theorists whom the war experience had not too well sustained. As Fleet Admiral Ernest J. King, wartime Commander of the United States Fleet and Chief of Naval Operations, growled to a Congressional committee, the Navy was willing to see its post-war plan revised downward by Congress, but "I may be perfectly blunt: I am not ready to say that it should be adjusted downward by the Army."

The Navy's case against unification at the service level was a serious one; undoubtedly there were many problems here which had not been properly examined and for which it was questionable whether unification could provide an answer. But this issue was to remain for a time in abeyance. President Truman accepted the Eberstadt recommendations on higher organization. He "endorsed fully," as he later wrote,[1] "the Navy's emphasis on the need for some means of more effectively meshing military planning with our foreign policy and agreed also that we needed to provide long-range plans for industrial mobilization consistent with the civilian economy. In other words, it was clear to me that a national defense program involved not just reorganization of the armed forces but actual co-ordination of the entire military, economic and political aspects of security and defense." So much, at least, had been accomplished. But when, in December, Truman sent in his special message on unification, he accepted, in effect, the Collins Plan.

The President's agreement with the Navy thesis is a good deal less clear in this message than he was later to make it seem in his *Memoirs*. He reflected the influence of the Eberstadt report: "We should adopt the organizational structure best suited to fostering co-ordination between the military and the rest of the government. Our military policy, for example, should be completely consistent with our foreign policy." But on the practical issues he accepted virtually everything which Forrestal and Eberstadt had opposed as likely to wreck the higher organization. He spoke for "parity for air power" (thus ignoring the large amount of air power within the Navy), for a single department, for a single Chief of Staff in over-all command. But there was to be no immediate decision. Senator

[1] *Memoirs*, Vol. 2, pp. 48-49.

Elbert D. Thomas (Democrat of Utah), chairman of the Military
Affairs Committee, retired into the Christmas recess with the record
of his hearings and the President's message, to prepare a unification
bill.

## DEBATE OVER ATOMIC ENERGY

"Being a President," Mr. Truman has observed,[1] "is like riding a
tiger. A man has to keep on riding or be swallowed." Seldom has
the tiger roared so voraciously or padded so furiously through great
issues and events as in the last four months of 1945. There were
the torrential problems of demobilization, both of the armed forces
and the war economy. Issues arising from the occupations both in
Europe and the Far East were rapidly accumulating. On October 3
the President called for an act regulating the domestic control of
atomic energy. On October 22, with the unification debate barely
joined, he called for the enactment of universal military training.
In mid-November Prime Ministers Attlee and Mackenzie King
were in Washington to discuss atomic energy with the President;
their communiqué was issued on the 15th. On the same day the
Congressional investigation into Pearl Harbor opened, and for
months was to hold the headlines with its testimony on military dis-
unity, failures of intelligence and conflicts of policy in 1941. On
November 20 the Nuremberg trials of the Nazi war leaders began.
On November 26 Patrick J. Hurley's intemperate resignation as
Ambassador to China not only forced the whole Far Eastern problem on the Administration's attention but also sounded the first gun
in what was to prove a long and bitter domestic controversy. There
were serious strikes at the same time, with half a million men idle
by December. In that month the new Secretary of State, James F.
Byrnes, set out for Moscow, where the Council of Foreign Ministers
was meeting; they were to get an agreement, of sorts, upon the
management of Far Eastern affairs, but the results were not aus-
picious. In January the first United Nations General Assembly was
to meet in London. And on December 20 Senator Brien McMahon,

[1] *Ibid.*, p. 1.

a Democrat from Connecticut, introduced his initial domestic atomic energy bill.

This background of confusing and conflicting issues, all inter-related yet all unavoidably having to be met on a more or less piece-meal basis, should be kept in mind in any assessment of the decisions of the time. To most in those days the greatest of all was the awe-some, the mysterious and the wholly novel issue of atomic energy. It had been presented suddenly and shockingly with the fall of the bombs on Japan in the last days of the war. Nobody understood it, had any grasp of its implications or of what to do about the startling new facts which it had apparently injected into the international world of war and policy. But it was an issue in which clearly military (or strategic) considerations appeared to come most directly into conflict with clearly non-military (diplomatic, economic, social and civilian) considerations. The debate over atomic energy, in the late fall of 1945 and the following winter and spring, presents one of the few instances in the post-war period in which problems of the civil-military relationship were explicitly, if nearly always confusedly, argued out. The manner in which American political and adminis-trative institutions dealt with this unparalleled question offers an instructive example of the operation of the civil-military relationship in our society.

Issues of civilian control were present from the beginning. In early 1945, as the two-billion-dollar gamble on a nuclear weapon was approaching what looked like success, Secretary Stimson had established the "Interim Committee" (composed mainly of civilian administrators, with some scientists and bankers) to advise upon the utilization of the terrible weapon. The Interim Committee not only recommended its military employment as soon as possible, thus con-tributing to the immolation of Hiroshima and Nagasaki, but went on to consider measures for the post-war control of the staggering new force. It prepared a bill (actually drafted by two lawyers, William L. Marbury, a civilian, and Kenneth C. Royall, another ci-vilian temporarily a brigadier general) to deal with the domestic aspects of this problem. The bill was circulated to the President and all interested agencies.

At the same time Stimson had been thinking about the international implications of atomic energy; and on September 11 (little more than a week after VJ-Day and a month after the revelation of the new horror to the world) he addressed a thoughtful letter to the President. The air was already full of argument over whether to "keep the secret" or "share it with the world." Stimson realized that what was involved was not "the world"; it was Russia.

> In many quarters it [the atomic weapon] has been interpreted as a substantial offset to the growth of Russian influence on the continent. We can be certain that the Soviet Government has sensed this tendency and the temptation will be strong for the Soviet political and military leaders to acquire this weapon in the shortest possible time. . . . [The result will be] a secret armament race of a rather desperate character. There is evidence to indicate that such activity may have already commenced.[1]

As early as September 1945 Stimson assumed that the Russians would sooner or later learn to produce atomic bombs, and saw that whether they learned sooner or later would make little difference. Russia was the issue, not the bomb itself; and whatever bomb policy we adopted would make sense only as it affected our relations with the Soviet Union. "I consider," he wrote,[2] "the problem of our satisfactory relations with Russia as not merely connected with but as virtually dominated by the problem of the . . . control of that bomb, . . . Those relations may be perhaps irretrievably embittered by the way in which we approach the solution of the bomb with Russia."

Like many others at the time, Stimson may have underestimated the embitterment that was inevitable in any event. But he was right in recognizing the vital political importance of the bomb.

He wanted to go direct to Moscow for an agreement which would "limit the use of the atomic bomb as an instrument of war" and also "encourage the development of atomic power for peaceful and humanitarian purposes." He believed the approach should be direct (with British support) rather than through any "general international scheme" involving all the small nations, which would not

[1] *On Active Service*, p. 643.
[2] *Ibid.*, pp. 643-44.

"be taken seriously by the Soviets." [1] Stimson, in short, was prepared
to face the power issue with the naked lack of hypocrisy which it
demanded. We would, of course, have to pay up on our side. In
return for the agreement he envisaged we might well have to stop
work on the development of atomic weapons, impound existing
bombs, exchange full information on peaceful development and
undertake under no circumstances to use atomic energy as a war
weapon. Stimson granted that there was risk in such proposals, but
argued that:

. . . if we fail to approach them now and merely continue to negotiate with
them, having this weapon rather ostentatiously on our hip, their suspicions
. . . will increase. It will inspire them to . . . an all-out effort to solve the
problem. If the solution is achieved in that spirit, it is much less likely that we
will ever get the kind of covenant we may desperately need . . . [2]

The prophecy was well borne out. The Secretary's distinction between merely "negotiating" with the Russians and seriously "approaching" them in the hope of a solution for what was already a
common problem, was acute. But that any better result would have
followed if his advice had been taken may be open to question. At
all events, in the confusions of late 1945 the Stimson approach was
not practical politics. With Stimson's letter before him, the President
called a full Cabinet meeting on September 21, to be devoted wholly
to atomic policy. Other administrative heads and the president pro
tem of the Senate were also invited. The President called first on
Stimson, who repeated his argument, but it seems not to have been
well understood. The discussion appears to have degenerated from
one over the critical question of how to deal with Russia, into a more
barren argument over Stimson's proposal for the second element in
a covenant with the Russians — "the development of atomic power
for peaceful and humanitarian purposes." The question was the
possible sharing of scientific knowledge, not information on how to
manufacture the bomb. According to Truman's much later account:

Secretary of the Treasury Fred M. Vinson took strong issue with the Secretary of War. Why, he asked, if we wanted to share any part of our knowledge

[1] *Ibid.*, p. 645.
[2] *Ibid.*, p. 644.

of atomic energy, would we not also want to share all the military secrets? He was opposed to that, and he expressed fear that an exchange of information would be a one-sided affair, . . .[1]

This was really beside the point, and further discussion seems to have confused the issue even more. Acheson (then Acting Secretary of State), Postmaster General Hannegan and Secretary of Commerce Wallace, who supported Stimson's desire for an attempt to secure agreement on the interchange of scientific information, found themselves strongly opposed by others, including Forrestal and Attorney General Clark and Secretary of Agriculture Anderson, who shared Vinson's views and believed that secrecy could and should envelop all our knowledge of atomic energy. Indeed, as the discussion grew more tense, the opponents tended to conclude that Stimson's supporters wanted to give Russia "the secret of the bomb." There was no true meeting of minds, and on this discordant note the Cabinet meeting broke up. It was Stimson's last. Already resigned as Secretary of War, he passed from the cabinet room into retirement. There had been no resolution of the vast policy issues before them; indeed, the issues themselves had scarcely been presented in any meaningful way. Subsequent leaks to the press merely transferred the confusion to a larger forum.

In the end, Stimson's advice was not followed. The President did not directly "approach" the Russians; instead, he decided to move first through the British and Canadians and thence through the United Nations — a course which, whether wise or not, was at least to have most of the unfortunate consequences Stimson had foreseen. But we could scarcely move at all on the international stage until we had established a domestic atomic policy as a base. On October 3 the President asked Congress for a domestic atomic control act. The haste was unavoidable, but again it was, perhaps, to have unfortunate results. The writing of the domestic atomic energy act, in the atmosphere of intense excitement, uncertainty and bewilderment which surrounded this subject in late 1945, contributed to the imprisonment of American atomic policy behind those bars of secrecy, rigidity and nationalistic fears and bellicosity which were to hamper

[1] *Memoirs*, Vol. 1, *Year of Decisions*, Doubleday, Garden City, 1955, pp. 525-26.

every subsequent effort at the solution of this gigantic world problem.

The message of October 3 laid down a basic policy:

> The hope of civilization lies in international arrangements looking, if possible, to the renunciation of the use and development of the atomic bomb, and directing and encouraging the use of atomic energy . . . toward peaceful and humanitarian ends.

But Truman recognized that "the difficulties in working out such arrangements are great," and seemed more impressed by the difficulties than the crucial importance of the goals. The hope of civilization lay in arrangements looking only "if possible" — a quite unnecessary and therefore all the more significant little verbal modification — to renunciation of the weapons. The message was a somewhat dubious chart for a dangerous course on which the future of civilization depended.

The Stimson letter had reflected an issue which was then prominent in many minds: using our atomic monopoly to secure from Russia an agreed abolition of the weapon, or using it to maintain our military supremacy. This issue the Truman policy tended to evade; we would try "if possible" to do both. Probably no other decision could have been taken in the climate of the times. But the object was impracticable. It was to prove, over the lengthy later history of United Nations disarmament wrangles, impossible to do both.

### THE MAY-JOHNSON BILL

Simultaneously with the message, the domestic bill prepared under the auspices of Stimson's Interim Committee was introduced into House and Senate as the May-Johnson bill. A civil-military issue immediately arose. Despite the fact that the bill had been drafted and sponsored by civilians, despite the repeated assurances of War Department spokesmen that its whole object was to relieve the military staffs of responsibility for atomic energy, it was to suffer throughout its career under the stigma of being "the War Department bill." The House as a matter of course referred it to the Military Affairs Committee, which opened hearings within a week. In the Senate there was objection to such a course. Arthur H. Vandenberg, the Michigan Republican who contributed so much to sanity in foreign affairs during these years, insisted that here were issues far too vast to be treated as simply a problem in military policy. Tom Connally, the Texas Democrat then chairman of the mighty Foreign Relations Committee, was piqued that Military Affairs should be "chiselling off" the prerogatives of his own august position. While House Military Affairs went forward with its hearings, the Senate, at the urging of Brien McMahon, established a Special Committee on Atomic Energy to which the whole matter was referred. The question whether this was essentially a military or a much larger and primarily civilian problem was thus already posed.

Respecting the President's demand for speed, House Military Affairs plowed ahead with the "War Department bill." The new Secretary of War, Patterson, urged it strongly. The scientific testimony, notably that of Leo Szilard, indicated a certain skepticism. The bill would have set up an Atomic Energy Commission of nine men, serving only part time and exercising only a general direction over a powerful Administrator and Deputy Administrator — the executive agents — both of whom might be military officers. The Administrator's post appeared to be tailored for Major General Leslie R. Groves, chief of the Army's "Manhattan Engineer District" to which the development and production of the bomb had been entrusted. To many it seemed obvious that the full-time military administrator would dominate completely the nine-man, part-time civilian commission; this looked like a bill, as Truman afterward put it,[1] "to set up a kind of permanent 'Manhattan District' under military control."

Nor was it only a matter of national policy. The top-flight scientists, who had labored manfully under the Army to produce something which most of them abhorred, who had at the same time acquired a strong distaste for the methods of military command and many of whom were in a state of something like rebellion over the use of the bombs — unnecessarily as they believed — against the live Japanese targets, were leaving the Manhattan District in droves. The work on nuclear energy was reaching a state of suspension, and

[1] *Memoirs,* Vol. 2, p. 2.

any attempt to continue it as primarily a military project, under the strict secrecies and rigidities of military command, threatened to wreck the whole future development. On the other hand, without some sort of bill to regularize the domestic position, the development could not be re-started at all.

J. Robert Oppenheimer was one of the scientific community who supported the May-Johnson bill, apparently on the ground that any bill would be better than none. Perhaps he saw that, however far-reaching the issues between the scientists and the soldiers might be, the terms of the May-Johnson bill were of no great significance to those issues. When Representative Chet Holifield (Democrat of California) asked him whether he would be "perfectly satisfied" to have a high Army officer as Administrator, he fenced in a rather evasive way, finally observing: "You see, this legislation is legislation to get control of the project out of the War Department, not to put it into the War Department." Holifield drily commented: "I am not so sure of that."

Neither were others. The argument that the May-Johnson bill was a vehicle for relieving the War Department of responsibility for atomic energy, yet keeping its development firmly under military control, was compelling. Indeed, the bill reflected the underlying evasion detectable in the Truman message. Harold Urey, the discoverer of heavy water, angrily summed it up: the bill should be "primarily what it purports to be, namely, an atomic energy bill for power purposes and not primarily what it actually is — an atomic bomb bill." But it was too much to ask the May Committee to wrestle with the subtleties in this distinction. On November 8 it dutifully reported the May-Johnson bill. "We thought," as Representative May said afterward, "we had done what the armed forces wanted, and I think yet that we did." Probably they had; and probably the nation would have supported them in the assumption that "what the armed forces wanted" should be the first test, with the demands of high civil and international policy only a secondary consideration. But international policy was assuming the center of attention; the May-Johnson bill disappeared into the Rules Committee, from which it never emerged.

The Prime Ministers of Britain and Canada were in Washington, and a week after the May Committee's report, a tri-partite declaration was issued to the world. The communiqué of November 15, signed by Truman, Attlee and Mackenzie King, defined American (as well as British and Canadian) policy with a precision which had been wanting in Truman's October message on a domestic bill:

We have met together to consider the possibility of international action:

(a) To prevent the use of atomic energy for destructive purposes.

(b) To promote use of recent and future advances in scientific knowledge, particularly in the utilization of atomic energy, for peaceful and humanitarian ends.

We are aware that the only complete protection for the civilized world from the destructive use of scientific knowledge lies in the prevention of war. No system of safeguards that can be devised will of itself provide an effective guarantee against production of atomic weapons by a nation bent on aggression. . . .

We have considered the question of the disclosure of detailed information concerning the practical industrial application of atomic energy. . . . We are not convinced that the spreading of specialized information, before it is possible to devise effective safeguards . . . acceptable to all nations, would contribute to a constructive solution of the problem of the atomic bomb. On the contrary, we think it might have the opposite effect.

The statement went on to propose a United Nations commission to submit specific proposals for the control of atomic energy to "ensure its use only for peaceful purposes" and for "the elimination from national armaments of atomic weapons."

In retrospect it seems clear that this, while high-minded, was a self-defeating statement. It announced that the West would retain a monopoly (admittedly bound to be only transitory) on atomic information; when this had forced the Russians to accept the abolition of war on Western terms, the peaceful benefits of atomic energy would be distributed to the globe. As Major General Groves, who had commanded the Manhattan District, crudely put it, the United States "should closely hold the secret of the bomb until all other nations have demonstrated their anxiety for peace." Such a policy was practically and psychologically impossible of success. The supposed monopoly of "the secrets" gave the West no such leverage over Soviet policy as was here implied; given the time which the West here indicated that it would afford, Russian science could be reasonably sure of penetrating whatever vital secrets of nature we had already unlocked. The statement seems to have operated as what it was — an urgent invitation to Stalinist Russia to provide itself with the atomic weapons with which it would be able to bargain equally once more on this new plane of power policy. As Stimson had foreseen, this was what Soviet Russia proceeded to do. Quite probably it would have done so in any event, but the statement did nothing to discourage it.

While none of this was clear at the time, the May-Johnson bill looked less and less adequate as a domestic foundation for international atomic policy. McMahon, in the Senate, decided that he would have to begin over again. He had been voted his Special Committee at the end of October; at the end of November it opened hearings. They were not hearings on the May-Johnson or any other bill; they were, rather, a high-level seminar on all aspects of atomic energy. The general ignorance on the subject was at the time comprehensive. Scientists, military officers, civilian administrators, paraded through the committee room, seeking to answer the basic questions. Were there really any "secrets"? How long could they be kept? What were the military potentialities? What were the possibilities of industrial application? Did we have a monopoly, and if so, how could it be used as an instrument of policy? As practical instruments of policy, what were the possibilities and limitations of the atomic weapons? Most of these questions had already been answered excitedly, confidently and wrongly in the press and in the popular mind. The McMahon inquiry could not overcome the huge publicity and now firmly established preconceptions, but it tried hard.

The Senator soon ran into the unresolved issue between control of atomic energy primarily for civilian and primarily for military ends. He reported, according to Truman,[1] that the military services felt strongly "that the control of atomic development should be

---

[1] *Memoirs,* Vol. 2, p. 3.

under their auspices, if not under their immediate jurisdiction." He asked for a conference, which took place at the White House on December 4, with Patterson, Forrestal, McMahon, Edward U. Condon (director of the National Bureau of Standards and scientific adviser to the committee) and the committee counsel, James R. Newman, present. McMahon's basic complaint was the refusal of the military departments to release the information vital for Congressional determination of policy — a highly significant issue in questions of control. Truman avoided this issue but gave his decision on the question of organization: "that the entire program and operation should be under civilian control and that the government should have a monopoly of materials, facilities, and processes."[1] In the light of this directive and of the hearings he had been conducting, McMahon on December 20, 1945 introduced his own bill, S. 1717, for the domestic control of atomic energy.

The hearings, conducted by an intelligent chairman, had been productive. In the light of all that has happened since, it would be hard to better Senator McMahon's summary of the problem as he saw it in early 1946:

(1) That the bomb is a weapon of appalling destructiveness . . . The bomb and the improvements on it which will certainly be made mean that another war in which atom bombs are used will threaten the existence not only of cities and nations but of civilization itself.

(2) Other countries will be able to make atomic bombs. The monopoly which we hold at present is precarious and is certain to be short-lived. [He put the period at from five to fifteen years.]

(3) No real military defense against the atomic bomb has been devised and none is in sight. . . .

(4) Some protection may accrue from faithful adherence to international agreements for the prevention of atomic bomb manufacture. . . . The real protection against the atomic bomb lies in the prevention of war. . . .

(5) The secrets which we hold are matters of science and engineering which other nations can and will discover. . . . We can give ourselves a certain temporary protection by retaining the secrets we now have. But that protection grows weaker day by day. . . .

(6) The peacetime benefits of atomic energy promise to be great indeed. . . .

[1] *Ibid.*

[but the] plants which produce power also produce material which constitutes the explosive element of bombs. . . .

(7) Military control of atomic energy, though necessary and useful during war, is a form of direction to which scientists in peacetime will not willingly submit. The continuation of such control will probably discourage further development and research. . . . On the other hand, the armed services are entitled to extensive participation in this development insofar as it relates to military applications of atomic energy. . . .

## THE MCMAHON BILL

These conclusions, all to be well justified by the history of the ensuing decade, supplied the foundation for the McMahon bill. It provided for a five-man, full-time and all-civilian Atomic Energy Commission; for an Administrator (not necessarily a military officer) to be chosen by the commission as its executive agent and therefore responsible to it; for complete government monopoly over all plants, fissionable materials, manufacture, patents and licensing, but with allowance for private research and private development of "source" materials (natural uranium or thorium), and for stringent measures to maintain secrecy and "security." The military services objected that this was entirely too much civilian control. The President backed McMahon with a letter (unpublished at the time) to Patterson and Forrestal, in effect ordering them to support both the all-civilian commission and the government monopoly. On January 22 McMahon opened his second set of hearings, this time on his own bill. They were to continue until early April 1946, running parallel most of the time to the politically sensational hearings on the Pearl Harbor disaster, to hearings on the unification bill and to the discussion of the Acheson-Lilienthal plan for the international control of atomic energy, which was published in March. It is inevitable that policy issues, however closely interlocked, have to be considered in compartments under the complex modern social organization.

As his second set of atomic energy hearings opened, McMahon was still feeling the pressure of military disapproval. On February 1, as Truman has recorded,[1] "he spent nearly two hours with me at

---

[1] *Ibid.*, p. 4.

the White House discussing his difficulties." This time the President supplied him with a letter which was released for publication, mainly reiterating the points he had made privately to the two Secretaries in January. While the hearings went on, now pretty much traversing old ground, the committee hammered at the bill clause by clause. When McMahon finally reported it on April 19, 1946, he could say that every word had received the unanimous approval of the Special Committee; every difference of opinion, and there had been several, had been resolved. With this assurance, the Senate on June 1 adopted the bill almost without debate.

It was in the House that it met its only important challenge. Representative May and his Committee on Military Affairs were chagrined that their own May-Johnson bill had been thrust aside. House Military Affairs reported out S. 1717 with a series of amendments, most of them very minor, and was promptly accused in the press of trying to "obstruct" it. This they hotly denied. They were all in favor of civilian control, of the international abolition of atomic weapons and the other objectives of the McMahon bill; but they insisted that it went too far both in excluding the military from matters vital to national security and in giving the administrative bureaucracy too great a voice in a development which might have commanding domestic economic and political effects. It was imperilling security and inviting socialism.

The House dissidents were here grappling, however dimly, with what was in fact a basic social issue which had been approaching over the past half century or so. War is, by its very nature, a communal or "socialistic" activity; as the demands of war and war preparation spread ever more widely and deeply through every aspect of our social, political and economic organization, it was inevitable that they should set up pressures for authoritarian and "socialistic" solutions. What is perhaps significant is the fact that in facing this issue the House — the representative, popular branch of the national legislature — was less suspicious of the professional military services than of their appointed civilian superiors. A similar attitude was reflected in the unbounded confidence which the congressmen were coming to place in the professional police of the

Federal Bureau of Investigation. One could trust the professional soldiers and policemen; one could not trust the civilian administrators to have sufficient regard either for the national security or the preservation of a free-enterprise economy.

If there was at least some substance in the issue, it was not, to be sure, here joined on any high plane. The principal committee amendment (which the committee recognized would provide the "bone of contention") went no further than to ensure that at least one of the Atomic Energy Commissioners would be a military officer. This was hardly a sufficient base on which to support the oratory with which J. Parnell Thomas, the New Jersey Republican then chairman of the Un-American Activities Committee, summed up the feeling of the dissidents: "S. 1717 is the creature of impractical idealists. I do not say that these one-world minded persons are unpatriotic. I say that their intense ardor for a better world has blinded them. Their faith in Russia is indicative." Partisan politics, notably absent in the Senate treatment of the subject, were rampant in the House. "We are," Dewey Short, Republican of Missouri, extravagantly exclaimed, "going to set up an Atomic Energy Commission and give it power of life and death over private industry in this country. . . . Destroy the New Deal — a rotten steal!"

Clare Boothe Luce, then a Republican Representative from Connecticut, could support the measure only "with a very heavy heart" because of its "socialistic character." But she restored a cooler perspective. She would support the Senate bill, because "we must"; she also saw that the matter of military representation on the commission was "a straw issue."

The true intent of this legislation . . . is to secure and promote, for as long as we can, or until international atomic control is achieved, our national monopoly of this fearful weapon. . . . Even if we deceived ourselves today into believing that this is preponderantly a bill for the peaceful development of atomic energy, we should not in the least deceive our world neighbors. . . .

The bill's intent is to enable our Nation to amass an adequate stockpile of bombs for the purpose of defense and attack in war . . . and to keep pace . . . with new processes in nuclear fission. It is the latter urgency which above all requires civilian control. . . . That is why we must not leave the matter in the hands of the military, who, while they can preserve the atomic status quo, can never make advances in this field.

She opposed all proposals for requiring military participation as "superfluous" at best and likely to hamper the scientific development. For her, the two "consolations" about this "socialistic, though I repeat necessary, legislation" were that it allowed the maximum practicable freedom for scientific advance and "permits, though it does not promote, the integration of domestic . . . control with a world plan for atomic control." While events have indicated that her fears as to the socialistic consequences of the bill were exaggerated, her analysis could hardly be bettered a decade later.

Big advertisements by a "National Committee for Civilian Control of Atomic Energy," summoning the House to "defeat the May Committee amendments" and signed by an imposing list of bishops, bankers, educators and other eminent persons, did not soothe the hostile congressmen. But in their stand for greater military control opinion seemed to be against them. The end was a compromise; the House withdrew its requirement that at least one commissioner should be a military officer; the Senate agreed that the head of the Military Applications Division (one of the five operating divisions established under the commission) should be an officer assigned from active duty. The bill went to the President on July 26, 1946. The all-civilian commission was to show no laxity either in preserving the atomic secrets or in developing the military potentials. Indeed, it was consistently the civilians in the Atomic Energy Commission organization who were to prod the military into new weapons development later on. The issue of civil-military relations in this form was not again to arise. As Representative Luce had said, it had been largely a "straw issue" from the beginning.


## ORGANIZATION PLANS

While some of the congressmen had been wrestling with these problems of the military future, others in near-by committee rooms had been dealing with those of the military present — and past. During the Christmas recess of 1945 Senator Thomas, chairman of the Military Affairs Committee, had produced his unification bill, S. 2044. The committee took the views of the Secretaries and top admirals and generals, including those of "a young general with flying experience," Lauris Norstad (later NATO Supreme Allied Commander Europe) and one of the rising admirals, Arthur W. Radford, later Chairman of the Joint Chiefs of Staff. They also heard the Director of the Budget Bureau, "whose contribution was extremely great." They worked over their bill with great industry, finally perfecting and publishing it on April 9, 1946. It was reported formally in May.

THE THOMAS BILL

The Thomas bill in general embodied the Collins Plan. Stemming from ideas adumbrated during the middle years of the Second World War and rooted in far older controversies over the role of the military airplane, it was virtually unaffected by the new military problems presented with the atomic bomb. It was not closely related, even, to the immediate military issues of 1946. The responsible administrators at the time were seriously worried by the precipitous demobilization. At a Cabinet meeting on January 11 Dean Acheson, then Acting Secretary of State in Byrnes' absence abroad, was "concerned" over the way in which the realities of power were draining away beneath the feet of policy. Forrestal wanted a major appeal to public opinion, through all the leading editors, publishers and news commentators, on "the seriousness of the present situation." But the Thomas Committee was studying future organization, not present problems of the kind with which the organization should be designed to deal. It was thinking primarily in terms of some supposedly distant and hypothetical "emergency." That was the mental frame within which it produced its proposal for a highly centralized Department of Defense under a powerful Secretary and an even more powerful single Chief of Staff.

The Navy maneuvered successfully for time by securing referral of the bill to Senator David I. Walsh's Naval Affairs Committee. In May Senator Walsh (the Massachusetts Democrat who had long presided benevolently over the naval interest) held hearings, through which the Navy's objections were vigorously publicized. On May 13 the President called the Secretaries of the War and Navy Departments and the principal naval and military advisers to the White House. He told them that he wanted the two services to identify their points of agreement and disagreement; that he was "not prejudiced in favor of one Service or the other," but that he wanted "a balanced system of national defense with particular reference to the integration of the budget." [1] The last was significant. Truman explained that after meeting the service of the national debt, no more than one third of the remaining federal revenue could be allocated to national defense, and that "this would mean the most careful screening of requirements." [2] It foreshadowed the policy, to which the President was to cling through the next four years, of adjusting military costs to a pre-determined fiscal ceiling, rather than adjusting the ceiling to the requirements of military policy. This is one method — indeed, the traditional method — of imposing civilian control on the military. When we reached near-disaster in 1950 it seemed at least open to question.

The President decided one major point at issue: he announced that he was against a single Chief of Staff as "too much along the lines of the 'man on horseback' philosophy." [3] For the rest, he asked Patterson and Forrestal to make another effort at agreement, and requested their report by May 31, 1946. The day after the White House meeting, Patterson, Forrestal, Eberstadt and Nimitz (then Chief of Naval Operations) met to take stock. It seems clear that with the Presidential decision on the single Chief of Staff, the Navy had taken the principal piece in the game. With Patterson's acquiescence in this, the area of agreement was really very large. The Army accepted most of the Navy's plan for a higher organization — a National Security Council, a National Security Resources Board, a Central Intelligence Agency. The Army accepted three autonomous departments — Army, Navy and Air — each to be headed by

---

[1] *The Forrestal Diaries*, p. 160.
[2] *Ibid.*
[3] *Ibid.*, p. 161.

its own Secretary, rather than insisting on a single Department of Defense. The Navy, for its part, recognized that there would still have to be one over-all defense "Director" or Secretary, even though no Department was created for him.

Two central obstacles remained. To the Army, this Director or Secretary of Defense was to be a "boss" of the whole establishment; the Navy insisted that he should have no powers of administration but should be a "coordinator" only. And the Navy felt that it was insufficiently protected in its right to its own aviation and to maintain its Marine Corps. Here the Navy saw two possible ways in which to make good its position. One was through limiting the powers of the Secretary of Defense, at the same time retaining Cabinet rank and direct access to the President for the Secretary of the Navy. The other was through a redefinition of the "roles and missions" of the several services with such precision that no conflict could arise between them. Each service would thus be entitled to retain whatever weapons or formations might be necessary to enable it to perform its assigned mission; each service would itself decide what the assigned mission required, and if the definitions were sufficiently clear and exclusive any service could appeal to them against threatened raids by another.

### PRESIDENTIAL INTERVENTION

The difficulty, of course, lay in writing the definitions. The Army wanted to restrict the Marine Corps mission to the narrowest of limits; and to confide to the proposed Air Force all land-based air missions, including those of anti-submarine warfare and the protection of ocean shipping. The Navy demanded a larger role for its Fleet Marine Force (whose divisions and corps had won so many Pacific victories) and strenuously resisted any surrender of its land-based reconnaissance and anti-submarine missions. But Patterson could not yield to the Navy view. On May 31 the two Secretaries addressed a joint letter to the President, setting forth their agreement on most of the issues and their differences on these two — which were, of course, the critical ones.

On June 15, 1946, the President released their letter, together with his own judgment, by which he expected both services to abide. Though an obvious attempt at even-handed compromise, this was a defeat for the Navy. Truman called for a single Department of Defense under a Secretary of Cabinet rank, with the three service Secretaries demoted to subordinate status. As to roles and missions, he confirmed the Navy in its maintenance of the Marine Corps as a combat force, but bestowed its land-based reconnaissance and anti-submarine aviation upon the Air Force. This last Forrestal knew that the Navy could not and would not accept; while the experience, in the early war period, with the attempt to combine Army aviation with naval anti-submarine warfare had strongly indicated that it was militarily impracticable. Forrestal's reaction, however, was temperate. He felt that a good deal had been gained and that time was on his side; and he knew that Congress was shortly to adjourn. He told the President that while he still had misgivings about the single Secretary of Defense "the essence of the matter was this: whether or not a law could be written which would clearly leave the Secretary of the Navy free to run his own department without kibitzing from above and while at the same time giving the Secretary of National Defense the global authority to make decisions on broad issues."[1] He discouraged newspaper criticism of Truman's position. At this time he was still, surely, thinking as a Secretary of the Navy; he could hardly have foreseen that he would himself be the first "Secretary of National Defense." But he was aware of the necessity for a "global authority" somewhere; it is possible that here were the first seeds of his later shift of attitude when, occupying the top position, he was to realize that considerable "kibitzing from above" might be unavoidable. At all events, the session was running out, and when Congress adjourned in early August the unification bill had not even reached the floor. Forrestal returned to his negotiations with Patterson.

The differences, though still in fact profound, were in appearance not unbridgeable. Eberstadt observed that "the Navy's position . . . could now be brought into consonance with the President's wishes,

[1] *The Forrestal Diaries*, p. 169.

the only question being the phrasing of language which would accomplish his objective of a so-called single Department, and ours the preservation of the integrity and economy of individual Services" [1] — a remark which irresistibly recalls the Lord Chancellor in *Iolanthe,* who "as an old Equity draftsman" knew that "the subtleties of the legal mind are equal to the emergency." And so it was to turn out. When the new (and now Republican) Congress met in January 1947, the President was able to present the legislators with a unification plan agreed to by both services. The Presidential directive of the preceding June had been quietly forgotten. Substantially, the Navy had won its major points.

The agreement rested upon a fairly elaborate compromise over the Secretary of Defense, and upon the Army's acceptance of the Navy's definition of roles and missions. The Navy accepted the single Secretary of Cabinet rank, but he would have no Department; he would preside instead over "the Military Establishment." The three service Secretaries would retain their departments, but without Cabinet rank; they would have access to the President and the Budget Bureau and would retain direct responsibility for the administration of their departments, but would sit in the National Security Council rather than in the Cabinet. As for roles and missions, these would be taken care of by an Executive Order rather than in the statute, and Patterson and Forrestal submitted an agreed draft of the order, to be issued simultaneously with the signing of the bill.

### ROLES AND MISSIONS

Roles and missions were an old problem, going back to the controversies of the inter-war years, when the Navy had disputed passionately with the Army Air Corps the precise number of miles beyond the coastline which the latter was to be permitted to fly. According to Admiral Nimitz, testifying in 1945, the respective roles and missions were first defined by the Army-Navy Joint Board in 1927; they were revised in 1935 and were "corrected" in August 1945. The admiral's testimony is here a little obscure. While Tru-

[1] *Ibid.,* p. 200.

man had, on August 21, 1945, demanded a JCS review of the services' post-war planning, it is not clear that any redefinition of roles and missions emerged. A year later, in August 1946, Patterson was using the failure of JCS to resolve this problem as an argument for a single Chief of Staff. The issue over roles and missions was the last to appear plainly, which may suggest that it lay at the real core of the problem.

For it was the issue between the three service organizations, each with differing skills, differing weapons and differing tactical and strategic theories. All recognized that in time of war the three would have to operate as a combined team under unitary direction, making the best possible use of the combined skills and weapons which each had to offer. But what they confronted was not war; it was a supposedly long period of peace. Preparing for war presents very different problems than does the waging of it. Each service knew that in peace there would never be enough money to develop its full potentialities; each dreaded that in the resultant competition one or another would seize the lion's share of the appropriations. This would not only weaken the power and prestige of the other two — a consideration which in institutional rivalries of this kind is unquestionably of effect — but would also weaken their ability to discharge missons which they believed, with complete sincerity and patriotism, would be vital to a successful national defense. It is shortsighted to regard the ensuing controversies as mere squabbles for money and power between rival and greedy institutions. They were matters of principle as well as of prestige. Every military officer is sworn to uphold the Constitution and the security of the state; and there was as deep and genuine a conviction in the Navy or the ground Army as in the Air Force that they had something essential to contribute to that end.

It is at least conceivable (though doubtful) that a really thorough and imaginative redefinition of roles and missions might have resolved the problem. The definition on which the two Secretaries agreed in January 1947 was hardly more than a semantic evasion. Thus, the Air Force, given large powers over every aspect of aviation, was required to "coordinate" its activities with the Navy and the ground Army, but there were no clear instructions as to how it was to do so. The Navy was authorized to maintain a Marine Corps sufficient for "limited land operations in connection with" the "seizure of bases" in "naval war." Did this permit the re-creation of a Fleet Marine Force of six divisions and many other units, such as had been developed for the Pacific war? The Marines' bloodiest operation had been the seizure of Iwo Jima, which was certainly a "limited land operation," but had no connection with "naval war"; that barren scrap of volcanic ash, of no significance whatever in naval strategy, had been taken at the cost of some 6,000 Marine lives solely to further the strategic Air Force war against Japan. The new definition of roles and missions bore little relevance to the actualities of war; it was drafted, with skill, to meet the requirements of peace-time military politics, not those of wartime strategy. The shrewd comment of the *Economist* of London upon "the remarkable structure of the agreement which conceals so many disagreements" was not inapposite.

But verbal agreement had at any rate been attained. It was to take another six months to grind the resultant bill through the committees and the Congress, and it was not signed until July 26, 1947. By that time the world had grown considerably more ominous than it had seemed when the original Collins and Eberstadt plans had been introduced in October 1945. As early as March 1946 Churchill, in his famous speech at Fulton, Missouri, had sounded the first tocsin of the cold war. During most of 1946 Marshall, as Special Ambassador, had been wrestling in futility with the seemingly insoluble problem of China. The hopeful Acheson-Lilienthal plan for the international control of atomic energy, although buttressed by the talents of Bernard Baruch and the energies of Herbert Bayard Swope, had been getting nowhere in the United Nations against the Soviet resistance which it was so well calculated to incite. In 1947 the month of March — a month so often and so curiously fateful in the affairs of our times — produced the crisis over Greece and Turkey, the "Truman Doctrine," the announced policy of everywhere supporting "free peoples who are resisting attempted subjugation by armed minorities or by outside pressures," and the pledge of $400

million in aid for the Greeks and Turks. Our possible military commitments were not only growing more immediate but were enlarging as they did so.

All this, however, had little effect upon the perfecting of the
National Security Act. No doubt, the darkening of the international
scene hastened its adoption. For better or for worse, we had to have
some consistent military policy, which was impossible so long as the
unification question remained hanging in the air. The congressmen
made some changes. In the interests of civilian control they went to
the length of prescribing that no person "who has within ten years
been on active duty as a commissioned officer in a regular component
of the armed services" could be eligible for appointment as Secretary
of Defense. Having thus fortified civilian authority, they went on
to write a good deal of the draft Executive Order on roles and
missions into the statute, thus confirming the several military interests involved in their control, or at least their veto power, over
what the civilians might ordain. The preamble specified that while
the three services were to be unified they were not to be "merged";
the powers of the Secretary of Defense were somewhat diluted and
those of the service Secretaries somewhat enhanced. It is suggestive
that these changes were all in the direction of strengthening the
military as against the civilians, but they were minor. The reorganization embodied in the National Security Act of 1947 was essentially
that agreed upon in January by Patterson and Forrestal; while in
large measure it was that proposed by Eberstadt in 1945.

The result was an integrated structure for the direction of all
aspects of American military, foreign and domestic mobilization
policy — a structure in which, it was hoped, every conflicting military, diplomatic, political and economic interest would have due
weight and influence, and no more than due weight and influence.
It was an intelligent exercise in chart-drawing. If the recalcitrances
of human nature were often to prevent the charts from coming to
life; if the basic disagreements concealed in the skillful compromises

were to thrust themselves back into our affairs, that cannot be held against the architects of the structure. It may still have represented the best possible answer to the problems of the time; and if it was not to work altogether as had been hoped, it may well have worked better than any other solution, practicable under the conditions of 1947, could have done.

## THE NATIONAL SECURITY ACT

With the National Security Act the post-war reorganization of the American military, diplomatic and political system was substantially complete. It was a reorganization which, of course, included many other elements — the Atomic Energy Act; the military appropriation acts which sought to establish a sound level of peacetime military expenditure; the proposals for universal military training and their failure; the reorganization of the civil government; the substitution of civil for military control in the occupied areas, and the Truman "loyalty" order, issued only nine days after the enunciation of the Truman Doctrine and for the first time establishing in the United States in peacetime a large-scale system of testing persons not for their acts but for their political beliefs. But of all these measures the Security Act was the most comprehensive and most conscious in its intent. It put the capstone, so to speak, on the new governmental structure deriving from the experiences of the Second World War. Subsequent developments were to flow, not from the experiences of the war but from the harsh lessons of the post-war period to which it led.

The National Security Act represented a kind of basic charter of civil-military relations and of security policy formation. The core of the new system was the National Security Council, with the President as chairman and a membership including the Secretary of State, the Secretary of Defense, the three service Secretaries, the chairman of the new National Security Resources Board and such other department or agency heads as the President might from time to time add to it. The Central Intelligence Agency was placed directly under the Council. While it retained some responsibilities in the "cloak and dagger" field, CIA's major function was to collect and "coordinate" (a distressingly frequent word) all intelligence coming into other branches of the government, to analyze it and make the distillate available to the President and the National Security Council.

The theory was that NSC, composed of the highest civilian officials responsible for diplomatic, military and industrial planning, and informed by CIA, would generate the basic policy recommendations in all matters affecting the national security. Accepted by the President, these recommendations would define the national policy and provide a clear, consolidated guide to action by the planning and operating agencies. With policy thus defined, the State Department would know how to conduct its international negotiations; it would also know the military potentials available to it. The now unified Military Establishment would devise the strategic and logistic plans necessary to support the agreed policy, or ensure (through its civilian representatives in NSC) that no policies were adopted making demands beyond the available military capabilities. The new National Security Resources Board, charged with all problems of industrial, manpower and raw material mobilization, would prepare mobilization plans to support the military strategy or (at least inferentially) keep the strategic planners within the bounds which the national resources would sustain.

## THE MILITARY ESTABLISHMENT

The Military Establishment itself was composed of three Departments, each independently administered by its civilian Secretary and each sustaining a military service under the command of its Chief of Staff. These were, however, now linked together by a whole series of "joint" and "coordinating" agencies. A common military direction was provided by the Joint Chiefs of Staff, where the three service chiefs (and the Chief of Staff to the President when there was one) would sit together. The Joint Chiefs of Staff, however, was much more than four (or three) eminent officers sitting around a table; it was an agency, provided with its secretariat, its Joint Staff, its many joint committees and groups and its intricate organization charts, all directed toward providing a structure of common planning and command. They would, theoretically, serve as advisers to both the Secretary of Defense and the President, and transmit Presidential decisions to the affected services.

Military administration, as distinct from military command, was in theory to be coordinated by the Secretary of Defense. His authority had been limited. He was given only "general direction, authority and control" over the departments; he was expressly forbidden to maintain a military staff and was allowed to appoint not more than three special assistants from civil life. To advise him, he was given a War Council, composed of the three Secretaries and the three service Chiefs of Staff. He was given two other agencies of common action: a Munitions Board to coordinate military procurement and a Research and Development Board to coordinate military research. Both were under civilian heads, responsible to the Secretary of Defense, but neither was well insulated from the military command authority embodied in the Joint Chiefs.

The Office of the Secretary of Defense (he had no Department) was thus kept to a minimum. But he was given one significant power — to "supervise and coordinate" the budget estimates. The new system quite plainly recognized the budget as not only the clearest expression of military policy but the controlling factor over its course and development. It sought carefully to mesh the military with the civilian responsibilities for the budget. With the policy decisions of NSC and the President as their guide, the Joint Chiefs would, in theory, prepare the strategic plans necessary to support them. They would then assign to the respective services both their strategic and their logistic responsibilities for fulfillment of the plans. The service departments would then independently make their own estimates of what they required in the way of weapons and force levels to enable them to meet the assigned responsibility. The result would be embodied in three departmental budgets. These would go back to JCS for review and consolidation. The result, with duplications and wastes eliminated, was supposed to represent a strictly military estimate of the minimum requirements for support of the policies received from NSC and the President.

But the civilian departmental Secretaries had already had a commanding voice in the preparation of the departmental estimates. The civilian Secretary of Defense was required to "supervise and coordinate" the whole process of military budget-making; and the civilian Comptroller in the Office of the Secretary of Defense was soon to become one of the most powerful officials in government. He (and the Secretary of Defense) reviewed the JCS budget before finally presenting it to the President and the Budget Bureau. In theory, military appropriations originated in the policy determinations of NSC and the President, these were translated into military terms by JCS, these were translated into money by the departments, this was reviewed by JCS and revised by the Secretary of Defense, to return to the White House and its Budget Bureau for final integration into the total national policy. There is a certain beauty in the theory. It is hardly necessary to say that it was seldom to appear in the practice.

Civil and military control had been intermingled all along the line. There was no point in the whole budget process at which the soldiers were not being ridden by the civilian budget-makers, and no point at which the civilian budget-makers were not being ridden by the soldiers, with neither in a position of clear responsibility for the results. It may be that such a situation is inescapable; at any rate, neither of the two obvious avenues of escape is attractive. One is to put the civilians in complete control, through the budget, of all questions of military plan and policy; the other is to put the military in complete control, through their estimates of the requirements of military plan and policy, over the budget. In the decade after 1947 the country was to wrestle with both ideas and was to accept neither. The budget, though a powerful regulator of civil-military relationships, is not a final nor altogether adequate one.

WEAK POINTS IN THE SYSTEM

While one must leave the question of the efficacy and success of the 1947 National Security Act to the later history, it may be useful to indicate here some of the ways in which it was to fail to meet the expectations entertained for it. The National Security Council proved the first weak point in the mechanism. This was due partly to Truman's disinclination to make full use of it; but mainly, perhaps, to the inherent difficulty of its assigned role. While it was to produce "policy papers" by the hundred over the next few years, they were not often to deal with the really big issues, and when they did, they lacked the precision and decisiveness necessary if they were to serve as guides to action. It may be that in a democratic society effective operating policy simply cannot be generated by a group of non-elected administrators passing in secret, in the light of secret information, on the secret productions of an anonymous planning staff. Or it may be that in our difficult and fluid world the very concept of a long-range, fixed "national policy" is defective and that it is impossible to arrive at policy determinations (or predictions) capable of providing a firm foundation for continuing military policy and military preparation. Whatever the reason, the soldiers have never ceased to complain since 1947 that they never receive the policy directives which would enable them to return clear military answers for the problems presented to them. Eisenhower reactivated NSC and infused into it a greater responsibility than it enjoyed under Truman. It is not clear that the net results have been much better.

If JCS received inadequate guidance from NSC, it also suffered under handicaps of its own. JCS had worked with rather remarkable though imperfect success in the conduct of a colossal war effort, and it was to work well again in the conduct of the Korean War, but it was not well suited to meeting the different and in some ways more difficult, because more uncertain, problems of an uneasy peace. After 1947, the nation looked to JCS to provide militarily sound answers for two broad and basic questions: How much of the nation's total resources should be devoted to military preparation? How should the determined amount be allocated among the services, the various weapons systems, the rival strategic theories? These questions were inherently unanswerable. There is no way of knowing how much should be given to preparation against a peril which can never be estimated with precision and which may never appear at all. And there is no way of deciding finally between weapons systems for each of which there are compelling arguments, none of which can be put to practical test, and all of which are highly uncertain in their probable effects.

It is asking too much of any military body to return technically "sound" replies to questions such as these; it was certainly asking too much of JCS. The Joint Chiefs were composed of the three service commanders (in addition to the Chief of Staff to the President, who at that time was not even *primus* among *pares*), each with his first loyalty to the service which he headed and passionately engaged as a partisan in the issues on which the JCS was supposed to give a corporate judgment. By their composition, the Joint Chiefs were almost constitutionally incapable of resolving the major problems which the National Security Act had confided to them. Since there appeared to be no other agency, in existence or imaginable, which could be relied upon to resolve these problems rightly, there was something to be said for leaving them to an agency which, rather than resolve them wrongly, would not resolve them at all. It is certainly better to leave unanswerable questions unanswered than to provide specious answers clothed in an appearance of technical authority. But this was not appreciated in the earlier years of the peacetime JCS, and the chiefs were to come in for much bitter criticism of their inability to arrive at a "sound" and unified strategic system.

Without clear policy guidance and unable to resolve the technical differences, JCS could hardly distribute to the three services their basic strategic and logistic responsibilities with much exactitude. Lacking such directives, each continued to build its budget requests around what it would like to have (and thought that it could get) rather than around clearly calculated "needs." When these requests were submitted to JCS for review, the Joint Chiefs (three of whom were the men making the requests) could do little more than "cut the pie" with approximate equality. The Secretary of Defense could do little more (aside from insisting on certain operating economies, generally of a minor kind) than cut the totals further to what he thought the Budget Bureau would stand for. The Budget Bureau's responsibility was to squeeze the whole thing under a pre-determined "ceiling"; this it could do only by hunting out what to its civilian mind looked like military "non-essentials." So it happened in the Truman years; so it happened again under Eisenhower. Out of this process there has never emerged a long-range, self-consistent military policy, clearly adequate to the military "need" and clearly consonant with the economic and political base. That such a policy could emerge is perhaps only another illusion. When real needs have in crisis imposed themselves the plans have been revised drastically upward to meet them; when they have passed, the pressures of economy have revised drastically downward all estimates of their possible recurrence.

NSC and JCS were the key elements in the reorganization, and both, with the later Department of Defense, have survived. The other agencies of unification were at best only partially successful. The National Security Resources Board was essentially an agency for stand-by planning against a possible future "emergency." As the realization slowly grew that our problems were not those of the future but of the present, NSRB tended to lose its significance and was never able to establish the prestige intended for it. It was ultimately abolished, and its powers transferred to the Office of Defense Mobilization. The Munitions Board and the Research and Development Board, while useful, tended to develop into service "log-rolling" agencies, and had difficulty in establishing satisfactory relationships with JCS. Robert A. Lovett, Truman's last Secretary of Defense, was critical of them, and the Eisenhower Administration superseded them with individual Assistant Secretaries of Defense. Little was heard of the War Council. Louis Johnson, when he succeeded Forrestal as Secretary of Defense, endeavored to revive it under a different name, but its achievements were not notable, and it appears to have been buried under the massive accretion of power in the Department of Defense. The "coordination" system envisaged in 1947, with the Secretary of Defense no more than a moderator among inter-service disputes, has yielded slowly but steadily to a centralization of power in the hands of the Defense Secretary.

Even the Central Intelligence Agency has fallen somewhat short of expectations, and it may be that the concept of "intelligence," like those of "policy" or "strategic plan," is a concept unable to carry all the burdens popularly assigned to it. It may be that nations, like men, will never be all-knowing, all-wise and all-powerful; and that the trinity of intelligence, policy and strategy, the one proceeding from the other, will never find any very valid counterpart in the real world of desperate expedient and stratagem in face of the unexpected and the unprepared-for — the world which we seem normally to inhabit.

The National Security Act, at any rate, could not transform the real world into one of order and precision. It was to fail to fulfill many of the hopes which had been entertained for it. Stimson's approving comment upon its enactment: "When the civilians and the soldiers are in cordial and sympathetic agreement, each conscious of his proper function and his proper relation to the other, there are few limits to the advances that can be made," [1] was not to be fully borne out. Indeed, it reflected a misconception; it echoed the great days of half a century before, when Elihu Root, a civilian, had forced a rational military organization upon the reluctant soldiers of 1900. It was not too relevant to the real issues of 1947. The underlying problem in the writing of the National Security Act was never to secure agreement between the military and the civilians; it was to secure agreement among the military men (and their civilian supporters), and this problem received little more than formal solution. But the signature of the act completed the post-war reorganization. We had constructed our new system. Almost immediately it was to be put to severe test.

[1] *On Active Service*, p. 522.

••••••••••••••••••••••••••••••••••••••••••••••••••••••••••••••••••••••••••••••••••

# CHAPTER 5

# Cold War

## OCCUPIED AND LIBERATED AREAS

The major problems which it was hoped that the National Security Act might meet had not, of course, waited upon its enactment. The rapidly rising tension between the United States and the Soviet Union had long since begun to pose issues of the gravest kind in the over-all employment of American political, military and economic strength, in the over-all national strategy. More particular problems were everywhere — in Korea, Iran, Trieste, Yugoslavia, Berlin, and in the trust territories of the Pacific atolls. The United Nations was an untried and dubious experiment. Occupation policies were creating tensions between the State Department and the War and Navy Departments, as well as with our late allies. While the big, theoretic issues of atomic energy, military unification and the appropriate level of the military budget were being debated in Congressional committees, many lesser but highly practical issues were demanding to be dealt with.

### GERMANY

The question of the civil administration of occupied territory had been raised well before the end of the war. Stimson, again reverting to the great precedents established by such military administrators as Root, Wood, Arthur MacArthur and Frank McCoy in Cuba and the Philippines, insisted on retaining the authority in the War Department rather than in State while the battle raged. Franklin Roosevelt had intended that a civilian officer should administer a conquered Germany, but had been brought by practical considerations to accept General Eisenhower as Military Governor — a decision which Truman, after the victory in Europe, did nothing to alter. With the conquest of Japan it was inevitable that Douglas MacArthur, as Supreme Allied Commander, should in effect become a military governor; while in China the continuance of civil war and the necessity for rounding up and repatriating the Japanese armies gave the American military commander, Lieutenant General Albert C. Wedemeyer, a major influence in the counsels of the diplomats and civilian officials.

As has been explained in Part I, Eisenhower's initial attempts in Algiers in 1942 and 1943 to govern a liberated territory through an odd civilian civil affairs section of his general staff at AFHQ had not proved successful, and Roosevelt on his voyage to Casablanca had made confusion worse confounded. The matter was straightened out with the President in Washington by Stimson himself, and in Algiers by McCloy on a trip there in February 1943. In the next few months, the Army's Civil Affairs Division was established, as was the Combined Civil Affairs Committee with McCloy as chairman. Here he provided an "invaluable bridge between military and political leaders." [1] The State Department in effect resigned itself to the situation; military considerations were of such paramount importance in virtually all the occupied areas that it might as well let the War Department run the show — in occupied Germany and elsewhere. While frictions arose between the military commanders and the many civilian assistants they were obliged to call in, the need for continued military government in Germany was not to be questioned for some years.

---

[1] Henry L. Stimson and McGeorge Bundy, *On Active Service in Peace and War,* Harper, New York, 1948, p. 559.

JAPAN AND KOREA

In Japan and Korea, where technically there was no military government, the situation was rather different. The towering personality and prestige of General MacArthur defied any diplomatic or political challenge to his conduct of affairs. In general, he worked well with the diplomats and civilian officials sent in to assist him. Portents of later trouble were not wanting. As early as October 1945 it seemed to his staff, according to Courtney Whitney,[1] that "[MacArthur's] superiors in Washington were the worst hindrance. . . . Washington evidently wanted to divide the unilateral authority it then exercised with the British and the Russians. . . . MacArthur opposed this idea wholeheartedly."

Here was a fairly basic issue of policy, in which Washington and the civilian direction were following a course which the military command in the field believed to be unwise. Yet insofar as MacArthur actually "opposed" Washington's idea, he was doing so in a political capacity, and using his military prestige only as a political weapon. But the matter did not come to a head at the time. Byrnes, the Secretary of State, journeyed to Moscow in December to secure an international control for Japan, to include an eleven-nation Far Eastern Commission to sit in Washington and a four-nation Advisory Committee (United States, Britain, Soviet Union and China) to sit in Tokyo and oversee the Supreme Commander. While MacArthur "concealed his irritation over such an ill-considered move" he "could not prevent his friends . . . from protesting vigorously."[2] But this was a problem of politics, not of war, and it was of little substance. As it turned out, the Far Eastern Commission was too ponderous and too remote to matter much; while the fact that each member of the Advisory Committee in Tokyo wielded veto power reduced that body to a satisfactory impotence. It continued to "harass" the Supreme Commander, and certainly did nothing to reduce the MacArthur irritation with the policy-makers in Washington; but whatever issues of civil-military relationships may be glimpsed here were to remain latent for the next five years.

[1] *MacArthur, His Rendezvous with History*, Knopf, New York, 1956, p. 297.
[2] *Ibid.*, p. 298.

CHINA

The problem of China was again altogether different. In face of
its appalling difficulties, involving military, political and economic
dilemmas alike, there was no question of a direct conflict between
military and civil interests. There was rather an equal bafflement
among all, and on all sides a much greater tendency to evade responsibility than to fight for the power of decision. "Problems like
those of China . . .," as Stimson observed,[1] "were not merely diplomatic — the State Department could not and *would* not assume the
whole labor of determining policy in areas where the military interest was so significant. Yet the military interest could not of itself
be wholly determinant; it was not proper that such questions should
be decided by the Joint Chiefs of Staff, as the *members of that body*
well understood."

"Vinegar Joe" Stilwell's efforts during the war to establish greater
cooperation with the Chinese Communists, and his contemptuous
differences with Chiang Kai-shek, to whom he was Chief of Staff,
may be regarded as an example of a purely military interest seeking
to override the dictates of civil policy. But if Stilwell was expressing
a military view, it was one supported by many of the non-military
officers of the Foreign Service. In early 1945 George Atcheson, Jr.,
then chargé at Chungking (and a diplomat who escaped the accusa-
tions of pro-communism which later clouded the careers of several
of his colleagues), reported that while the policy of refusing in any
way to cooperate with the Chinese Communists was "diplomatically
correct," it was also practically "dangerous." He felt that "If this
situation continues, . . . the probable outbreak of disastrous civil
conflict will be accelerated and chaos in China will be inevitable."
He suggested that while continuing to support Chiang and his Nationalists we should at the same time aid the Communists and any
others "who can aid in this war against the Japanese." There was a
"tremendous internal pressure for unity" in China "based upon
compromise with the Communists"; and Atcheson was intimating

[1] *On Active Service,* p. 561 (emphasis added).

that the United States should try to utilize this pressure rather than stubbornly oppose it.

It was not a military officer but the Ambassador, Patrick J. Hurley, then absent in the United States, who vigorously opposed this suggestion from the chargé. (Hurley was, to be sure, a former military officer — an example of the difficulty of distinguishing between "military" and "civilian" factors in policy.) The Ambassador's reasons were not military but political; he had already resisted an earlier proposal to supply arms to Communist guerrillas on the ground that "such help would be identical to supplying arms to the Communist armed Party and would, therefore, be a dangerous precedent." It was as hard for the civilians as for the military men, in this period, to pick and choose between the military and the political dangers. The difficulty was that there existed no way of bringing the two sets of considerations — military and political — into consonance, and since military men and civilians were to be found on both sides, this difficulty would have existed regardless of any civil-military organization charts which might have been devised.

Hurley returned to Chungking by way of Moscow; there he received from Stalin himself what Hurley thought were assurances that Russia, wanting only a stable government in China, was uninterested in the Chinese Communists and would firmly support Chiang Kai-shek. This seems to have convinced the Ambassador that there was no need to make concessions to Mao Tse-tung in order to avert "disastrous civil conflict." If only Hurley were properly supported from Washington, he could buttress Chiang and the Nationalists into a position where they could take care of the Chinese Communists.

Yet if this was the reasoning, it was mistaken; indeed, nearly everyone seems to have been mistaken in this crisis, at once so vast and so vaguely apprehended for what it really was. By November 1945 the acceleration of the civil chaos, compounded by the problem of getting the Japanese troops out of the country, was too painful to be evaded. It was the soldiers who forced the issue, but only by asking, quite properly, for orders. Wedemeyer, commanding the

United States forces in China (then consisting mainly of some 50,000 Marines in the North China–Manchuria area), had been directed to disarm and repatriate the Japanese, continuing until such time as the Nationalist government could assume the responsibility. But the Nationalists were showing no signs of being able to assume the responsibility. Many of the Japanese had been disarmed and shipped into forced labor in Russia; some were defending themselves against the Communists until they should find an opportunity of surrendering to the United States. What was to be done?

On November 20, 1945 the Secretaries of State, War and Navy met to find an answer. The objective was simple. They wanted to get the Japanese out of Manchuria and establish the authority of the Nationalist government over the whole country. The means, unfortunately, were obscure. They were under heavy pressure to "bring the boys home." They knew that if they withdrew the Marines they risked "a vacuum of anarchy in Manchuria" [1] into which the Russians would inevitably flow; but they did not know what real chance there was that the Nationalists would be able to fill the vacuum. On top of this, the State Department — the voice of civil as distinct from military policy — was most anxious to avoid entanglement in the Chinese civil war. Mao's Communists seemed to have large popular and nationalistic forces behind them; while from Stalin's assurances they were apparently not direct agents of Moscow. To intervene against them on behalf of Chiang's now reactionary and corrupt regime would be "imperialist meddling" of the worst sort, which would not only place us in a bad light before the world but would very probably commit us to a losing horse in China. What the statesmen really hoped for was that Chiang himself would extricate them from their difficulties by reforming his strategy and his administration and starting to win rather than to lose his civil war. But they hoped that he could do it without direct American participation in the war. The answer to Wedemeyer's appeal for instructions did little more than state this series of embarrassing dilemmas and urgently ask Wedemeyer for his views.

[1] *The Forrestal Diaries*, Walter Millis (ed.), Viking, New York, 1951, p. 108.

They did not get much help; Wedemeyer was a soldier, not a politician. On some points he was incisive. He lent no support to the idea that Chiang Kai-shek could extricate Washington from its dilemmas; we could not at the same time uphold Chiang and remain uninvolved in the "fratricidal" war he was waging upon the Communists. "There can be no mistake about this," Wedemeyer wrote. "If the unification of China and Manchuria under Chinese National forces is to be a U. S. policy, involvement in fratricidal warfare and possibly in war with the Soviet Union must be accepted and would definitely require additional U. S. forces far beyond those presently available in the theater to implement the policy." This was certainly military advice in its clearest, most crisp and most appropriate form. But it did not, as the statesmen apparently hoped that it would, answer their problems. The general's final recommendation was either to evacuate China at once or to announce full support for Chiang, the consequences of which he had so frighteningly depicted. This simply handed the question back to the civil authorities — in the first instance, the civilian Secretaries of War and the Navy.

On November 26, 1945 War and Navy completed a long memorandum for the Secretary of State on the Chinese problem. It was scarcely a model of either clarity or decision. It recommended the retention of the Marines in North China for the time being, despite the admitted dangers of their involvement in "fratricidal strife"; all aid to the Generalissimo in getting the Japanese repatriated; and an attempt to secure an international agreement with Soviet participation on the future of China and Manchuria. The State Department, it hopefully concluded, should "provide a definitive policy to cover the next few years in China." This was easier said than done.

The problem was not eased when on the following day Ambassador Hurley sent in a wholly unexpected and sizzling resignation, in which he accused unidentified but supposedly pro-Communist elements in the State Department of sabotaging his efforts to reunite China under Chiang. At the Cabinet luncheon on the 27th there was no other topic of conversation. The solution for the immediate crisis came from Clinton Anderson, the Secretary of Agriculture. He "said he believed the appointment of George Marshall would take the headlines away from Hurley's resignation the following day." Forrestal seconded the suggestion and the consensus was that the wartime Chief of Staff would make an "able ambassador." [1] That took care of the headlines. It did not meet the problem of policy.

On the same day there was a State-War-Navy meeting to consider the military departments' memorandum of the day before. It is hardly surprising that Dean Acheson, then Under Secretary of State, felt that it failed to cover the whole field. He was "convinced that we cannot 'yank the Marines out of Northern China now,' but he said that he feels that the situation is not adequately understood by the public in this country. He inquired whether we could not talk the matter over realistically with the Russians." But Byrnes was "puzzled" as to what to say to them. Perhaps, he finally suggested, "the wise course would be to try to force the Chinese government and the Chinese Communists to get together on a compromise basis," threatening Chiang with a withdrawal of aid if he did not accede. It might even be well "to tell Russia what we intend to do and to try to line them up with this policy." [2] It thus appears to have been the very conservative Byrnes who actually generated the policy that was to guide the Marshall mission. That a statesman like Byrnes could even have toyed with the idea of co-opting Russia in such an enterprise is eloquent, not only of the climate of opinion in late 1945 — so different from that which was to rule only a year or two later — but also of the great ignorance, still existing among many Americans of all shades of opinion, as to the real nature and motivation of Stalinist foreign policy. Not until the impasse over the Baruch plan for the control of atomic energy and the complete failure, in April 1946, of Byrnes' offer to Russia of a twenty-five-year guarantee against German rearmament did a clearer understanding begin to emerge.

THE MARSHALL MISSION

At all events, the Marines would remain temporarily in North China; we would help the Generalissimo to move his own forces

---

[1] *The Forrestal Diaries,* p. 113.
[2] *Ibid.,* p. 123.

into Manchuria, but not otherwise directly assist him in the fratri-cidal war with the Communists. Marshall would be sent out with the mission of bringing that war to an end on terms that would permit the re-establishment of the Nationalist government's au-thority throughout the country. That this was an impossible mission was insufficiently realized, especially by the younger Chinese experts in the State Department who drafted the instructions, or by Byrnes and Truman, who endorsed them. Yet Wedemeyer, the soldier, had already told them that they would either have to support the Gen-eralissimo in full-scale warfare, with many more American troops than anyone dreamed of committing, or in effect surrender the colossal population of China to Communist conquest. Our total policy-making machinery — military, diplomatic, administrative and legislative — was simply incapable of facing and clearly resolving such a dilemma; instead, a weak compromise solution was adopted. Four years later the Communist conquest of China was completed under circumstances which made it far more menacing to the United States, and with consequences far less easily controlled, than might have been the case had the possibilities been clearly grasped and the situation resolutely dealt with at the beginning. It was just such failures in basic policy-formulation which it was hoped that the National Security Act would correct. The hopes were to be largely disappointed, but the continuing deterioration of our position in China during 1946 and early 1947 was another indication of the need for a higher organization of our military-diplomatic policy.

General Marshall had not been chosen for his military back-ground — Secretary Anderson's inspiration was of a political and propagandist nature — though it may have been felt that as a mili-tary man he would have special competence in arranging what would in the first instance be a war armistice. He did, indeed, secure an armistice; his difficulty was that neither side would keep it. This was not for military reasons. They would not keep it because the armistice, like the general's own instructions, left unresolved the great political and power issue over which the two sides were fight-ing. The Generalissimo and his Nationalists, if they were to have any hope of survival, could accept nothing less than the complete subordination and ultimate destruction of the Communist movement. Mao Tse-tung, similarily, could accept no "compromise" peace which did not assure him freedom to infiltrate and ultimately capture the Nationalist government. This had been the central issue in China for some twenty years — ever since Chiang and his Kuomintang had broken with their Soviet-oriented origins and their Communist colleagues far back in 1927 — and no armistice which failed to decide it could possibly terminate the struggle. Even less could it be done by a diplomacy which had evaded the issue and sent out its emissary under instructions that he was to take sides for neither party to it.

"The complex problems in China," as the State Department's celebrated "White Paper" later put it, "fell largely under three heads — political, military and economic — but they frequently became so entangled that discussion of them cannot be separated. This was particularly true of the political and military problems." In addressing them there was little conflict between the soldiers and the civilians, or between the civilian heads of the military departments and the heads of State or the other civil agencies concerned. Indeed, except for Hurley's explosive resignation, there was not much conflict of any sort in 1946; only in embittered retrospect did the differences between "the China lobby" and the State Department's "China hands," between the Truman Administration's distrust of the Generalissimo and its opponents' impassioned anti-communism, develop into lethal debate — not over what ought to be done but over what ought to have been done. In 1946 hindsight was not available either to guide policy or to envenom controversy. The truth is that no one knew what ought to be done at a time when decision might conceivably have affected events; the failure, if such it was, was not a failure of civil-military relationships but a failure of the whole mechanism of policy formation.

In the summer of 1946 Marshall returned for a visit to the United States, hoping in that way to bring pressure on the disputing factions in China; but the gesture was useless and the Nationalist cause continued to disintegrate. As the year ended, Byrnes turned in his resignation. In January 1947 President Truman announced Marshall's appointment to the office. He was the first professional soldier, professionally trained and with a lifetime in the Army behind him, to serve as an American Secretary of State. But it was not for that reason that Truman had called him to the post. The President enormously admired his wisdom and judgment; he was to think him among the greatest of American statesmen. But in that tangled and politically stormy time there was much, too, in the remark which Stimson remembered Theodore Roosevelt once making: "The great thing about an Army officer is that he does what you tell him to." Efficient loyalty also has its place in civil administration. Truman could be confident that Marshall would be both wise and loyal.

## THE BUDGET OF FISCAL '48

Little more than a week after the announcement of Marshall's appointment, the President made public the War-Navy agreement on the National Security bill. It was not to be enacted for another six months (Forrestal, though confirmed as the first Secretary of Defense in July 1947, did not take the oath of office until September 17). But while the machinery of unification thus remained to be erected, the basic military structure was now clearly adumbrated. And the defense budgets, which would give this structure its shape and scale, could not wait. Through the latter part of 1946 and early 1947 the departmental budget-makers, the Budget Bureau and the appropriations committee were laboring on the budget for fiscal '48 with the new military structure very much in mind.

The '48 budget was in several ways critical in the development of our military policy. A year before the huge war surplus of airplanes, combat ships and weapons had for the most part been serviceable; the men were being demobilized, but so far as equipment was concerned, it was mainly a question of how much to retain out of existing stocks. Now it was apparent that obsolescence was already far advanced. The heavy bombers, like the Flying Fortress, that did most of the war's work had been outmoded well before the war was over by our own development of the B-29, while still more powerful and formidable designs were on the way. The jet fighter plane, introduced by the Germans as the war was ending, clearly spelled the fate of the piston-engine fighter. It was the same with the war designs of submarines, tanks, aircraft carriers and much else. Despite billions of dollars worth of weapons left in the "pipelines," all the services had to think seriously about replacement; and their success in securing appropriations for new building would determine not only their prestige but the authority with which they could speak in the still undecided strategic and tactical controversies and their actual ability to discharge the strategic missions which they claimed for themselves. The whole future of the soon-to-be-independent Air Force or of the Navy as a sea-air arm might turn upon the new building allowed them.

The Budget Bureau, on the other hand, was committed to economy and to the President's concept of a fixed ceiling on defense expenditure. The war had ended in the early months of fiscal '46, and the Truman Administration had succeeded in reducing total defense expenditure for that year to $45 billion. Fiscal '47 would show an expenditure of only $14.25 billion. After the Budget Bureau had done its work, the budget for fiscal '48 (presented by the President in January 1947) called for an estimated expenditure of only $11.25 billion. The Navy had begun planning on a giant carrier, intended to enable it to keep up with the impending jet age, as well as on various lesser prototypes; it also wanted to complete the large tonnage from the war programs which had been unfinished on VJ-Day. The Budget Bureau told it that it could not have the super carrier. The Army Air Force demanded its seventy-group program; it was reduced to a request for only fifty-eight full groups. The ground Army's troop strengths and formations were to be still further reduced; it was allowed little or nothing to replace the tanks, troopcarriers and other weapons and vehicles which the last days of the war had shown to be already obsolete.

The congressmen, however, were even more deeply committed to economy than the Administration. This was the first session of the celebrated Eightieth Congress, which the Republicans had captured in the fall elections, and their chairman of the House Appropriations Committee, John Taber of New York, was a famous ax-wielder. The

Republicans were out to make an economy record; unfortunately, they, like many others, were increasingly alarmed by the rising military threat of Soviet communism. In February the British announced that they would be forced to lay down the burden in Greece; and on March 12 the President appeared before Congress not only to ask for $400 million for economic and technical aid and weapons for Greece and Turkey, but to proclaim the "Truman Doctrine" calling for the assistance of free peoples everywhere to resist Communist infiltration and subversion. At the Cabinet meeting at which this policy had been discussed a few days before, the consensus had been "that we should support Greece to the extent that we can persuade Congress and the country of the necessity."

Congress was persuaded of the necessity; but it was also persuaded of the necessity for staying out of war, for economy, for popular but expensive domestic programs of social service. Amid such conflicting emotions, "The treatment which Congress gave the military budget for 1947-1948," as Elias Huzar puts it,[1] "was the most thorough — and, for the War Department, one of the most uncomfortable — in the years since 1933. . . . Congressmen . . . never explored the connections between military and foreign policies so extensively in the decade and a half after 1932 as they did in 1947." But while the exploration was thorough, one cannot feel that it really threw much light on the underlying civil-military problem. Some thought that to strengthen our military posture would invite war; others, that it was the chief means for averting one. Some wanted to enlarge aircraft building because that would impress the Russians with our power; a few opposed this on the ground that it would simply play into Soviet hands by wrecking our own economy. For some, the principal standard seemed to be whatever was required to maintain a prosperous and adequate aircraft and munitions industry. Hardly any seemed to conceive the problem as one of providing a currently sufficient military force to meet the current military-political issues with which we were confronted.

No one, of course, even considered large-scale military interven-

[1] *The Purse and the Sword*, Cornell University Press, Ithaca, 1950, p. 171.

tions abroad of the kind which alone could have stayed the Chinese Nationalist collapse or guaranteed success in the Greek government's resistance to the Communist civil war that was being waged (largely from foreign bases) against it. The impulse was toward some general improvement in the military posture, not toward specific military answers for specific political issues. The painful dichotomy between the desire to provide "adequate" defense and the desire to save money in doing so was resolved, in general, along two lines. One was the traditional hunt for minor economies — a sterner insistence than before on "justification" for every item and a stern excision of everything which might seem deferrable, regardless of its effect on long-range military planning. The other was to put whatever could be allowed for improving the military posture into aircraft production, especially Army aircraft production, on the assumption that aircraft represented the modern and economically most efficient embodiment of military power. The House Appropriations subcommittee did make a rather drastic cut in the request for Air Force appropriations, but much of this was ultimately restored. The Congressional changes reduced the estimated expenditures for fiscal '48 by only about half a billion dollars; their distribution as between the three services was not markedly altered. But if the Air Force failed to get its seventy-group program it did, at least, establish itself in a very strong position as against the Navy and the ground Army. It seems fair to say that the budget for fiscal '48 had the effect of launching the independent Air Force on its career as the dominant element in American military policy. Air Force strategy was, of course, not devised as an economy measure. Yet partly because it seemed economical, thereafter the Air Force was to come first with Congress; increasingly the military policy of the nation was to be framed around the dreadful, and in most situations inapplicable, Air Force concept of "strategic" bombing with mass-destruction weapons.

Three or four years later, with the development of the Soviet arsenal of atomic and hydrogen bombs, this increasingly exclusive preoccupation with strategic bombing was to seem a valid, indeed a necessary, decision. Perhaps none other could have been taken even at that time. It is still questionable whether it was a valid decision in early 1947. For the crises which lay immediately ahead, the strategic Air Force was to prove a nearly useless military instrument. It could not help in a situation like that presented in Greece; it could not stay the Communist conquest of China; it was of no value in the field in Korea; we did not dare use it in Indo-China. The Korean disaster in particular might well have been averted had we maintained in the area larger, better equipped and better trained ground Army forces (with naval and tactical air support); in this and later crises the Strategic Air Command has no doubt helped to "hold the ring" and prevent smaller wars from growing into greater ones, but it has not in itself proved a practicable instrument of positive policy. However that may be, the fiscal '48 budget, representing a collaboration between the Democratic officials of the Truman Budget Bureau and the Republican representatives in the Congressional committees, much more than any contribution of professional military expertise, set the basic pattern of American military policy which was to rule, substantially, down to June 1950.

## THE CRISES OF 1948

It was a pattern, needless to say, with many loose ends. The National Security Act was still to be passed and signed. If the military budget had rather clearly delineated the future, it was still, as always, a compromise. But the Air Force was already virtually independent, and so accepted on all sides. The top administrators had long since adjusted themselves to the new situation; and the informal relationships which existed among them were providing a cement for the new unification more powerful than anything which was to be supplied by the statutory enactment.

Secretary of War Patterson, Secretary of the Navy Forrestal and Robert A. Lovett (Assistant Secretary of War for Air during the conflict, who was to become Under Secretary of State in July 1947) were close friends, men of similar backgrounds and outlook. They all respected Marshall's abilities and welcomed his appointment as Secretary of State; they were all able to work loyally with the President, even when they might disagree with his absorption in partisan politics. Vannevar Bush, the outstanding scientific statesman of the war, was intimate with them; so were most of the top admirals and generals. They were served by brilliant "Indians" — like George Kennan or Paul Nitze in State, or Wilfred McNeil or Marx Leva in Defense, or many more. The civilians and the flag officers lunched frequently together in the more exclusive recesses of the Pentagon; Forrestal in particular cultivated the Congressional leaders of both parties and the press.

The top administrators of American civil and military policy in these years were all friends; they shared a common apprehension of the Soviet Union and a common conviction that the answers were to be found primarily in foresight, planning and cooperation.

### THE MARSHALL PLAN AND CONTAINMENT

It was Marshall who early in 1947 set up the Policy Planning Staff in the State Department under George Kennan — in a way a forerunner of the National Security Council staff. On April 29, 1947, before the Policy Planning Staff had even had its first meeting, the Secretary of State demanded from Kennan a policy adequate to meet the impending crises of Greece and Turkey, of a collapsing Europe and a collapsed China. The next day the Secretary called Kennan in and said he wanted the policy within ten days or two weeks. One result was the "jelling" of what was later known as the Marshall Plan. The idea had been in the State Department for months and Dean Acheson in May flew a "trial balloon" at Cleveland, Mississippi. Kennan and the Policy Planning Staff put it into concrete terms; it was announced in Secretary Marshall's address at Harvard on June 5, and was an instant success. The July issue of *Foreign Affairs* carried Kennan's celebrated "Mr. X" article adumbrating the policy of "containment." American foreign and military policy were being given shape and substance. Planning, forethought, cooperation between the agencies of foreign policy and military and economic power were paying dividends even before the enactment of the statutory measures intended to insure these things.

But they were partial dividends. The developing crisis in world affairs was larger, more vague, more ominous than anything with which our institutions were equipped to deal. In July 1947 General Wedemeyer was sent back to China to ascertain and report on the facts of that increasingly alarming situation. In the fall the President set up a commission under Thomas K. Finletter, to report on the quite different but hardly less alarming problem of air policy in an age which had produced the air-borne atomic bomb. Another commission had already returned an elaborate report on universal military training (of course strongly favoring the proposal) about which nothing was ever done. The National Security Act was finally passed in late July. The President frankly, if rather crudely, told Forrestal that he had offered the post of Secretary of Defense to Patterson but that the latter had refused on the ground that he had to make money, and that therefore he would send in Forrestal's name. Forrestal accepted, and was confirmed on the same evening (July 26-27, 1947).

FORRESTAL TAKES OFFICE

He was in no hurry to take office; much of what had to be done could be done under the old hat as easily as under the new one. But the tensions of the cold war were rising. A now almost forgotten crisis over Trieste, precipitated in September by the Yugoslavs, led to orders from the President (at the moment returning from a visit to Brazil) that Forrestal should be sworn in immediately and should take action to see that all available reinforcements were provided for the American command at Trieste. There were few if any available reinforcements and the crisis happily passed; but in the result Forrestal was sworn in on September 17, 1947, and the machinery of the unification act was brought into full operation. At this formative moment there were many doubts. At a luncheon on September 16 General Lauris Norstad confirmed Forrestal's impression "that State under Acheson's leadership had been very dubious about the creation of the [National Security] council and would undoubtedly try to castrate its effectiveness." But Norstad at the same time expressed "considerable misgivings about the extent of military participation in diplomatic decisions." The trouble was "the paucity of trained people in the State Department and the consequent necessity of drafting people from the military to fill in the gap." If this went on, according to Norstad, the Military Establishment would be attacked "as exercising too powerful an influence upon our foreign policies," whereas in fact it was "usually the military people who had to hold back the sporadic and truculent impulses of political people and diplomats who do not realize the consequences of aggressive action." It was to meet such situations, Forrestal said, that the National Security Council had been created.[1]

## THE WEDEMEYER REPORT

In the next two or three months there were to be few "sporadic and truculent" initiatives from the political people; and while few could doubt the ominous appearance of the international situation, there were no crashing crises and no imperative demands for policy decisions in the international sphere. Under the guidance of its new Secretary of Defense, the Military Establishment ground out the budget requests for fiscal '49, again scaled to the exiguous ceiling imposed by the Administration. Events in China were running an appalling course, but what could be done? In September 1947 General Wedemeyer returned from the China theater with his finding. Its principal feature was a recommendation for a United Nations trusteeship over Manchuria, to be exercised jointly by the United States, the Soviet Union, Britain and France. At the moment, the United States was in propaganda difficulties in the UN over its policy in Greece, where we were trying to prop up a "reactionary" government against Communist insurrection. There was a move for a UN investigatory commission, which the Soviet Union was promoting as a means of getting its finger in the Grecian pie. The Wedemeyer proposal to invite Russia into a joint trusteeship for Manchuria, coming when we were doing all in our power to keep the Russians out of Greece, threatened to upset this policy, and the Wedemeyer report was suppressed.

[1] *The Forrestal Diaries*, pp. 315-16.

It had contained no real solution for the China problem; for there was none, anywhere between a commitment of American men and money vastly greater than the country would accept or a deal with the Chinese Communists of a kind which the country would find equally abhorrent. From this dilemma there was no exit; and during the latter part of 1947 American statesmen and soldiers alike could only watch as the Chinese Communists began to expand their essentially guerrilla warfare into more formal operations with larger and larger masses of maneuver. The shifting of the balance against the Nationalists became more and more painfully apparent, and by December Mao was able to declare with confidence that the Nationalists were on the run. The State Department's energies were engrossed at the time with Greece, with aid for Turkey and with putting the Marshall Plan into operation. Another foreign ministers' meeting to secure a German and Austrian peace treaty ended in a total failure which sufficiently accentuated the chasm between East and West and the menaces of Soviet policy. But the problems these presented still seemed to lie in the diplomatic and economic fields; few as yet realized that they might have immediate military implications.

THE FINLETTER COMMISSION

In January 1948 the Finletter Commission on Air Policy published its report. It was still oriented toward the future rather than the present; but the future which it examined was a frightening one and not now more than a few years away. The debates over atomic policy of two years before had been tentative and theoretical; now this all-civilian commission publicly and forcefully placed the nuclear arsenal at the center of practical strategic plan. Its conclusions were uncompromising:

[The] Military Establishment must be built around the air arm. Of course, an adequate Navy and Ground Force must be maintained. But it is the Air Force and naval aviation on which we must mainly rely. Our military security must be based on air power.

The basic reason was that:

Atomic weapons will not long remain our monopoly. . . . It is known that other nations are working diligently on the problem of atomic energy. . . . It would be safe to assume, in making our plans for the next two years, that possibly hostile powers will not be producing atomic weapons in substantial quantities before the end of 1952. . . . The conclusions of the Commission thus fix as the target date by which we should have an air arm in being capable of dealing with a possible atomic attack on this country as January 1, 1953.

Here was a clear, unequivocal recognition that the political and strategic concepts of the Second World War — and, indeed, of most of the military history of the race — were subject to fundamental revision. It also tended to emphasize the extent to which then current military policy was built on sand. It rested on a nuclear monopoly which was certain to be short-lived. On the assumption that our possession of the monopoly would probably prevent another major war, and in any event would give us an irresistible weapon for winning one should it break out, we had reduced our conventional forces to mere occupational, police and training cadres; but we had not even maintained the capability to deliver the "sustained and powerful air counteroffensive" with atomic weapons on which this strategy was based. The Finletter report did not so much recommend a new strategy as point to our failures to implement a strategy already largely accepted, and in particular point to its fatal flaw. Once the Soviet Union had acquired a nuclear arsenal of its own, the strategy of monopoly would be in ruins. And this time was very near.

The Finletter report exposed a basic issue; but it did so in a way that was in some respects unfortunate. It was, to begin with, an Air Force report. The assignment had been to study "air policy" alone; the commissioners were not given the whole field of combined military policy, and even within the narrower limits of their mandate they paid relatively little attention to that important segment of "air power" represented by naval aviation. They consulted extensively with Air Force officers, and could not conceal the fact that they were responding mainly to the Air Force's somewhat parochial view of problems which already far surpassed the competence of any single service. Their uncompromising conclusion that security must henceforth be based on "air power" was phrased in a revealing way: "Of course, an adequate Navy and Ground

Force must be maintained. But it is the Air Force *and naval aviation* on which we must mainly rely." The words here italicized were only too obviously an afterthought, put in to soothe the sailors, and painfully inconsistent with the preceding offhand statement that "of course" an "adequate" Navy would also have to be maintained. Given a Navy which was already carrying a large proportion of its fire-power on wings, it would seem that any study of "air policy" should have given closer attention to what constituted an "adequate" naval component. There were many, not only in the Navy but outside it, who were not convinced that all strategic wisdom resided in the young generals of the Air Force.

Even within its terms of reference, moreover, the report was open to the charge of superficiality. Its uncomplicated solution for the appearance of a Soviet air-atomic capability was simply more air-atomic power on our side. By the beginning of 1953 we should have "an air arm in being capable of dealing with a possible atomic attack." But our own strategy had been based on the assumption that there was no way of "dealing" with an atomic attack; the atom bomb was the "ultimate weapon," against which there was "no defense." If the assumption was valid, more air-atomic power on our side would be no reply to the appearance of an atomic weapons system in Soviet hands; if it was fallacious, then much more thought would have to be put into the problem of defense, of alternative military means, of total rather than merely air-power strategy, than either the Air Force generals or the Finletter Commission had given to such questions. Most of this remained beyond the purview of the Finletter Commission. In effect, what it said was that within about five years the Russians would have an effective atomic arsenal; and that the American reply should be the Air Force seventy-group program of retaliatory and "deterrent" air power. When it added that this was no real solution, and that there was no real solution save in the abolition of war, it still further weakened the impact of its findings. The Finletter Commission quite clearly stated the problem; but its analysis sounded more like propaganda than a guide to action, and the report was to leave little visible trace in the practical struggles of JCS, the Budget Bureau and the appropriations committees with the immediate strategic issues.

## NEW DIFFICULTIES

In time of major war, military policy is made primarily in the "war rooms" and chiefs-of-staff committee meetings in the top levels of military command, and in constant contact with the Commander in Chief; in times of non-war it is made mainly in the conferences of the budget officers and the hearing rooms of the military affairs committees. In war, the difficulty is to keep the military demand within the limits of what the civilian economy can produce and supply; in non-war, the difficulty is to determine the proper allocation of production as between civil and military demands. At the beginning of 1948 it was apparent to informed people that our military policy was badly out of adjustment with the actualities of the perilous world which we confronted. But in spite of the new machinery of the National Security Act, there was no easy way in which to reconnect the two.

The Finletter Commission had called for a great new effort of air-atomic preparedness. On February 18 Major General Alfred M. Gruenther, then head of the JCS Joint Staff, gave a "briefing" at the White House on the exiguous state of our conventional forces. Aside from the occupation troops in Germany and Japan (numbering about 250,000 men but neither organized nor trained for combat and excluded by the Army Department from its calculations as "political" forces only) we could muster only about two and a half part-strength Army divisions and a few Marine battalion landing teams as forces available to meet emergency. And Gruenther discerned several "explosives points" around the world — Greece, Italy, Korea and Palestine — where emergency might at any moment arise. If it did, he noted, "the employment of anything more than a division in any area would make partial mobilization a necessity." [1]

This was a situation which the Finletter report had not considered. Perhaps no one had really considered it; it was so extraordinarily

[1] *The Forrestal Diaries*, pp. 374-76.

difficult to combine the atomic bomb with a working military policy for the urgent present. In December and January 1948 a series of secret conferences with British representatives, held at Blair House, had clarified the relations of the two countries in atomic development — relations which had been reduced to considerable ambiguity by the Atomic Energy Act of 1946, which, with its extreme, seclusive provisions for secrecy, had been superposed on the more informal wartime understandings. These had given Great Britain a veto power over the use of the atomic weapon in war; it was agreed between the two countries that "we will not use it against third parties without each other's consent." The British now surrendered this power of control in return for an American undertaking to permit a certain limited "exchange of information" on non-military atomic development. The discussions were amicable, and the result removed some dangerous uncertainties; but it did nothing to resolve the basic strategic problems presented by the development of nuclear warfare.

Forrestal tried to force the Joint Chiefs to face up to these problems. The Finletter report (and the very similar conclusions of a joint Congressional committee on air policy, which appeared in March) put a renewed public pressure behind the Air Force demand for its seventy-group program. This in turn undermined the proposal for universal military training (UMT), so much desired by the Army, which the President had laid before Congress. If we were to rest our security on the atomic bomb, what need was there for an expensive and intensely unpopular system of mass military training, with all its connotations for permanent peacetime conscription? Meanwhile a bitter contest was developing between the Air Force, which believed that it should have sole responsibility for atomic warfare, and the Navy, which believed that it should also have access to the atomic weapons and could use them in many situations to better advantage than could the Strategic Air Command. The issue was practical, and growing acute. In the spring of 1948 the Atomic Energy Commission, at its Eniwetok proving grounds, fired the first test bombs that had been exploded since the Bikini experiment two years before. They reputedly developed six times the power of the

Hiroshima and Nagasaki weapons. The agreement on "roles and missions," promulgated by the President when he signed the National Security Act, was no longer adequate to the strategic problems latent in such developments. Forrestal resolved to force the Joint Chiefs to devise a better one. If they would not or could not decide, he would "make my own decisions." [1] His plan was to drag the Joint Chiefs away from their Washington desks and telephones and sit them down for a two- or three-day conference in some secluded place where they could really grapple with the underlying issues confided to them by the Security Act. "Certain decisions must be taken about who does what with what weapons."

THE KEY WEST CONFERENCE

The conference was to meet at the isolated Key West naval base on March 11, 1948; before it could do so, however, there intervened a series of startling and ominous events which were to lend to its deliberations an unexpected urgency. Our efforts to defeat Communist rebellion in Greece were going badly. In early February the Communists in South Korea had precipitated a wave of strikes, riots and sabotage which, though not widely noticed in the United States, was menacing for the future. On February 24, 1948 democratic Czechoslovakia was captured by her internal Communist conspiracy in a *coup* which did profoundly shock the United States and the whole non-Communist world. And on March 5 there arrived a top-secret telegram from General Lucius D. Clay, commanding in Berlin:

> Within the last few weeks, I have felt a subtle change in Soviet attitude which I cannot define but which now gives me a feeling that it [war] may come with dramatic suddenness. [2]

The American public was to know nothing of this until long afterward, but at the time it threw all the higher military and administrative echelons in Washington into a consternation which helps explain many of the subsequent events. Just to make things com-

[1] *The Forrestal Diaries*, p. 390.
[2] *Ibid.*, p. 387.

plete, there was a gloomy report on March 8 from the American Embassy in Nanking: there was "increasing evidence" that the Generalissimo would soon be forced either to make a negotiated peace with the Communists or else find himself "discarded" altogether; the "present criminally inept and wasteful [Chinese Nationalist] strategy" might temporarily postpone disaster but could not "indefinitely" stave it off.

The Clay telegram arrived on a Friday. The Senate Armed Services Committee had called a meeting with the military chiefs for Monday, March 8, to discuss their proposal for universal military training and tell them that they would have "to get a more realistic approach" to this subject "from a budget point of view." Budgetary considerations were not absent from Monday's discussion, but in face of the suddenly heightened international tension they were beginning to appear in a new light. "Senator [Wayne L.] Morse [of Oregon, then of the Republican Party] said he felt there was a need for a review and presentation to the country of the facts about the world situation and our present military weakness." The senators were told that UMT had become "mandatory"; the facts, as Forrestal privately commented a few days later, were "grim enough." [1] The committee voted unanimously to institute hearings on UMT.

On Thursday, March 11, the Joint Chiefs met with Forrestal in the tropic spring weather at Key West. It is difficult to feel that they rose to the strategic problems confronting the nation with the largeness of vision that had been expected of them; they did, however, work out a compromise of their inter-service issues that might suffice to get them through the budgetary difficulties ahead. By noon on Sunday they had arrived at certain "broad, basic decisions": For "planning purposes" the Marine Corps was to be limited to four divisions, with the proviso that they were not "to create another land army." The Air Force recognized the "right" of the Navy to proceed with the development of an atomic capability, although it was not to create "a separate strategic air force," this being reserved ex-

[1] *Ibid.*, pp. 388-89.

clusively to the Air Force. But the Navy was "not to be denied use of A-bomb" and was to be allowed to continue with its projected super carrier, then mainly desired as a platform from which the heavy planes required to deliver the early atomic weapons could be launched. This patched up the Navy–Air Force quarrel. It was only in the remaining half hour or so before lunch on Sunday that Gruenther brought up the Army's problems. Existing war plans called for larger ground forces than were even authorized; the active Army had sunk well below the authorizations; voluntary enlistment was clearly a failure, while UMT, whatever its utility as a long-range project, could not furnish men needed immediately. The Joint Chiefs agreed to support a recommendation for reactivating selective service (the draft) in order to bring the Army at least to authorized strength. They also agreed that the President should ask for a supplemental military appropriation to bring the armed forces as a whole to a state more nearly commensurate with the ominous "realities of the world situation." [1]

Forrestal reached Washington on Monday, March 15, and saw the President the same afternoon. A good deal had been happening in his absence. The suicide, as it was declared to be, of Jan Masaryk in Czechoslovakia had intensified the shock and anger over the country's fall. On Friday, in Brussels, Britain, France, Belgium, the Netherlands and Luxembourg had reached agreement on a fifty-year treaty of mutual defense, the Brussels Pact. On the same day two junior Republican representatives, Richard M. Nixon of California and Charles J. Kersten of Wisconsin, announcing their desire to "give solemn warning to the conspiracy in the Politburo that any further step of aggression . . . will be actively resisted by every means at our disposal," had brought in a joint resolution authorizing the United States to enter into defensive military alliances. The idea that the United States would have to make much larger financial, if not military, commitments to the defense of the West than had been contemplated was already active. In the midst of the Key West conference a telegram was handed in announcing that Ernest Bevin, the

[1] *Ibid.*, pp. 392-93.

British Foreign Minister, was proposing the expansion of the Brussels Pact into a larger structure of "Atlantic security." There was an already lively private debate among congressmen as to whether more than merely economic reconstruction of Western Europe might not be needed. Late Saturday the Senate adopted, 69 to 17, the $5.3 billion authorization for Marshall Plan aid.

THE PRESIDENT'S NEW PROGRAM

On Monday afternoon Forrestal found the President prepared to make a strong statement favoring some measure of rearmament and a revival of the draft. The Secretary had gone to Key West mainly with the idea of beating the Joint Chiefs' heads together on the technical issues of service functions; he returned to find that the Key West decisions were expected to provide the basis for an immediate strategic plan to meet the suddenly urgent immediate issues. There is an indication of how urgent they seemed to be in the fact that not until next day, Tuesday, March 16, did the Central Intelligence Agency, frantically studying the implications of the Clay telegram, feel free to come up with a prediction that war was not probable over another sixty days. It was another two weeks before CIA felt justified in extending this rather slim prophecy of peace.

The President had engaged himself to speak at the St. Patrick's Day dinner in New York on Wednesday, and had intended to devote the occasion to a plug for UMT. It was Marshall who convinced him that the strategic problem, now far transcending the limited question of UMT, was too critical for such a forum; and Truman shifted his major effort to an address before a joint session of Congress at 12:30 on March 17, 1948. This, of course, added an immense weight to his words, and the result was to be a decisive policy statement. For the first time, the President identified the Soviet Union as the "one nation" blocking all efforts for peace. He described Russia's "ruthless course of action," and saw behind it an apparently "clear design" to subjugate the remaining free nations of Europe. We must, he declared, "meet this growing menace." The position of the United States "should be made unmistakably clear.

. . . There are times in world history when it is far wiser to act than to hesitate."

The words were forceful; unfortunately, there was not much in the way of "action" which the President or his Administration was prepared to recommend. He advanced only three specific proposals: prompt adoption of the Marshall Plan program; adoption of UMT, and a "temporary" re-enactment of selective service. The speech was widely hailed as a call for a firm foreign policy and for the rearmament which would be necessary in support of it. But when Forrestal and the other civilian chiefs of the Military Establishment went before the Senate Armed Services Committee next day, they had little to offer beyond generalities. Forrestal told them that the aggregate in service (1,384,000 men on March 1) was 350,000 short of authorized strength. But what, specifically, was needed would have to wait upon further consideration by the Joint Chiefs.

It was nearly a week later (March 25) that Forrestal, accompanied by his three service Secretaries and their three Chiefs of Staff, appeared before the House Armed Services Committee to present what he described as "a specific program, which is solely designed to achieve one great objective: to avert war, whether it be open or covert." It was presented as a program not for weapons but for "manpower" — for "a balanced strength in manpower — on the ground, on the sea, in the air." It was to be a demonstration to the world less of organized and equipped military might than of the fact that our "fields" of human and spiritual reserves "will not lie fallow, but that we shall keep them planted for a quick harvest of strength and will, not next year or next month, after the rich prizes of northern Italy and the Ruhr and Sweden and France may have fallen, but now."

Since strength and will are comparatively helpless without weapons, organization and training, this was largely rhetorical. Forrestal appears to have been groping here with his difficulties over UMT (in which he had little faith), his doubts of the Strategic Air Command's strategy of annihilation, his need for some immediate power in the world political balance, his embarrassment over the still unresolved inter-service quarrel. The actual budget proposals which

JCS had worked out and which Forrestal presented on March 25 were scarcely calculated to permit a "quick harvest" of our human resources in emergency; in retrospect they seem a feeble response to the realities of the world situation. The program called for reviving the draft to yield the 350,000 men required to bring the Army up to strength; the Air Force would get the men and planes it needed to fill the authorized fifty-five groups, but not the desired seventy. A sum of about $775 million was asked for additional Air Force and Navy aircraft procurement and for air research and development. Forrestal supported UMT only as a "long-term" proposal, thereby killing what little chance it had for adoption. He made it clear that what he wanted was some improvement in the immediate military posture; but the whole supplemental requested an expenditure of only about $3 billion over the $11 billion in the regular budget. This was regarded as about the maximum which the economy — or at any rate the taxpayers and the politicians — could "afford." But even so it was to have rough going.

The Air Force objected. Stuart Symington, the first Secretary of the Air Force, and "Tooey" Spaatz, about to retire as Air Chief of Staff, continued to demand the full seventy groups, and argued that these would require no more than a further $800 million. The next few weeks were a time of trial. It was not, in fact, an issue between the military and the civilians; it was an issue created by the new service's challenge both to older military patterns and to the civilian requirement for economy. There were civilians on both sides, while the Joint Chiefs, as the corporate fount of military advice, was more or less in the middle.

### BALANCED FORCES

Forrestal tried to escape through his concept of a "balanced" force. It was generally admitted that we could not put our whole faith in the Air Force's strategic bombers. As the Finletter report had said, "of course" adequate ground and naval forces were necessary. But what was adequate? On this the proponents of land-based air power had not spent much thought. To many it seemed that the answer should lie in establishing an appropriate balance between the three services; then, if it appeared that the national security dictated any specific level of strength for one service, the two others could readily be adjusted upward or downward accordingly to yield a balanced structure of defense. Forrestal may not himself have accepted such a simplistic view of the problem, but at least it offered him a possible way out of his difficulties. He asked the Joint Chiefs to determine what the adoption of a seventy-group Air Force would require in the way of additional Army and Navy strengths in order to keep the entire structure in balance.

Unfortunately, it was an unanswerable question. Confronted as they were by basic conflicts of strategic theory, the Joint Chiefs were no more able than Forrestal or the Budget Bureau or the newspaper editors to assign relative weights to the different views. Given a concrete military problem, a Second World War theater commander could estimate with at least some accuracy how much air, how much ground and how much naval force he would require to take an objective. To make a "militarily sound" estimate of that kind amid all the unknowns and imponderables of cold war strategy was virtually impossible. When Forrestal asked for an estimate of an over-all defense system balanced around seventy rather than fifty-five air groups, about all JCS could do was to increase Army and Navy appropriations roughly in proportion to the increases for Air. This "cutting the pie" worked out to a supplemental of about $9 billion, which was politically and (it was assumed) economically impossible.

It was certainly impossible, as Forrestal was acutely aware, without either raising taxes or continuing, at a time of full employment and prosperity, to run a deficit and thus invite what Forrestal feared would be a run-away inflation. With all the other military or quasi-military demands, present or in prospect — for European recovery, for atomic energy, for stockpiling, for increased military aid — we had, as Forrestal put it,[1] "a barrel that is completely full now, and one blow of the hammer is going to bust the bungs on it." The House did not ease matters by appropriating $822 million for air-

[1] *The Forrestal Diaries*, p. 429.

plane procurement outside both the supplemental and the regular budget requests, the intention of the statesmen being to force a seventy-group program whether the Joint Chiefs or the President would accept it or not. Forrestal strove to get the Joint Chiefs to put the seal of professional approval on a supplemental budget of something less than $9 billion — a redistribution of funds and force levels which would stay somewhere near the $3 billion supplemental first proposed. But this was asking them to revise a "military" opinion under "political" pressure, something forbidden by the accepted mythology.

## THE NEW BUDGET

How mythological this distinction between the "military" and "political" spheres had actually become is suggested by the adroit device which JCS, with Forrestal's help, found to resolve the dilemma. It clung to its professional conclusion that $9 billion was the irreducible minimum supplemental required by military security; but it recognized that the expenditure of this amount was a matter of "phasing" which had to be adjusted to economic considerations, the capacity of the munitions and airplane industries and so on. This phasing was a problem for the politicians, not the soldiers. And when asked what they would immediately recommend, granting that political decision would keep the supplemental in the neighborhood of $3 billion, they consented "unanimously" (that bound the Air Force) to an immediate supplemental program of $3.48 billion for fiscal '48, and to a regular budget for fiscal '49 of about $14.5 billion in all. Practically, this provided for increasing the active strength by 411,000 men (most of them to the Army) for an aggregate of 1,795,000 and for activating sixty-six rather than fifty-five Air Force air groups. This last was to be done, however, mainly by bringing Second War B-29 bombers out of mothballs rather than by new construction. The President authorized Forrestal to present this program to Congress, but at the same time sent it to the Budget Bureau for further study.

While Forrestal was fighting before the committees for this program, the Budget Bureau was to develop its own ideas; so was Congress, which enacted and sent to the President the $822 million extra-budgetary appropriation for new aircraft, though with a proviso allowing Truman to determine the time and rate of its expenditure. The confusing jumble was not finally resolved until May 13, 1948, when the President called Forrestal, the service Secretaries, the Chiefs of Staff and the Budget Director to the White House to read them a memorandum. The rather curious gist of it was that while Truman would accept both the $3.48 billion supplemental (the least to which JCS would set their hands) and the $822 million for new aircraft, he would not fully spend them.

The memorandum (which had actually been written by Forrestal's own assistant, McNeil, to White House and Budget Bureau specifications) made Truman's position plain. In a conference of the week before Marshall had declared that "the policy of this country was based upon the assumption that there would not be war and that we should not plunge into war preparations"; Truman had strongly approved and said that "he wished to make it very clear to all present that the increases on which he had given the green light . . . were not to be construed as preparation for war — 'that we are preparing for peace and not for war.' " [1] In the memorandum [2] he now said that his address of March 17 had contemplated no more than "the development of a military posture which would give evidence of continuing firmness in world affairs" — a rather curious downgrading of a speech which had proclaimed that this was a time when "it is far wiser to act than to hesitate." He had thought that a sufficient gesture could be made on a supplemental budget of no more than $1.5 billion. When the Military Establishment had come back with a request for $3 billion, he had consented "to go along"; but when Forrestal had finally presented the compromise program of $3.48 billion, he had felt it necessary to re-examine the problem. This review had yielded two conclusions: With other demands, a continuing military expenditure of about $15 billion a year was all the economy could stand "without large-scale deficit financing"; and

---

[1] *The Forrestal Diaries*, p. 432.
[2] The report of this memorandum is from *ibid.*, pp. 436-38.

while the programs now presented were still within this limit, they would generate force levels and procurement policies which would call for much larger expenditures in later years.

If the contemplated force levels were achieved by the end of fiscal '49 either the budget for fiscal '50 would have to be enlarged far beyond the stated ceiling or else there would have to be a "demoralizing demobilization" on June 30, 1949. Truman in effect accepted the shelving of UMT in order to secure re-enactment of the draft. He also accepted the proposed supplemental and regular budgets. But speaking explicitly as Commander in Chief he ordered the Military Establishment to spend no more of these funds than would keep the total spending permanently within the $15 billion annual limit. They were to review their programs in September and again in December (just before the presentation of the fiscal '50 budget) to ensure this. Truman himself was in effect to impound the Congressional appropriation for added aircraft procurement. These policy decisions were substantially followed. Indeed, the budget for fiscal '50 was to put even more restrictive limits on military spending; and it is an irony of fate that just six days before the end of that fiscal year there was to burst the Korean crisis, which destroyed this whole budgetary and fiscal approach to the problems of military preparedness in the increasingly dangerous world. If this episode represents to any degree a triumph of the civilian over the military elements in policy, it cannot be said that the triumph was a wholly fortunate one.

## AFTER-EFFECTS OF THE 1948 CRISES

To the public, Forrestal seemed a badly battered if not a defeated figure. He had failed to establish his concept of a balanced defense structure against the insurgency of the Air Force. " 'Unification,' " as Hanson Baldwin said, "becomes a joke when the Secretary of the Air Force goes over the head of the Secretary of Defense and [to Congress] over the head of the President himself." Congress had torpedoed UMT but was showing no haste to adopt the draft act for which UMT had been sacrificed. No coherent, consistent military-political strategy for the cold war had been devised; and as the tensions of mid-March had tended to evaporate, there was less and less likelihood that any would be found. Forrestal thought that in mid-March a determined effort could have secured the re-enactment of selective service "in three days," but in late May he was still fighting for the bill, unsure of the outcome.[1] As he wrote to Marshall at this time, the Soviet peril seemed less acute, and this factor, combined with "the political stresses of an election year," had tended to produce a "dangerous complacency on the part of certain elements in the country."

FORRESTAL'S ACCOMPLISHMENTS

Yet Forrestal had accomplished something. Congress was finally to give him the renewal of selective service, and with it a modest increment of usable military strength "in being." He had helped divert both the Congress and the country from an all-out commitment to strategic air power alone; and if he had not created an Establishment capable of meeting the actual crises which were to lie ahead, he had kept the general course of military planning and military appropriations on bearings which were to preserve us from disaster. The budgetary problem was doubtless insoluble. In moments of danger the country will make sacrifices and vote huge amounts of money; when peril is not obvious it will not, and there is little which military technology can do to alter matters. But Forrestal's insistence on "balance," though much derided, was to leave us with at least the elements of those forms of military power which Korea was urgently to demand. At the end of May in a private conversation with Senator Taft he found Taft agreed that the proper allocation of funds among the services was "probably the most serious job in government," but still saying that there was a "general impression" in Congress of "waste and extravagance in military spending because of the lack of any criterion by which efficiency could be proved or disproved." [2] The Senator might, perhaps, have considered the precise limits of Congress' own responsi-

---

[1] *The Forrestal Diaries*, p. 444.
[2] *Ibid.*, p. 446.

bility here. The allocation of funds was in fact a reflection of the military criterion of what constituted waste and what constituted efficiency, in a military rather than a cost-accounting sense. If Congress could not or would not itself do the "most serious job in government" it was hardly entitled to nibble around the edges of the job done by others. But in the early summer of 1948 few statesmen were prepared to think in such terms. ·

The March crisis had already faded, but it had left its effects behind it. The Brussels Pact was a reality. All during the spring the project of a Western union, founded on the Brussels Pact, and to which the United States would contribute arms if not more solid political guarantees, had been active. The probable requirements of large "lend-lease" expenditure on military aid for Europe had been prominent in the debates over what we could afford for our own rearmament. The problem of Palestine was acute; it seemed possible for a time that the United States might have to move troops (which we did not possess) into that tortured ground. And on the last day of March there had come the first hint of what was to become the Berlin blockade.

Clay messaged that the Russians were instituting a new system for the control of traffic between the East and West Zones of Germany, amounting to the assertion of a right to inspect Western personnel and material going through the agreed corridors into the Western sectors of Berlin. It looked so serious that there was a meeting on March 31 of Forrestal, the service Secretaries and Chiefs of Staff, the Under Secretary of State (Lovett) and two State Department assistants. Several possible courses of action were considered, starting with an idea that the President might send a message direct to Stalin threatening war. Clay was ordered not to permit the Russians to inspect his trains; and the Russians stopped all trains. Food was flown into Berlin on April 1. But on the same day the Embassy in Moscow reported that while Russia had the capability of overrunning Western Europe, it could not take on the whole Western Hemisphere. On April 2 the Central Intelligence Agency extended indefinitely its prognosis of peace. Then the Russians relaxed the restrictions. Again a threatening storm appeared to have passed. But the irritations continued, until finally on June 24, 1948 — the day that Thomas E. Dewey was nominated at the Philadelphia Convention as Republican candidate for the Presidency — the Russians struck. They halted all remaining rail and road traffic between the West and the Western sectors of Berlin, leaving some 2 million Berliners almost wholly dependent on air transport for their food and fuel.

NEW POLICY ISSUES

The last six months of 1948 were to be occupied by three or four really major foreign issues, all involving serious problems of military-political strategy and none simplified by the fact that a Presidential election was in progress. There was the Berlin blockade — an immediate and lethal threat to the whole position which the Western powers had been endeavoring to erect upon the victory of 1945. There was the growing collapse of Nationalist China, which by the latter part of 1948 was both unmistakable and apparently unpreventable by any means open to Washington statesmanship. There was the initiation of a North Atlantic defensive alliance, powerfully encouraged by the Vandenberg resolution of June 11, in which the Senate in effect called for the commitment of American military strength to regional alliances under Article 51 of the United Nations Charter. And there was the issue of the military application of the nuclear weapons — an issue deeply obscured in secrecy and in the continuing dispute between the Navy and the Air Force over control of the weapons, over strategic theory and over the allocation of the reduced military appropriations.

These great issues were all intimately related. Taken together they would seem (in the clear light of hindsight) to have called for just that kind of broad, correlated and "global" policy which the National Security Act had been designed to produce. In fact, they appear to have been dealt with by the responsible officials in a piecemeal and *ad hoc* fashion, not markedly different from the way in which great issues were dealt with before 1947. CIA's information may have been better than that which had been assembled for Franklin Roosevelt, but it was clearly deficient — in relation, at least, to the ideal entertained for it, if not in relation to the limitations upon all "intelligence" in a practical world. The effect of NSC is not prominent; NSC no doubt considered the staff papers, debated policy and arrived at recommendations, but every glimpse we have been given of the actual policy-making process in this period shows Defense, State, the Budget Bureau, the White House, making the independent determinations — usually on a hasty if not extemporaneous basis — which really counted. And in this process it is not possible to discern any clearly "military" interest in conflict with any clearly "civilian" authority. On one occasion Clay, a military officer, closed the East-West frontier, which should have been a political decision. He did so, however, not in an effort to undermine State but simply because he could not get a decision of any sort out of State and felt that he had to act.

The soldiers and the civilians at least cooperated in writing off the Chinese Nationalists, since neither saw anything else to be done. They cooperated likewise in the negotiations which were to lead to the North Atlantic Treaty Organization. Here was a movement in which military and political considerations were obviously and closely interlinked, and in which military and political officers were closely associated. Indeed, it may have been the creation of NATO much more than the organization charts of the National Security Act, or any other single factor, which cemented the modern military-civil relationship. NATO was to have an effect upon internal political-military organization and plan at least comparable to its effect upon combined international planning. But not until the following year was the NATO treaty to be signed.

A NEW EUROPEAN POLICY

The problems of atomic energy were more obscure; in them were involved not only the old inter-service rivalry but differences among the politicians, the scientists, the administrators and the legislators. Here, no more than in the other fields, was there any clear decision. Yet by January 1949 there had developed here, as elsewhere, a patently new formulation of national political-military strategy, quite different from the policies we had been following in January 1948. The crisis of the Berlin blockade had been substantially mastered by means which, though military, were non-violent; the heroism of the air crews, which numbers of them demonstrated with their lives, was more effective than if it had been expended in war. For the time being, it settled the problem of Germany; both sides accepted the division of the country, with an iron curtain running between East and West, and both segments left to develop as they might within the respective power constellations. The Soviet power play, in short, had failed, and in failing was to leave a certain stability behind it.

But the Western success here was in the realm of tactics rather than of grand strategy. While mastering the blockade the United States achieved at least three fundamental strategic decisions. The first was to found the military security of the United States upon a military defense of Western Europe. The principle had been implicit in the Marshall Plan of 1947, while it was not to be translated into concrete terms until the signing of the North Atlantic Treaty in April 1949. But the powerful contribution of Senator Vandenberg, culminating in the resolution of June 11, had in effect decided the issue, and by the turn of the year the treaty negotiations were already far advanced.

CHINA WRITTEN OFF

The second strategic decision was that Nationalist China could not be saved. By the end of 1947 Mao Tse-tung knew that he had won; by the end of 1948 Washington knew it also. As early as August 13 Secretary Marshall was advising the American Embassy in Nanking that it was unlikely that the situation would permit us "at this juncture to formulate any rigid plans for our future policy in China." The policy with which the Marshall mission of two years before had been charged was now abandoned; there would be no American support for a coalition government including the Communists. The Generalissimo would have to go it alone. The State Department was mindful of the danger that he might now be driven toward coalition in order to avoid being "discarded" by his own people. The Embassy was told to "overlook no suitable opportunity to emphasize the pattern of engulfment which has resulted from coalition governments in eastern Europe." It was a little like impressing upon a mouse the fact that the cat's jaws are dangerous, without being able to offer any protection against them. Admonition seemed all that could be offered.

The policy which Dean Acheson was later accurately, if infelicitously, to describe as that of "letting the dust settle" had perforce been adopted. In September there came the first big defection of Nationalist troops to the Communists (taking with them all their American-supplied material); by the end of the year, Mao's forces, which had begun 1948 with an inferiority 1 to 3 against the Nationalists, were enjoying a 1½ to 1 superiority. As early as October 1948 Washington felt compelled to face the problem of Formosa — a year before the Generalissimo's retreat to that sanctuary. The decision was that while it was strategically important that the island should not fall into hostile hands, no strategic gain would follow from our occupying it ourselves; it was not practicable to commit any American armed forces to its defense, and it would therefore be protected against hostile occupation by diplomatic and economic means alone. This remained the China and Formosa policy down to the attack upon Korea eighteen months later.

## COMMITMENT TO ATOMIC WARFARE

The third basic strategic decision arrived at by the latter months of 1948 was never clearly stated and many of its aspects are still obscure. But it amounted to committing American defense and foreign policy ultimately to the atomic bomb — which three years before we had undertaken to banish, if possible, from international affairs. While Forrestal had been trying to get a little more conventional ground strength in being against immediate emergencies, the nuclear weapons were more and more plainly moving into the forefront of long-range strategic planning. At the Blair House conference concluded in January 1948 the United States freed itself from Britain's wartime veto power over the military use of atomic bombs.

The Key West conference of the Joint Chiefs in March had turned mainly on the question of which service would control the nuclear arsenal. The development of the bombs themselves had meanwhile been revived and was advancing rapidly under the Atomic Energy Commission. At Eniwetok in the spring of 1948 the first test shots were fired since those at Bikini two years before. Senator Edwin C. Johnson (Democrat of Colorado) let slip the statement that we now had a weapon six times as powerful as the Nagasaki bomb. Though never so stated, it seems probable that in the early planning for NATO it was considered that the atomic bombs would represent the principal American military contribution to a Western European defense.

The sudden crisis at Berlin in June seemed to make some immediate reinforcement essential, but the United States had virtually nothing with which to reinforce except the big B-29 strategic bombers, which were known throughout the world as the atom bomb carrying planes. On Sunday, June 27, 1948, the Pentagon decided to sound out both General Clay and the British on the dispatch of B-29 groups to Europe. Clay, who already had a squadron of B-29's, responded with eagerness, and his strength was raised to a group. But somewhat to the surprise of the Americans the British Foreign Office was also cordial to the suggestion, and on June 28 Truman indicated that he would favor sending two groups to the airfields in England. But at the Cabinet meeting on July 2 there was some further discussion of this. Secretary of State Marshall said that our Ambassador, Lewis Douglas, had been instructed to ask the Foreign Minister whether the latter had "fully explored and considered the effect of the arrival of these two groups in Britain upon British public opinion." Marshall himself felt that he had to weigh further "the implications and inferences" of the move. Not until July 15 did NSC recommend the dispatch of the B-29's to British bases. According to Forrestal's summary,[1] one reason for doing so was that "We have the opportunity *now* of sending these planes, and once sent they would become somewhat of an accepted fixture, whereas

[1] *The Forrestal Diaries*, pp. 455-57.

a deterioration of the situation in Europe might lead to a condition of mind under which the British would be compelled to reverse their present attitude."

Thus the atomic bombs, in effect, at least, were introduced into Europe. It has never been made clear whether the B-29's actually carried the weapons in their bomb bays, but the point is hardly material. The "custody" of the bombs was still vested in the Atomic Energy Commission, not in the Air Force; and a week after the NSC recommendation to send the bombers Forrestal was presenting the President with a "formal request of the National Military Establishment for an executive order" to transfer custody. Truman decided in the negative. He said "that the responsibility for the use of the bomb was his and that was the responsibility he proposed to keep"; as he had said earlier, he did not propose "to have some dashing lieutenant colonel decide when would be the proper time to drop one." [1] A few days later he intimated to Forrestal that "after the election" he might review the question as between the Air Force and the AEC, but the matter of custody was more legal then practical. The apparatus of atomic warfare had gone to England as well as Germany; the nuclear weapons were now central to our military and diplomatic strategy.

## THE NEWPORT CONFERENCE

Forrestal was to manifest a certain uneasiness over this development. In the summer of 1948 he would ask visitors to his office whether they thought public opinion would support the use of the bomb in war. In spite of Key West the Navy–Air Force dispute over the weapon was growing more bitter. At the end of July Forrestal concluded that another JCS conference on the issue was necessary, "and if they were not able to decide it, I would." He recalled to active duty the two leading elder statesmen of Air Force and naval aviation — General Spaatz and Vice Admiral John H. Towers — and asked them to define the issues. With the Spaatz-Towers report completed, Forrestal again wrested the Joint Chiefs from their Wash-

[1] *Ibid.*, p. 458.

ington desks, for a meeting, this time, at the Naval War College in Newport, in the latter part of August. The gain was not, it would seem, very great. While the primary control of the Air Force over atomic warfare was confirmed, it was also declared that "the exclusive authority and responsibility in a given field do not imply preclusive participation." [1] What this somewhat ponderous language appeared to mean was that the Navy was still free, as under the Key West agreement, to develop its own atomic capabilities, including the super carrier for launching atomic bombers, while the Air Force, though in sole charge of "strategic" warfare, was obligated to utilize the strategic atomic capabilities which the Navy might develop. It was not really very satisfactory, but it stilled the dispute for the rest of Forrestal's term of office.

The Secretary of Defense was still dubious of public opinion. On September 14 he assembled a dinner of twenty of the nation's leading newspaper publishers and editors, together with Marshall, Army Chief of Staff Omar Bradley, Under Secretary of State Robert A. Lovett and "Chip" Bohlen, Counsellor of the State Department. The ostensible purpose was to brief the press on the Berlin crisis and the Soviet menace; and there was much talk about the Berlin situation. But the real object may perhaps be read in Forrestal's diary note: ". . . unanimous agreement that in the event of war the American people would not only have no question as to the propriety of the use of the atomic bomb, but would in fact expect it to be used." [2]

So far had we come from the Truman declaration of October 1945 that "the hope of civilization lies in international arrangements looking, if possible, to the renunciation of the use and development of the atomic bomb." American foreign-military policy at the beginning of 1949 may be briefly summarized: Let China go, holding only Japan and Okinawa by direct military means; on the other hand, back the defense of West Germany and Western Europe with a formal military alliance; but rest our military contribution in both areas primarily upon our monopoly, as we then supposed it to be, of nuclear weapons. Other forms of military power would be cut

[1] *Ibid.*, p. 477.
[2] *Ibid.*, p. 488.

back to what could be sustained without either an increase of taxes or a risk of inflation. These basic policies were obviously neither "purely military" nor "purely civilian" in their inspiration; many factors had gone into their construction and many men and institutions had participated in the result — soldiers, diplomats, administrators, economists, congressmen, the press and public opinion.

But to a greater degree than any of them, probably, fully realized, the keystone of the arch thus erected was the atomic monopoly. Many voices, from the Finletter report onward, had warned that the monopoly could not endure long. Within the year, the keystone was to crumble; within eighteen months, the policy was to be in ruins.

# CHAPTER 6

# New Men and New Methods

## NEW DEVELOPMENTS

### NEW MEN

The early months of 1949 were to bring new men, new organizational structures, new turns of controversy to civil-military relationships. President Truman had, unexpectedly, been re-elected in November 1948, which minimized the changes in the executive branch; but he had brought back a Democratic Congress with him, thus restoring the Democratic leadership to its former seats of power in the foreign affairs, military and appropriations committees. Even in the executive branch there were inevitably new faces. Marshall, ailing, had asked for release from the burden, and in January 1949 the President announced the nomination of Dean G. Acheson as Secretary of State. Acheson was both brilliant and experienced; he was also a skillful counsellor to and executant of the underlying Truman attitudes. He lacked Marshall's enormous professional authority over the military hierarchy and at the same time lacked Marshall's prestige with Congress. As it turned out, Acheson, of wholly civilian background, was to find it much easier to work with the Pentagon than with Capitol Hill. What troubles he had with the soldiers were negligible beside his troubles with the congressmen. The soldiers recognized in him another professional, serving like themselves in an ordered structure of duly constituted authority; he irritated the congressmen, on the other hand, by his quickness of mind and dislike of cant, while he represented to them the menace of an administrative bureaucracy escaping, by its knowledge and expertness, from their efforts to maintain political control.

Forrestal was not to resign as Secretary of Defense until early March, but both his resignation and his replacement by Louis Johnson were being confidently predicted by the turn of the year; and Johnson was already in a position of power within the Military Establishment before the official change took place. Johnson had been Assistant Secretary of War a decade before, in the later years of the inter-war period, but he had never established himself, as Forrestal had done, in the affections and loyalties of the armed forces. To military men, the civilian Secretaries always come rather as ambassadors from an alien and potentially hostile world; they look eagerly for signs to indicate whether the new plenipotentiary will be basically sympathetic or hostile toward them. Johnson did not seem sympathetic.

There were other changes. When Marshall resigned, Lovett resigned as Under Secretary of State, and for a time was to pass from the scene. He was replaced by James Webb, Forrestal's "opposite number" in the Budget Bureau. The Budget Bureau went to Frank Pace (later Secretary of the Army). In March Admiral Leahy retired as Chief of Staff to the President, leaving the Joint Chiefs as, officially, only a three-man body until August, when the 1949 amendment to the National Security Act was to restore JCS as a four-man board on a permanent and statutory basis. Eisenhower, then president of Columbia University and in civilian status, was unofficially to fill the gap left by Leahy during much of this period.

## DEFENSE REORGANIZED

Reorganization of the security structure had been in prospect since the latter part of 1948. During that year the first Hoover Commis-

sion on governmental reorganization had been at work. It had first
been intended to exclude the Military Establishment from its purview, on the ground that the system was too new for proper evaluation; but the continuing strains within the Establishment and the
mounting international tension combined to alter this decision. A
"task force" under Ferdinand Eberstadt (a principal author of the
1947 act) was set up to examine the workings of the new military
system. At the same time Forrestal, conscious that the purely "coordinating" powers on which, as Secretary of the Navy, he had insisted, had left him, as Secretary of Defense, with deficient authority
to meet the real problems, was groping for some enhancement of
the Office of Secretary of Defense. The task force recommended no
drastic change in basic organization, but it, too, felt that "coordination" had not been wholly successful. It believed that the hand of
the Secretary of Defense should be strengthened by removing the
adjective "general" from his statutory authority to exercise "general
control" over the Establishment; by giving him the help of an Under
Secretary and a somewhat strengthened staff. It also strongly urged
improved accounting and administrative procedures, intended to
make more effective the Secretary's budgetary control, which was
recognized as the civilian authority's most powerful weapon over
military policy.

The Secretary of Defense would have to be upgraded. On March 5,
1949 Truman called for an amendment to the 1947 act "to accomplish two basic purposes: First, to convert the National Military
Establishment into an executive department . . . and, second, to
provide the Secretary of Defense with appropriate responsibility and
authority and with civil and military assistance adequate to fulfill
his enlarged responsibility." The result was a Senate bill, introduced
on March 16 and referred to the Military Affairs Committee, which
after extensive hearings reported a measure supporting the Presidential demand for a Department of Defense and also the Eberstadt
task force recommendations for improved budgetary and accounting
practices. The House had already started a bill embodying the
Eberstadt fiscal proposals. Much of the summer went into con-
solidating and perfecting these measures, but the Act Amending
the National Security Act of 1947 was signed on August 10, 1949.

It decreed some significant changes. The anomaly of a Secretary of Defense with no department to support him was done away with; the Military Establishment was superseded by a Department of Defense, over which the Secretary would have unqualified "direction, authority and control." He would also be given a Deputy Secretary and three Assistant Secretaries to enable him to discharge this responsibility. The three service Secretaries were removed from the National Security Council and their departments were downgraded from "executive" to "military" departments, which were to be "within" the executive Department of Defense. The Vice President was added as a statutory member to NSC; while a statutory Chairman (without vote) was added to the Joint Chiefs of Staff, thus restoring that institution as a four-man body. A Comptroller was authorized for the Department of Defense and comptrollers for the three departments; while rather elaborate provisions, worked out under Eberstadt's supervision, prescribed uniform accounting and budgetary procedures, the use of stock funds for better control of the unmanageable inventories, and a corporate type of organization for such quasi-industrial operations as shipyards or military transport systems.

JOHNSON AS SECRETARY OF DEFENSE

Thus there began the accretion in the power of the civilian Secretary of Defense which has continued steadily from that time. When Secretary Johnson took office in March 1949 he was already prepared to wield the powers which the 1949 amendment was later to give him in statutory form. Like so many civilian secretaries of the military departments before him, he was energetic, prepared to lay about him to reduce "waste and extravagance" and, admittedly, devoted to the end of maximum military efficiency only at minimum cost. But as in the case of his predecessors, neither the energy of the individual officer nor the breadth of the powers afforded him provided any automatic answer to the military problems of the time.

The former order had rested on a close collaboration and a large degree of mutual confidence between Truman, Marshall and Forrestal. It is an understatement to say that Secretaries Acheson and Johnson were not sympathetic. Whatever the reasons for his appointments, Truman was not able to create with the new men the harmonious "team" that had so well served him during the prior two years. Acheson, the skillful lawyer-diplomat, and Johnson, the intensely ambitious and at times erratic lawyer-politician, did not move along parallel lines. Acheson was relatively unpopular with Congress but enjoyed the President's complete confidence and firm support; Johnson found his most vocal support in Congress, which was basically anti-Truman even on the Democratic side, and he was relatively unsuccessful with a military hierarchy which was uncertain of his motives and sensed that his loyalty to the Administration might be limited by personal interest.

Like many men who launch their fragile rafts on the seas of politics, Johnson was to be unfairly assailed for his bad luck as well as more properly criticized for his bad judgments. A more creative Secretary of Defense might have taken a more imaginative view of the global problem in early 1949 and urged more imaginative solutions. Instead, he did what he thought he had been assigned to do; and it is hardly his fault that the assignment turned sour, leaving him, when emergency arose, under savage criticism for not having provided the armaments which the people and their political representatives had been unwilling to pay for. But if it is not to his blame, neither is it to his credit that he had no greater vision than anyone else.

He suffered unduly under the old illusion that "military" and "political" factors could be and must be rigidly compartmented. One of his earlier contributions to the smooth working of military-civilian relations was his curious order that there was to be no contact between the Departments of Defense and State except through their Secretaries. He was alarmed over "the political domination of Defense in many ways by State"; it distressed him to discover in some top-level conference that State had already been talking to his own "Indians" on whom he was relying for guidance, or that, even worse, "there were one or more men from the Military Establishment who were over in the State Department, working there, who were giving advice, which disturbed the Joint Chiefs of Staff very much because that advice was one colonel's advice over there, not seeing all the documents the Joint Chiefs had." His order disrupted that fruitful intercommunication among the "Indians" which, as Paul Nitze has pointed out, provides one of the principal powerhouses in which effective and correlated policy is generated. Amid the serious policy issues now arising, the Johnson edict could not be fully enforced and did not long endure, but it symbolizes the fragmenting effect of Johnson's advent.

The policy issues were serious. The developing debacle in China, though already producing its recriminations, was scarcely perhaps an issue, since no one had proposed an alternative to the courses being followed. The evacuation of southern Korea, which was to be completed in June 1949, had been accepted on the advice of the Joint Chiefs, and even Douglas MacArthur had approved. As he later explained his position, Korea "was not a proper place for the employment of American ground troops, . . . it involved inherent dangers to place United States ground troops in continental Asia," and they should not be left there "because they might be trapped." Formosa had already been left to merely diplomatic or economic defense. Toward the end of 1949 Chiang Kai-shek and what remained of the Chinese Nationalist armies were to take refuge on Formosa; but on four different occasions JCS was to repeat its finding that we could not undertake a military defense of the island. The policy of withdrawal and consolidation in the Far East seemed inevitable at the time; and even when the State Department on July 30 published its celebrated "White Paper," in effect pulling the last fringe of the rug out from under the Generalissimo, the popular reaction in the United States was not adverse. There was much criticism of past policies, but as Senator Vandenberg said, it was of a "post-mortem" nature. Most agreed with the *Minneapolis Tribune* that further aid to Chiang would be "Operation Rathole." It was distressing that the Generalissimo had to be abandoned, but there seemed nothing else to be done.

## THE DEVELOPMENT OF NATO

Much more formidable, at the time, were the issues surrounding the formation of the North Atlantic military alliance. NATO can hardly be regarded as a product of the "military mind," though its roots ran far back into the combined military planning of the Second War years. The civilians of the State Department who worked on it in the formative period are inclined to give the soldiers the credit; the soldiers are inclined to ascribe the parentage mainly to "Dean Acheson and his people." It seems clear that the signing of the Brussels Pact in March 1948 precipitated ideas which had been in suspension in State, Defense, Congress and even in the public mind. The Vandenberg resolution in June 1948 constituted an impressive Congressional contribution to the development of the policy.

To Brigadier General G. A. Lincoln and some of his Army colleagues, it had long been obvious that the American frontier was now on the Elbe and could be defended only by a military alliance. The British, and in particular the Royal Air Force, were even more vividly aware that their defenses "lay upon the Rhine," and the defense of Britain now meant the defense of our own advance air bases, which had been supporting, since the summer, our atomic bombing planes. The Joint Chiefs, at their conference in Newport in August 1948, had contributed two (then secret) suggestions. The first was that the Brussels Pact powers be urged to set up immediately a central military command; this was in fact done with the appointment of Field Marshall Viscount Montgomery as commander in chief for Western Europe. The second was that "in the event of war" there should be a "Supreme Allied Commander-in-Chief (West) who should be an American." [1] This was an early suggestion of the office to which General Eisenhower was to be called in 1950.

The civilians in the State Department were prompt to build on these military decisions. But the implications were not clear. Quite early there arose an argument between the "dumbbell theory" — which envisaged the alliance as simply a connecting bar between two massive centers of power, one in Western Europe and the other

[1] *The Forrestal Diaries*, Walter Millis (ed.), Viking, New York, 1951, p. 478.

in Canada and the United States — and an integrated concept in which the whole Atlantic littoral, interconnected by sea communications, would be brought into a single defensive system.

In the spring of 1949 an American military mission with State Department representation in the person of Paul Nitze journeyed to Europe to investigate the practical requirements. The results were sobering. They destroyed the "dumbbell theory," for they showed that the West European center of power did not exist. To bring Western Europe into an effective defensive position vis-à-vis the Soviet Union would call for an expenditure of something like thirty to forty billion dollars a year, which the Europeans could not possibly provide. The integrated concept of a single Atlantic community (at least reminiscent of the cultural, though not political, organization which had ruled in the eighteenth century) would have to be accepted. But if the Europeans could not find the sums required for rearmament, the American Congress certainly would not. A complete and sufficient defense could not be established; the most that seemed feasible was to bring Western Europe into a somewhat more respectable "posture" of defense. This could at least prevent a Russian sneak attack with the divisions they had ready in Central Europe; it would require them to make a considerable effort of mobilization before they could hope to overrun the West, and so insure some measure of warning. It was about the best that could be done. When the mission reported in this sense, it was something of a shock to the Pentagon. The defense of the West had to be unitary, but there was no visible means of filling it with firm military content. The NATO treaty was signed on April 4, 1949. But through the ensuing year, as the ratifications were exchanged and the machinery put into operation, NATO was to retain much more the character of a political and economic than of a military alliance.

## THE GREAT DEBATE

### THE FISCAL '50 BUDGET

Another major issue of these months revolved around the redesign of the military system to bring its costs within the limits of "what the economy could afford." Here everybody — civilians and military, the Congress, the White House, the departments, the staffs, the newspaper editors and columnists — was to take a hand; controversy was to rage violently, with an arresting disregard of the actual strategic problems then visible on the horizon. The underlying issue was, of course, Truman's continuing $15 billion ceiling on defense expenditure; but it was rarely addressed in these terms, while it had a baffling tendency to split (like the uranium atom) into many highly charged sub-issues, each with its own constellation of shattering effects.

The separate budget estimates for fiscal '50, as developed in the latter part of 1948, had totted up to an "impossible" $30 billion. Forrestal's budget officers had worked this down to just under $17 billion, but the White House stuck to the ceiling, and the budget presented in January 1949 called for only $14.2 billion. Nor was that all. The President had accepted the then current (fiscal '49) budget only on the proviso that it was to be reviewed to ensure that the services were not building empires which would require greatly increased expenditure later on. As a result of this review he imposed, in December, drastic limits not merely on the expenditure but on the force levels for which the services would be permitted to plan. The Air Force, which had never abandoned its goal of seventy groups, was cut back to forty-eight. The Navy suffered similar blows, but that did not prevent each service from feeling that the other was grabbing the money that should have gone into its own weapons system.

CARRIERS AND BOMBERS

The Air Force was particularly resentful of the Navy's giant carrier, capable of launching the atomic bombers which the Air Force regarded as solely in its province. "Uncle Carl" Vinson of Georgia, who as chairman of House Naval Affairs had long, benevolently and expertly presided over the Navy's interests, was now chairing the combined House Armed Services Committee. On the first day of the session, to the Navy's shock, he introduced a bill not only authorizing the seventy-group Air Force but also prohibiting the

Navy from building any super flat-tops without express authorization from Congress. A strong movement developed in both houses to insist upon the seventy-group Air Force regardless of what might happen to the rest of the military system. As Representative Clarence Cannon, chairman of the House Appropriations Committee, was later to put it:

> If there should be another war, . . . the outcome would be decisively determined by atomic warfare in three weeks or less. But . . . neither the Army nor the Navy could reach Moscow with the first atomic bomb in three weeks — or three years. Only land-based bombers could reach Moscow with a lethal charge. . . . The only way to avoid war is to have available at any instant the means of striking swiftly. . . . And the atomic bomb, serviced by land-based bombers, is the only weapon which can ensure that protection.

It was a strategic theory which the Navy could not accept; and the Navy more and more felt itself under unfair and unwarranted attack. The Navy began to prepare a counter-offensive. In January Captain Arleigh A. Burke (the redoubtable "Thirty-one Knot Burke" of the Pacific war) was assigned as "Assistant Chief of Naval Operations in charge of the Organizational Research and Policy Section known as Op-23." The principal function of Op-23 — whose precise history remains somewhat obscure — was to do battle with the Air Force.

At Norfolk on February 18 the Navy ceremoniously laid the keel of its giant carrier, U.S.S. *United States*. On March 1 the Air Force riposted with an even more spectacular development. Utilizing the new in-flight refueling techniques, it flew a heavy bomber non-stop around the world. While Air Force sources continued to criticize the super carrier, Navy sources grew more caustic on the Air Force's preoccupation with long-range strategic bombing, and in particular on the big, six-engine B-36 bombers which it was making the backbone of its Strategic Air Command.

These arguments grew no less acrimonious as Louis Johnson took over and began to wield the economy ax. His problem was not only to hold down the fiscal '50 budget, then on its way through Congress, but to plan the foundations for that of fiscal '51. In early April the Joint Chiefs again adjourned to Key West to discuss matters with General Eisenhower, who was there recuperating from an intestinal disorder. Though Eisenhower was still at Columbia University, he had continued, as has been said, in the role of a military elder statesman and unofficial chairman of JCS. Johnson joined the conference on April 10. One of the subjects discussed was the Navy's giant carrier, whose keel had just been laid. Eisenhower, who was usually rather cool toward the Navy, apparently joined with Bradley and Hoyt Vandenberg (the Army and Air Force Chiefs of Staff) in concluding that the big carrier was a development which could be dispensed with. After some further consultations, which did not, unfortunately, include the Secretary of the Navy, Johnson laid this suggestion before the President and received Truman's authorization to proceed with it. On April 23 the Secretary of Defense cancelled the big carrier. The explosion was immediate and violent.

Johnson had insufficiently appreciated the Navy's already embittered state of mind, the symbolic as well as practical importance of the carrier to the future development of the Navy, and the delicacy of the balance of forces over which he was presiding. The Secretary of the Navy, John L. Sullivan, was meeting a speaking engagement in Texas when the news reached him; he flew back to Washington and, pausing only long enough to be briefed by the Chief of Naval Operations, Admiral Louis E. Denfeld, sent in his resignation. A period of vicious bureaucratic infighting was to ensue. In the office of Dan Kimball, Under Secretary of the Navy, a civilian assistant began to assemble an all-out attack on the Air Force's B-36. Cedric R. Worth was a former newspaperman and reserve naval officer. He had help from some active naval officers as well as from the Glenn L. Martin airplane firm, which had seen some of its own orders cancelled to permit a larger procurement of B-36's from the rival Consolidated-Vultee. But Worth testified that he had told his superior, Kimball, nothing about what he was doing. His reason was interesting: "My opinion was that he [Kimball] should not know. . . . Because it would do him no good. . . . He would have to tell me not to do it." Worth was "sure" of this, yet he went ahead anyway. It provides a small, vivid glimpse into the actualities of policymaking in Washington at this time.

Worth's memorandum was anonymous. It not only argued that the B-36 was an inefficient weapon, incapable of performing the strategic mission which the Air Force had assigned to it, but advanced spicier allegations to the effect that improper influence had contributed to its procurement. (Johnson was a former counsel to Atlas, Floyd Odlum's holding company which controlled Consolidated-Vultee.) Worth, with the assistance of some active naval officers, began to circulate this paper. In May he gave it to Representative James Van Zandt (Republican of Pennsylvania), a former Marine officer and a strong supporter of the naval interest. On May 26 Van Zandt brought in a resolution for a special investigation of the disturbing "rumors" which were rife concerning the B-36 and the B-36 contracts. Vinson quickly moved to secure the investigation for his own Armed Services Committee (of which Van Zandt was a member), but the matter could no longer be suppressed.

Unable to do anything about the disease, Secretary Johnson struggled only more frantically with the symptoms. In mid-April he issued his "gag" order controlling public information and centralizing in his own office the security review of the outgivings of the warring services. For years each service had been accustomed to observe its own annual "day" as an occasion on which to celebrate its achievements and make propaganda for itself. After Army Day (April 6) Johnson abolished the separate observances and decreed a unified Armed Forces Day to be celebrated thereafter on November 11. In June he ordered the service departments to slash their public information personnel by nine tenths and to transfer much of the surplus to his own Public Information Officer staff in the Office of the Secretary of Defense. However salutary, such palliatives could neither still the service quarrel (easily waged from the retired list when the active officers were silenced) nor answer the fundamental question of how best to organize a military establishment that must not cost more than $15 billion a year.

## CONTAINMENT AND LIMITED WAR

In July 1949 George Kennan, then head of the State Department's Policy Planning Staff, sought to warn the Joint Chiefs that while they were more and more committing themselves to a strategy of all-out atomic retaliation, the existing policy of "containment" implied the likelihood of limited, local wars to which this strategy would be inapplicable. Kennan wanted two, possibly more, fully mechanized ground divisions to be available in any emergencies for which an atomic holocaust would be an excessive answer. Not everyone in State agreed with Kennan — the force seemed too weak for Germany and no one had foreseen Korea — but the point was academic. The reply came back through the JCS staff that economy put any such ideas out of the question.

While the Atomic Energy Commission was at work on an extensive program of weapons expansion, Secretary Johnson was laboring still further to reduce the allowances for the conventional forces, both in the fiscal '50 budget (still in Congress) and in the planning for fiscal '51. He was claiming that he could save a billion dollars in management and organizational reform — in just "cutting the fat" — but when in early August he set up a special National Defense Management Commission in the Defense Department, the most it could find for him by such relatively painless means was hardly half that amount. To get under the ceiling by the target date of June 30, 1950 would compel cutting far below the "fat" into the bone and sinew. It was soon apparent that the Navy was to be a major subject of the surgery. Its carrier air groups were to be cut from fourteen to six; the eight large carriers in commission were to be reduced to four, and there were to be further large reductions in active strengths. The Secretary had made a concession; he had promised to modernize two more of the *Essex* class carriers, thus enabling them to handle jet airplanes. But this would not, at that period, restore the atomic capability of U.S.S. *United States.* Johnson thought the Navy ought to be satisfied with the conversions; the Navy thought that Johnson was finally excluding it from the possibility of development into a decisive weapon in the warfare of the future.

The truth was that the really basic strategic problems — of atomic weapons, conventional forces, strategic as against tactical air, Navy as against Air Force — were simply going unanswered. Even less was any broad answer being provided for the problem of fitting our military establishment, whatever its character, into a grand military-political national strategy. We had surmounted the Berlin crisis with the airlift. We would meet the remaining dangerous situations, like that in Greece, or potentially dangerous situations, like those in Korea, Formosa or Indo-China, with moral support, military and economic aid and advice, but not with troops. When the NATO treaty was signed in April 1949, few contemplated any significant American military commitment to the alliance. At the end of June the last American forces, except for a Military Assistance and Advisory Group contingent, evacuated South Korea; and on July 30 the State Department published the White Paper on China which left that unhappy country to its fate until the dust should settle. And none of this aroused any important public alarm or protest — at the time.

### THE HOUSE COMMITTEE HEARINGS

In early August the House Armed Services Committee, under the shrewd eye of its chairman, Vinson, opened its first series of hearings on the B-36. This was to be an investigation only into the charges made by the "anonymous document" and repeated by Representative Van Zandt, not into the larger strategic issues involved. A long procession of Air Force officials laid bare the whole history of the B-36 and the B-36 contracts. The huge plane actually dated from before our entry into the Second War, since design had begun in 1941; and the testimony made it rather plain that it was much less than a satisfactory solution for the problem of an intercontinental atomic strategic bomber. But it was also rather plain that the B-36 was the best thing available as a stop-gap until a long-range jet bomber could be developed; while, as Vinson summed it up, there had not been "one iota, one scintilla of evidence . . . that would support the charges that collusion, fraud, corruption, influence or favoritism played any part whatever in the procurement of the B-36 bomber."

That sufficiently finished Mr. Cedric Worth. But the Navy, except for Worth, had not been heard; the committee had not considered the Navy's criticism of the Air Force's strategic concepts or of the policies which were being adopted in consonance with those concepts. The Navy after having been convicted, in effect, of circulating a scurrilous document of no merit, had been denied any opportunity to state its case. The hearings ended on August 25. Vinson, while aware of the more serious issues, intended to defer further hearings until the atmosphere might be calmer. Boiler pressures in the naval sections of the Pentagon, however, rose toward the bursting point, and in September the explosion came.

Captain John G. Crommelin, Jr., a wartime naval aviator then serving on the JCS Joint Staff, was a first-class combat pilot and leader, a man unshakable in his courage but somewhat deficient in his political judgment. On September 10 he called in the reporters; he told them that he had assisted in drafting the Worth document. He went on to say that the Pentagon was "emasculating the offensive potentiality of the United States Navy"; that the Navy was "being nibbled to death"; that "this means my naval career. But I hope this will blow the whole thing open and bring on another Congressional investigation." Two days later Fleet Admiral William F. Halsey (then in retirement) ostentatiously supported Crommelin. The whole thing was blown open. But there was to intervene a far more shattering detonation than Crommelin's. On September 23 President Truman announced that an atomic explosion had taken place in the Soviet Union. The Russians had the bomb.

THE SOVIET BOMB

There was to ensue one of the truly great debates of our times over military and foreign policy, perhaps more significant to history than the great debates over the League of Nations, over the approach to the Second World War or over the United Nations. But in two ways it was extraordinary: it was almost wholly secret, hidden in the upper recesses of government; while its decisions, insofar as they were arrived at, were administrative rather than political in character. The Congress, the press and the public — the great organs of modern democratic government — were only peripheral parties to an argument upon which the whole future of American and Western society might well turn. Public opinion, in the autumn of 1949, did not even seem to be greatly interested; after all, this was only a test "explosion" and it might be years before the Russians turned it into a usable weapons system of transportable bombs, carriers, defenses and all the rest. But to the responsible men in government the shock was extreme, even though the event had long been foreseen.

They knew that once a Soviet atomic industry had been successfully started, the materials and weapons would proliferate as rapidly as might be desired; it was a question only of the money and energy put into the development, and none doubted that the Soviet Union would put in all the money and energy it required. They knew that at a stroke the whole military-political situation had been transformed. Probably not many had fully realized the extent to which the atomic arsenal had already been built into our own defense structure, or the extent to which the wisdom of this policy had rested upon the supposed monopoly. So long as we alone wielded the thunderbolt, we could afford a Jovian disregard of minor and passing developments; we could skeletonize our active forces, "disengage" in the Far East or look with complacency upon the military weakness of Western Europe. Now we were, or certainly soon would be, a Jove against whom the thunderbolts could be flung back. The potential holocausts upon which we had come more and more to rely as our principal instruments of military power would now be mutual. The whole international policy equation had been abruptly and terribly altered.

Here was a central issue in civil-military policy — that is, in the adjustment of the civil to the military requirements in the life of a modern state. What was to be done? How was the United States, regarded as a great community owing responsibility — moral, political, military and economic — to its membership, to deal with a new development in history, at once appallingly dangerous and appallingly uncertain in its possibilities? To thoughtful men, whether in uniform or out of it, the announcement of September 23, 1949 presented a crisis — intellectual, moral and technical — far transcending the usual crises of international affairs. In the record of the AEC hearings *In the Matter of J. Robert Oppenheimer* (held in the spring of 1954), one may read much of the history of the truly agonizing reappraisals, soul-searchings, often passionate differences and suspicions of motive, among the men charged with the high direction of American policy in the autumn of 1949. It is a great and, in some respects, tragic record of the actual processes of policy formation in the modern age. It records with precision the manner in which some of the more basic decisions of our times were arrived at; at the same time making clear the extent to which all these responsible officers had to operate in secret, to make their decisions in secret, to arrive at judgments on which they knew the nation's if not civilization's future might depend without the political officer's normal support in public argument and expression.

## THE B-36 HEARINGS REOPENED

The public knew virtually nothing about the discussions — so vital to its own welfare and survival — which went on in JCS, NSC and AEC. The accident of the B-36 imbroglio did provide a public forum in which at least some of these issues were debated in October. Vinson had ended the first series of hearings in the latter part of August. On October 5, a week and a half after the announcement of the Soviet explosion, he reconvened the House Armed Services Committee, crisply closed out the charges against the B-36 and the B-36 contracts, and on the following day opened hearings into the Navy's strategic case. It was well-organized and forcefully presented. The Navy had brought Admiral Arthur W. Radford, then commanding the Pacific Fleet, back to Washington to mount the demonstration; and he did it with thoroughness and effect.

The committee had originally posed a series of specific questions: whether the B-36 was a satisfactory weapon; whether the decision to cancel the big carrier was sound; whether the Air Force was concentrating unduly on strategic as against tactical aviation; whether the JCS procedures in weapons evaluation (in which, it seemed to the critics, any two services appeared to have the right to decide whether a weapon desired by the third service was necessary to it) were valid; the effectiveness of strategic bombing and the wisdom of the concept underlying it. For six and a half days a procession of naval officers were to testify to these subjects. Radford marshalled his forces as if they were a task group, with technicians, strategists and naval administrators following one another upon the stand in a prearranged order. Radford's own opening statement was powerful:

> The kind of war we plan to fight must fit the kind of peace we want. We cannot look to military victory alone, with no thought to the staggering problems that would be generated by the death and destruction of an atom blitz. . . . The B-36 has become, in the minds of the American people, a symbol of a theory of warfare — the atom blitz — which promises them a cheap and easy victory if war should come. . . .
>
> Less than 6 percent of Air Force research and development funds is earmarked for tactical and fighter types. . . . Strategic bombing should be a primary role of the Air Force. However, the United States is not sound in relying on the so-called strategic bombing concept to its present extent . . . In the minds of our citizens this fallacious concept promises a short-cut to victory. Our citizens must realize that its [sic] military leaders cannot make this promise.

Under "any theory of war," the admiral argued, the B-36 was a "bad gamble with national security." It was relatively slow and vulnerable; this would force it to operate only at night and from high altitudes, which would make precision bombing of military targets impossible and compel it to rely for its effect on general "population" and "area" bombing. Even so, did it have "a reasonable chance to attack successfully without sustaining unacceptable losses? If it has not, the B-36 is a billion-dollar blunder." Admiral R. A. Ofstie, denying that the Navy wanted to "encroach" upon the Strategic Air Command's preserve, was even more blunt: "We consider [that] the strategic air warfare as practised in the past and as proposed in the future is militarily unsound and of limited effect, morally wrong and decidedly harmful to the stability of a post-war world."

Admiral Ofstie advanced an argument that was to assume added force in later years:

> Much emphasis has been placed upon the instantaneous character of an offensive using atomic bombs. Among laymen this has produced an illusion of

power and even a kind of bomb-rattling jingoism. . . . The idea that it is within our power to inflict maximum damage to the enemy in a short time without serious risk to ourselves creates the delusion that we are stronger than we actually are. . . . In recent weeks we have been made aware of the fact that we are not alone in our possession of the atomic weapon, which had been the basis of this illusory strength.

Through the following days the naval witnesses drove home their case. There was not much discussion of the Soviet atomic explosion, but the grim fact edged everything that was said. Unfortunately, the public paid relatively little attention. The Air Force was allowed a couple of days for rebuttal testimony, and the hearings finally wound up on October 19 with General Bradley's celebrated outburst against the Navy: "Our military forces are one team — in the game to win regardless of who carries the ball. This is no time for 'fancy Dans' who won't hit the line with all they have on every play unless they can call the signals." It was neither fair nor discerning. The Navy had advanced a serious criticism of ruling strategic ideas at a moment when those ideas were in a state of utmost uncertainty and when every high policy agency in Washington was looking frantically for guidance. Bradley knew no more than Radford or Ofstie or anyone else what the "rules of the game" might prove to be or what the next play should be. Yet he reduced the Navy's case to a mere "admiral's revolt" — a rebellion by disgruntled sailors — and so the public was largely to accept it. The committee produced a judicious report, but it attracted little attention. Crommelin was first exiled to the West Coast, and when he refused to keep silent was rusticated to his home in Alabama. Vinson had stipulated that no Navy witness was to suffer for his testimony, but after Congress adjourned the President was to manifest his displeasure by abruptly relieving Denfeld, the Chief of Naval Operations. The Navy was in the doghouse. The strategic issues which it had raised were still unsettled.

Such was the result of the principal public debate. The private debate had been intense from the beginning. Unfortunately, it was to take shape around an issue which probably should not have been the central issue and which, if the various policy-forming mechanisms of the National Security Act—NSC, NSRB, JCS and the rest of them—had operated as it had been hoped that they would operate, would not have been the central issue. The real question was of the broadest possible kind. It was a question of how to reorganize American military and diplomatic policy to deal with the fact that the Soviet Union had unlocked the secret of atomic energy. In the fall of 1949 it came down to something much more limited: should the United States proceed with an all-out, "crash" program to develop a hydrogen bomb?

## THE SILENT DEBATE: PUBLIC ATTACKS

### DEBATE OVER THE HYDROGEN BOMB

From the early days it had been known to everybody (including the Russians) that a thermonuclear or "fusion" reaction could produce enormously greater releases of energy than the fission reaction, on which the wartime effort had centered. Work had never ceased on the thermonuclear reaction, but it had been overshadowed in the latter 1940's by the successes with the development of fission weapons. In the summer of 1949 the AEC had been developing a major program for expanding research and production facilities, for improving the quantity and quality of the atomic stockpile. We had the fission weapons, and saw great opportunities for further development. The fusion weapon, on the other hand, was something completely vague; it was a theoretic possibility, but no one had brought it within range of practical engineering and no one even knew whether it could ever be produced. It was an idea which might prove to be totally impossible of realization. It was the "Super" which had often been discussed, on which a lot of work had been done, but which in October 1949 remained a theory only.

But when the Russians exploded their atomic device in the late summer of 1949, "Super" leapt at once into many minds. The Russians had knocked our strategic position into a cocked hat; we had lost our "lead" in atomic energy, and the best way to regain it was at once to produce the thermonuclear giant weapon. Many people converged upon Washington. Edward Teller, the nuclear physicist most deeply committed to the "Super" program, hastened to the Capital; so did L. W. Alvarez and E. O. Lawrence. They button-holed everybody, from scientists to senators, sufficiently "cleared" to be talked to. Vandenberg, the Chief of the Air Staff, put the pressure on the Joint Chiefs. "On October 14, 1949, the Joint Chiefs met with the Joint Congressional Committee on Atomic Energy, where General Vandenberg, speaking for the Joint Chiefs, strongly urged the development of this thermonuclear weapon." The Atomic Energy Commission was at the time perfecting its large expansion program for atomic weapons. In a memorandum "about October 5 or 6" Lewis Strauss, one of the Commissioners, urgently recommended that this program should be supplemented by "an all-out program on the H-bomb."

Opinion in the Air Force was by no means unanimous, but most had a "very definite interest in going forward with it if indeed it proved technically feasible." But nobody knew whether it was technically feasible or not, "so there was a very animated controversy about it," as John von Neumann said, which "lasted for months." Though the answer may have seemed obvious to the less complicated minds among the military, the problem was actually an intricate one. On October 11 David E. Lilienthal, chairman of AEC, and under pressure from Strauss, addressed a letter to Oppenheimer, who was then head of AEC's General Advisory Committee. His question was whether, in the light of the Soviet explosion, AEC's planned expansion program "constitutes doing everything that it is reasonably possible for us to do for the common defense and security."

Though not so phrased, this was in effect asking whether to undertake a thermonuclear crash program. And while this was in the first instance a technical question, it was clearly more than merely technical; inevitably military and political if not "moral" factors must enter into any responsible judgment. The General Advisory Committee met for two days, October 28 and 29, 1949, to thresh out the issues. As to feasibility, their best guess — it was scarcely more than that — was that there was slightly better than a 50-50 chance of success. (This, it may be noted, was overoptimistic; no success was ever achieved with "Super" as such.) A crash program seemed to mean two things: a much heavier concentration of effort on thermonuclear research, and a start upon the production facilities which would provide the required materials, such as heavy waters, in the amounts which it was then thought would be necessary if the problem were solved. The first meant the diversion of scarce scientific manpower from the expanded atomic program which was just about to get under way; the second meant the diversion of production facilities from the manufacture of the plutonium needed for the new atomic bombs.

The atomic program was highly promising. It was in fact vastly to enlarge the atomic stockpile, to raise the energy of the fission weapon to twenty-five times the power of the Hiroshima and Nagasaki bombs, greatly to improve the efficiency of production processes and to develop whole "families" of lesser and militarily more usable atomic weapons. Was it even militarily sound to cripple a program with such possibilities in order to launch another for which there was no certainty of success and which, even it it did succeed, might produce only a bomb too ponderous to be delivered and too colossally destructive to be of any true military utility?

On technical grounds alone there was an argument against the crash program. But undeniably the serious and responsible men who composed the General Advisory Committee took more than technical factors into consideration. A super bomb was no real response to the problem created by the atomic bomb race; it would simply raise the contest to new and more appalling levels. If the United States launched a massive thermonuclear effort, it was certain that the Russians would do the same; if the United States succeeded, it was all but certain that Russian science would succeed as well. The Russians were then believed to be a long way behind in the atomic race; a thermonuclear race would give them the opportunity to "cut the corner," much as had happened in the pre-World War I naval race when Britain's development of the dreadnought battleship rendered obsolete her great existing preponderance of battleships and thus enabled Germany to draw abreast at a bound.

Moreover, behind such calculations there lay a deep feeling that a "bigger bang" was no solution for a problem created by the fact that the "bang" was already far to big for society to survive it. There was a troubled, perhaps a moralistic, hope that the development of war could somehow be diverted from the terrible atomic "strike" upon the world's great population centers into less totally destructive methods. Oppenheimer was to say later that at the time he over-estimated the effect which our refraining from the crash program would have on Russia, and underestimated the likelihood that the Russians would develop a thermonuclear bomb regardless of our action. But some of his colleagues do not agree. Obviously, the point cannot be resolved. At all events, the General Advisory Committee, while assuming that the existing thermonuclear research would continue, unanimously reported against a crash program for the "Super."

On November 9, AEC transmitted its Advisory Committee's report to the President, at the same time setting forth its own views. AEC felt that this was a policy issue which only the President could decide, and therefore made no recommendation as a body, merely stating the individual conclusions of the members. Commissioners Strauss and (to a lesser degree) Gordon Dean favored the crash program; Commissioners Lilienthal, Pike and Smyth were against the crash program "at this time." Truman's response was to appoint Lilienthal, Acheson and Louis Johnson as a special committee of the National Security Council to advise him.

Acheson urged a broad review of the entire political and strategic problem through NSC. This study, with the work largely being done at the top staff level in NSC, State and Defense, was eventually energetically pressed, but it took several months to complete. Meanwhile, through the NSC special committee, Lilienthal was for the first time coming in close touch with both the military and the State Department. He was shocked when General Bradley told him "rather flatly that they had no reserve except the A bomb in the event of aggression against us any place in the world. . . . We had, it seemed to me, falsely relied upon the security of merely a stockpile of A bombs." It made him less rather than more eager to plunge into the thermonuclear unknown, and more interested in the broad review of military policy stimulated by the State Department. Within the special committee he was inclined to feel that the crash program should wait upon the completion of this major reappraisal; Acheson thought that the H-bomb program could be begun simultaneously with the work of reappraisal; Johnson, like most of the military, wanted no delay. In the end, they reached a unanimous report, the gist of which, according to Truman, was "that I should direct the AEC to take whatever steps were necessary to determine whether we could make and set off a hydrogen weapon. Concurrently with this, the Special Committee recommended a reexamination of our foreign policy and our strategic plans both diplomatic and military." The crash program had been adopted. On January 31, 1950 the President announced publicly: "I have directed the Atomic Energy Commission to continue its work on all forms of atomic weapons, including the so-called hydrogen or super-bomb. . . . We shall also continue to examine all those factors that affect our program for peace and this country's security." [1]

Nothing was to turn out as had been foreseen. While the Los Alamos laboratory immediately stepped up its work on "Super," putting about a fifth of its personnel on the project, the atomic program did not suffer. It was realized that the proposed big Savannah River production plant could be designed for a dual purpose; this, together with great improvements in the efficiency of the plutonium plants, promised to yield enough material for both programs, especially since so little progress was being made in the research on the thermonuclear bomb. Early in the year a new series of calculations appeared to demonstrate that "Super" was an impossibility, and it was in fact never built. The work lagged, while the atomic program went rapidly forward. But then in May 1951, amid a series of atomic test shots, a device was fired at Eniwetok which achieved a fusion reaction; it was not of itself of use in a weapon, but it revived the interest and the excitement. Gordon Dean, now acting chairman of AEC, felt the time had come to pull the whole H-program together; and in June 1951 (just as the Korean truce talks were

---

[1] Harry S. Truman, *Memoirs*, Vol. 2, *Years of Trial and Hope*, Doubleday, Garden City, 1956, p. 309.

beginning) there was a two-day convocation under Oppenheimer at Princeton of everyone with ideas upon the subject. It was to this that Teller and others brought a "wholly new approach"; and after two days of intense discussion and blackboard work, "everyone in the room" was convinced that "at least we had something for the first time that looked feasible." Dean himself was so enthusiastic that four days later he made a commitment for a new plant — for which he had no money available. The first megaton device was fired little more than a year later, and the first Soviet thermonuclear explosion took place in August 1953; the first "droppable" American bomb was fired in the following March.

NSC 68

Meanwhile, the broad NSC policy review was being developed through the winter and spring; embodied in a paper known as NSC 68, it was completed in early April 1950. As a policy-making or policy-formulating agency, the National Security Council with its staff seems still to have been in a somewhat indeterminate position. For advice on the crash program Truman had not used NSC itself; he had used its machinery to set up an *ad hoc* committee. For a major, long-term policy review, such as was provided in NSC 68, where most of the groundwork had to be laid in the secondary or policy-planning levels of the departments concerned, NSC could lend a certain coherence to the interdepartmental staff work (of a kind that must have gone on anyway) and place upon the product a stamp of authority that would otherwise have been lacking. Those who worked on the project feel that NSC provided a convenient mechanism, a probably useful development in the now lengthy history of interdepartmental policy planning. But it had not yet attained the rigidity of organization and performance which the Eisenhower Administration was to give it; while the true role of its own staff in the processes of policy-formulation remained deeply hidden within the growing secrecy of all governmental processes.

For it is striking that this major effort at the reorganization of American military and foreign policy in the light of the Soviet explosion was carried out in profound secrecy. Like the inner arguments over the H-bomb policy, NSC 68 was never published. In general, it analyzed the new world situation and called for large expansions of our military, diplomatic and economic effort in meeting it. State wanted to publish the paper, and, indeed, prepared a version for the purpose with only a few obviously essential security deletions. But Defense objected, for the interesting reason that if published it might constitute a commitment — an indication of what our ablest military and political thinkers considered a minimum answer to the actual international problem — and if the commitment, for budgetary or other reasons, could not thereafter be met, the consequences would be embarrassing. This would seem to have limited the effectiveness of the paper — major policy determinations can never be operative without public understanding and support.

The secret decisions as to both the thermonuclear and the atomic arsenals were intensely practical decisions and, whether right or wrong, were to have important consequences for the nation and the world. The conclusions of NSC 68, more general or theoretical in character, were to have less visible result. Yet they also had a later history. After the completion of NSC 68 in April, the military planning staffs were put to work to translate its recommendations into military budgets and force levels. Whether the policy paper or the resultant plans would have sufficed to break through the Truman budgetary ceiling when it came to the hard business of writing the fiscal '52 budget seems highly dubious. But the question was not to be put to the test. A little more than two months after the completion of NSC 68 the Russians and North Koreans effectively shattered the Truman ceiling. The military staff work begun in the spring of 1950 was to provide the foundation for the enormous expansion of the military structure which took place in late 1950 and 1951.

THE ANTI-COMMUNIST CAMPAIGN

Thus in the fall of 1949 and the winter of 1950 the nation had faced a major tranformation in the world scene and its administrators had secretly made or prepared drastic changes in its military and foreign policies. Yet the first six months of 1950 were to pass in a mood of tranquility. The President and his Secretary of Defense continued to hold the active forces to a rigid and crippling economy. The occupation forces in Germany continued to be not only trained but deployed as an internal constabulary. Those in Japan were largely skeletonized, the divisions being cut from three regiments each to two, and left without their heavier tanks because Japanese bridges would not carry them. There was, to say the least, complacency as to any Communist threat upon the international world. Unfortunately, a divisive excitement over the internal menaces of communism was rising to altogether new heights. On January 25 Alger Hiss (indicted over a year before) was finally convicted, in his second trial, of perjury — a verdict which most took as proof that he had been a dangerous Soviet spy. Less than a month later Senator Joseph R. McCarthy opened his meteoric career as an anti-Communist with his speech at Wheeling, charging that there were "200 card-carrying Communists" — or some such number — in the State Department. The charge was patently absurd, but fortune favored the Senator. In March, the British arrested the German-born physicist, Klaus Fuchs, as an atomic spy. Fuchs confessed to having transmitted atomic information to the Russians in 1945 and 1946.

The sequence was overpowering. As far back as 1945, Igor Gouzenko, a code clerk in the Soviet Embassy in Ottawa, had defected and revealed a good deal about the Soviet espionage systems in America; the British scientist, Alan Nunn May, had been convicted for imparting what seemed rather minor atomic information to the Russians. It was not taken too seriously at the time. But then in August 1949 the Soviets fired their explosion. In January Hiss was convicted on what amounted to a charge of espionage. In February McCarthy announced that the State Department was riddled with Communists. And in March the British arrested Fuchs, who confessed. Could anything be more obvious than that the Russians owed their mastery of the bomb to the theft of "the secret" and that the major shock they had administered to our diplomatic and defense position was ascribable solely to Communist treason? The inference was natural and persuasive; the fact that it was certainly exaggerated and oversimplified and perhaps untrue escaped most Americans at the time.

The image arose of a vast and lethal fog of Communist conspiracy, infiltration, espionage and betrayal, at work everywhere in the national community and especially in the Democratic Administration. That this was seriously to distort the more normal processes of policy formation in the military and diplomatic fields can scarcely be doubted. Tightened "security" measures were to divorce the public even further from participation in major policy issues, of which they might now be kept in almost total ignorance. Public confidence in the State Department was seriously undermined. The collapse in China, which had been rather generally accepted as inevitable at the time it occurred, was now explained on the grounds of communism or pro-communism within the Department. State was weakened in the public eye by comparison with Defense; and in a nation supposedly devoted to the principle of civilian control, almost any military advice or decision took priority — with public and Congress — over those of the diplomats or civil administrators. The seeds of much of this were planted in the opening months of 1950. The noxious weeds of division and suspicion which sprang from them were to proliferate through the storms that lay immediately ahead.

# Truman and MacArthur

## THE BEGINNING OF THE KOREAN WAR

The Korean War was to bring the most dramatic, the most complex and most illuminating issue of civil-military relationships since the end of the Second World War. It was not often clearly argued in these terms, and the central episode, the relief of General MacArthur, never in fact represented a direct clash between the military and the civil power in the state. It was in part a clash between the traditionally independent field general and the Washington top military command. But mainly it was a clash between personalities and partisan political interests. Had any other of the leading American generals of the time been in command in Tokyo, or had another president — particularly another president of a different party — been in office, it could hardly have arisen. Turning as largely as it did upon the individual men and the particular political situation involved, it was not typical of American military-civil development; it would be somewhat idle to base institutional or organizational changes upon this almost unique episode.

Yet it is still instructive in the basic principles of civil and military authority in the modern democratic state. All elements which go to make up total national policy were involved in it — the troops, who must be prepared to die in support of great national ends; the theater commander who not only directs them but is responsible for them; the high command at the center anxiously aware of its responsibility for the broader political and economic consequences of its military decisions; the diplomats whose political achievements must justify and make good the expenditure of military force; the Chief Executive, who must see that military and political means are kept in consonance toward viable national ends; the Congress and the people, who are supposed to be the final regulators of the entire process. The events of late 1949 and early 1950 were a case history in the reaction of a modern democracy to a revolutionary, but long-range, shift in the international power balances. Korea was a case history in its reaction to an immediate military crisis.

The attack of June 24, 1950 upon South Korea came as a virtually complete surprise. The possibility, of course, had been long foreseen. Only a day or two before, John Foster Dulles (then a special representative of Dean Acheson's State Department) had been inspecting the South Korean defenses along the 38th Parallel. The situation had seemed uneasy and dangerous ever since the withdrawal of the American occupation forces in the previous year. But the recognized peril had not entered into the substance of American military and diplomatic planning. Rather like the Japanese attack on Pearl Harbor, it was a danger accepted in theory but never translated into practical policy. In his later famous speech before the National Press Club in Washington in January 1950, Acheson had omitted both South Korea and Formosa from his description of the American defensive perimeter in the Far East. He could hardly have done otherwise; we had recently withdrawn our troops from Korea and JCS had decided that it was impossible to put any into Formosa. The Secretary of State could not offer to defend areas which both the political administration and its military advisers had felt need not be defended. The speech was an accurate statement of the policy established at that time. But it emphasizes the extent to which the known dangers in the Far East had neither been fully appreciated nor provided against.

The response to the crisis was, however, creditable to the power and flexibility of our military-political institutions. The news of the assault reached the State Department at 2 P.M., Saturday, June 24. Acheson reported it to the President (then in Missouri) by telephone and suggested that the UN Security Council be called in an emergency session to declare an act of aggression. On Sunday morning Acheson telephoned again: an all-out invasion was clearly under way; the UN Security Council had been called and would probably declare a cease-fire, but this would probably be ignored. Truman responded that he would immediately fly back to Washington and directed that meanwhile the Secretaries of State and Defense and the Joint Chiefs should start work upon recommendations to be submitted on his arrival.[1]

The UN Security Council, under American urging and in the fortuitous absence of the Russians, adopted that Sunday afternoon its resolution declaring that a breach of the peace had occurred, calling for a cease-fire and the "withdrawal" of the North Korean forces and calling upon all members to "render every assistance" to the UN in furthering the purposes of the resolution. At Blair House on Sunday evening the President met with his advisers. It was decided to employ available American naval and air power south of the 38th Parallel to cover the evacuation of American nationals. Forrest Sherman, Chief of Naval Operations, was later to testify that the directives on this Sunday evening were "predicated entirely . . . on the cover for evacuation"; but the decisions seem to have gone rather further than that. Acheson had been ready with three proposals: evacuate American personnel, but in order to do so keep Kimpo and other airfields open; order MacArthur to get ammunition and supplies to the South Korean armies; order the 7th Fleet into Formosa Strait to prevent the spread of hostilities. This, especially the last, implied a good deal more than a mere rescue of imperilled nationals. As Truman long afterward recorded it,[2] there was "complete accept-

[1] Harry S. Truman, *Memoirs,* Vol. 2, *Years of Trial and Hope,* Doubleday, Garden City, 1956, p. 332.

[2] *Ibid.,* pp. 334, 335.

ance" at Blair House on Sunday evening of the fact that "whatever had to be done to meet this aggression had to be done." Truman adds that "Vandenberg and Sherman thought that air and naval aid might be enough. Collins said that if the Korean Army was really broken, ground forces would be necessary." The President issued orders to put the Acheson program into effect. But MacArthur was also told to send a survey party into Korea to find out what aid was needed, while the President (by his own account) "instructed the service chiefs to prepare the necessary orders for the eventual use of American units if the United Nations should call for action against North Korea."

So far, they had nothing to go on beyond the UN resolution calling on members to "render every assistance" in effectuating a cease-fire and withdrawal. Monday morning was an anxious time. In the course of the day there was a dispatch from MacArthur: "Tanks entering suburbs of Seoul. . . . our estimate is that a complete collapse is imminent." [1] He had been compelled to recall the survey group he had been directed to send to Korea. On Monday evening there was a second conference of the Secretary of State, the service Secretaries, JCS and others at Blair House. Seoul had fallen. President Truman's memory is that he ordered Johnson to call MacArthur on the scrambler telephone and direct him to use American air and naval forces, not merely to cover an evacuation but "to support the Republic of Korea"; [2] he was also to put the 7th Fleet into Formosa Strait. Operational command in Korea and the rest of the Far Eastern theater was vested in MacArthur that evening.

Early on Tuesday morning a UN commission fortunately present in Korea reported that the invasion was "well-planned, concerted, and full-scale." [3] The President summoned a meeting of the Congressional leaders to read them a statement he proposed to deliver at noon. The participants could not afterward recall that there was any objection or any demand for a different procedure. At noon on Tuesday, June 27, the President announced: "I have ordered the United

[1] *Ibid.*, p. 337.
[2] *Ibid.*
[3] Leland M. Goodrich, *Korea: A Study of United States Policy in the United Nations,* Council on Foreign Relations, New York, 1956, p. 112.

States air and sea forces to give the Korean Government troops cover and support." He added that he was ordering the 7th Fleet to protect Formosa from attack and, "as a corollary," calling on the Chinese Nationalist government to cease all attacks on the mainland.[1] The UN Security Council did not meet until 3 in the afternoon; and not until 10:45 in the evening did it adopt the American draft resolution recommending that members "furnish such assistance as may be necessary to repel the armed attack and to restore international peace."[2] Thus the action in support of South Korea was not formally endorsed in the UN until after the American decision to supply that support had been taken.

There was still a considerable obscurity as to what both the Blair House and the Lake Success decisions had decided or what they implied. Clearly, the United States was now lending military support to South Korea and had the Security Council's approval in doing so. But the scope and purpose of the support were uncertain. At 5 in the afternoon of Thursday, June 29, there was a meeting of the (United States) National Security Council. Secretary Johnson proposed a directive for MacArthur which "intimated" the possibility of a war with the Soviet Union. The President objected: "I wanted to take every step necessary to push the North Koreans back behind the 38th parallel. But I wanted to be sure that we would not become so deeply committed in Korea that we could not take care of such other situations as might develop." Frank Pace, Secretary of the Army, thought that the greatest caution should be exercised in authorizing any military action north of the parallel, and Truman agreed, "pointing out that operations above the 38th parallel should be designed only to destroy military supplies, for I wanted it clearly understood that our operations in Korea were designed to restore peace there and to restore the border." Just what they were in for and how deeply they were in for it would still seem to have been unclear.

As this meeting was being held in Washington on Thursday afternoon it was already early Friday morning, June 30, in Tokyo. Mac-

[1] *Memoirs,* Vol. 2, p. 339.
[2] Goodrich, *Korea,* pp. 112-13.

Arthur, placed in operational command two or three days before, took off in the face of dangerous weather for a personal inspection in Korea. Thus he was actually in Korea while the conferees were sitting around the table Thursday evening in Washington. MacArthur spent some eight hours on the front with President Syngman Rhee. Long before the inspection was over he was persuaded that the air and naval support ordered by Truman could not do the job. He returned to Tokyo; and a long telecon conversation with the Pentagon ensued. (It was 5 P.M. June 30 in Tokyo, but 3 in the morning of June 30 in Washington.) The general laid it on the line. The South Korean Army was "completely disintegrated and was in full flight." If so authorized, he said, it was his intention to land an American regimental combat team in Korea to serve as the nucleus of a "possible build-up of two divisions from Japan 'for early offensive action.'" At shortly before 5 that Friday morning (Washington time) Secretary Pace got this information to the President. Truman immediately authorized the use of the regimental combat team and called a meeting of his advisers to consider the commitment of the two divisions. The President was inclined to think that the Chinese Nationalists could be used instead of American troops. Both Acheson and the JCS were against this — Acheson thinking of the political difficulties it would involve and the JCS of the military deficiencies of these untried, ill-trained and ill-equipped forces. After discussion Truman acceded and General MacArthur was "given full authority to use the ground forces under his command."

It was this decision on the morning of June 30 which turned the Korean Incident into the Korean War. The decision was implicit in a great deal that had gone before; but up until this commitment of the ground army the United States was at least technically in a position from which it could have withdrawn, recalling the air and sea forces and washing its hands of further complications. But with the Army on the ground, this would no longer be possible. Once troops were sent in, they would have to stay — until they were destroyed or driven out.

In this way the Korean War was launched as an international police operation. The position was to be confirmed on July 7 when the UN Security Council recommended that members supplying forces in pursuance of the June 25 and 27 resolutions should make them available "to a unified command under the United States" and requested the United States to designate a supreme UN commander. The designee was, of course, MacArthur. But he became the UN Supreme Commander only after he had been conducting the war for some two weeks as an officer of the United States. It is apparent that the new designation sat lightly on his shoulders.

## THE TURN OF THE TIDE

If both military intelligence and political foresight may seem to have been deficient, the crisis when it did break was handled with courage, skill and effectiveness. Truman maneuvered promptly and adroitly, both to throw in military force and simultaneously to secure UN authorization for doing so. State and Defense functioned smoothly and cooperatively to bring forth agreed recommendations; Congress raised no objections; public opinion seemed overwhelmingly behind the decisions taken, and Acheson was later to think it probable that he might have got a war resolution by acclamation, and perhaps regretted that he had not risked the attempt. MacArthur was later to emphasize his conviction that the President had acted rightly in accepting the Communist challenge. During the desperate July days when the lines were being swept away, when MacArthur's estimate that he could hold the Han and undertake "an early offensive" with two skeletonized divisions was being grimly disproved, when immediate crisis overcame all other considerations — the Commander in Chief Far East, the Joint Chiefs, the State Department, the White House and Congress operated in a harmony that left nothing to be desired. But the Pusan perimeter was held; crisis began to relax, and other elements began to creep slowly into the situation.

## MACARTHUR

Douglas MacArthur was a "political soldier" — a phenomenon comparatively rare in American experience, though by no means previously unknown. Because of the difference in backgrounds, the American political soldier has differed considerably from his European counterparts. We have never had a Cromwell to turn out a Parliament with bayonets or a Boulanger to act the man "on horseback." Because the military interest has never been a major institution in our state, we have never had a Waldersee or Ludendorff or Schleicher to assert the paramountcy of "the army" in political or diplomatic affairs. MacArthur never had "the Army" (much less the Navy or the Marines) behind him; he never spoke for a military interest as such, even though many military men were to agree with his positions, and there was never a time when he could be fairly compared to the European or Latin American political soldiers.

Yet he was a military politician. From an early date he had taken a close interest in partisan politics; he was prepared to use his prestige as a soldier to influence civil policy decisions, and the arguments of military necessity to override the diplomatic or political objectives of his civilian superiors. As Samuel P. Huntington puts it:

. . . MacArthur had been a brilliant soldier but always something more than a soldier; a controversial, ambitious, transcendent figure, too able, too assured, too talented to be confined within the limits of professional function and responsibility. As early as 1929 his name was mentioned in connection with the Presidency, and in 1944, 1948, and 1952 he was on the fringes of the presidential political arena.[1]

His was a complex, arrogant and forceful character. He was a military leader of indisputable ability, yet in his enormous reputation there was an element of propaganda myth, dating from the dark days of early 1942 when the American people had desperately needed a hero and MacArthur, defending Bataan, was the only figure available for the role. It can only have been galling to that proud personality. It may have intensified his natural egotism and sensitivity; his constant insistence upon the importance of the Far East

[1] *The Soldier and the State,* Harvard University Press, Cambridge, 1957, pp. 369-70.

as opposed to the European theater (where much less brilliant men, like Eisenhower or Bradley, were to earn greater laurels); his scorn of the politicians, and his almost compulsive drive to be always alone, supreme and unfettered.

This was the remarkable personality who presented what Forrestal, in the later stages of the Pacific war, once described as "the MacArthur problem." It was a problem with which most Washington staffs and administrators had long been familiar. Everybody knew that it had to be handled with gloves. Franklin Roosevelt had been adept at managing it; while the Truman State Department, alike under Marshall and Acheson, had experienced comparatively little difficulty with it during the long proconsulship in Japan. But fate now decreed that General MacArthur should become the chief executive agent of policies with which he did not agree, laid down by a Commander in Chief to whom he was politically opposed and whom he appears to have regarded with contempt. Something of the same kind had happened in the days of Lincoln and McClellan.

At the beginning, all went well so far as command relationships were concerned. The two divisions first deployed in Korea were swept back; but by late July a position was stabilized in the Pusan perimeter in the extreme southeast corner of the peninsula; reinforcements arrived; MacArthur reported that he now held "a secure base," and by August he was planning the brilliant counter-stroke at Inchon. MacArthur had to argue the Joint Chiefs into accepting this military gamble; but it seems fair to say that so far national policy, diplomacy, grand strategy and tactics in the theater had run in close harness. But now, with the immediate crisis apparently under control, issues of policy and politics raised an ugly head.

In the UN resolution of July 7, calling upon members to assist in repelling the aggression and to place their forces under the American UN commander, Chiang Kai-shek had seen an opportunity. The Generalissimo had offered 33,000 Chinese Nationalist troops to the common cause. MacArthur had agreed with the Joint Chiefs that it would be unwise to accept the offer. It was unlikely that these poorly trained and worse equipped formations would be "effective" in Korea; besides, they were needed to hold Formosa against a possible descent by the Chinese Communists. There were other considerations, of which State was particularly aware. One of the first decisions taken in the Blair House conferences was that Formosa should be neutralized. The United States had never before committed itself to defend Formosa against an attack from the mainland; now that it was about to do so by sending the 7th Fleet into Formosa Strait, it seemed essential to make it clear that we would not permit Formosa to be used as a base for a descent upon Communist China. To introduce Chinese Nationalist troops into Korea, where they would have a direct land approach into Manchuria, would vitiate this policy. The Chinese Communists were known to be extremely sensitive about Manchuria, where their position vis-à-vis the Russians was none too secure. Even in these early days, the possibility of a Chinese Communist intervention in the Korean War could not be disregarded. Nothing seemed more likely to invite it than the arrival of large Chinese Nationalist forces in the peninsula.

## THE VISIT TO FORMOSA

But the decisions of June 25 and 26 in Washington had made MacArthur, for the first time, responsible for the whole Far Eastern defense, including Formosa as well as Japan and Korea. Toward the end of July MacArthur informed Washington that he intended to inspect the Formosan addition to his command. JCS tried tactfully to suggest that since the State Department was dealing with the sensitive international problems of Formosa, MacArthur might prefer to send a senior staff officer to make the military survey rather than go himself. MacArthur brushed this idea aside, and visited the island on July 31.

According to his faithful aide, General Courtney Whitney, "It did not dawn on MacArthur that his visit to Formosa would be construed as being sinister in any way." [1] Unfortunately, it dawned on nearly everybody else; and the world press immediately took the visit as an effort by MacArthur, if not by the United States, to revive the Chinese Nationalist forces as an instrument for a full-scale attack on

[1] Courtney Whitney, *MacArthur, His Rendezvous with History*, Knopf, New York, 1956, p. 372.

Red China. This was not at all what our allies had had in mind in supporting our resistance to North Korean Communist aggression within the confines of Korea. MacArthur may have been as naive in this instance as Whitney represents him; but MacArthur was never a naive character. The reaction of the world press was fairly violent, and on August 5 Louis Johnson dispatched a directive instructing MacArthur once more that United States policy was both to protect Formosa against Communist attack and to prevent any attack upon the mainland by the Generalissimo. MacArthur answered that he "understood" and would be governed "meticulously" by the directive. But the Administration was uneasy. It dispatched Averell Harriman, as special representative of the President, in the hope of arriving at a better understanding.

Harriman reached Tokyo on August 6 and had several long sessions with the Commander in Chief Far East (CINCFE). "For reasons," he reported, "which are rather difficult to explain, I did not feel that we came to a full agreement on the way we believed things should be handled on Formosa and with the Generalissimo. He accepted the President's position and will act accordingly, but without full conviction. He has a strange idea that we should back anybody who will fight communism, even though he could not give an argument why the Generalissimo's fighting Communists would be a contribution towards the effective dealing with the Communists in China." MacArthur made the rather pointed suggestion that he was "prepared to deal with the policy problems," but added that he would "conscientiously deal only with the military side unless he is given further orders from the President." It was an early sign of a dangerous ambiguity in the situation. Through the four and a half years of his rule in Japan, MacArthur had combined the functions of a five-star general with those of the principal American political officer in the Far East. His experience and position entitled him to "deal with the policy problems"; what it did not entitle him to do was to control policy issues in the guise of giving "purely military" advice.

The newspapers were now interpreting MacArthur's visit to Formosa as a sign that the general had "rejected" the President's policy of neutralizing the island. Since MacArthur had privately agreed to be good and go along, Truman issued a statement that he and the general "saw eye to eye on the Formosa problem." Naturally, this only created more hostility between two forceful personalities who were actually seeing eye to eye on almost nothing. On August 10 MacArthur issued a scorching declaration on his visit to Formosa:

> This visit has been maliciously misrepresented to the public by those who invariably in the past have propagandized a policy of defeatism and appeasement in the Pacific. I hope the American people will not be misled by sly insinuations, brash speculations and bold misstatements invariably attributed to anonymous sources, so insidiously fed them both nationally and internationally by persons 10,000 miles away from the actual events, if they are not indeed designed, to promote disunity and destroy faith and confidence in American purposes and institutions and American representatives at this time of great world peril.[1]

Though elusively worded, like so many MacArthur statements, it sounded very much like an accusation of defeatism and appeasement against the Truman Administration; at the very least, it seemed to represent a claim by MacArthur to comparable authority with Truman's in the development of Far Eastern policy. Clearly, there were rifts ahead.

### THE VFW MESSAGE

The military position, on the other hand, seemed increasingly hopeful. While UN forces had been compressed into a perilously narrow perimeter around Taegu and Pusan (in the extreme southeastern corner of the peninsula), they were holding and reinforcements were arriving. The 24th, 25th and 1st Cavalry Divisions from Japan were in Korea; the 1st Marine Division, representing the initial reinforcement from the United States, had begun to arrive on August 2. By mid-August MacArthur was concerting his plans for a counter-attack. At this moment an invitation arrived in the Tokyo headquarters to prepare a message for the annual convention of the Veterans of Foreign Wars. A theater commander in the full tide of dangerous action is scarcely required to respond to such requests. But "MacArthur decided," in the somewhat incredible words of

---

[1] Whitney, *MacArthur*, p. 375.

Whitney, "that this was an excellent opportunity to place himself on record as being squarely behind the President." [1]

His method of doing so was curious. The message to the VFW carried several implied barbs for Administration policy. "Nothing could be more fallacious than the threadbare argument by those who advocate appeasement and defeatism in the Pacific that if we defend Formosa we alienate continental Asia." At the moment, Tokyo dispatches were quoting "reliable sources" to the effect that MacArthur felt that the United States should "take more aggressive action against communism not only in Korea but elsewhere in Asia." Our UN allies were already nervous over the idea that the Korean police action might be expanded into a general crusade against communism in the Far East that would precipitate the third world war. Before the United Nations, the Soviet Union was resoundingly accusing us of "aggression," not only in Korea but because of our alleged designs on Formosa; the MacArthur message could be (as later it was) used as powerful ammunition in this propaganda war. Truman first saw it on August 26, two days before its intended release. He has later said that he thought then of relieving the general. The matter was so serious that he summoned the Secretaries of State and Defense, the Joint Chiefs and Secretary of the Treasury John W. Snyder. They were all "shocked," but apparently none dared at that point to suggest the relief of the towering figure of the Commander in Chief Far East. Instead, the President instructed Johnson to send him a message directing that he "withdraw" the statement. Truman knew that it was already in type (in the *U.S. News and World Report*) and so could not be suppressed; the withdrawal order was intended simply to limit the damage, so far as possible, by making it clear that MacArthur was not speaking for the Administration. [2]

According to Whitney, MacArthur was "utterly astonished." He withdrew the statement in an abrupt telegram of acquiescence; but began to see himself the victim of conspiracy. In the eyes of the Tokyo headquarters it seemed "logical," again according to Whitney,

[1] *Ibid.*, p. 377.
[2] Truman, *Memoirs,* Vol. 2, pp. 354-56.

that the VFW statement had "innocently" run afoul of "plans being hatched in the State Department to succumb to British pressure and desert the Nationalist Government on Formosa. . . . in the event that the State Department was conspiring with the British to hand over Formosa to the Communists, it is easy to see how the statement to the VFW would cause consternation." [1] Here, as elsewhere, it is difficult to know how accurately General Whitney, writing after the event, represents the state of mind obtaining in Tokyo at the time. If his report is trustworthy, it would seem to indicate that already an impossible situation had developed between the Commander in Chief Far East and his superiors, both military and political, in Washington. The episode, says Whitney,[2] gave MacArthur "his first clear illustration of the devious workings of the Washington-London team." A theater commander in wartime who really believed that the civil authorities were "conspiring" against him with a foreign power would surely be compelled to resign. But MacArthur did not resign; and the issue passed.

WAR OBJECTIVES IN KOREA

In mid-August, General Collins and Admiral Sherman, representing the Joint Chiefs, were in Tokyo to discuss the planned offensive. MacArthur's proposal of an "end-run" amphibious landing at Inchon seemed bold to them, but they were persuaded to accept it and the planning went rapidly forward with a target date of September 15. But though accepted by the military, it was a plan which raised new worries for the civil policy-makers. If successful, it would bring the fighting back to the neighborhood of the 38th Parallel, thus forcing a policy question which had so far gone unanswered and raising a threat which had so far not received much consideration. In reaching the great decisions on June 25 and 26 it had been assumed by all parties that the objective was simply to push the Communists back again behind the 38th Parallel boundary — in Truman's words, "to restore peace there and to restore the border." This was certainly State's view at the time and apparently that of the soldiers. How-

[1] *MacArthur,* pp. 380-81.
[2] *Ibid.,* p. 384.

ever, the UN Security Council resolutions (as drafted, of course, in the State Department), not only calling for the repulse of "aggression" and the restoration of "peace," but also noting the longstanding purpose of the UN to bring about "the complete independence and unity of Korea," were at best ambiguous. Did these license not merely the restoration of the parallel boundary, but the destruction of the North Korean regime and the reunification of the country?

If the latter was now to be taken as the objective, it would obviously heighten the interest of the Chinese Communist government in the struggle. So far, the North Koreans had apparently been deriving their support only from the Soviet Union. But as early as August 20 the Chinese Communist Foreign Minister, Chou En-lai, telegraphed the UN Secretary-General, Trygve Lie, that "the Chinese people cannot but be most concerned about the solution of the Korean question." [1] He had been following this up with similar hints. The threat of a Red Chinese intervention was at least menacing enough to lead Truman, in his statement of war aims on September 1, to include a hope "that the people of China will not be misled or forced into fighting against the United Nations and against the American people." Both the policy problem and the threat were submitted to the National Security Council; it came up with a paper, approved by Truman on September 11, which seems (from the former President's paraphrase) to have been something of an evasion:

General MacArthur was to conduct the necessary military operations either to force the North Koreans behind the 38th parallel or to destroy their forces. If there was no indication or threat of entry of Soviet or Chinese Communist elements in force, the National Security Council recommended that General MacArthur was to extend his operations north of the parallel and to make plans for the occupation of North Korea. However, no ground operations were to take place north of the 38th parallel in the event of Soviet or Chinese Communist entry.[2]

This really begged the question; and Johnson's later testimony, to the effect that up to the time he left the Defense Department (in mid-September) "there was no definite policy lined out as to what

[1] Goodrich, *Korea,* p. 138.
[2] *Memoirs,* Vol. 2, p. 359.

our action should be and how we were going to end this thing," would seem to have been well justified. The NSC finding placed upon MacArthur responsibility for decisions which should have been faced by the high command in Washington. If Washington was to commit our troops to the "occupation of North Korea" then it should have been prepared to accept the possible consequences, already foreseen; if the risks were too great, then the commitment should not have been authorized. The finding quite failed to provide against the highly likely contingency which in fact materialized — that only after MacArthur had been allowed fully to commit himself would there occur the intervention which was the condition on which the commitment was not to take place. MacArthur's later complaints of his inability to secure clear policy directives from Washington were not without substance.

At the time there were no complaints; MacArthur was fully prepared to accept whatever responsibility was left to him. The JCS directive embodying the NSC finding was dispatched on September 15, the day of the brilliantly successful Inchon landing. Ten days later the military situation had been transformed. Seoul had been liberated by Xth Corps; 8th Army, breaking out of the Pusan perimeter, had destroyed or dissipated most of the North Korean army and joined up with Xth Corps to establish an irregular line (still at most points well south of the parallel) across the Korean peninsula. The war to rescue South Korea from aggression seemed virtually won. But the question whether to go on and capture North Korea from the Communists was now acute, and being debated in every capital of the non-Communist world.

To MacArthur it was no question. He had assumed from the beginning that the UN resolutions of June and July had authorized the reunification of the country. In the September 15 directive JCS had authorized him to "plan for the possible occupation of North Korea, but to execute such plans only with the approval of the President." On September 26 this was enlarged; JCS gave him as his military objective "the destruction of the North Korean armed forces," and in attaining it authorized him to "conduct military operations north of the 38th Parallel." But this was accompanied by the most

strict injunctions not to permit any of his forces to cross the Manchurian or Russian borders. In no circumstances were air units to be
allowed to pass the frontiers, and it was suggested "as a matter of
policy" that only Republic of Korea ground troops should be em-
ployed in areas near the border. MacArthur replied two days later
with a brief outline of his plan: 8th Army to advance on the west
and capture Pyongyang, the North Korean capital; Xth Corps to be
withdrawn from Inchon for another amphibious landing, this time
at Wonsan on the east coast, whence it would advance through
North Korea in a wide sweep to a "juncture" with 8th Army. The
plan was approved. But there was a good deal of uneasiness in
Washington.

It was known that the Chinese Communist government, beginning
at about the time of the Inchon landing, had been concentrating its
best army units along the Yalu frontier. On September 30 Chou
En-lai, in a broadcast from Peiping, announced that Communist
China could not "supinely tolerate" a crossing of the parallel, and
warned that she "would not stand aside" if North Korea were invaded by the UN forces.[1] On the same day MacArthur reported to
Washington that he intended to issue a public directive to 8th Army's
commander, declaring that the parallel was no longer a factor —
"to accomplish the enemy's complete defeat, your troops may cross
this parallel at any time." Nervously, JCS instructed him to "proceed
with your operations without any further explanation or announcement . . . Our government desires to avoid having to make an issue
of the 38th Parallel."

ACTION IN THE UN

Not only did the government wish to avoid making an issue of the
parallel; for too long it had avoided the issue itself. It is difficult to
respect the rather blurred and fuzzy processes by which, when in
September it became inescapable, it was finally made. Both in Washington and Lake Success there was much division of opinion. Our
UN allies were already concerned lest we convert the war in Korea

[1] Goodrich, *Korea*, p. 139.

into a general war on communism. The general whom we had appointed as UN commander had rather plainly indicated his leaning toward such a course. At the same time, the presence of the Chinese forces along the Yalu made the danger of Chinese intervention a real one, and continued threats from Peiping underlined it. The Indian representatives, convinced that the Chinese meant business, were trying in every way possible to keep the war below the parallel in order to avert the general war which a Chinese intervention might bring.

Yet there were countervailing arguments, at Lake Success as well as in Washington. To settle for a mere restoration of the *status quo* would be to accept the restoration of a demonstratedly unstable situation; simply to drive the Communists behind the parallel (not a militarily defensible feature) would only leave them free to rebuild and re-equip for renewed attack. There were other considerations. Many, not only in Washington or among the allied UN delegations but in the general public, saw in the Korean issue a golden opportunity for establishing the moral authority and effective power of the United Nations. Merely to repel a military aggression would be a modest gain; but if the UN could show itself equal to dealing with the total situation, eliminating the division which was at the root of the trouble and re-creating a free and united Korea as a viable unit in the international community, it would be impressive proof of the moral leadership and practical strength of the international organization. Many who had little sympathy with MacArthur's political views were to combine in abetting his conquest of North Korea.

The general had been authorized to cross the parallel, but only in order to destroy the North Korean army and only if Russia or China did not intervene. The State Department devoted itself to securing more definite authority from the UN for the new course. On October 1 ROK troops made the first small penetration of the parallel, at its extreme eastern end. Next day the *New York Times* carried a curious lead editorial. The issue of the parallel was now "settled," this observed, as far as the South Koreans were concerned. But the position as to non-Korean UN forces was not yet "clearly established." It would be utter folly, the *Times* argued, for the Chinese

Communists to intervene at this point; but it suggested the weakness of the argument by merely hoping "devoutly" that they would not. The *Times* revealed both its fears and uncertainty as to the proper role of the United States in the situation by suggesting that it would be "advantageous" if forces sent across the parallel were confined mainly to "Koreans and other Asiatics." The editorial reflects a dubiety that extended far beyond the offices of the *Times*.

At Lake Success, in the meanwhile, the American representatives were laboring hard to secure from the General Assembly (it was now useless to appeal to the Security Council, since the Russians had returned to that body) a resolution specifically announcing the objective of establishing "a unified, independent and democratic government" in all of Korea. MacArthur's somewhat florid demand of October 1 for the surrender of the enemy — "The early and total defeat and complete destruction of your armed forces and war-making potential is now inevitable. . . . I . . . call upon you and the forces under your command, in whatever part of Korea situated, forthwith to lay down your arms" — was initiated in Washington, as Acheson later testified, and "was issued by him at the direction of this government." In the UN the British and Commonwealth representatives had accepted the American policy and were, with others, to sponsor the resolution.

On October 3 the Chinese Communist Foreign Minister issued an even stronger, though still somewhat cryptic, warning; he told the Indian Ambassador at Peiping that if United States or United Nations forces crossed the parallel, China "would send troops to the Korean frontier to defend North Korea," but that this action "would not be taken if only South Korean troops" passed the parallel. There were reports from other sources to the same effect. But they were discounted in Washington as only a bluff, intended to obstruct the UN resolution. Meanwhile, South Korean forces, with express authorization from 8th Army, were across the border and pushing rapidly up the east coast road against slight opposition. On October 7 the UN resolution (sponsored by Britain, Australia and six others, though largely drafted by the United States) passed by a vote of 47 to 5 with seven abstentions. (The Soviet bloc voted in the negative; Yugo-

slavia, India and five Arab states abstained.)  On the same day
American troops, patrols from the 1st Cavalry Division, crossed the
parallel for the first time.  The ROK's by that time were approaching the important port of Wonsan, far up the eastern coast.  Perhaps
the one most critical decision of the Korean War had been taken.
But it had been taken in the worst way, for confused reasons, on
deficient intelligence and with an inadequate appreciation of the
risks.

With the passage of the resolution MacArthur issued another
pronunciamento calling upon the North Korean forces to surrender
and "to co-operate fully with the United Nations in establishing a
unified, independent, democratic government in Korea."  Unless
there was immediate response, he would "at once proceed to take
such military action as may be necessary to enforce the decrees of the
United Nations."  The General Assembly, of course, had no power
to issue "decrees," and the statement may seem at best to have been
somewhat overconfident.  But while MacArthur was in complete
agreement with the decision to attempt the occupation of North
Korea, he cannot fairly be held responsible for it.  In no way did he
exceed orders drafted in Washington and endorsed in Lake Success;
and the widespread idea that the general, by appealing to "military
necessity," had forced a reluctant civil administration into a dubious
political adventure was without foundation.

But to Washington the adventure was already looking more and
more dubious.  The North Koreans did not respond to the demand
for surrender; but the Chinese did.  On October 9 there was a broadcast from Peiping: the UN resolution was illegal; the American invasion of North Korea was a serious menace to the security of
China; "We cannot stand idly by. . . . The Chinese people love
peace, but, in order to defend peace, they never will be afraid to oppose aggressive war." [1]  And it was in these days that they began
secretly to pass their divisions across the Yalu to build up for the
counter-stroke.  Washington, like Tokyo, was in complete ignorance of this movement; but Washington was disturbed.  By this time

[1] Goodrich, *Korea*, p. 139.

Truman appears to have trusted MacArthur as little as MacArthur trusted Truman. On the day of the Peiping broadcast another JCS directive went off, again strictly enjoining the general against any "military action against objectives in Chinese territory." According to Acheson, the preponderant view in Washington was still that a Chinese Communist intervention, while possible, was "not a probability," though some, like Kennan, were prophesying trouble. And the President felt that he must have a personal interview with the great military figure whom, despite several invitations, he had never met face to face.

## THE WAKE ISLAND MEETING

The meeting at Wake Island was outwardly cordial. In their first (and private) conversation the President found the general "very friendly — I might say much more so than I had expected." Just what he had expected, Truman does not explain. The general said he was sorry if the VFW statement had caused embarrassment; the President assured him it was a closed incident, and the general declared "that he was not in politics." Later, at the conference table, the general assured the President that the war in Korea was all but won; that he did not believe that either the Russians or the Chinese would intervene; and that even if the Chinese tried to do so they could not get more than fifty or sixty thousand troops across the Yalu. "General MacArthur stated his firm belief that all resistance would end, in both North and South Korea, by Thanksgiving. This, he said, would enable him to withdraw the Eighth Army to Japan by Christmas." [1]

The two men separated with no apparent rift between them, and in fact up to this point the command relationship had been correct and effective. MacArthur had voiced his policy differences with the Commander in Chief in the matter of Formosa (as well as a barely concealed contempt for the Administration) but he had not put these on military grounds. He had been restless under the restrictions placed upon his operations in Korea by what he thought was

[1] *Memoirs,* Vol. 2, pp. 365-66.

a timid and pro-British State Department; he felt that Washington had been unduly parsimonious with reinforcements in the Far East, apportioning too much to NATO and to Europe, where there was no war. But the great victory at Inchon had cured most of these discontents. Despite all of Washington's irritating failings, the end was now in sight; and MacArthur alone had done it. According to Whitney,[1] the general saw no sense in the mid-Pacific conference with the President; could not understand why Truman should have wasted MacArthur's time, and flew back to Tokyo believing that the whole thing had been merely a "political ambush," designed to appropriate something of the MacArthur glory for Truman and the Democrats, who were facing the November Congressional elections. Outwardly, the meeting had been cordial. But it left further dangerous rifts within the American policy and command structure.

## THE CHINESE ATTACK

Meanwhile Washington was preoccupied with a great deal more than the Congressional elections or even the Korean War. It was obviously necessary to support and reinforce MacArthur; but the overriding fear of that summer and fall was that Korea simply foreshadowed a Soviet attack upon the Western world. Korea could be, and apparently was being, held with the available bits and pieces of the World War II military machine. But to hold the free world itself it seemed suddenly urgent to convert the new NATO alliance into an effective instrument of defense; to raise and re-equip American military forces for its support and, even more, to raise the American military production potential to a point at which we would be reasonably prepared to face the possibility of a third general war.

### MARSHALL AS SECRETARY OF DEFENSE

The American reaction to this global problem will be discussed later. But it was obvious from the onset of the Korean crisis that the days of Louis Johnson as Secretary of Defense were numbered.

[1] *MacArthur*, p. 395.

Johnson's relations with Acheson were already dangerously strained; while it was plain that the man who had been so assiduously economizing the services into incapacity was not the one to preside over the major rearmament effort now demanded. Under Presidential pressure, Johnson resigned on September 15, as the Marines were going ashore at Inchon; and Truman turned again to George C. Marshall, the one public servant whose abilities he most respected and whose integrity he most deeply trusted. The provision of the Security Act excluding professional soldiers from the office of Secretary of Defense had to be hastily amended to permit the nomination; this produced some partisan by-play, but the amendment was adopted without real difficulty and confirmation was immediate. Marshall took office on September 18.

It was a singularly suitable appointment. During the Second War Marshall had been the country's outstanding military statesman; and the success of the Joint Chiefs (as also of the Anglo-American Combined Chiefs) as a corporate direction of that conflict was certainly in large measure due to his wisdom and influence. In 1950 Marshall had his civilian experience as Secretary of State behind him. At the same time, he had not lost the respect of his former military colleagues nor the touch of his old command authority over them. Under him a harmonious relationship between Defense, State, NSC and their staffs was established. This was, no doubt, facilitated by the fact that in August the President had strengthened NSC with a "Senior Staff" composed of some of the ablest men from State, Defense, Treasury, JCS, the National Security Resources Board, the Central Intelligence Agency.

In the subsequent Congressional hearings, Marshall was to describe the mechanism of policy formation as it operated in later 1950 and 1951. Beginning with UN resolutions, JCS would prepare precise military directives (of course with the assistance of its own Joint Staff with its complex structure of joint planning committees). If of a minor nature, they were approved by the Secretary of Defense and then carried direct to the White House by Bradley, who regularly met with the President at 10 in the morning. The Chairman of the Joint Chiefs got the President's approval and the directives were sent.

If, however, the matter "involved precise political consideration it was discussed as a rule with members of the State Department or sent them and their reaction awaited." After formulation between State and Defense, the policy paper would go to NSC, where the new Senior Staff, including high-level representatives of all interested agencies, would study the question and "final action would be taken." (Legally, NSC was only advisory and there could be no "final" action except upon approval by the President; here Marshall may have been telescoping a bit.) In transmitting the resultant directive to the theater commander (MacArthur), General Collins, the Army Chief of Staff, acted as the executive agent of JCS, and the channel through whom all communications passed. The men who operated within this system testified later as to its efficiency. Marshall and the individual Chiefs of Staff were to say several times that it produced smooth and agreed military solutions, and that they were never overborne by the civilian diplomatists of State. Acheson was to say, in response to a question, "Yes, sir, it has been a very satisfactory relationship throughout."

The record would appear to bear out these statements. The Joint Chiefs of Staff, under the sensitive hand of the Secretary of Defense, were consistently to support the civil-political direction; State was consistently responsive to the military considerations presented by JCS, and there was a warm personal relationship between Acheson and Marshall. In regard to Korea, the Joint Chiefs were to show themselves keenly aware of the larger policy problems which led the Truman Administration to insist upon a limited war — much more so, it is interesting to note, than MacArthur and most of the field commanders. In the MacArthur crisis in the coming spring these professional soldiers not only loyally supported the civilian Commander in Chief (as the Constitution required them to do) but indicated rather strongly their personal agreement with Truman. At the same time they worked out and brought in the massive estimates for new military spending and for foreign military aid required to buttress the NATO system — estimates which were in large measure dictated by political rather than immediate military considerations and for which State rather than Defense carried the immediate responsibility. Issues between rearming ourselves or rearming our allies — of a kind which were rather prominent in the year before Pearl Harbor — were not wholly absent in 1950-51, but were to play a minor role. Except for the partial and peculiar exception of the MacArthur crisis, civil-military relations in the difficult Korean period were to operate with remarkable harmony and success.

### APPEARANCE OF THE CHINESE TROOPS

Unforeseen by any of the parties, that crisis was now in the making. Eighth Army had crossed the 38th Parallel on October 7, headed generally northwestward along the more or less open valleys of the "invasion route" leading to Pyongyang, the North Korean capital. Resistance had been stiffer and progress slower than the optimism after the recapture of Seoul had suggested; but by October 20 MacArthur, back from Wake Island, felt that the *coup de grace* was about to be delivered, and flew to Korea to witness it. He dropped units of the 11th Airborne Division beyond Pyongyang to cut off the defenders' support (actually there was none), and observed 8th Army units occupy the enemy capital. This time the war really was won. He started Xth Corps (originally intended to make a flanking "juncture" with 8th Army) fanning out in a separate operation from the east coast ports of Wonsan, Hungnam and Iwon across the vast, mountainous and largely valueless stretches of northeastern Korea. Tenth Corps' advance was ordered not as one arm of a combined attack but as an occupation and police operation.

Eighth Army was launched up the west coast "invasion route," which trends north for some fifty miles above Pyongyang, then angles northwestward with the coast for another eighty miles or so to Sinuiju and Antung, standing on the opposite banks of the Yalu where that river enters its estuary to the sea. The route crosses the Chongchon just where it turns the angle. In Pyongyang, as the forward movements began, they were interrogating nine prisoners, indubitably Chinese, who had been picked up by the ROK IId Corps just as MacArthur and Truman were meeting at Wake Island. They said they were forced "volunteers" from the Chinese into the North Korean army, and did not seem to amount to much.

By October 24 advance elements of the American 24th Division were within a few miles of Sinuiju and the Yalu; far to the northeast, the 7th Regiment of the 6th ROK Division had slid down the hills and taken a bottle of water from the Yalu itself. The UN forces were now widely scattered in thin groups and spearheads, and Washington was more worried than ever. On the 20th, Central Intelligence had come up with an estimate that the Chinese Communists would move in far enough to cover the Yalu hydro-electric installations, apparently jeopardized by the change of plan for Xth Corps, much of whose output was consumed in Manchuria. State thought the proper answer was a statement by MacArthur that he did not intend to interfere with the hydro-electric plants; JCS vetoed this on the ground that it would unduly hamper MacArthur's freedom of military operation. How the Central Intelligence Agency arrived at the estimate, at once alarming and deceptively complacent, has not been stated. It is evident that CIA, State and Defense alike were already well behind the actual events.

For a week or so UN troops had been meeting with only occasional skirmishes as they ranged freely across North Korea. But on October 24, when the advance element of the 6th ROK Division had been filling its canteens in the Yalu, another element of the same division, some fifty miles behind them to the southeast, had run into a trap at Unsan, on the upper reaches of the Chongchon. The American 1st Cavalry Division started northward in relief. On the night of October 26 it, likewise, ran into an ambush. One squadron lost a great part of its men. "Both traps," says S. L. A. Marshall,[1] "had been sprung by Chinese troops in superior strength," but of the prisoners taken at Unsan only two were Chinese. Their stories were like those of the earlier prisoners. They were forced "volunteers" in the North Korean armies. But they said that the units with which they had crossed the border were not mere regimental groups; they were full-sized Chinese divisions.

Lieutenant General Walton Walker, commanding 8th Army, had already sensed trouble ahead. The scattered advance to the Yalu was dangerous; his supply situation was already difficult, and he

---

[1] *The River and the Gauntlet*, Morrow, New York, 1953, p. 10.

ordered a reconcentration of 8th Army behind the Chongchon River line, eighty miles from the Yalu. Twenty-fourth Division retreated without difficulty; but the 7th ROK Regiment, returning from the upper Yalu, ran into one of the Chinese columns which were now entering Korea in strength. It lost 500 men and most of its equipment. Walker pulled back and established himself on the Chongchon. He did not know that while the UN command had been fanning out across North Korea, the Chinese had slipped through the thin and widely dispersed UN columns a massive concentration of some 200,000 soldiers. They were now in ambush around the headwaters of the Chongchon, on Walker's right flank, and near the Chosin Reservoir, which Xth Corps was approaching.

Washington, Tokyo and 8th Army were alike ignorant of the true situation. In 8th Army, as S. L. A. Marshall says,[1] "there was a sense of impending change and a realization that the army must replenish toward it." But there was no firm intelligence. They knew that organized Red Chinese units were in the field, but whether this meant only "the beginning of a commitment in piecemeal fashion" or the beginning of "open intervention . . . to defeat UN forces in Korea" they did not know. Eighth Army's intelligence periodic of October 29 concluded lamely that "At present, the evidence is insufficient to say." Without being asked by the theater command, the Joint Chiefs dispatched another group of F-86 jet fighters and some Navy jets to help meet a Chinese threat "if it came." The President asked JCS to get an estimate of the Chinese danger from MacArthur. On November 4 the general replied that "it is impossible to authoritatively appraise the actualities of Chinese Communist intervention in Korea." There was the possibility of "all-out intervention" but there were "many fundamental logical reasons against it and sufficient evidence has not yet come to hand to warrant its immediate acceptance."

EVALUATING CHINESE INTERVENTION

That there was at least some Chinese intervention was now obvious to all. On November 5, the day after the inconclusive report

[1] *Ibid.*, pp. 12-13.

to the President and JCS, MacArthur addressed an angry "special report" to the United Nations Security Council: "It is apparent to our fighting forces, and our intelligence agencies have confirmed the fact, that the United Nations are presently in hostile contact with Chinese Communist military units deployed for action against the United Nations." To support this, a whole series of incidents was summarized, beginning on August 22 when anti-aircraft fire from the Manchurian side of the Yalu had attacked our aircraft; including instances in which enemy aircraft had retreated across the Yalu to receive sanctuary on the Chinese airfields; including the identification of small Chinese "volunteer" units, up to regimental size, in the North Korean forces. By November 4, this report stated, thirty-five Chinese Communist prisoners had been taken.

More than this, there was a "special communiqué" issued to the world on November 6.[1] This announced that the war had been won; with the capture of Pyongyang and the invasion of northeastern Korea "the defeat of the North Koreans and destruction of their armies" had become "decisive." But at this point the Chinese had intervened:

. . . the communists committed one of the most offensive acts of international lawlessness of historic record by moving, without any notice of belligerence, elements of alien Communist forces across the Yalu River into North Korea and massing a great concentration of possible reinforcing divisions with adequate supply behind the privileged sanctuary of the adjacent Manchurian border.

A possible trap was thereby surreptitiously laid, calculated to encompass the destruction of the United Nations forces . . . This potential danger was avoided with minimum losses only by the timely detection and skillful maneuvering of the United Nations commander responsible for that sector, who with great perspicacity and skill completely reversed the movement of his forces in order to achieve the greater integration of tactical power necessitated by the new situation and avert any possibility of a great military reversal.

The last sonorous sentence sounded a great deal better than the time-worn "our troops affected a strategic withdrawal" or "our lines were rectified to improve the tactical position," but it meant exactly the same thing. In short, it covered Walton Walker's retreat to the Chongchon. But the whole communiqué suggests today that the

[1] The following report of this communiqué is from Whitney, *MacArthur*, p. 405.

general was losing his touch with reality. The Chinese concentrations were still only a "possible" reinforcing group beyond the Yalu; MacArthur obviously did not know that they had passed the Yalu many days before and were actually massing in the midst of his own forces. The "trap" had not been avoided; the real trap had not yet even been detected.

## THE YALU BRIDGES

The sequence is rather striking. On November 4 MacArthur reported to his government and his military superiors that it was "impossible to appraise" the danger of an all-out Chinese intervention, and that "many logical reasons" were against it. On November 5 he appealed to the United Nations and on November 6 to world opinion on the assumption that such an intervention was about to take place. It was also on November 6 that MacArthur ordered his air commander, Lieutenant General George E. Stratemeyer, to mount a strike of ninety "strategic" B-29 bombers on the Yalu bridges at Sinuiju, and advised Washington of the order. In Washington it caused consternation. The President was in Missouri, to cast his ballot in the Congressional election. Acheson got him on the telephone; the Under Secretary of Defense, Lovett, was in Acheson's office with MacArthur's message.[1]

It was then about 10 in the morning, and the bombers were to take off in three hours. Lovett said that "from an operational standpoint he doubted whether the results to be achieved would be important enough to outweigh the danger of [accidentally] bombing Antung or other points on the Manchurian side of the river." There were other considerations. "Dean Rusk pointed out that we had a commitment with the British not to take action which might involve attacks on the Manchurian side of the river without consultation with them." On the basis of the MacArthur report of November 5 State had already requested an "urgent" meeting of the UN Security Council to consider the Chinese intervention, and a bombing attack meanwhile which hit Manchuria might wreck further chances of

[1] The report of the telephone conversation which follows is from Truman, *Memoirs*, Vol. 2, p. 374.

progress through the UN. Acheson said that he and Lovett were agreed that "this air action ought to be postponed until we had more facts about the situation there"; Truman's reply over the telephone was that he would not approve the strike unless "there was an immediate and serious threat to the security of our troops," of which MacArthur had given no indication. At 11:40 A.M., JCS, in conformity with this instruction, dispatched a directive to MacArthur, ordering the postponement of all bombing of targets within five miles of the Yalu and asking his reasons for mounting the attack.

This evoked a sizzling, and somewhat curious, reply:

> Men and material in large force are pouring across all bridges over the Yalu from Manchuria. This movement not only jeopardizes but threatens the ultimate destruction of the forces under my command. . . . The only way to stop this reinforcement of the enemy is the destruction of these bridges and *the subjection of all installations in the north area supporting the enemy advance to the maximum of our air destruction.* Every hour that this is postponed will be paid for dearly in American and other United Nations blood. . . . I am suspending this strike and carrying out your instructions. . . . [But] I cannot overemphasize the disastrous effect, both physical and *psychological,* that will result from the restrictions which you are imposing. I trust that the matter be immediately brought to the attention of the President as I believe your instructions may well result in a calamity of major proportion for which I cannot accept the responsibility without his personal and direct understanding of the situation.[1]

This seems to have baffled both the President and the Joint Chiefs, as well it might have done. Two days before, the general had reported that logic was against any large-scale Chinese intervention; now, two days later, "men and material in large force" were "pouring across" the Yalu bridges and he had already ordered a major transformation in the whole character of the war to meet not only the new military problem but also the "psychological" factors it involved. The MacArthur reply violated a fundamental canon of command relations by using a sudden threat of the destruction of his forces as a lever to compel a change of orders. (On an occasion in World War II George Patton met a similar maneuver on the part of a division commander by asking him, first, if he had any

---

[1] *Ibid.,* p. 375 (emphasis added).

recommendation as to his successor.) It implied an effort by Mac-
Arthur to go over the heads of his superiors, JCS, to the President.
Worst of all, it sought to justify a new strategy and tactics, which
he had already ordered, by an appeal to a change in the situation
which he had not reported, and which he did not now explain. Had
MacArthur really foreseen "a calamity of major proportion" he
would have done much more than order a bombing strike at Sinuiju.
He would, first, have advised Washington of the facts; he would
then have formed a defensive position along the Chongchon and put
Xth Corps into a posture of defense to the eastward. He would
immediately have adjusted his military strategy to State Department
and UN policy. But he did none of these things. Both JCS and the
President were not unwarranted in believing (as apparently they
did) that MacArthur was trying to impose his own political policies
upon the government of the United States under the guise of a
"military necessity" which the general had failed to establish.

The conduct of civil-military policy as regards Korea had reached
a serious breakdown. Perhaps this was the point at which the problem should have been faced. The actual decision was less heroic.
Since MacArthur "felt so strongly," Truman told the Joint Chiefs
to give him "the go-ahead." [1] In the resultant directive JCS noted
somewhat pointedly the discrepancy between the November 4 message ("impossible . . . to . . . appraise the actualities of Chinese
Communist intervention") and the November 6 message ("Men
. . . are pouring across all bridges over the Yalu") but nevertheless
authorized him to bomb Sinuiju and the bridges up to the middle of
the river. The previous restriction of air action to a limit five miles
within Korea was removed.

But Washington also had to consider where this new situation
was to end. If the Chinese Communists were really "pouring"
troops across the Yalu, the policy would obviously have to be re-
adjusted. Assuming that the new attack (if in fact there was to be
a new attack) could be held by the UN lines now established along
the Chongchon and in the Chosin Reservoir area, the United Nations
would be in a strong position to offer a peace which, while leaving

[1] *Ibid.*, p. 376.

to the Communists a "buffer" area, the hydro-electric plants and the barren expanses of northern and northeastern Korea, would preserve to the Republic of Korea almost all the productive parts of the country. Proposals in this sense were already being advanced in London, at Lake Success and in Washington. But this was precisely the outcome which MacArthur believed should be prevented. About this time he discharged an emphatic "warning" against "the widely reported British desire to appease the Chinese Communists by giving them a strip of Northern Korea." The warning (according to Whitney, who does not give date or addressee) continued:

> To give up a portion of North Korea to the aggression of the Chinese Communists would be the greatest defeat of the free world in recent times. Indeed, to yield to so immoral a proposition would bankrupt our leadership and influence in Asia and render untenable our position, both politically and militarily. . . . From a military standpoint, I believe that the United States should press for a resolution in the United Nations condemning the Chinese Communists for their defiance of the United Nations' orders . . . calling upon the Communists to withdraw forthwith . . . on pain of military sanctions . . . should they fail to do so. I recommend with all the earnestness that I possess that there be no weakening at this critical moment and that we press on to complete victory which I believe can be achieved if our determination and our indomitable will do not desert us.[1]

MACARTHUR RESUMES THE OFFENSIVE

MacArthur here appealed to the "military standpoint"; yet this seems clearly a political rather than a military recommendation. He was not asking for support for his military command against a new threat (which he still did not seem to take seriously) but for an alteration of national policy to permit "sanctions" against Communist China, essentially political in character, which his government had not theretofore contemplated. Washington had reason to feel that it was MacArthur, rather than the Chinese, who was trying to start a "new war" in Asia, and that the order to bomb Sinuiju may have been motivated as much by this desire as by a military need to interdict Chinese reinforcements. Such feelings cannot have been lessened when on the next day, November 7, the general reported

---

[1] *MacArthur*, pp. 411-12.

that he had been confirmed in his belief that the Chinese were not launching a full-scale intervention, and that he proposed to resume the offensive, in order to take "accurate measure . . . of enemy strength." [1]

In Tokyo, MacArthur was still supremely confident, and urging Walker, who remained dissatisfied with the condition of his army and supply, to hurry on with the planned offensive. There had been no significant change in the intelligence picture. Tenth Corps was beginning its march northward from the east coast ports into the unknown; and its 7th Division was in fact to reach the headwaters of the Yalu itself. But Washington in mid-November was extremely anxious; and there seemed an increasing opacity between the planners in the State Department and the Pentagon and the executants in Tokyo and Korea.

While Tokyo was boldly committing itself to the offensive, the discussion in Washington seems to have been almost wholly in defensive terms. JCS advised the President that "Every effort should be expended as a matter of urgency to settle the problem of Chinese Communist intervention in Korea by political means, preferably through the United Nations, to include reassurances to the Chinese Communists with respect to our intent, direct negotiations through our Allies and the Interim Committee with the Chinese Communist Government, and by any other available means." Meanwhile, there should be no immediate change in MacArthur's directive, but all planning should be "on the basis that the risk of global war is increased." At a National Security Council meeting on November 9, Bradley speculated on the three possible purposes of the Chinese: simply to hold a buffer area along the Yalu; to force us into a war of attrition that would commit us so deeply in Asia as to assure a

---

[1] It was also on November 7 that MacArthur reported that hostile planes were operating in increasing numbers from the inviolate Manchurian airfields and asked that our pilots be authorized, under the long-established international law rule of "hot pursuit," to follow these hit-and-run enemies for two or three minutes' flying time across the border. To Washington, this seemed only reasonable: Marshall "urgently" approved, Acheson agreed and the President directed the State Department to inform our allies of the intended authorization. The allies reacted so strenuously in the negative that the plan was held in abeyance; and within a few weeks our forces were driven so far from the border that the matter was reduced to the academic.

Soviet victory in a global war; to drive us completely off the Korean peninsula. If the last was the purpose it would mean a third global war, since the Chinese could not do it alone and would have to bring Russia into the conflict. Bradley gave it as the Joint Chiefs' opinion that we could probably hold in the existing Korean positions, though if the pressure increased we might well have to attack the Manchurian bases. Acheson thought that while the primary interest of the Chinese was "to keep us involved" they also had a strong secondary interest in holding the border area and its power plants. He thought we ought to "explore privately" the possibility of securing a settlement on the basis of a twenty-mile demilitarized zone along both sides of the Yalu, under a UN commission. But he recognized, as a major difficulty here, the fact that we had so few means of making direct contact with the Chinese Communists.[1]

MacArthur was not a party either to these deliberations or to these doubts. He was committed to the offensive; and it had been agreed that there should be no change in his directive. This introduced another factor. There was now a firmly established tradition (dating mainly from Pershing's independence in the First World War) that once a field commander had been assigned his mission there must be no interference with his method of carrying it out. If he bungled it, he could be relieved; but until he was relieved, there could be no back-seat driving from the Pentagon or the White House. This, coupled with MacArthur's tremendous military prestige, made JCS extremely reluctant to intervene in the events which were now to transpire.

On November 20 Walton Walker published to 8th Army his directive for the offensive, set for the 25th. On the next day, November 21, JCS did go so far as to "request information" from MacArthur about the coordination of 8th Army and Xth Corps, which were being separately commanded from Tokyo. Under the etiquette, a "request for information" was an indication from the high command that it thought the field commander was going wrong. An answering "request for clarification" was the field commander's indication that he thought his superiors were being silly. In this

[1] Truman, *Memoirs,* Vol. 2, pp. 378-79.

case, MacArthur did not immediately reply. Instead, on November 24, he flew to the Chongchon to launch Walker and 8th Army on their way, with a resounding communiqué which he was later to regret:

> The United Nations massive compression envelopment in North Korea against the new Red armies operating there is now approaching its decisive effort. The isolating component of the pincer, our Air Forces of all types, have for the last three weeks . . . successfully interdicted enemy lines of support from the north so that further reinforcement therefrom has been sharply curtailed and essential supplies markedly limited. The eastern sector of the pincer . . . has steadily advanced in a brilliant tactical movement and has now reached a commanding enveloping position, cutting in two the northern reaches of the enemy's geographical potential. This morning the western sector of the pincer moves forward in general assault in an effort to complete the compression and close the vise. If successful, this should for all practical purposes end the war. . . .

Visiting one of the forward headquarters, he told the corps commander, General John B. Coulter: "If this operation is successful, I hope we can get the boys home by Christmas." [1] Emplaning for his return to Tokyo, he ordered the pilot to take him on a personal reconnaissance along the Yalu frontier. On the snow-covered roads and bridges and fields he saw no signs of military activity, no indication that troops had passed the river or were intending to do so. It was the day after Thanksgiving.

But in Tokyo that evening the general found another "disquieting" [2] message from JCS. The gist was that there was "growing concern" in the UN and in Washington over the possibility of another general war; the top command felt that they must close out the Korean War, and that this might be accomplished if MacArthur would halt "short of the border," taking only the approaches to the Yalu and holding these only with ROK troops. MacArthur replied immediately and (as usual) at length, indicating that he had no such intention. He advanced the military argument that the hills overlooking the Yalu were unsuited to defense. To this he added the political argument that a failure to recover the entire body of

---

[1] Whitney, *MacArthur*, p. 416. Other versions of the remark make it less conditional.
[2] *Ibid.*, p. 417.

Korea "would be . . . regarded by the Korean people as a betrayal . . . and by the Chinese and all of the other peoples of Asia as weakness reflected from the appeasement of Communist aggression." He informed JCS that "it is my plan" to consolidate along the Yalu, and only thereafter to replace "as far as possible" American with ROK troops. When this had been done, it was "my plan" publicly to announce the return of American forces to Japan and the parole of all prisoners of war, leaving the question of the unification of Korea to its own people, with the advice and assistance of the United Nations. In the context of Washington's problems at the moment, this outgiving was not, it must be granted, very helpful. But it made no difference. Two days later all the plans were abruptly vetoed — by the Chinese Communists.

Walker had barely started forward on November 25 when his right flank was heavily hit by strong Chinese units; by next day he was under the heaviest kind of pressure, and the grim truth was soon apparent. Before it had got off the ground the 8th Army offensive had collided with a Communist offensive carrying the weight of at least six Chinese armies behind it. By November 28 Walker's right was collapsing; retreat had become inevitable; crisis was extreme; and MacArthur was issuing a communiqué in terms very different from those used only four days before. It was now recognized and proclaimed that there were as many as 200,000 organized Chinese Communist troops already in Korea; the UN was facing "an entirely new war." The general concluded:

This situation, repugnant as it may be, poses issues beyond the authority of the United Nations military council — issues which must find their solution within the councils of the United Nations and the chancelleries of the world.


## THE NEW WAR

Here was a crisis not only of war but of policy, and one unquestionably complicated by MacArthur's remarkable personality. "Within a matter of four days," Truman observes,[1] MacArthur "found time to publicize in four different ways his view that the

---

[1] *Memoirs,* Vol. 2, pp. 382, 384.

only reason for his troubles was the order from Washington to limit the hostilities to Korea. . . . This," the former President adds with some justice, "was simply not true." Indeed, up to this point the general himself, while expressing his resentment of the "extraordinary inhibitions" imposed on him, had done so primarily on political grounds, regarding them as evidence of appeasement and weakness. He had made no great issue of them as military limitations. Despite the cancellation, in early November, of his order to bomb the Yalu bridges, he had declared in the November 24 communiqué that his air forces had "successfully" interdicted the enemy lines of communication. Collins, searching the record afterward, could find no instance either before the disaster or after it in which MacArthur had specifically asked for authority to carry the strategic air war into Manchuria. Until November 28 MacArthur's pressures toward enlarging the war had been political rather than strategic in motivation; it was only after the debacle that the "extraordinary inhibitions" became prominent as an excuse for the military failure. The element of self-justification which now entered the correspondence did not lessen the corrosive want of confidence between Washington and Tokyo, nor ease the problem of devising a new policy and strategy.

The first interchanges were not helpful. On November 29, later described by MacArthur as the day of "the highest crisis" when "it was not certain just what losses I would sustain in my strategic withdrawal," the Commander in Chief Far East appealed to JCS to accept Chiang Kai-shek's offer (made at the beginning of the war) of 33,000 Chinese Nationalist troops. The Joint Chiefs seemed surprised. MacArthur himself had agreed that such troops would be "ineffective" in Korea; and JCS now had the report of the survey party which the general had sent to Formosa after his own visit and which strongly confirmed this opinion. JCS replied that they were "considering" the proposal, but that "world-wide consequences may be involved." Next day, November 30, there was another communication from CINCFE. Prior to the debacle the Joint Chiefs had "requested information" as to the lack of coordination between 8th Army and Xth Corps. MacArthur now brusquely replied that it was "quite impractical to have a continuous line across the neck" of the peninsula; and that while his forces might seem to be over-extended, the nature of the terrain made it "extremely difficult for an enemy to take any material advantage thereof." This was too much for JCS and they replied, not with hints but with a flat directive: The advanced elements of Xth Corps "must be extricated from their exposed position," while the entire region northeast of the waist of the peninsula was henceforth to be "ignored" save for strictly military considerations. At this time, Xth Corps had not yet been hit, and illusion still reigned in Tokyo. At a command conference on December 1 they were still "optimistic" and even thought (according to Whitney [1]) that they could send the 1st Marines right across the peninsula to fall on the rear of the forces attacking 8th Army. That day they were disabused. The Chinese delivered their ambushed blow at the Marines in the Chosin Reservoir area, and Xth Corps' tragedy began.

THE NEW HISTORY

In Tokyo two operations were going on. On the one hand it was necessary to rewrite the history — which had been so largely provided by MacArthur himself — and on the other to rewrite the policy and strategy to meet the "new war." Apparently, these two operations became to a certain extent confused. The new history began to issue in communiqués and public statements from December 1 onward. The "massive compression envelopment" of the November 24 communiqué became only a "reconnaissance in force" to "develop" Communist strength; the "successful" air interdiction became an example of the "extraordinary inhibitions . . . without precedent in military history" under which MacArthur had been laboring; Xth Corps' "pincer" movement into a "commanding enveloping position" became its "fortunate presence" on the enemy's flank which "forced" him to "divide his forces and thus weaken his offensive capabilities"; the advance into the Chinese trap which was to end the war by Christmas became a "fortunate premature disclosure of enemy build-up operations." Before the month was out

[1] *MacArthur*, p. 423.

CINCFE had convinced himself that, as he officially assured the United Nations in his report of December 26, the operations initiated with the November 24 offensive were "possibly in general result the most significant and fortunate of any conducted during the course of the Korean campaign." And in the spring, when he appeared before the Congressional committees, he declared with every appearance of sincerity that "the disposition of those troops, in my opinion, could not have been improved upon, had I known the Chinese were going to attack. . . . Had I been permitted to use my air, when those Chinese forces came in there, I haven't the faintest doubt that we would have thrown them back."

## THE NEW STRATEGY

If the history had to be rewritten, the rewriting of the strategy to preserve 8th Army was somewhat more urgent. Washington was arguing for a general retreat and regroupment of 8th Army and Xth Corps on some defensible line across the peninsula. In a long message on December 3 MacArthur rejected this idea — which would, of course, have reflected upon the wisdom of dividing the two in the first place. He advanced technical reasons; the junction of the two forces would "jeopardize the free flow of movement that arises from the two separate logistical lines of naval supply and maneuver." But when he added that he refused to accept such a "defensive" concept, it could only suggest that the self-justification was getting involved with the strategy. He went on:

I do not believe that full comprehension exists of the basic changes which have been wrought by the undisguised entrance of the Chinese Army into the combat. . . . This small command actually . . . is facing the entire Chinese nation in an undeclared war, and unless some positive and immediate action is taken, hope for success cannot be justified and steady attrition leading to final destruction can reasonably be contemplated.

This last was serious. It was also puzzling. Did MacArthur actually foresee the "final destruction" of his forces, or was he merely using this as a threat, possibly in an effort to cover his own military defeat, to force the all-out war with Communist China at which he had so often hinted? Collins, again in Tokyo, had a long conversation with MacArthur which he reported to Washington:

[MacArthur's] basic position was that the United Nations should not fail to accept the new challenge of Communist China's aggression and that the full power of the United Nations should be mounted at once. If reinforcements could arrive in time, the most advantageous action would be a withdrawal in successive positions, if necessary, to the Pusan area; otherwise, the command should be evacuated.

Collins was back in Washington on December 7 with a more detailed report. It was a delicate moment. The President, at his press conference on November 30, had been trapped into an intimation that the use of the atomic bomb in Korea had been considered. There was a world-wide sensation; and so violent a reaction in Great Britain that the Prime Minister, Clement Attlee, flew to Washington. He arrived on December 4. He was reassured as to the atomic bomb; but the dramatic trip only emphasized the mounting distrust in the free world of American policies, particularly as executed by the United Nations Commander in Tokyo. Collins returned as the conferences with the British were ending, and Truman called him in to brief the combined group of British and American statesmen. According to Truman,[1] Collins (not unnaturally) gave a comforting picture: ". . . the situation in Korea was serious but no longer critical." Collins was confident that Xth Corps could be evacuated by sea and added to 8th Army. He reported that Walton Walker was convinced that he could hold "a sizable part of Korea for an indefinite time," that MacArthur "shared this confidence" and that Collins himself agreed with them.

But Collins' report to the JCS on MacArthur's attitude was in slightly different terms. Fundamentally, CINCFE's view was that if he was to continue under the "restrictions" which had been imposed upon him, the war was lost, evacuation was inevitable and there was no point in seeking an armistice with the Chinese as our troops could be got off without one. If, however, the United States and the United Nations would accept all-out war with China — including naval blockade, the bombardment of the Chinese main-

[1] *Memoirs,* Vol. 2, p. 410.

land, the maximum use of the Chinese Nationalists, air reconnaissance over Chinese territory — MacArthur would be willing to
recombine Xth Corps with 8th Army and "hold a position across the
peninsula as far north as possible." For men in responsible charge
of global military-political decisions this was at best ambiguous.
CINCFE was apparently saying that if his views as to enlarging
the war against China were accepted, he would be able to re-form
a line — something which had seemed to him "quite impractical"
on November 30. Would the removal of the "inhibitions" so completely alter the military situation in Korea? Was the "final destruction" or evacuation of 8th Army otherwise in fact inevitable? Mac-
Arthur, as he was afterward to claim, was never technically "insubordinate" — indeed, he was to tell the congressmen that he was
probably the "most subordinate" soldier in history — but he was resistant. As the Chief of Naval Operations, Forrest Sherman, was to
to testify: "Throughout this period the conduct of affairs was made
difficult by a lack of responsiveness to the obvious intentions of the
directives which were transmitted out there and a tendency to debate
and in certain cases to criticize."

THE RIFT WIDENS

At the moment when CINCFE was maneuvering for an all-out
war on China as the reply to the disaster into which he had run, the
high civil and diplomatic command was taking the opposite direction. As has been said, Attlee reached Washington on December 4.
On December 5 Lester Pearson, the Canadian Foreign Minister,
stressed the need for negotiating a peace with Asian communism.
Nehru continued urgently to advocate a cease-fire in Korea and a
settlement. At the same time, "The attacks currently being made on
the Administration's China policy by its domestic critics suggested
that within the United States powerful forces were bent on pushing
the country into open and all-out conflict with Communist China."[1]
MacArthur's statements and communiqués, though always carefully
veiled, were a prominent cause of this impression. A serious issue

[1] Goodrich, *Korea,* pp. 157-58.

of high policy — between a probably major war on China or a cease-fire and settlement which would necessarily accept more or less the *status quo* — had been joined. How far was it appropriate to allow a military commander to employ his military prestige in weighting the decision?

On December 6 JCS dispatched to all theater commanders a directive ordering them to exercise "extreme caution" in their public utterances and to clear all speeches, press releases or statements concerning foreign or military policy with the Department of the Army before publication. It was, of course, for MacArthur's benefit, but was given a common address in order not to make this too obvious. CINCFE indicated both his understanding of the intent and his contempt for the order by elaborately submitting his next routine communiqué for clearance. Naturally, he was told that this was not required; and he was to use this reply as justification for his freedom with later statements which, unlike the communiqué, did directly concern foreign and military policy.

Meanwhile, the policy decision was being taken. On December 8 the Truman-Attlee conference ended with a communiqué announcing complete agreement: "There can be no thought of appeasement or of rewarding aggression in the Far East or elsewhere." But "we are ready, as we have always been, to seek an end to the hostilities by means of negotiation." It added that every effort would be made to achieve the UN purposes of a free and independent Korea by "peaceful" means. This was the critical point. The aim of clearing all Communists out of North Korea and reuniting the country, which had been embodied in the UN resolution of October 7, was here tacitly abandoned. The United States, with its UN partners, was now willing to end hostilities not by "victory" but by "negotiation." In effect, this meant a settlement on whatever lines the armies might have reached when "negotiation" became effective. Attlee had suggested that "perhaps we could limit our negotiations to the question of keeping the Communists on the 38th parallel" and the Americans had not seriously rebutted the idea.[1] Meanwhile, the unification and

---

[1] Truman, *Memoirs*, Vol. 2, p. 407.

democratization of Korea would have to wait upon "peaceful" means. In essence, this was a decision to settle for the *status quo ante*. When on December 12 India brought into the General Assembly a resolution, supported by thirteen Arab and Asian states, to set up a three-man committee to explore the basis for a cease-fire in Korea, the United States supported it.

In his initial announcement of the "new war" MacArthur had declared that it posed issues beyond the competence of the military command — "issues which must find their solution within the councils of the United Nations and the chancelleries of the world." The solution which had now in effect been returned by the UN and the chancelleries of the world was not in the least what MacArthur had in mind. Through the next month or so an extraordinary and baffling correspondence flowed back and forth between Washington and Tokyo, as Washington sought to translate the new policy and the new military strategy into directives which MacArthur would carry out, and as MacArthur sought to use his military recommendations as a means of changing policies with which he did not agree.

It was during the last two or three weeks in December that the Administration, on the one hand, stiffened its new policy, while the Commander in Chief Far East, on the other hand, developed the policy and strategy which he was to advance, after his relief, as his justification. The military situation at this time is significant for both processes. The initial Chinese onslaught had expended its force, and there was something of a lull on the battle lines which everyone knew to be only temporary. Eighth Army had lost Pyongyang, but it had formed a position of sorts above the parallel and covering Seoul. Tenth Corps was making its bloody and bitter retreat into the Hungnam perimeter, losing much of its equipment on the way. Its evacuation had not yet been accepted as inevitable, but the possibility that the UN armies might be driven completely from the peninsula was acute in every mind. "Bug-out fever" was epidemic, not only on the fighting fronts but in many headquarters. As early as November 28 the Joint Chiefs had initiated a staff study of what could be done in case the armies were expelled from Korea.

MacArthur's message of December 3 and Collins' glosses upon it had left Washington in a quandary. The problem, according to Acheson, "led to discussions between the Secretary of Defense and Chiefs of Staff and myself during the latter part of December." Marshall was to provide a vivid little sketch of civil-military relations in this difficult period:

We had a great many discussions. It has been a rather common procedure for the Secretary of State and one or two of his principal men, Mr. Lovett [Under Secretary of Defense] and myself and the Chiefs of Staff to meet in the Chiefs of Staff room and hold discussions of two and three hours over these various matters, generally with some specific document. . . . Then we would investigate it, or the Chiefs of Staff had, through their lower working levels, and then their reply had gone back informally [to State], and then this meeting would occur. . . .

We always reached agreement, and it was an agreement where the Chiefs of Staff sat on one side of the table, and Secretary of State Acheson, with his people, and Lovett and myself sat on the other; in other words, the civilian discussing it from our point of view, as nearly as I was civilian, and the military across from us.

Now those were carried either to the Security Council or direct to the President. . . . and I do not recall a case where the President overrode the Secretary of Defense or the Chiefs of Staff . . . to the advantage of the State Department.

On December 22 Walton Walker, commanding 8th Army, was killed in a jeep accident. General Matthew B. Ridgway was snatched from his family's Christmas observances and rushed to Korea to replace him. Conferring with MacArthur in Tokyo on Christmas Day, Ridgway was attacked by CINCFE with the idea that the Chinese Nationalists on Formosa should be "used" as a diversionary force in "mainland China" — something of a new suggestion, as the previous (and rejected) proposals had been for the employment of such troops in Korea. Ridgway, new to the theater and to the Far East, sent a cautious personal memorandum to Collins, explaining that he accepted "the logic" of this proposal, considered "entirely as related to my responsibilities . . . for ground operations." He made it rather plain that the memorandum was sent only to insure that silence would not be construed as opposition to his new theater commander. But whatever Ridgway thought, the incident shows that a new buttress was being established for the MacArthur strategy.

## THE NEW DIRECTIVE

The directive of September 15 (issued on the now far-distant day of the Inchon landing) had instructed CINCFE that the United States "would not permit itself to become engaged in a general war with Communist China" and, in the event of Chinese intervention, had authorized MacArthur only "to continue military action as long as it offered a reasonable chance of successful resistance." This, if not completely out of date, at least seemed no longer to be controlling in CINCFE's mind. On December 27 Marshall completed a draft directive to meet the new situation. It was discussed among Truman, Acheson, Bradley, Rusk and Marshall during the following day; it was put into final form and dispatched on December 29:

It appears from all estimates available [these, it must be noted, were mainly MacArthur's estimates] that the Chinese Communists possess the capability of forcing United Nations forces out of Korea if they choose to exercise it. The execution of this capability might be prevented by making the effort so costly to the enemy that they would abandon it [was this a reference to the strategic atomic bombing of China?], or by committing substantial additional United States forces to that theatre, thus seriously jeopardizing other commitments including the safety of Japan.

We believe that Korea is not the place to fight a major war. Further, we believe that we should not commit our remaining available ground forces to action against Chinese Communist forces in Korea in face of the increased threat of general war. However, a successful resistance to Chinese–North Korean aggression at some position in Korea and a deflation of the military and political prestige of the Chinese Communists would be of great importance to our national interest, if they could be accomplished without incurring serious losses.

Your basic directive [to assist the Republic of Korea and restore peace and security] . . . requires modification in the light of the present situation. You are now directed to defend in successive positions [subject to safety of your troops as your primary consideration *], subject to the primary consideration of the continued threat to Japan, to determine in advance our last reasonable opportunity for an orderly evacuation. It seems to us that if you are forced back to position in the vicinity of the Kum River . . . and if thereafter the Chinese Communists mass large forces . . . with an evident capability of forcing us out of Korea, it then would be necessary under these conditions to direct you to commence a withdrawal to Japan.[1]

The directive concluded with a request for CINCFE's views and a statement, which Tokyo thought "ominous," that "definite direction on conditions for initiation of evacuation will be provided when your views are received."

### MACARTHUR'S COUNTER-PROPOSAL

MacArthur, according to Whitney,[2] received this directive "in utter dismay." It declared that Korea was not the place to fight a major war. "Was it, then," in Whitney's words, "a policy that we would meet Communist aggression in Asia only if we could do it without too much trouble?" MacArthur, reading this formal directive from his superiors, made two deductions: first, that the Administration had "completely lost the 'will to win' in Korea"; second, that it was trying to offload upon the general's shoulders its responsibility for the "shameful decision" to evacuate the peninsula. The Commander in Chief Far East sat down late on the night of December 30 to compose an excoriating reply:

It is quite clear now that the entire military resource of the Chinese nation, with logistic support from the Soviet, is committed to a maximum effort against the United Nations command. . . . Meanwhile, under existing restrictions, our naval and air potential are being only partially utilized and the great potential of Chinese Nationalist force on Formosa and guerilla action on the mainland are being ignored. . . .

Should a policy determination be reached . . . to recognize the state of war which had been forced upon us by the Chinese authorities . . . we could: (1) blockade the coast of China; (2) destroy through naval gunfire and air bombardment China's industrial capacity to wage war; (3) secure reinforcements from the Nationalist garrison in Formosa to strengthen our position in Korea *if we decide to continue the fight for that peninsula;* and (4) release

---

[1] Whitney, *MacArthur*, pp. 429-30. There are two versions of this directive. One was a paraphrase read into the record of the MacArthur hearings (*The Military Situation in the Far East,* Hearings, 82d Cong., 1st sess., p. 2179), the other that given (without source) by General Whitney. Since the Whitney version reads much more clearly and intelligibly, it is presumably the original, and has here been used. But the starred phrase, in brackets here, does not appear in the Whitney version, where there are three dots. It has been inserted from the paraphrase of the hearings.

[2] *Ibid.,* pp. 430-31.

. . . the Formosan garrison for diversionary action (possibly leading to counter-invasion) against vulnerable areas of the Chinese mainland.

I believe that by the foregoing measures we could severely cripple and largely neutralize China's capability to wage aggressive war and thus save Asia from the engulfment otherwise facing it. [Emphasis added.]

The general went on to intimate that once this general war had been opened upon Communist China, we could evacuate Korea and "effect a strategic displacement of our forces [to] . . . the littoral island chain" without embarrassment. The same officer had hotly insisted only a few weeks before that to leave even a five-mile buffer strip along the Yalu would be "appeasement" and "so immoral a proposition" as to bankrupt our influence in Asia. As to whether the proposed retaliation on China would bring on Soviet intervention, CINCFE felt that to be a matter purely "of speculation." He believed that a Russian decision for or against a general war would depend solely on the Russians' own estimates of relative strength; that it would, in other words, in no way be affected by anything that we did. Yet he had just seen the full force of the Red Chinese army thrown against him because of an American advance which had changed the Chinese calculations of strength and interest.

MacArthur ended by giving what Whitney, inaccurately, calls a "cold, professional estimate": Unless the "restrictions" were removed and the proposed all-out war on China were accepted, then the plan of a successive retreat into the Pusan beachhead was "tactically sound." In execution of this plan it would be unnecessary for JCS to make an "anticipatory decision for evacuation"; the implication was that when they had been forced to the beachhead, evacuation would be inevitable anyway.

## RIDGWAY TAKES COMMAND IN KOREA

This, surely, was a remarkable reply by a field general to his higher military and civil command. What not only Truman but the Joint Chiefs of Staff wanted, and desperately needed, to know was whether MacArthur could and would hold on in Korea under the conditions — or "restrictions" — which had been imposed upon him for what were believed to be the most compelling reasons of high policy. What they got was not a "cold, professional" answer to this question; it was in effect an announcement that MacArthur would not play unless both the policy and the strategy were transformed in accordance with his liking. Ridgway was in these hours touring the front lines of 8th Army. It is not surprising that he was shocked by the state of morale which he encountered. It was an army of beaten, apprehensive men who had lost not only their aggressiveness but their alertness. They were "not patrolling as they should"; they knew nothing about the enemy before them; they did not know the terrain; they were not preparing rear lines of defense against the attack which everyone expected to come, and they did not know what they were fighting for or why they should be expected to continue.

Ridgway flung himself into the task of infusing a new spirit. When he met President Syngman Rhee his first words were: "Mr. President, I am glad to be here. And I've come to stay." [1] It was not the mood in Tokyo, where they were considering the abandonment of the peninsula and a retreat to "the littoral islands."

Shortly after dark on New Year's Eve (the day after MacArthur's reply to JCS) the Chinese delivered the expected attack. Despite Ridgway's efforts, 8th Army was still spread too thin and was too dispirited to stem it; on January 2 the hard decision to evacuate Seoul had to be taken; the UN forces retreated south of the Han into central Korea, but the prepared lines which Ridgway had urged were enough to hold against the diminishing enemy attack. The Hungnam perimeter was abandoned and Xth Corps rejoined 8th Army. A position was reconstituted across the peninsula. It was far south of the 38th Parallel, but it was also far north of the Pusan beachhead into which CINCFE had intimated that he must inevitably be driven. Temporarily the situation had been stabilized. No one knew whether or how long it could be maintained.

## REJECTION OF THE MACARTHUR PROGRAM

For MacArthur's superiors in Washington, both military and civilian, his message of December 30 posed a formidable problem.

---

[1] Matthew B. Ridgway, *Soldier*, Harper, New York, 1956, p. 204.

They were being compelled to deal in these days with issues of re-armament, of NATO, of global defense and global policy, in which Korea was only a part, yet into which Korean policy had to be fitted with care if the whole was to succeed. Yet they had to deal with the Korean aspects through this unusual man, with access to strong popular and political forces, the workings of whose subtle mind they did not easily follow and whose motivations they had been taught by experience to distrust. CINCFE's demand for an all-out war on China (accompanied by the hint that under cover of such a war they might evacuate Korea altogether, thus reducing the American casual-ties) clearly raised two major questions. One, which was to be end-lessly discussed after MacArthur's recall, concerned the danger of bringing on Soviet intervention and a third world war, or at the very least of fragmenting the UN and NATO alliances and leaving us naked to a Soviet-dominated world. The other, which received com-paratively little public attention, concerned the effectiveness of Mac-Arthur's strategy, regarded strictly from a military viewpoint.

In his message of December 30 MacArthur had advanced four specific proposals. The first, a naval blockade of China, could not interrupt the main line of Chinese military supply, which was over-land from the Soviet Union, and could add little to the embargo which we were already organizing. The second, destruction of China's industrial capacity by air bombardment, could have had only a long-delayed effect upon the operations in Korea. It might ulti-mately have put so much pressure upon the Mao regime as to lead it to abandon the Korean War and retire behind the Yalu in order to escape further punishment; but all World War II experience with "strategic" and "population" bombing combined to suggest that such a result, if attained at all, could be attained only at the cost of a slaughter of Chinese civilians and a devastation of the country so vast that our own people would rebel at the horror while our name would become anathema throughout the world.

It is interesting that when MacArthur returned to lay his program before the Congress and the country, he suppressed this proposal for the destruction of China's "industrial capacity to wage war," doubtless because its real implications were too obvious. On the other hand, in his December 30 message to JCS he wasted no words over the demand for an attack upon the "sanctuary" bases in Manchuria, of which so much was afterward to be made. Doubtless this was because it would be apparent to the experienced military men in JCS that, with his air demonstrably unable to interdict the 200-mile enemy communication line now running from the Yalu to the military frontier, the extension of the air attack across the river, while it could have helped, would hardly have been decisive.

As to the third and fourth points in the MacArthur program, the "use" of Chinese Nationalist troops in Korea had been rejected by everyone on the ground that they would be "ineffective"; while it required a belief in military miracles to imagine that they could create any significant diversion by guerrilla operations in South China. "We are not prolonging this war," as Bradley was later to put it, "just for the fun of it. The only difference is General Mac-Arthur thinks that to do certain additional operations would be decisive, and we do not think they would be decisive. They might help a little bit, but to offset that you must run the risk of opening up World War III." But enmeshed as they were in "security," the Joint Chiefs were never able to get this point of view over clearly to the public. The military-technical aspects of the MacArthur program (if it can be called a "program") were always its most obscure facet.

In Washington, as the new year came in, the public was not yet a factor in the argument, and the Joint Chiefs had no difficulty in appraising the MacArthur recommendations. What they could not clearly judge, through the fluent prose of CINCFE's telegrams, was the extent to which they might be risking the destruction of 8th Army by following their own policy — which was, essentially, to hang on in Korea as long as possible with the means available in the hope of securing an acceptable cease-fire. They were not on the ground; and the great tradition of independence for the theater commander forbade them from questioning his reports. Their uncertainty about the real position of 8th Army was MacArthur's greatest weapon against them; and it is hard to doubt that CINCFE at least tried to use it to secure the policies he believed necessary.

KOREA 1951: THE PHILIPPINES 1942

On January 9 the Joint Chiefs of Staff, with the approval of the President and the Secretary of State, produced another official directive. CINCFE was told that his proposed retaliatory measures against China could not be permitted, and was again directed to "defend in successive positions" subject to "the safety of his troops and his basic mission of protecting Japan." But it added: "Should it become evident in the judgment of CINCFE that evacuation was essential to avoid severe losses of men and material, CINCFE was at that time to withdraw from Korea to Japan." The reception of this message in Tokyo reflects the curious state of mind now ruling in that proud, defeated and withdrawn headquarters. What they saw in it was not an order but, in Whitney's words, a "booby-trap"! The pro-British if not pro-Communist conspirators in Washington were trying to throw on MacArthur the onus for the Korean debacle and the evacuation which, as a result of it, might become inevitable. "MacArthur refused to be so easily taken in,"[1] and on January 10 sent an angry yet subtle reply:

There is no doubt but that a beachhead line can be held by our existing forces for a limited time in Korea, but this could not be accomplished without losses. . . . The troops are tired from a long and difficult campaign, embittered by the shameful propaganda which has falsely condemned their courage and fighting quality in misunderstood retrograde maneuver, and their morale will become a serious threat to their battle efficiency unless the political basis on which they are asked to trade life for time is quickly delineated, fully understood and so impelling that the hazards of battle are cheerfully accepted.

One cannot help contrasting Ridgway's efforts to restore morale and fighting spirit at the front with this attempt by the theater commander to use the alleged dissatisfactions of his troops to achieve his political ends. CINCFE went on to tell JCS that he was in full agreement with "their" estimate that the limitations imposed on him would eventually render evacuation unavoidable. "In the absence of over-riding political considerations, under these conditions the com-

[1] Whitney, *MacArthur*, p. 435.

mand should be withdrawn from the peninsula just as rapidly as it is feasible to do so." There was a final turn of the screw:

Under the extraordinary limitations and conditions imposed upon the command in Korea . . . its military position is untenable, but it can hold, if over-riding political considerations so dictate, for any length of time up to its complete destruction. Your clarification requested.

This threw Washington into a consternation comparable to that which had been caused nearly a decade before by a similar message from the same officer under similar circumstances. In February 1942, at the height of the defense of Bataan, MacArthur had shocked Washington by supporting a proposal from President Quezon that the Philippines be neutralized and the American troops evacuated. Then, as in 1951, the apparent purpose was to compel the dispatch of reinforcements (which were not yet in existence) and force a reversal of high policy, from the strategy of "Europe first" which had at that time already been adopted to one of "the Far East first." In 1942 MacArthur was told, immediately and emphatically, that "American forces will continue to keep our flag flying in the Philippines so long as there remains any possibility of resistance"; and that put an end to the maneuver. Under the political and psychological conditions of 1951 it was difficult for Washington to be so forthright.[1]

[1] The parallel between the two episodes is so close that it deserves elaboration for the light it throws on MacArthur's attitude in Korea. In 1942 as in 1951 the general was careful to evade any direct responsibility for the proposed evacuation. He encouraged and assisted Quezon to make the proposal, to which he merely appended his own "comments." In these he said: "Since I have no air or sea protection, you must be prepared at any time to figure on the complete destruction of this command. . . . The temper of the Filipinos is one of almost violent resentment against the United States. Every one of them expected help and when it has not been forthcoming they believe they have been betrayed in favor of others. . . . the plan of President Quezon might offer the best possible solution of what is about to be a disastrous debacle. It would not affect the ultimate situation in the Philippines for that would be determined by results in other theaters. . . . Please instruct me." The instructions were prompt; and the "violent resentment" of the Filipinos, which he had used as an argument just as he used the low morale of the 8th Army a decade later, evaporated. The military debacle which he prophesied was unavoidable (as it proved not to be in Korea), but few would hold today that either the national interest or his own reputation would have been served by adopting the proposal which, for whatever reason, he abetted and supported. (Henry L. Stimson and McGeorge Bundy, *On Active Service in Peace and War*, Harper, New York, 1948, pp. 397-404; Richard H. Rovere and Arthur M. Schlesinger, Jr., *The General and the President and the Future of American Foreign Policy*, Farrar, Straus & Young, New York, 1951, pp. 58-59.)

According to Admiral Sherman, the Chief of Naval Operations, "the character of that reply of the 10th January was such as to pre-cipitate an immediate meeting of the Joint Chiefs on the 11th, a further meeting on the 12th; the preparation of a new military direc-tive which was then dispatched, and then the Department of State . . . arranged to send their message. That period of January 9, 10, 11, 12 and 13 was a very difficult one." Washington was not inter-ested in "booby-trapping" General MacArthur. These high military and civilian officials were carrying a tremendous responsibility, trying desperately to reach correct solutions for desperately serious issues of national policy and strategy. At this juncture the Com-mander in Chief Far East had presented them with the deadliest threat which a military commander — in a democratic society at least — can raise against his military and civil superiors: the threat of the "complete" and useless "destruction" of the armies under his command. That the Joint Chiefs' position was indeed "difficult" is plain. MacArthur's motivations, on the other hand, are more ob-scure. But whether his real purpose was to force an enlargement of the war or to force an immediate evacuation, one cannot help noting another obvious consequence of his recommendations. Whatever Washington might do, they would have the effect of putting Mac-Arthur in a position in which he would be free of responsibility and free of blame.

Should Washington enlarge the war, this would validate Mac-Arthur's contention that his defeat had been solely due to the inhi-bitions under which he had suffered; while since this would be a "political" decision which the general had insisted was beyond his "military" competence, any resultant disasters would be the fault of the politicians. Should Washington elect for an immediate evacua-tion, that would equally exonerate him of the military reverse and prove him right in maintaining that Korea could not be held under the limitations imposed upon him by the politicians. But since he had expressed his willingness to fight to "destruction" if the poli-ticians so ordered, he could not be blamed for the evacuation. If Washington ordered him to stay on the restricted basis, then Mac-Arthur would be free to wash his hands of the consequences. What-

ever disasters might ensue could not be blamed on him; but neither
— as this brilliant mind only tardily realized — could subsequent
successes be laid to his credit. It may seem invidious to imply that
General MacArthur made so personal and egoistic a calculation of
the immense responsibilities of his office; yet we have the faithful
Whitney's word for it that he saw in the January 9 directive only
a personal "booby-trap" and that the January 10 response which
caused such alarm in Washington was dictated by a refusal "to be
so easily taken in." When Admiral Sherman was later asked whether
there had not been at this time a "failure of teamwork" between
MacArthur and the Joint Chiefs, his reply, emphatic as it was, must
seem an understatement:

> At this period, possibly better than any other indication [sic], the normal
> relationships which are desirable between one echelon of command and another
> had been seriously impaired.

### THE NEW INSTRUCTIONS

The crisis produced three documents. The first was another directive, sent on January 11, which repeated the previous instructions,
or "in other words," as Bradley later put it, told him "to stay in
Korea." The second was a JCS "memorandum" dated January 12,
on possible courses to be followed in case we should be forced back
into the Pusan beachhead or compelled to evacuate. This paper had
its source in the staff studies which JCS had ordered on November 28, a month and a half before; as finally evolved and approved
(after two revisions) it clearly reflected some of the MacArthur
ideas. It was submitted to the National Security Council, but a copy
went to CINCFE. The third was a message direct from the President to MacArthur, sent on January 13. MacArthur had repeatedly
insisted that he must have "political" decisions. "In the absence of
over-riding political considerations, . . . the command should be
withdrawn," and so on. It had been intended to explain the political
considerations to him in the military directive, but to the purists in
the Pentagon this was a forbidden commingling of the two spheres.
After anxious discussion between the President, State and the Joint
Chiefs, the "military part" was "pulled out" and sent as a directive;

the political part was embodied in Truman's message of January 13, seeking to expound to the general the serious political considerations which underlay his military orders. But no one by that time could have supposed that what MacArthur really wanted was explanations, or that he would be materially affected by any given him. The really critical question was no longer CINCFE: it was 8th Army — its morale, its capabilities, its adequacy as an instrument of the policy not of General MacArthur but of the United States. As Truman's message was dispatched, General Collins was emplaning for another visit to the Far East to find out what was really going on.

It seems not too much to say that with Collins' arrival in the Far East, MacArthur's influence was largely finished. Perhaps this was the real end of that overshadowing career. Collins is represented by MacArthur's supporters as having been under the impression when he landed in Tokyo that evacuation was inevitable. If so, he realized by the time he reached the front in Korea that the peril had been grossly exaggerated. Ridgway had restored 8th Army to a fighting outfit, while MacArthur had been sitting withdrawn in Tokyo, knowing really very little about the armies he commanded, nursing his personal grievances against an Administration which he detested. From the moment of the retirement in early January into the prepared lines below the Han, Ridgway had started his people on aggressive patrolling. The Chinese at the same time had spent their drive and outrun their communications. Ridgway had felt out the opposition against him, first with platoon and company units, then with battalions and regimental combat teams. On January 25, only ten days after Collins' arrival in the Far East, Ridgway launched a full-scale attack on a two-corps front that "was never stopped until it had driven the enemy back across the Parallel." [1] MacArthur had provided for every contingency save one — the contingency of success.

Belatedly, MacArthur appeared to realize that he was in an untenable position; just as he had realized in the case of his maneuver in the Philippines a decade before. In 1942 he had quickly shifted

[1] Ridgway, *Soldier*, p. 216.

his stance; he had carried on the great defense of Bataan, and although disaster was inevitable he had emerged from it as the hero of the Pacific war. In 1951 a similar shift was attempted. With the messages from Washington and Collins' arrival it was clear that the MacArthur program of evacuation under cover of an expanded war against China had no future; with the growing success of 8th Army it was clear that the Washington policy was promising. MacArthur seized upon the President's "political" message of January 13 as his avenue of retreat. As Whitney maintained then and thereafter, this was the "first" indication the Tokyo command had received that Washington intended them to stay in Korea — something which Washington had for weeks been urgently desiring that they should do if possible. Whitney even put an added twist on this contention; during the controversy later in the spring he was quoted in the newspapers:

General MacArthur's spokesman said today that until January 13 this year, MacArthur believed Washington officials wanted our forces evacuated from Korea and made a scapegoat for some political advantage. Major General Courtney Whitney, MacArthur's aide, said a January 13 message from President Truman was the Government's first clear statement to MacArthur to hold in Korea.

But it was too late by that time. The general could no longer emerge as the hero of policies which he had so persistently obstructed; and the further course of the Korean War passed beyond the influence of the Tokyo headquarters. The controlling factors thenceforth were to be, after the President, State, JCS and Ridgway.

KOREAN OBJECTIVES RECONSIDERED

In mid-December the UN had adopted the resolution looking toward a cease-fire in Korea; in mid-January it was considering the "five principles" submitted by the Canadian Foreign Minister, Lester Pearson, looking toward an immediate cease-fire with a "united Korea" to be established later by diplomatic negotiation. The Canadian resolution was adopted on January 13, and immediately rejected by the Chinese Communists. "Now," said Acheson, "we

must face . . . the fact that the Chinese Communists have no intention of ceasing their defiance of the United Nations"; and the
United States demanded a UN resolution formally declaring Red
China, as well as North Korea, an aggressor.[1] But this was not a
declaration of war; and it was a reluctant General Assembly which
in early February adopted even this much. According to the *New
York Times* report:

> The aggression was undeniable, but most of the Asian and Arab countries
> held back to the last, and the Western European nations accepted it only with
> the reservation that they would oppose almost any further action.

Under the circumstances, the condemnation had little meaning.
MacArthur continued to issue statements or inspire newspaper
stories demanding the "use" of the Chinese Nationalists, complaining of his "inhibitions" or calling for "decisions far beyond the scope
of the authority vested in me as the military commander, . . . but
which must provide on the highest international levels an answer
to the obscurities which now becloud the unsolved problems raised
by Red China's undeclared war in Korea." But as the nightmare
of forced evacuation receded, as 8th Army under Ridgway continued
to forge ahead, despite the "inhibitions" and "obscurities," it seemed
increasingly probable that we could bring the Chinese Communists
to negotiate for a cease-fire on terms relatively favorable to the UN.

Beginning on February 6 there were informal meetings once a
week between representatives of State and JCS, considering ultimate
objectives in Korea. As the battle once more approached the 38th
Parallel it was realized that serious decisions would once more have
to be made; but the soldiers and the diplomats were agreed that they
could not be made until the real balances of power became clearer.
MacArthur was already publicly implying that, despite Ridgway's
successes, the best that could be hoped for was simply an endless
military stalemate and an endless drain of blood. Both the civilians
and the soldiers in Washington thought it better to wait and see.
State could not define rational political objectives until it knew
what were the military capabilities on which it would have to rely;

[1] Goodrich, *Korea,* pp. 160-62.

JCS could not determine a "suitable" course of military action until it knew what political objectives would be adopted. This did not represent a conflict between the civilian and the military viewpoints, but a mutual understanding that decisions, for each, would have to be kept in abeyance until the situation, in Korea and on the global stage, was clearer.

## THE RELIEF OF MACARTHUR

By the middle of March Seoul was being retaken and the armies were again close to the parallel. Our UN allies felt that we should not again invade North Korea without an attempt at a settlement; and State, with the concurrence of Defense, recommended another effort to secure a cease-fire approximately on the parallel. On March 20 General MacArthur was advised that a Presidential announcement was being planned to the effect that the United Nations were prepared to discuss "the conditions of settlement" in Korea. It was explained to CINCFE that this would be done because of the UN belief that a diplomatic effort should be made before another military crossing of the parallel; but that Washington, on the other hand, recognized that the parallel had no military significance and did not want unduly to restrict MacArthur's military operations in the interests of this essentially diplomatic move. State desired MacArthur's recommendations as to how much freedom of military action it should preserve for him over the next few weeks in respect to this artificial boundary. CINCFE replied at once that since he could not clear North Korea in any event with his existing force, his directives required no modification.

### MACARTHUR DEMANDS SURRENDER

A draft for the Presidential statement was thereupon prepared; and it was still being elaborately discussed between State, Defense and the allied representatives in Washington when on March 24 General MacArthur in Tokyo issued his own public demand for a cease-fire. It was very different from that being debated in Washington:

Even under the inhibitions which now restrict the activity of the United Nations forces . . . Red China . . . has been shown its complete inability to accomplish by force of arms the conquest of Korea. The enemy, therefore, must by now be painfully aware that a decision of the United Nations to depart from its tolerant effort to contain the war to the area of Korea, through an expansion of our military operations to its coastal areas and interior bases, would doom Red China to the risk of imminent military collapse. These basic facts being established, there should be no insuperable difficulty in arriving at decisions on the Korean problems if the issues are resolved on their own merits, without being burdened by extraneous matters not directly related to Korea, such as Formosa or China's seat in the United Nations.

The Korean nation and its people . . . must not be sacrificed. This is a paramount concern. . . . I stand ready at any time to confer in the field with the commander-in-chief of the enemy forces in the earnest effort to find any military means whereby realization of the political objectives of the United Nations in Korea . . . might be accomplished without further bloodshed.

Thus adroitly did CINCFE torpedo the Washington political initiative of which he had been privately advised. Unable or unwilling to climb back upon the Washington policy, he was apparently determined to destroy it. With this statement, he transformed what had been intended as an offer to negotiate into what could only come as a demand for surrender, on pain of sanctions which neither Washington nor the UN had any intention of applying and in the interest of an objective (the military unification of Korea) which both Washington and the UN had long since abandoned. Perforce, the draft of the Presidential statement had to be laid aside. In his *Memoirs* [1] the former President recalls the anecdote which Lincoln produced when confronted by a somewhat similar move on the part of General McClellan: ". . . it made me think of the man whose horse kicked up and stuck his foot through the stirrup. He said to the horse: 'If you are going to get on, I will get off.' " Like Lincoln, Truman was in no doubt as to who was going to get on and who would get off. "By this act," he writes, "MacArthur left me no choice — I could no longer tolerate his insubordination."

[1] Vol. 2, pp. 442, 443.

Acheson, Lovett and the Joint Chiefs met immediately to consider this latest MacArthur crisis; later on the same afternoon they discussed it with Truman. The only immediate action to result was an icy message from JCS: "The President has directed that your attention be called" to the order of December 6 requiring clearance for statements dealing with policy. In view of the private information given him on March 20, "any" further statements by the general "must be coordinated" as therein prescribed. Truman had not yet fully decided on his course, but within a day or two his mind was made up: MacArthur would have to be relieved. There is some reason to believe that Marshall may have arrived independently at the same conclusion, also well before the next incident, which was to provide the opportunity.

### THE LETTER TO MARTIN

In February the House Minority Leader, Representative Joseph W. Martin, Jr., had delivered a violently and explicitly partisan attack on the Truman foreign policy, turning mainly on a demand for the employment of "the anti-Communist forces of the Republic of China" — forces which the Minority Leader put somewhat extravagantly at "800,000 trained men." There was, he said, "good reason to believe" that MacArthur favored their use, and that there were "people in the Pentagon" who favored it likewise. Martin shipped his speech to the general with a request for comment. On March 20 (the day he was advised of Truman's proposed offer to negotiate) MacArthur responded with his usual fluency. The Congressman's views on the "utilization" of the Chinese Nationalists were in conflict neither with "logic" nor the "tradition" of invariably "meeting force with maximum counterforce." He continued:

It seems strangely difficult for some to realize that here in Asia is where the Communist conspirators have elected to make their play for global conquest, and that we have joined the issue thus raised on the battlefield; that here we fight Europe's war with arms while the diplomats there still fight it with words; that if we lose this war to Communism in Asia the fall of Europe is inevitable, win it and Europe most probably would avoid war and yet preserve freedom. As you point out, we must win. There is no substitute for victory.

The general did not ask that these views be held in confidence; he did not add such a request after he had read the message about the forthcoming offer to negotiate. Nor did he follow the letter with such a request when, a few days later, he received the peremptory directive, ordering him to clear all policy statements. Martin read the letter on the floor of the House on April 5, 1951, and next morning, a Friday, it was being headlined throughout the country and the world. MacArthur, as the *New York Times'* report put it, "struck at the very basis of the Administration's concept of how the tide of Communist imperialism is to be rolled back. With barbed words he asserted that he was fighting Europe's war with arms . . ." The President moved to action.

## THE DECISION IS MADE

Bradley had been alerted, he could not remember by whom, on Thursday afternoon, and had held a brief meeting of the Joint Chiefs to warn them that they had better begin studying "the military aspects." Before the Cabinet meeting on Friday morning Truman conferred with Acheson, Marshall, Bradley and his own special assistant, Averell Harriman. All apparently agreed that MacArthur ought to be relieved, though Marshall expressed caution and the arresting thought that if the general were dismissed "it might be difficult to get the military appropriations through Congress." These were, of course, the huge appropriations for rearmament and NATO. Acheson foresaw "the biggest fight of your administration." After the Cabinet meeting these same men had a further discussion. Truman was "careful not to disclose that I had already reached a decision"; and it was determined to seek the views of the Joint Chiefs on "the military aspects." [1] The rituals had to be meticulously observed. It was not military usurpation which was the danger at the moment; it was that any assertion of civilian control in seeming disregard of military advice would be used by opposition politicians to attack the civil Administration.

[1] *Memoirs,* Vol. 2, p. 447.

The same group met again briefly on Saturday, April 7. According to Truman,[1] Marshall who had been reading the files, now said that MacArthur should have been fired two years before. They discussed the possibility of giving the command in Korea to Ridgway while retaining MacArthur in his essentially political post in Tokyo; but this they rejected as impracticable. Truman sent them away to think it over, while Bradley got the Joint Chiefs together Sunday afternoon. They were, he reported, unanimous in the opinion that from a strictly "military" point of view, MacArthur should be relieved. It was necessary to have a theater commander "more responsive" to JCS control from Washington; besides, they thought the general insubordinate in failing to comply with the directive to clear his statements, and they believed that "the military must be controlled by civilian authority in this country." Truman called the original group back to the White House on Monday; Bradley reported these views of JCS; all declared their conclusion that the general should be relieved, and the President announced his decision to relieve him.

On Tuesday afternoon, April 10, they discussed the drafts of the messages and announcements. To soften the blow as much as possible, they arranged for its delivery through Frank Pace, Secretary of the Army, who was then in Korea. But there was a foul-up of communications; Pace, visiting the front lines, could not be reached; Washington feared that there had been a leak, and the announcement was given to the press at 1 A.M., Wednesday, April 11. In Tokyo, it was about 3 in the afternoon of the same day. The news reached MacArthur, rather brutally, by way of the commercial news broadcasts, which were brought to him as he sat at the end of a luncheon. The famous general had been summarily dismissed.

If this had never really represented a conflict between the "civilian" and the "military" elements in the control of the national policy, it at least threw considerable light upon the actual (as distinct from the theoretical or rhetorical) relationships between them. Whether or not they dealt wisely, Truman and his advisers, in uniform and out of it, had at least dealt firmly and effectively with a complicated

[1] *Ibid.*, p. 448.

problem of policy, politics and personality affecting civil-military considerations of great difficulty and delicacy. As far as the Administration was concerned, the "MacArthur problem" had been solved, for good or ill. But the Administration, of course, represents but one element in the formulation and control of American military and foreign policy. There remained the Congress, the political party system, the press and the public. Not the least instructive aspect of the MacArthur episode is the manner in which these other great instruments of policy formulation responded to it.

## THE MACARTHUR HEARINGS

Douglas MacArthur returned to the United States in an enormous fanfare of publicity in which partisan political pressures — which the general had seldom sought to discourage — were prominent. He was invited to appear on April 19 before a joint session of the two houses of Congress, where he was received with the utmost deference, and where he delivered a self-justification (in some respects rather less than frank) and an attack upon the Administration's conduct of a foreign war of a kind not often permitted to top generals just relieved for insubordination to the civil authority.

Had the American people believed themselves to be engaged (as in fact they were) in a large-scale war effort for the attainment of vital national objectives, the MacArthur address to Congress could hardly have been given. But because Korea represented a struggle which the Administration was trying to keep within the bounds of limited warfare; because there was no grasp of the fact that even limited warfare might produce major political results; because there was almost no understanding of the real nature of the enemy's strength and, consequently, almost no appreciation of the advantages which our internal dissensions were daily providing him; because there seemed no overriding national peril to silence the petty bickerings of personal or party interest, it was possible both for the general to make the address and for it to be received as a major contribution to statesmanship.

MAC ARTHUR ADDRESSES CONGRESS

It was more skillfully constructed than most of his hearers could have realized. In general, it was a résumé of the political and strategic ideas which MacArthur had been perfecting and publicizing since his defeat on the Chongchon. He advanced five specific recommendations. "Apart from the military need as I saw it to neutralize the sanctuary protection given to the enemy north of the Yalu," he proposed four other measures:

First, the intensification of our economic blockade against China.

Second, the imposition of a naval blockade against the China coast.

Third, removal of restrictions on air reconnaissance of China's coastal areas and of Manchuria.

Fourth, removal of restrictions on the forces of the Republic of China on Formosa, with logistical support to contribute to their effective operations against the Chinese mainland.

This suppressed MacArthur's proposal to destroy China's "industrial capacity to wage war," converting it into an innocuous "reconnaissance" of coastal areas and Manchuria; it suppressed his suggestion for an evacuation of Korea; it made no mention of whatever proposals there may have been (Whitney hints obliquely at them) for the use of atomic weapons; while the general's statement that "no man in his right mind" could advocate sending American ground troops into China at least glossed over the fact that no commitment of Chinese Nationalist forces to the mainland could possibly be "effective" without massive American support and the probable ultimate embroilment of our ground forces.

Having thus elusively described his program, the general continued:

For entertaining these views, all professionally designed to support our forces . . . and bring hostilities to an end . . . at a saving of countless American and Allied lives, I have been severely criticized in lay circles, principally abroad, despite my understanding that from a military standpoint the above views have been fully shared in the past by practically every military leader concerned with the Korean campaign, including our own Joint Chiefs of Staff. [Applause, the members rising.]

This was a curious declaration. The MacArthur program, from whatever motives it sprang, had certainly not been "professionally" designed to bring hostilities to an end — indeed, as he described it, it seemed obviously incapable of doing so. His views had been criticized in much more than "lay circles, principally abroad"; while the Joint Chiefs had never "fully" shared them, of course, at any time. MacArthur rested his "understanding" that in the past they had done so on the JCS memorandum of January 12 — the document which evolved out of the staff study, begun in November, of possible courses in the event that evacuation of Korea became imminent. This top-secret memorandum had advanced in all sixteen proposals. From these MacArthur, in his address, selected and revealed to the world four recommendations: To intensify the economic blockade of China (which was already being done); to "prepare now" to impose a naval blockade as soon as a beachhead was stabilized "or when we have evacuated Korea"; to "remove now" restrictions on air reconnaissance of China and Manchuria; to "remove now" restrictions on Chinese Nationalist forces and give such "logistical" support as would contribute to effective Chinese Nationalist operations against the Communists.

This paper of three months before, prepared under conditions very different from those obtaining in April to meet eventualities which had not taken place and now quoted only in small part, was cited by the general as proof that JCS had "in the past" fully shared his views as to strategy in the Far East. Even what was quoted was certainly far from sustaining the allegation; and when he added that "as far as I know," JCS had never changed the conclusions of January 12, he was well aware that in fact they had. The general concluded the impressive address with the cliché he had already found serviceable — "there is no substitute for victory" — but the precise nature, design, purpose or effect of the victory he had in mind he failed to make clear.

It is a curious fact that, despite the enormous and generally favorable attention which this address received, it had no measurable influence over the course of Far Eastern policy and strategy. After Collins' visit to 8th Army in January MacArthur had largely ceased to be a force in strategic plan; after the address to the joint session of Congress he largely ceased to be a force in policy. His prescription, whatever exactly it might be, was too vague, too seemingly dangerous, too loosely connected with the realities in the Far East and the world, to be influential with American opinion. On May 3 the Senate Foreign Relations and Armed Services Committees were to open their joint hearing into *The Military Situation in the Far East;* and for two months this remarkable spectacle was to continue in daily session, with the transcripts (only mildly censored for security) released each evening to the press. But the so-called "MacArthur Hearings" were in large measure a partisan political enterprise rather than a serious inquiry into the policy and strategy of the Far East; and while they were illuminating in many ways, they failed to resuscitate Douglas MacArthur's power and authority in American affairs.

### THE HEARINGS BEGIN

Through the first three days MacArthur, as opening witness, reiterated and defended his position dramatically, skillfully, at times evasively. The Administration's policy of waging a limited war to a reasonably satisfactory end was denounced as "appeasement."

> The concept I have is that when you go into war you have exhausted all other potentialities of bringing the disagreements to an end . . . [If the Administration's concept is that of] a continued and indefinite campaign in Korea, with no definite purpose of stopping it until the enemy gets tired or you yield to his terms, I think that introduces into the military sphere a political control such as I have never known in my life.

The last was rhetorical; most wars have ended when one side or the other has "got tired," and students from Clausewitz on down have recognized it as the function of the political authority to determine the end, as well as the beginning, of military action. MacArthur's "concept" would in fact have introduced into the political sphere a military control altogether novel in American affairs. This may not have been immediately apparent to the congressmen; but the general's position compelled him to make extreme claims for the military authority:

> When all other political means fail, you then go to force; and when you do that, the balance of control . . . is the control of the military. A theater commander . . . is not merely limited to the handling of his troops; he commands that whole area, politically, economically and militarily. . . . At that stage of the game you must trust the military. . . . When men become locked in battle, there should be no artifice under the name of politics which should handicap your own men, decrease their chances of winning and increase their losses.

This evaded the fact that MacArthur had actually been in conflict with his own military superiors as well as the political authority; it represented a claim to absolute and irresponsible authority in the *theater* commander which few other soldiers of the time would have supported. Nor would many have supported the claim that "once you go to force," force and its military exponents become supreme. MacArthur did not really support it himself; questioned later on, he quickly backtracked:

> At no time in our system of government is there any question of the civil administration being in complete control. What I said was meant to convey the idea that there should be no non-professional interference in the handling of troops in a campaign. . . . Any idea that a military commander in any position would possess authority over the civil functions of this government is a treasonable concept in my mind.

This was quite different from what he had said a couple of days before. But such inconsistencies were at the time difficult to detect through the turgid streams of uncorrelated questions and answers which flowed interminably through May and June.

MacArthur was followed on the stand by Marshall, Bradley, Acheson, the three Chiefs of Staff, Hurley, Louis Johnson and numerous lesser military and diplomatic figures. Toward the later stages public interest seriously flagged. When MacArthur was asked at the end whether he would like to reappear (since much adverse testimony had been introduced against him), he declined. He had made his case in the first days; it was a work of art, and there was no reason to impair its perfection by rebutting subsequent criticisms to which few had paid much attention anyway. Partly for this reason, much in the record was left inconclusive and unelucidated. And as the interminable rounds of questioning went on it became apparent that almost no one — with the exception of Wayne Morse of Oregon, then on the Republican side, and Brien McMahon, the Connecticut Democrat — was interested in the facts of the "military situation in the Far East."

To most of the Republican senators the hearings were chiefly a means through which they might exploit MacArthur's relief to the maximum damage of the Truman Administration; while the cautious Democrats were mainly conducting a kind of delaying action. They dared not seem too critical of the great military figure who enjoyed so enormous a public reputation; the most they could do was to turn some of his and the Republicans' shafts. The skill with which Senator Richard B. Russell (of Georgia), the chairman, managed this has often been noted, and it undoubtedly helped to preserve the nation from courses which might have been disastrous. But the Democrats evidently felt it inadvisable to enter a positive and challenging support of the Truman foreign policies or of MacArthur's dismissal — some of them probably did not want to — and in consequence, although the great majority of the witnesses were favorable to the Administration, the Administration's case was seldom clearly or effectively brought out. Nor were the underlying issues of civil-military relationships with which nearly everyone struggled in one way or another in the course of the hearings.

## CONFUSION CONFOUNDED

There was never any real clarification of the technical military factors involved. When McMahon asked the general whether he thought we were "ready to withstand the Russian attack in Western Europe today?" the answer was: "Sir, I have asked you several times not to involve me in anything except my own area." That was a question which he felt should be addressed to the Joint Chiefs — although it would seem to have been rather critical for MacArthur's own recommendations as to policy in the Far East. Toward the end of the hearings Major General Emmett ("Rosie") O'Donnell, Jr., was to testify that when he went out in command of the strategic bombers in the early stages of the war, it was his "hope" that everything could be wound up with one "very severe blow on the North Koreans." The air general's idea was that, "with advance warning, perhaps, . . . we now have at our command a weapon that can really dish out some severe destruction"; using it, we should "go to work on burning five major cities in North Korea to the ground" and destroying completely "every one of about eighteen major strategic targets." The idea was vetoed at the time by MacArthur's air commander, on the ground that everything available had to be put into tactical support of the troops. The senators did not press O'Donnell on the vital questions of how his proposed destruction would have affected the military results or helped to solve the basic policy problems presented by Korea. The testimony was simply allowed to stand as a presumably serious contribution to the question of how the Korean War should have been, but was not, fought.

When Senator Styles Bridges (Republican of New Hampshire) asked the Air Chief of Staff, Hoyt Vandenberg, whether we could "win" without full use of air power, Vandenberg replied by asking what he meant by "win."

Bridges: Let's say drive the Communists out of North Korea, out of all Korea.

Vandenberg: I wasn't aware that was our objective.

Bridges: I am not either, but I haven't been able to find out what our objective is.

Vandenberg: I believe our objective is to kill as many Chinese Communists as is possible without enlarging the war at the present time in Korea. I believe that there are reasonable chances of success in achieving a negotiated peace without endangering that one potential that we have, which has kept the peace so far, which is the United States Air Force.

Thus the technical question went unanswered, while the policy question beneath it was scarcely clarified. The Republicans found a promising line of attack in accusing the Truman Administration of having incompetently intervened for "political" reasons into the mysteries which should remain the sole province of the military men.

This might have brought the hearings close to the heart of the civil-military relationship in a modern society; about all it actually did was to yield many pages of bad argument, equally confused on both sides. Thus, Bridges asked Bradley: "If it reaches a time in this country where you think the political decision is affecting what you believe to be basically right militarily, what would you do?"

Bradley: Well, if after several instances in which the best military advice we could give was turned down for other reasons, I would decide that my advice was no longer of any help, why, I would quit.

Bridges: Would you speak out, tell the American public?

Bradley: No, sir . . . I am loyal to my country, but I am also loyal to the Constitution . . . and I wouldn't profess that my judgment was better than the President of the United States or the Administration.

Bridges: Would it not be on a military subject?

Bradley: Yes.

Bridges: Should you not speak out?

Bradley: I would, yes, to the constituted authorities.

Bridges: But you would stop there?

Bradley: Yes.

It is apparent that the Senator was trying merely to make a case for MacArthur, the general trying to make a case for Truman. But beneath the interchange there lay real and difficult issues both of policy and of morals. They were not well elucidated by the Mac-Arthur hearings; and the chief result of this and many other similar questionings would seem to have been to demonstrate the inextricable intermingling on all top command levels of the military and the political factor.

The possible uses and limitations of military force in achieving desired policy ends was a vital question which became almost totally fogged in the partisan interchanges. Acheson, appearing for the first time on June 1, defined this issue in his crisp, intelligent way:

Our objective is to stop the aggression, and the attack on that [South Korean] government, restore peace. . . . The United Nations has since 1947 and the United States has since 1943 or 1944 stood for a unified, free and democratic Korea. That is still our purpose . . . I do not understand it to be a war aim. In other words, that is not sought to be achieved by fighting, but it is sought to be achieved by peaceful means.

This might well have served as the starting point for an examination into the potentialities of force in the situation we were then confronting. But the question was lost in further theoretical discussions of the civilian and military roles in policy-making, like that introduced by General Wedemeyer when he appeared on June 11. Wedemeyer's testimony is of singular interest. He began by advancing the extreme military claim, which few military men actually supported, that "a commander in the field should be given no restrictions *whatsoever* in carrying out his mission, sir." (Emphasis added.) Wedemeyer's position seemed to be that once the mission had been assigned, the government must stand committed to support any and every military means which the field commander thought necessary for fulfilling it, even though the requested means might undermine other vital policies and the mission might on that account have been revised. Again, this was rhetoric. It was a claim to a military absolutism which no American officer would advance unless his personal and political emotions were deeply engaged.

But Wedemeyer's emotions were so deeply engaged that he went on to startle the congressmen with a recommendation for an immediate evacuation of Korea. His testimony well illuminates the tangled intellectual roots out of which the policy of the neo-isolationists — a policy of which Wedemeyer was to become a spokesman and which left a clear impress upon the earlier days of the Eisenhower Administration — was to grow.

General Wedemeyer had indicated his belief that a truce providing for a cease-fire generally along the 38th Parallel would not be "victory"; it would be "tantamount to a defeat, sir, psychologically." Senator J. W. Fulbright (Democrat of Arkansas) then pressed him to say what, in his view, would represent an "acceptable minimum" of success in Korea. Wedemeyer tried to evade the blunt issue, but after much verbal fencing was finally brought to the critical point:

Now I am going to step out of the realm of an Army officer and tell you this, sir, that in my judgment we ought to get out of Korea; and I would do it because I just don't think that we are going to get anywhere. I want to take the strategic initiative away from that enemy, and I want the Americans and their allies to take actions in the political, the economic, in the psycho-social and in the military fields at times and places of our own choosing, and the kinds of action that we take will be coordinated to accomplish our national aims.

Fulbright not unnaturally pointed out that this sort of retreat would represent a much worse defeat than an acceptance of a truce along the parallel line. Wedemeyer answered:

But you must take counter-steps in other fields. I would break off diplomatic relations with them. I would go into full mobilization. And I would clearly lay it all before the world. . . . And I would go further; I would go to the real perpetrator of all this . . . in the Kremlin. And if we permit them to call the tune to which we shall dance, our form of government would be in jeopardy.

Wedemeyer explained that he would break relations with Russia and her satellites "concurrently" with his proposed withdrawal from Korea and would do it all in order to "explain to the world my future actions. 'I am going to take the initiative away from these people.'"

This was, essentially, the MacArthur program reduced to an intelligible statement — a statement, one cannot help adding, which MacArthur himself had been far too intelligent, too shrewd, to present. It revealed (as subsequent experience has pretty clearly demonstrated) a serious misapprehension of the actual military, political and psychological forces available to both the United States and the Soviet Union in their world struggle. The strategy of headlong flight as a means of taking "the strategic initiative away from the enemy" has seldom proved a valid one. But at least Wedemeyer recognized (where MacArthur had concealed) the essential corollary. If valid at all, it required that while decamping from the field of battle we should take massive "counter-steps" — "full mobilization," a "clear" challenge direct to the Kremlin. And for this, the American people had no stomach.

In its earlier days, the Eisenhower Administration was to take over, even to the terminology, the first part of the Wedemeyer program. The disengagement of our own troops from such fields as

Korea; action otherwise "at times and places of our own choosing," the destruction of the enemy's "strategic initiative" by withdrawal of our own; the resort to "psycho-social" as well as political and economic means as a substitute for bloodshed — all these ideas were prominent at least in the earlier period of the Eisenhower Administration. But Wedemeyer's "full mobilization" and all-out challenge to the Kremlin were, of course, no part of the program after the Republican return to office. In their absence, the other devices were to prove relatively ineffective. The Wedemeyer testimony survives to make clear the extent to which the complicated motives and emotions of the MacArthur crisis tended to channel the policy of the United States into courses which, though perhaps not mistaken, were to prove relatively barren of result. New ideas and initiatives would still have to be developed by those who profited most from the MacArthur crisis and the great charade of the MacArthur Hearings.

On June 23, four days before the MacArthur Hearings reached their tortured and, by this time, tiresome and neglected end, Jacob Malik, the Soviet delegate to the United Nations, threw out the suggestion in a UN radio talk that a truce in Korea was possible. A week later, Ridgway broadcast an offer to the Chinese commander to consider a truce. The UN and United States command had in effect asked for peace. It was to take another two years to get it and many lives were to be sacrificed in the interim. But the whole character of the Korean War was now altered.

From this point on, the American national objective was no longer either "victory" or a reunification of Korea; it was simply and solely a cessation of hostilities. Against this simple desire, MacArthur and his supporters could make no headway. The hearings had generated enormous amounts of political ammunition for discharge against the Democratic Administration; what they had quite failed to generate was any significant public pressure for reversing the course which that Administration was following. The salient fact is that the American people did not accept the veiled MacArthur prescription for "victory"; they did acquiesce in the Truman policy of a limited war for limited ends, and were grateful for Eisenhower's conclusion of the war on these terms. They had listened to General MacArthur with the enormous respect claimed by his character, his career and his achievements; but they hardly lifted a finger to promote the courses which he appeared to recommend. "Victory," in the terrible modern contexts, had become too barren a goal to pursue.

# The Global Problem

## A NEW MILITARY POLICY

If the MacArthur problem was mainly a personal and political one, having little relevance to the fundamental relationship of civil to military power in the state, it was at the same time set in the context of a global issue by which this relationship was profoundly affected. The aggressive Soviet moves in the spring of 1948 had brought the Brussels Pact into existence and set American policy on the path which led to the North Atlantic Treaty Organization. The Soviet atomic explosion in the summer of 1949 had compelled a review in depth of the American position; it had produced the hydrogen bomb program and NSC 68, with its proposals for a serious and large-scale rebuilding of American military power. But NATO, the hydrogen bomb program and NSC 68 were all alike in a tentative, almost faltering stage when in June 1950 the Soviet Union, for the first time since 1948, unleashed naked military aggression in support of its aims.

### A NEW BUDGET

"Communism," as General Bradley told the House Appropriations subcommittee in July, "is willing to use arms to gain its ends. This is a fundamental change and it has forced a fundamental change in our estimate of the military needs of the United States." It was at the same time to force an equally fundamental change in the civilian estimates of the capacity of the economy. Secretary Johnson put it succinctly: "In the light of the actual fighting we have reached the point where the military considerations clearly outweigh the fiscal considerations." When the Communist onslaught came the United States was maintaining armed forces of about 1.5 million men. We were entering a fiscal year for which $13.5 billion had been made available for defense; we were planning a forty-eight-group Air Force and an expenditure of about $1.5 billion on Mutual Defense Assistance — two thirds of this for NATO and the rest distributed among Greece, Turkey and our Far Eastern satellites. These sums, and force levels, were patently insufficient for meeting the costs of war in Korea, to say nothing of the global peril which seemed so suddenly to impend. The Truman "ceiling," the calculations of the Budget Bureau, the power of the civilian comptrollers in Defense, were scrapped by the immediate decision of the civilians themselves. Now and for the next two or three years defense budgets were again to be based (as they had been during the First and Second World Wars) primarily on the military estimates of requisite force levels rather than on the civilian estimates of the economic limitations.

This represented the critical decision. Unavoidably, it at once promoted the Joint Chiefs of Staff into a position of authority which they had not held since 1945. While MacArthur was struggling against the famous "inhibitions" imposed on his action in Korea, the far more disabling "inhibitions" upon military power under which the Pentagon had labored since the end of the Second War were quietly and almost by common consent removed. This is not, of course, to say that JCS was given unlimited power, or that the new estimates were uninfluenced by civilian suggestions or considerations of civil policy. The civilians were, indeed, often to take the lead in urging the military to enlarge their planning. The foundations for the new programs had been laid in NSC 68, in which the State Department had been a prime mover; as Johnson was to testify, the new military proposals were "based upon studies which began immediately after the President's announcement of the Soviet atomic explosion last September . . . The minimum desired forces which these studies showed to be required — normally a matter that would have been provided for in next year's budget — are being requested at this time." In the development of the NATO defense, State continued to carry the main responsibility, but of course consulted the Pentagon at every step.

In an address broadcast on July 19 the President announced the basic responses he proposed to make to the crisis. They were three: to limit the fighting strictly to Korea; to make a massive increase in the American military potential, and to use this increase largely in support of our allies in Western Europe. The object, he declared, was not to prepare for war but to avert one on any major scale. On July 24 he asked Congress for a defense supplemental of $10.5 billion and on August 1 he requested an additional $4 billion for the Mutual Defense Assistance Program (MDAP), seven eighths of it for the NATO powers. Congress, the final citadel of "civilian control," was to accede with little hesitation. In the House Appropriations subcommittee the main concern seemed to be whether these huge new sums would be enough. The Defense spokesmen reassured the legislators that the bill carried more than they believed would be necessary for Korea, while the provisions of the general military build-up accorded with the pre-Korean JCS planning. But Bradley explained that the JCS were under orders "to keep these matters under continuous study." If revision became necessary, *"we* will inform the Congress as quickly as possible"; and the pronoun here italicized seems indicative of the new strength of the Joint Chiefs' position.

It was Secretary Acheson who appeared on August 2 as the first witness for the MDAP supplemental. "The details of this program," he was obliged to say, "are still being worked out, but the magnitude of the task is already apparent . . . This amount will enable us to proceed with those measures which are immediately required during the fiscal year of 1951, as our part of the initial phase of this defense program . . . Our deputy to the North Atlantic Council, Mr. [Charles M.] Spofford, is now engaged in active consultation with the representatives of other nations in the North Atlantic Treaty

Organization to work out what each of us can and will do now to increase our common defense capabilities."

## THE NEEDS OF NATO

There was, however, more than monetary totals to be worked out. Well before Korea, it had become apparent that the creation of an effective NATO defense would turn chiefly on three related military issues: American willingness to supply a supreme commander (thus fully involving the United States in the common enterprise); the willingness of all the members to flesh the organization with troops (which in turn raised the question of an American troop contribution); and the rearming of West Germany. Serious studies of these issues had begun in several agencies after the President, at the end of January 1950, approved the preliminary NATO defense plans and thus put the first MDAP appropriations into effect. But when NATO met in Paris in May it seemed unlikely that satisfactory solutions could be found.

Both the reluctance of the member states to make heavy troop contributions of their own and the simple logic of West European geography combined to indicate that an effective defense would be impossible without West German troops. But the political difficulties, both international and internal, in the way of German rearmament seemed at the same time insuperable. Both Truman and Acheson were on record against the idea, not only because of the resistance of Germany's neighbors but also because of domestic opposition. Less than three weeks before the Korean crisis, Bradley, falling back on the old evasion, told the House Military Affairs Committee that while "from a strictly military point of view" the inclusion of West Germany in the defense was essential, "there are political considerations that enter into it." These were "something entirely out of military hands," to be "decided on a higher level." Three weeks later it was the JCS who were on the "higher level" and the unreal distinction between the political and the military had once more disappeared.

It is true that the post-Korean reversal in regard to German rearmament was by no means a matter merely of the dictates of the military. Defense, no less than State, had been absorbed by the problem of nuclear war; the shock of Korea brought State, no less than Defense, back to the problem of immediately available conventional forces, in which West German troops seemed critical. McCloy, now High Commissioner in Germany, was seriously alarmed by the build-up of the East German Communist "police"; and had put his own staff to work on the question of rearming West Germany. In July the State Department, learning of this, brought some members of McCloy's staff back to Washington to help. One was an Army officer, Colonel H. A. Gerhardt. By August State had worked out a "package" plan, including an American supreme commander, five to eight American divisions in Europe and a defense line established east of the Rhine. Johnson was still Secretary of Defense and his edict banning communication between the lower levels of Defense and State was still theoretically in force; but Gerhardt got this plan "almost surreptitiously" to the Joint Chiefs. Their response was favorable; but they insisted that a rearmed West Germany must be included, as otherwise we would be committing the American supreme commander and his American divisions to probable disaster.

Acheson had opposed German rearmament, but was now prepared to accept the necessity for it. The question, unfortunately, had to be promptly decided, since the North Atlantic Council (composed of the twelve NATO foreign ministers) was to meet in New York in mid-September. As matters began to look brighter in Korea, however, new pressures were arising against the whole NATO concept. Johnson was convinced that the Europeans were dragging their feet. While a large body of public opinion was hostile to rearming the late enemy, opposition politicians on the farther right, like Senator Kenneth S. Wherry, the Nebraska Republican, were seeing an opportunity. They were demanding that Europe be compelled to accept a rearmed Germany as the price of any further MDAP appropriations. The NATO idea, abruptly reinvigorated at the end of June, was again languishing by the end of August. At Acheson's suggestion, Truman on August 26 summoned him, Johnson and the Joint Chiefs to tell them that they must produce an agreed State-Defense policy on NATO immediately. (This was the meeting at which Truman also presented them with the problem of MacArthur's message to the Veterans of Foreign Wars.) State and JCS were already in sufficient rapport; the difficulty was with Johnson, the civilian Secretary of Defense.

## THE NATO PACKAGE

State dispatched a task force to the Pentagon which came back with an agreement: Defense would supply an American supreme commander and a large American reinforcement for Germany if State would undertake to make West German military manpower available for the common defense. German rearmament, in short, was the condition on which the military command would permit the essentially civilian and diplomatic NATO policy to go forward. Acheson thought the condition was more rigid than was either necessary or desirable, but he was bound to it. The agreement went to the President by September 8; he submitted it to his usual advisers and secured their approval. But by this time it was too late to allow for proper preparation of our British and French colleagues. They were due to arrive in New York on September 12. Acheson was left in the dilemma that he could not give them adequate warning of what amounted to a major shift of American policy; yet he did not believe that he could honorably conceal from them at this meeting the fact that the shift had taken place. He chose to make the demand for German rearmament central to the proposals which he laid, first, before the Big Three foreign ministers and, later in the week, before the full NATO Council when it met at the Waldorf-Astoria in New York.

As a result, the Secretary was accused of using surprise tactics and the surprise was blamed for the failure of the policy. The French Foreign Minister, Schuman, could not accept the rearmament of Germany — whether he could have done so with even the fullest preparation may today remain a question — and the issue was in effect side-stepped, thus being left to harry NATO policy for years thereafter. The military, for "purely military" reasons, had demanded immediate implementation of an essentially political condi-

tion which some, at least, of the political men had felt to be of dubious practicality. To this rather small extent they had overridden
civilian control. Yet the sequel is instructive. Seven years later there
were still no effective, formed German troops in the NATO defense
system; through the interval, however, that system was to be successfully established and was to grow greatly in strength and influence.
The conclusion would seem to be that neither "purely military" nor
"purely political" wisdom, nor even the rather close combination of
the two illustrated in this episode, can provide more than a dim
guide to the future.

## THE ROLE OF CONGRESS

The second week of September 1950, during which the NATO
conference took place, was one of unusual drama and significance. It
began with the President's announcement on Saturday, September 9,
that he had approved "substantial increases" of American forces in
Europe contingent upon a matching effort by the Europeans, and
with his broadcast the same evening outlining a program of moderate economic controls — higher taxes, restrictions on housing and
consumer credit, military priorities for materials in short supply, and
the possibility of wage and price controls should these prove necessary. The National Security Council recommendation to advance
beyond the 38th Parallel was approved by the President on Monday,
September 11. The Big Three foreign ministers met on Tuesday in
New York; that evening Truman "startled Washington" by announcing that Louis Johnson had resigned, and that George Marshall
would be nominated as Secretary of Defense as soon as the National
Security Act could be amended to permit the appointment of a professional officer to that post. Wednesday morning's newspapers
brought the first reports of an offensive being launched out of the
Pusan perimeter. That day the Senate Armed Services Committee
reported out the bill permitting Marshall's nomination; while the
Senate Appropriations Committee reported out the defense supplemental, which the House had raised from the requested $10.5 billion
to nearly $17 billion. On Thursday morning the banner headlines

proclaimed the air-sea bombardment of Inchon. On Friday morning the full story of the Korean maneuver was out; the Marines, backed by the Army's 7th Division, had landed successfully; they were well on their way to Seoul; while the North Koreans, outflanked, were crumbling. The full North Atlantic Council met that day in New York. The Administration policy of a quick, limited war in Korea accompanied by a massive build-up of the Western defenses seemed likely to end in brilliant success.

But here an unexpectedly discordant note was struck by the more right-wing Republicans. In any working structure of civil-military policy formulation, the Congress, and more especially its opposition elements, are obviously no less vital factors than the military chiefs and the civilian administrative heads. The Republicans in Congress were not too well pleased with these triumphs of the Democratic Administration in a year which was to bring the mid-term Congressional elections. But there was little that they could criticize in Democratic military and foreign policies which were not only apparently succeeding but also closely paralleled their own. Thus Senator Henry Cabot Lodge of Massachusetts had suggested that we might have to send as many as twenty divisions to Europe only the day before the President announced that large reinforcements would be sent. Clearly, this presented Senator Taft, the Minority Leader, with something of a dilemma. He could hardly disavow Lodge or the other Republicans who shared such views; yet he could not support the Democratic President. Taft endorsed the raising of fresh divisions, but argued that we should be "slow" in sending them to Europe until we should be "able to tell what the European countries are going to do for themselves. I am willing to send more troops to Europe, but I want to know first what is needed."

### THE MARSHALL ENABLING BILL

At this juncture, the Marshall enabling bill provided the Republicans with what looked like more solid ground. When it was introduced on Wednesday, September 13, Taft indicated that he would oppose it in the name of "civilian control." But he added that he would also oppose it because returning Marshall to the Cabinet would strengthen Acheson "in relation to the Chinese Communists." The Republicans already intended to fight the Congressional elections — now less than two months off — on the argument that the Democratic Administration had been "soft" on communism in the Far East. The Marshall mission to China in 1946 was one of their leading exhibits for this enterprise; and the general's reappearance as a saviour of the country in a war against communism in 1950 would be less than helpful.

The Senate debate on the bill — it took place on Friday — was astonishingly "bitter." The main argument of the opposition was the necessity of preserving civilian control, but the fact that this had almost nothing to do with the question did not escape the reporters. Senator William E. Jenner of Indiana delivered an hour-long diatribe against the general so outrageous that Jenner's Republican colleague, Saltonstall of Massachusetts, arose at the end to dissociate himself as emphatically as he could from what had been said; while the Democratic Majority Leader (Scott Lucas of Illinois) called it "the most diabolical speech . . . I have ever heard in sixteen years here." The bill passed without difficulty, but on a division which quite clearly indicated how little the constitutional issues of civil as against military authority were concerned. It was adopted by a virtually straight partisan vote (in the Senate, McCarran of Nevada was the one Democrat in opposition; while in the House only five Democrats joined the one hundred Republicans against the bill), and Marshall's appointment was promptly confirmed when it reached the Senate. The fact that Marshall had spent his life as a professional soldier would seem to have been almost the last consideration in the minds of the statesmen who opposed the enabling bill.

Through the rest of September and October the Korean operations progressed most hopefully; there were no signs of a Soviet attack, and though the Pentagon staffs were laboring on the huge regular appropriation requests for fiscal '52, Bradley had seen no reason to return to Congress for more money to be made currently available. In London the NATO Council deputies, under Spofford's chairmanship, were working hard to perfect an integrated defense structure, including some resolution for the impasse over German rearmament. But among our own politicians and our NATO partners there was a rather general relaxation of the tensions of five months before. And then disaster struck along the Chongchon.

## THE GLOBAL IMPACT OF CHONGCHON

The effects of Chongchon upon the Korean War have been described; its effects upon the larger problem of global policy and defense were almost as dramatic. President Truman was, as usual, prompt in crisis. On November 30, before the full scale of the Korean debacle was apparent, he issued a statement to the nation:

Because this new act of aggression in Korea is only a part of a world-wide pattern of danger to all the free nations of the world, it is more necessary than ever before to increase at a very rapid rate the combined military strength of the free nations. It is more necessary than ever that integrated forces in Europe under a supreme commander be established at once.

With respect to our own defense I shall submit a supplemental request for appropriations . . . I expect to confer tomorrow with Congressional leaders.

To a correspondent of the *New York Times* it seemed likely that evening that "a confused and even rather frightened Congress, but a Congress ready to support any sort of military appropriations," would approve "in quick order." After the conference with the legislative leaders next day the second supplemental request went in; this time for another $16.8 billion for defense and over $1 billion for a "substantial" increase in the Atomic Energy Commission's productive capacity. This was not, Truman explained, "a war budget. That would obviously require far more money. However, the immediate approval of these funds will permit us to make the fastest possible progress in increasing our strength." There was to be some increase in force levels. The aggregate strength of all services was to rise from 2.5 to 3.5 million men by mid-1951, and the Air Force goal was raised to sixty-eight groups; but the supplemental request was mainly directed toward "partial mobilization" — that is, toward expanding the production base so as to make large-scale industrial procurement possible should it later be needed. The Pentagon was not preparing for war. But a week after the Chinese attack JCS was advising all American forces abroad that the danger of general war had "greatly increased" — a warning taken so seriously in the Mediterranean that the 6th Fleet went to sea.

The pressure on the NATO planners immediately intensified. The Truman-Attlee conference gave one afternoon session (December 6) to the Western defense; on the following day the Council deputies in London announced themselves in agreement and ready to discuss concrete plans with the Military Committee. Admiral Sherman flew to join the Military Committee as American delegate. Within a week the plans were completed, and Acheson with Frank Pace, deputizing for Marshall, departed for a formal meeting in Brussels of the North Atlantic Council and the Defense Committee, called to approve the planning. On the evening of December 15 Truman, after much conferring with Congressional leaders, announced his "austerity" program of moderate wage and price controls and tax increases, to support the big new budget requests. He created the Office of Defense Mobilization and named Charles E. Wilson ("General Electric Wilson," not "General Motors Wilson") to head it. Next day he proclaimed a "national emergency," a matter about which there had been much hesitation and debate; he gave Wilson large powers and called for a "mighty production effort." On December 18 the NATO meeting in Brussels reached agreement on the integrated defense plan; on December 20 the President named Dwight D. Eisenhower as Supreme Commander Allied Powers Europe, and declared that more American divisions would be dispatched to Europe as soon as possible. The solution that had been found for the German problem rested on the idea of brigading the Germans into the Western forces in regimental combat teams. Bonn had already made it clear that it would not accept this; but the point was more or less overlooked at the time. The correspondents thought that the integrated plan might yield a formed NATO force of upwards of seventy ready divisions.

Even this was not the end. In mid-January 1951, when the Administration presented its regular budget for fiscal '52, it was to ask a third massive supplemental — $10 billion — for fiscal '51. A year before, $13.5 billion had seemed the maximum which the nation dared appropriate for defense. This third supplemental, as Truman now explained, would bring the total for fiscal '51 to $52 billion; and in the regular budget for fiscal '52 he was asking $61 billion for defense together with $11 billion for the Mutual Defense Assistance Program. Within the executive branch, the civilian "power of the purse" had been put into reverse gear to secure a maximum military effort.

## CONGRESS AND THE BUDGET

There remained the Congress, which in general responded as the *New York Times* correspondent had predicted it would. In mid-December the House had passed the colossal second supplemental by a voice vote, barely two weeks after it had been submitted to them. The House and Senate, working chiefly through the armed services subcommittees of their Appropriations Committees, are experienced and expert in dealing with the minutiae of military budgets. In any more or less stable international situation they can, and do, bring sharp knives to the paring of lesser extravagances, duplications and anomalies from the military requests. Yet they are unequipped for, perhaps by their nature incapable of, dealing with those basic issues of military policy which the military budget is supposed to control. They had gone over the original and modest fiscal '51 budget with the customary fine-toothed comb. But when the Administration had, first in July and then in December, demanded massive revision of the basic military and fiscal policies of the state, the Congress and its committees could only accede.

Anyone who examines a report of hearings by the armed services subcommittee of the House Appropriations Committee must be struck by the inordinate time and attention given to very minor items, often involving no more than a few hundred thousand dollars, in contrast to the failure to bring any real criticism against the basic structure of the budget requests, which determines the expenditure of billions. The legislative power of the purse would not seem to have much significance unless it is a power which can be applied in the determination of the underlying military policy issues; otherwise it becomes little more than a power to insist on proper accounting procedures and the avoidance of obvious wastage. This is a useful power; but its limitations are not always realized. In 1950 and early 1951 Congress voted the big budgets, usually trying to assert its authority by making them bigger rather than smaller; but in giving its votes it knew very well that what it was doing was merely approving basic policy changes necessarily made elsewhere.

It would not be fair to say that "the military" were in control from the latter part of 1950 to the spring of 1952; but it is reasonable to suggest that military considerations were dominant in this period and that military men necessarily exercised an authority over diplomatic, political and fiscal policy not normally desired by nor accorded to them. Congress, like the State Department, the Budget Bureau and the civilian Secretaries in the military establishment, was forced to acquiesce. But the Congress, and especially the opposition elements within it, were not happy in doing so. The right-wing Republicans and conservative anti-Truman Democrats set out to assert "civilian control" less by opposing the great measures for which the Truman Administration was calling than by obstructing them. And it is perhaps a weakness of our system that while it offers so few opportunities for an opposition to oppose, it offers so many to obstruct.

As Rovere and Schlesinger have observed,[1] December was not only a "momentous" but also a "zany" month. While the President was declaring a national emergency and asking for huge new military appropriations and military commitments in Europe, a draft board in Montana was refusing to call another man until MacArthur had been authorized to use atomic bombs in China as he saw fit. As the Truman-Attlee conference was concluding, twenty-four Republican senators voted for the Kem resolution demanding full information on the "secret commitments" the President was making to the Prime Minister. On the day the House passed by voice vote the $17 billion defense supplemental, the Republicans of both houses also voted overwhelmingly to demand the immediate resignation of the Secretary of State in order to cement "national unity." And influential Republican newspapers seriously supported the idea. The brief debate on the Marshall enabling bill had struck a note which was to

[1] Richard H. Rovere and Arthur M. Schlesinger, Jr., *The General and the President and the Future of American Foreign Policy,* Farrar, Straus & Young, New York, 1951, p. 156.

deepen. In early December, Senator Taft had said that while he favored raising new divisions for Europe he would not send them there until he had better assurance as to the Europeans' own contribution. On December 20 former President Hoover, in a radio address, was to carry this thought to a point perilously near the absurd. For the United States to send any more troops or money to Europe, Hoover argued, would be to "invite another Korea." We should send neither, therefore, until the Europeans had first armed themselves to form "a sure dam against the Red Flood." To many the logic of this appeal — which seemed to demand that we do nothing until such a time as others had relieved us of the necessity of doing anything — was not apparent.

## THE REPUBLICAN ATTACK

As the great tide of bigger appropriations, rearmament, larger foreign commitments, swept on, there was little which the opposition could do except express frustration. The Congressional opposition wanted desperately to have some share in the control of events, but it lacked more than votes. It lacked any philosophical or principled basis on which to take its stand. In January 1951 Senator Wherry, the Nebraska Republican, brought in a complexly worded but shrewdly designed resolution. It provided that the Senate Armed Services and Foreign Relations Committees should meet jointly to "consider and report recommendations on whether or not the Senate should declare it to be the sense of the Senate that no ground forces of the United States should be assigned to duty in the European area for the purposes of the North Atlantic Treaty pending the adoption of a policy with respect thereto by the Congress." The sense is obscure; but the significance, as Tom Connally, chairman of Foreign Relations, pointed out, was plain enough. If adopted, it would mean that "essentially the control of our troops under the North Atlantic Treaty" would be "turned over to Congress." Interestingly enough, Senator Connally did not treat this as raising a high constitutional issue over the separation of powers and the locus of authority within the state; his objection was the more earthy and practical one that the enemy, in the event of war, would know "everything about the

plans, from time to time, as they were determined by the Congress."
Yet this observation, limited as it may seem, perhaps did after all go
to the heart of the problem. Congress could not take over control of
the NATO divisions because it was imcompetent to do so. It was
incapable of functioning as a general staff, and therefore could not
assume a general staff's role.

Egged on by its right-wing Republicans, the Senate was to make
two major attempts to assert its authority over military and defense
policy, as against both the uniformed soldiers and the civilian (and
Democratic) bureaucrats. In each the instrument was the same — a
joint hearing by the Foreign Relations and Armed Services Committees. The first was the hearing on "the Assignment of Ground Forces
of the United States to Duty in the European Area," conducted during February 1951; the second was the far more spectacular Mac-
Arthur hearing in May and June. Neither was to have much visible
effect on the Truman policies or the popular support for them; and it
may be said that as vehicles for asserting senatorial power in this field
both were largely failures. In 1951 Senator McCarthy was already
demonstrating with what deadly effect the powers and prerogatives
of a senator could be brought to bear, when wielded by sufficiently
unscrupulous hands, upon national policy. But there is a difference
between the power of a senator and the power of the Senate. In
these moments of quite serious national crisis, when great changes
were being made in American military and foreign policy, both the
Senate and the House, as institutions, would seem to have been relatively ineffective. The Congress could be querulous, difficult and
dangerous to the administrators, like Truman and Acheson and
Marshall; but it could offer them no promise of support in alterna-
tives to the arduous and onerous courses which they felt compelled
to take. At critical moments — as in the case of the Vandenberg
resolution — it could lend powerful assistance. But in the current
conduct of policy it was a constant annoyance, a drag and disability;
it could not be a partner — and since it could not assume responsibility, it gave no hope that it could ever be made a partner — in the
great task of managing the destiny of the nation. The legislature, on
which the authors of the Constitution placed so much reliance as the

final regulator of civil-military affairs, has in modern times proved unsuited to discharge the function.

The Senate committee hearings on the assignment of American forces to Europe opened on February 1, 1951 with testimony from General Eisenhower, just back from his first quick survey of his new command. The new Supreme Commander, speaking with an opacity which later press conferences were to make familiar, felt that his "real duty" was to "generate a morale." He was disinclined to talk in crass terms of force levels, numbers of ready divisions, German rearmament and similar details. "If I can play a part in helping allied morale that will make certain that all of us are trying to contribute our maximum to the security of the free world, then it becomes necessary that there be a certain flexibility in action." When it came to cases, the flexibility became so flexible as to be somewhat unintelligible. On the hard-core problem of the Germans the former president of Columbia observed that:

I personally think that there has to be a political platform achieved and an understanding reached that will contemplate an eventual and earned equality on the part of that nation before we should start to talk about including units of Germans in any kind of agreement.

The senators seemed to find this kind of thing rather difficult to deal with; but when Richard B. Russell of Georgia, admitting his "confusion," asked whether the general's mission to Europe had been "as commander-in-chief, or was it in a dual capacity, to investigate political questions and to arrive at political decisions as well as military?" he received an instructive answer:

I spoke in every country to the prime minister and foreign minister on their request, and then I talked to the defense ministers and their chiefs of staff. There is no escaping the fact that when you take an area such as is involved in all western Europe and talk about its defense, you are right in the midst of political questions, financial questions, economic, industrial as well as strictly military, and you couldn't possibly divorce your commander from contact with them.

There was no escaping the fact that the military were deeply involved in political issues, or the unhappier fact that the Congressional politicians had little chance to get their fingers into this resistant pie.

A few days later there was an interchange between Senator Harry F. Byrd of Virginia and Secretary Marshall:

> Byrd: In other words, you do not think Congress should have any voice in the question of sending troops?
>
> Marshall: You always have a voice, . . . in the appropriations.
>
> Byrd: What kind of voice do you think Congress should have, if it can't establish a general policy?
>
> Marshall: You are putting it on a question of policy. You are getting into a debate which I do not care to carry one side of.

It was, the Secretary of Defense insisted, a debate between the Congress and the President, not with himself or the military officers. It was an issue of "policy." And the senators had to leave it there. It was not until February 15 that Truman was even willing to tell them how many American troops he intended to send to Europe. On that day Marshall testified that he had the President's authority to say that the Joint Chiefs had recommended, and the President had approved, a policy "which looks to the maintenance by us in Europe of approximately six divisions." Two were already there; the equivalent of four more would be sent. It was the moment, it should be noted, when General Collins' arrival in Korea was clarifying that muddled situation. Whatever that may have had to do with it, the result was that a decision which really dated back to the State-Defense agreement of early September was not even exposed for senatorial judgment until five months later. Senator Taft might angrily declare that "I do not accept [the JCS] as experts. . . . I suggest that the JCS are absolutely under the control of the Administration." But there was little that he or any other of the senators could do about it. The six divisions were established in Germany, with or without the approval of "the most august legislative body in the world."

As has already been indicated, the Senate's intervention in the MacArthur affair was equally ineffective from any practical standpoint. Passions continued to run high, but few actually paid much attention to the closing days of the hearings. And it was neither by nor with the advice and consent of the Senate that the two really great events of June 1951 took place. One was the Russian hint at peace negotiations, and Ridgway's request on June 30 (in accordance with instructions) for a truce in Korea. The other was the meeting of scientists at Princeton on June 20-22, from which they emerged with the conviction that the problem of a usable hydrogen, or megaton, weapon was on the road to solution.

But the Senate, of course, knew nothing about this. The development of American policy thereafter, both in Korea and on the global stage, was to owe little to the senators or the representatives. Whether as critics or supporters, they were in general to trail after policies made in the White House, State, Defense or AEC which they were powerless to dominate or to alter. When in early 1952 another shift was to come, when fiscal considerations were to assert themselves once more and the "stretch-out" was to begin to reduce the authority of the military planners and promote that of the Budget Bureau, Congress had little to do with it. The senators were often to show themselves effective critics; and a Vandenberg, a McMahon, a McCarthy could as individuals wield great power for good or ill. But the Senate had no principled grounds on which to criticize and no clear philosophy which might have enabled it to control the subsequent history. The Congress was probably the least important factor in the developments which were to come.

## THE NEW CIVIL-MILITARY EQUILIBRIUM

Two rather bloody years were to follow the request for an armistice in Korea. Each recorded only about half the American casualties and much less than half the American battle deaths of the first year, although ROK casualties were often very high. It is obvious that through these two years the American professional soldiers on the level of field command were baffled by the problem presented to them. They were required to wage a war which they were not "allowed" to win, basically because the political administration believed that the costs and risks of "victory" were incommensurate with the political gains which victory might achieve. They were engaged in a form of war which had never been taught at West Point, Annapolis or even in the higher war colleges; a war not waged for the classical military objectives of territory and power, but for political and propaganda objectives that were beyond the training and outlook of the typical American soldier. Truce negotiations had begun in mid-summer of 1951. Their unbelievably tortuous and quite unexpected difficulties arose from the fact that the Chinese Communists were trying to achieve political goals (for which they had not the slightest hesitation in sacrificing their coolie troops by the thousands), while the UN command was trying only to stabilize a military situation (for which they hesitated to sacrifice any men at all), the political consequences of which had never been clearly foreseen or analyzed by anyone on the Western side.

It gave rise to the paradoxical situation in which the UN forces were, essentially, trying to club the Communists into signing an armistice. It is hardly too much to say that, after the shift of policy in early December, the UN and the United States were no longer trying to exact surrender from the Chinese; they were trying to force the Chinese to settle on terms which would not be too disadvantageous to the Western interest. This is never an easy operation; and since the only club which Ridgway and Van Fleet (Major General James A. Van Fleet, commanding 8th Army) were allowed to wield was the strictly limited-objective offensive at minimum cost in life, the result was, naturally, the long stalemate. As it happened, more lives — American and more particularly South Korean lives — were to be expended than anyone had foreseen; and it may still be argued that an all-out drive for victory in Korea in June of 1951 (something, it must be noted, quite different from what was recommended by MacArthur) would have been cheaper in the end. Such are the calculations which statesmen, compelled to trade life for power, must confront. It still seems a dubious argument; and it seems improbable, even more, that the United States or the UN could in the latter half of 1951 have risen to such an effort.

RELAXING TENSIONS AND NEW PLANS

It was not only in Korea that events seemed to mark time between the opening of the truce negotiations in the summer of 1951 and the American Presidential elections in November 1952. In Paris, General

Eisenhower was trying to set up a viable Western European defense. But the task was not easy. There had been a considerable relaxation of the near-panic of the year before. It was now more and more generally accepted that this time, at least, the Russians were not going to march; that left more time for everything; there was less hurry and pressure about setting up an effective NATO system, though no one seriously proposed abandoning the basic policy which NATO embodied. Yet even while this effort to build a "conventional" European defense went on, the atomic scientists and engineers were undermining it. They had left their meeting at Princeton in June convinced that a super weapon — not the original "Super" but a fission-fusion-fission device of similarly gigantic power — could be produced. It was not for another year that this idea could be field-tested; but in the meanwhile the rapid expansion of the production of fission, or atomic, bombs, and the success with which they were stepped up to ten times the energy releases which had devastated Hiroshima and Nagasaki, or reduced to package sizes which could be fired through guns or delivered by small airplanes and missiles, were putting a quite new face on war. Despite the existence of State, JCS, NSC, AEC, and their subordinate policy-making agencies, there seemed to be no place in government that these developments could be analyzed and applied accurately to the solution of the problems of the American people. And by the end of 1951, both the President and the Congress were more interested in the 1952 Presidential election than in the policy issues before the nation.

It was an indication of the relaxing tensions when, on September 17, 1951, after just a year in office, Marshall again laid down the burdens of state and his long-time coadjutor, Robert A. Lovett, was sworn in as the fourth Secretary of Defense. It was perhaps symbolic that one of Lovett's first acts was, according to Washington report, to take the issue of the future strength of the Air Force out of the hands of the Joint Chiefs, who were deadlocked over it, and confide it to the three civilian Secretaries. The Pentagon saw the rule of the Joint Chiefs drawing to an end; this seemed a "noteworthy" indication that the new Secretary of Defense "intended to bring the Secretaries of the Army, Navy and Air Force back to fullest participation in policy making" — something which they had less and less enjoyed since the advent of Louis Johnson in 1949.

## NUCLEAR POWER AND BUDGETARY REVISION

While this report was perhaps premature, it foreshadowed the future. Not only were the international pressures relaxing; the internal economic pressures were going up. In the throes of the Korean debacle, the Congress had raised military appropriations for fiscal '51 to some $52 billion, and Truman had asked about $60 billion for fiscal '52. But the regular appropriations bill made slow progress; it was not finally passed and signed until October of 1951, some three months late, and then provided only $57.2 billion, some of which could not be expended until subsequent fiscal years. It did not, however, provide for the current costs of the Korean fighting, for which it was believed that another $5 billion supplemental appropriation might be necessary. These were coming to seem rather staggering sums. It was obvious that appropriations were running far beyond what could actually be expended — it was said that the fiscal '52 bill had been predicated on a consumption of aluminum and other strategic materials greater than the entire world supply — and in September 1951 Senator Paul H. Douglas, the Illinois Democrat, put up an impassioned battle for defense economies.

It was on September 18 (the day after Lovett took office) that Brien McMahon of Connecticut brought in a bill calling for a vast expansion of the nuclear weapons program, accompanying it with a thunderous speech. His theme was that the mass production of atomic weapons of all varieties had now become possible; that this meant a revolution in military fire-power, and that here in turn was the way in which to achieve "peace power at bearable cost." The Senator, somewhat inconsistently, concluded with a plea that the United States should make a major effort in the UN to end the nuclear armaments race; but what caught the Congressional and public imagination was his demand for a six-fold increase in the expenditure on nuclear weaponry (then about $1 billion a year) and the argument sustaining it:

At the rate we are moving I can see ahead only two ultimate destinations: Military safety at the price of economic disaster or economic safety at the price of military disaster . . . The atomic bottlenecks are being broken . . . There is virtually no limit and no limiting factor upon the number of bombs which the United States can manufacture given time and decision to proceed all-out.

This was the first clear announcement to the nation of the arrival of that appalling horror, "the age of atomic plenty." It was the first emphatic statement of the policy later vulgarly known as that of a "bigger bang for a buck." McMahon insufficiently considered the possibility that the Soviet Union, which he said already had many more men at work on nuclear science and weaponry than we did, might be breaking the bottlenecks as fast as we were. He had not fully worked out the consequences of the nuclear armaments race into which he was urging the country. But his underlying contention — that to avoid "economic disaster" we should pin our defense policy on the nuclear arsenal, cheaper per unit of energy release than conventional weapons — was to be of powerful effect.

One speech, of course, could not reverse the majestic trends of conventional military policy. But many besides the Senator were beginning to think that we were heading for "military safety at the price of economic disaster." With the fiscal '52 budget completing its passage through Congress, Lovett's first problem was the fiscal '53 budget, which would have to be presented in January 1952. The service requests had totted up to $70 billion. In view of the difficulty the services had experienced in spending what had already been allotted to them, Lovett felt that these estimates could be scaled to more modest sums. There were two main factors involved. One was the contemplated force levels, a matter complicated by the fact that the Air Force had for months been campaigning for an increase of its authorized goal from 95 groups to 150 or more. The other was the pace at which the force levels should be achieved.

Lovett brought the Joint Chiefs to agree to a modified schedule of force levels which was adopted by the National Security Council on October 1. This called for 21 Army divisions, 409 active Navy combat ships, 3 Marine divisions with their air wings and 143 Air Force groups, to be completed by June 1954. When Senator Lodge declared on the floor on October 2 that the Joint Chiefs had assented to an Air Force strength of "about 140 groups" it was taken as a considerable triumph for the new Secretary of Defense. It meant that the "roll-back" or "stretch-out" was already beginning. Wilfred McNeil, the pleasant, expert and astute administrator who had ruled over Defense finance since the days of Forrestal (and was to continue long thereafter), realized that the peak of defense production generated by the big appropriations of 1950 and 1951 would have to be levelled off. It was both necessary and practicable to push forward the spending heights in order to fill the yawning valleys that would otherwise open before them. Lovett suggested that the fiscal '53 budget could appropriately be based on a level of about $45 billion. In the end it came out at $55 billion, which the President reduced to $52 billion at the cost of stretching forward the completion date for the 143-group Air Force. The power of the Budget Bureau was reviving, and was to grow greater. This fiscal '53 budget, submitted in January 1952, would be ruling when the winner of the 1952 Presidential election took office a year later. It was already showing the signs of the retrenchment which the Eisenhower Administration was later to enforce.

NATO REORGANIZED

In other areas civilian considerations and civilian administrators were asserting themselves. When the North Atlantic Council met at Ottawa in the latter part of September 1951, it reflected a growing concern over the costs of all this new defense apparatus. It turned to examine "the danger of inflation, the burden which increased defense efforts place on the balance of payments and the obstacles to an adequate defense arising from price and allocation pressures on raw material supplies." A Temporary Council Committee of civilian officials from each of the member states (known popularly as the TCC or "Twelve Apostles") was established to combine a "militarily acceptable" defense plan with the "realistic political-economic capabilities" of the several nations. The work was done mainly by an executive committee, the "Three Wise Men," headed by Averell Harriman for the United States with Sir Edwin Plowden and Jean Monnet as his colleagues.

It was at this same meeting that the North Atlantic Council first took formal cognizance of the European Defense Community, or EDC — a plan, originally advanced by the French and already endorsed by the Big Three foreign ministers, for assimilating West Germany into the Western defense structure. EDC, essentially a system for a common European army in which the Germans would share with all the others, was to complicate the whole Western defense problem over the next five years and come only to failure in the end. But throughout, the difficulties were primarily political; it was the diplomats and the political men who were to deal with these difficulties, with a minimum of either interference or help from the soldiers acting on "purely military considerations." It seems unnecessary here to follow the tortuous history of EDC; it is enough to cite it as another example of the way in which primarily diplomatic and political considerations, and the civilian officers who were charged with them, were reasserting the political authority briefly abandoned to military considerations in the crisis months of late 1950.

Not until the Council meeting at Lisbon in February 1952 did NATO finally assume shape and structure as a major program for organizing the civil-military relationships of the whole Western coalition. The "Three Wise Men" and the TCC had submitted their report in December. It was based on a principle distinctly novel in the long history of defense planning — that the "prime requisite for carrying out the defense program" was "a satisfactory rate of general economic expansion." This was doubtless sound; but it involved war with economics (and therewith politics) to an extent which had rarely been contemplated by either the military men or the politicians of the past. The Lisbon meeting made or approved numerous significant decisions. It approved a Supreme Allied Command for sea warfare (SACLANT, set up at Norfolk under the American admiral, Lynde D. McCormick, and comparable in its responsibilities to SACEUR, the Supreme Allied Command in Europe, under Eisenhower at Rocquencourt). It accepted the accession of Greece and Turkey to the alliance. It approved the TCC report, and agreed that the conflicting demands of security and economics might be satisfied by a European defense of fifty divisions, in varying but "appropriate" states of readiness, plus 4,000 aircraft and "strong" naval components. "In principle" it approved EDC.

But it went on to reorganize the NATO structure itself. It increased the responsibilities of Eisenhower, as Supreme Commander, but at the same time strengthened the civilian organization behind the military command. The Council Deputies, over whom Spofford had presided since 1950, were abolished, and a council of "permanent representatives" was set up in their place. But its real powers were gathered together into the hands of a Secretary-General (who would also be permanent Vice Chairman of NATO), a post which was entrusted to Lord Ismay. "Pug" Ismay, a man of pleasant mien and unusual competence, had been Military Secretary of Churchill's War Cabinet during the Second War, and was at the time Secretary of State for Commonwealth Relations. Within the NATO organization, he was to provide a capable political counterpart for Eisenhower, the Supreme Commander.

The system appears to have worked well, though it has certainly not produced the massive defenses of Western Europe which were contemplated in the winter of 1952. In Korea at this time, the fighting "had tapered off into a monotonous routine of patrol clashes, raids and bitter small-unit struggles for key outpost positions." Ridgway, who had succeeded MacArthur as CINCFE, had halted any further "offensive ground operations in Korea," because the cost of major assaults on the now dug-in Chinese positions would be more than the results would justify, and because of the possibility that peace might come anyway out of the reopened armistice talks. The statesmen concerned with NATO, feeling that the Soviet threat was diminishing and that they were left with what was, obviously and unavoidably, both a political and a military problem of probably long duration, were falling back on what were neither "purely political" nor "purely military" solutions. They tended to interweave the two factors into a complex system in which neither is at any time clearly discernible. At the annual NATO conferences the foreign ministers (including the American Secretary of State) carry all the burdens of the authority and the publicity. The generals, and even the civilian Defense Secretaries, are rarely heard to speak loudly. Yet in this country, and presumably elsewhere, a vast interchange goes on between the military and the civilian authorities and their staffs and "Indians."

Nelson Rockefeller, who at the behest of the Eisenhower Administration was to preside in early 1953 over a committee which re-examined the Defense organization, testified to the burdens to which the civilians were subjecting the Joint Chiefs of Staff:

> Any time the State Department is going to have an international meeting . . . they may feel there are military aspects to their questions. So, they will send to the Joint Chiefs of Staff a long list of questions, not ones that are on the agenda for discussion, but ones that might come up, on which they would like to have a military point of view. . . . Now you have the United Nations' problems. . . . The State Department in its current activities has constant contact with the Joint Chiefs in order to get advice and counsel.

One is reminded of the chaotic days of 1946, when neither soldiers nor civilians would or could take responsibility for the great decisions which then had to be made, and when the "buck" was passed rapidly around among the agencies concerned. But this development was rather different and perhaps more serious. It reflected a new caution on the part of the civilian administrator in taking any decision affecting military factors for which he did not have the military imprimatur. It was not that the military would demolish him if he disregarded their advice, but that the Congress and the press might do so. Both through NATO and through domestic budget planning, non-military factors were asserting a greater authority; but State had been trained — mainly by the censorious congressmen — to go to Defense on any question which might have "military" significance; and Defense, overwhelmed as it was in its own special problems, did not know how to answer questions for which only a "political" solution could be valid. Acheson and Marshall had once agreed that any of their subordinates who used the phrases "purely political" or "purely military" would be required to leave the room immediately. The emergence of NATO and the problems of the UN only emphasized an issue which would have been present in any event in our own tasks of policy formulation.

NATO was an organization of the national anl international security systems which rendered the old civil-military dichotomy more or less meaningless. Eisenhower, on his first visit to his command, had found the prime ministers and foreign ministers insistent that he see them before making contact with the defense ministers and military staffs. His problems thereafter were far more political than military in character. Admiral Robert B. Carney, established at Naples as Commander Allied Forces Southern Europe, was to have the same experience; from his palm-fringed headquarters looking out over Vesuvius and the Bay, he was to struggle with all the complications of Italian, Greek and Mediterranean politics much more than with the strategy of Southern Europe. Much the same was true of the other commands — McCormick's SACLANT at Norfolk, Norstad's AAFCE (Allied Air Forces Central Europe) at Fontainebleau and the innumerable lower echelons in which American and allied staff officers were intermingled. Even the purely American operational commands, like 7th Army in Germany, were deeply involved with the political authorities and politics of the countries in which they were established.

After 1918 the civilians, alike in the Congress, in State or the military departments, had entertained no doubts of their competence to exercise control over the uniformed forces; nor had the professional officers entertained any doubts of their competence to advise in the purely military field. After 1945 this confidence, on both sides, tended to diminish; after Korea it was further weakened. The civilian diplomat or administrator hesitated to risk decisions for which he did not have the firm support of the military technicians on all "military aspects" involved; the high military officers, on the other hand, felt that this placed them under a responsibility for which they were ill-equipped. They felt themselves obliged either to underwrite or to oppose political decisions which they thought beyond their competence and which they felt they should not be asked to determine. It has been said that every defense budget since 1945 has presented the Joint Chiefs of Staff with a searing moral crisis.

In the depths of the Korean wretchedness the State Department and the civilian bureaucracy were accused of hazarding the national security by flouting the expert advice of the military professionals. But the military professionals were at the same time accused of hazarding the national security by their subservience to the political administration — which they were, of course, sworn to uphold. Many officers, especially the older ones like Bradley or, in some of his moods, Eisenhower, have sought to escape the dilemma by retreat into the old division between "political" and "military." An impracticable retreat at best, it became virtually impossible with the rise of NATO. Our own Defense Department, National Security Council, National Security Resources Board, Munitions Board and dozens of other agencies, had created a plethora of staffs, boards and committees in which civilian and military representatives sat together, in which the civilians believed that they had to take military advice and the military believed that they had to tailor the advice to civilian considerations. NATO now piled dozens, if not hundreds, of such joint committees and command posts on top of these. In them, not only State but Treasury, Agriculture, Commerce, CIA, the Information Agency and other civil departments were involved. But they all looked now to the paramount authority, if not of the Department of Defense, at least of the military factors for which Defense was the chief spokesman. And Defense was uncertain of its role. About 25,000 individuals go to work in the Pentagon every morning; there is probably not one, in uniform or out of it, who is not conscious of the overriding civilian authority; and there are very few, if any, who know just where the line between civilian and military considerations should or does lie.

It was in the early '50's that the Army, Navy and Air Force began to realize the enormity of the obligations that were being thrust upon them. They had to produce not simply competent combat commanders and staff specialists in logistics, but a whole corps of military statesmen, capable of filling the innumerable politico-military staff positions in the Pentagon, in the UN, in NATO, in the trust territories, in the MAAG groups, which were yawning after and devouring politically-aware military personnel. The five national war colleges (and even their subordinate staff schools) more and more shaped themselves to produce men who would be, it was hoped, capable of filling this rather new type of command and staff position. Their old function of training commanders for success in battle action receded far into the background. The checkered "game board" at the War College at Newport (where the Navy instituted the whole system of higher military education) has become mainly a place for the "coffee break" between lectures on large issues of global strategy. One has to go to places like New London or Pensacola to see the intricate combat trainers in which men are now taught how to fight ships or airplanes in combat action. The war colleges have advanced to higher issues.

## THE DOUGLAS-BRADLEY DEBATE

This development in military education was paralleled by a less formal education of civil and diplomatic officers in military factors — which a generation before they would have ignored. But the commingling of the two spheres was not easily recognized. Korea, NATO, the huge budgets, the draft, the onerous requirements of secrecy and security, the prominence of JCS in all policy issues, added up to produce a sense of public unease and dissatisfaction. Whatever the reason, the military seemed to be taking over. In March 1952 the uneasiness found expression through the voice of Associate Justice William O. Douglas of the Supreme Court. In an article in *Look* magazine, a medium of mass communication not often used by Supreme Court Justices, he bluntly declared that "The increasing influence of the military in . . . our affairs is the most ominous aspect of our modern history." He continued:

Our Government was designed to keep the military in the background, reserving them for the days of actual hostilities. . . . We indeed do the military great disservice by thrusting civilian tasks on them, by placing on them the burdens of peace. . . .

The military mind . . . has two distinctive characteristics — first, it tends to put every problem in the perspective of war; second, it tends to regiment people, to have one orthodox creed and to leave no room for diversity of opinion . . . That we have taken the military rather than the political approach to these [world] problems is powerful proof that we have become victims of the military mind. . . . the civilian heads by and large are merely spokesmen for what the military want.[1]

The same issue of the magazine carried a rebuttal from Omar Bradley. Almost plaintively, the Chairman of the Joint Chiefs made the point that the government's current "dependence on military counsel is not of the soldiers' choosing." Everywhere, moreover, it was the civilians who were in final charge:

> Economically, politically and militarily, the control of our country resides with the civilian executive and legislative agencies . . . When you have civilians like these in charge, no military clique can develop. And when you have trained and skilled businessmen and scientists advising the military as frequently as we have had since 1940, admirals and generals are not likely to influence unduly the policy and plans of our Government. . . . I also am sure that as soon as civilian agencies are organized to take over such civilian problems, the military will gladly withdraw to its purely professional duties.[2]

This argument was simply beside the point, in the context at which the nation had arrived by the late winter of 1952. Bradley's wistful vision of a time when the soldier might once again "withdraw" into his "purely professional duties" was as unreal as Douglas' no less wistful vision of a time when the soldier could be reserved "for the days of actual hostilities."

Justice Douglas' strictures upon the militarization of our politics, economics and society were no doubt valid, but were misdirected in being trained against the largely non-existent influence of a "military mind." General Bradley's defense — that the civilians were everywhere still in control — was also doubtless valid, but also misdirected, in that it failed to recognize that, whoever was in control, the military factor was bound to assert an importance in our affairs beyond anything known in the past. It was quite true that no "military clique" of flag officers was likely to rise to dominance in American government; but this fact would not, after all, meet Justice

[1] *Look,* March 11, 1952.
[2] *Loc. cit.*

Douglas' basic criticism — that our society was being unwisely and unnecessarily militarized. Both men expressed a sense that the country's attitudes and policies were becoming unduly military. Each felt that he and the forces for which he spoke were not responsible. Neither knew, practically, what could be done about it, or was fully aware of the pressures behind the changes which both deplored.

This interchange in *Look* magazine was only part of a wider debate — or perhaps one should say of a wider fumbling with issues about which no one had any very clear idea of the avenues along which practicable solutions might be found. Hanson Baldwin devoted his powerful column in the *New York Times* to pointing out the great numbers of military men, active and retired, who were serving as diplomats, administrators, high officers in civil government or private industry. In the spring and summer of 1952 the Congress seemed alarmed, restless and conscious of its own ineffectiveness before the issues of civil-military policy which were presented to it. When Eisenhower returned to run for the Presidency, it was obvious that military and defense policy would be, if not exactly an issue (no one could dispute the conqueror of Europe on any question of defense policy), at least a leading theme in the campaign. But the ideas on all sides of such questions were fuzzy, unformed, wanting in creative significance or force.

## THE KOREAN WAR: THE LAST STAGE

In the meanwhile the Korean War was grinding on, with considerably less bloodshed than in the earlier stages but with less visible hope that it could ever be brought to a conclusion. The American public reacted with ennui and an increasingly intense desire that the distasteful business could somehow be wound up. The professional soldiers involved in the unforeseen morass reacted variously. Van Fleet, the 8th Army commander, was later to return to the United States with the complaint that he had been stopped in the moment of victory. He was to testify before the Senate Armed Services Committee that in June 1951 his army had the Communists retreating "in a panic" and that he was "crying" to be released in pursuit, but was instead ordered to halt. "Though we could readily have followed up our successes," as he said elsewhere, "and defeated the enemy, that was not the intention in Washington; our State Department had already let the Reds know that we were willing to settle on the 38th Parallel." Others in Korea at the time — some, even, on Van Fleet's own staff — were inclined to disagree with this estimate of the situation as of June 1951; and the Chinese Communists were soon dug in so deeply as to render any renewal of the advance impossibly costly.

Ridgway, in his memoirs,[1] reached the conclusion that "If we had been ordered to fight our way to the Yalu, we could have done it — if our government had been willing to pay the price in dead and wounded . . . From the purely military standpoint the effort, to my mind, would have not been worth the cost." In May 1952 Ridgway was promoted to replace Eisenhower as Supreme Allied Commander Europe when the latter returned to run for the Presidency, and General Mark Clark took over in Tokyo as Commander in Chief Far East. Clark was given a "defensive" mission. "I was given neither the authority nor the military resources to achieve victory. I was instructed, rather to bend every effort toward realizing an armistice quickly."[2] Clark soon did what any professional soldier would do under the circumstances. If his job was to club the enemy into granting us an armistice, then he would have to have a "big club," and he put his staff to work developing a plan which in effect would produce victory as a prelude to an armistice.[3] But the cost estimates turned out to be very high. When the staffs had worked out the price in lives, planes, ships and strategic policy (the bombing of the trans-Yalu bases would have to be included) for an all-out push in Korea, Clark realized that "heavy losses" would be certain. Was the purpose worth it?

Clark's conclusion at the time was that the prospective losses "would be far less than losses we would have to take eventually if we failed to win militarily in Korea and waited until the Communists

---

[1] Matthew B. Ridgway, *Soldier*, Harper, New York, 1956, p. 219.
[2] Mark W. Clark, *From the Danube to the Yalu*, Harper, New York, 1954, p. 69.
[3] *Ibid.*, pp. 69 ff.

were ready to fight on their own terms." [1] Washington disagreed, and never permitted him to mount his "broad plan" for winning the war. This, too, became a part of the unhappy post-mortem. In his memoirs (published in 1954) Clark declared himself as still of his original opinion. But by 1957 — five years after Clark's arrival in Tokyo — there had been little to indicate that a great sacrifice of life in Korea in 1952 would have averted greater sacrifices later.

## COMMUNIST BLACKMAIL

The civilians in Washington can hardly be blamed if they were perplexed by a military situation which baffled the generals. Clark's arrival in Tokyo coincided with one of the strangest episodes of the war. The day he landed was the day on which the Communist prisoners of war on Koje Island staged a spectacular revolt, captured the camp commander, Brigadier General Francis T. Dodd, and in effect held him for ransom. Their price was not money, but political and propaganda advantage. This was a problem for which our military people were quite unprepared. A sterner strategy might immediately have sacrificed the unfortunate Dodd and made political and propaganda capital for the West out of the episode; but that would have been contrary to our whole political and military ethic and the position we were seeking to establish before the world. Dodd was finally retrieved unhurt, but at the cost of some lamentable concessions to the Communist prisoners. In Tokyo and Washington there was to be much unhappiness over the handling of the incident, but even more bewilderment. And it was, indeed, only a special case of the larger problem.

Like General Dodd on Koje, the United States and the UN in the Korean War as a whole were being held for ransom. What we regarded as a war and thought of in the conventional terms of past wars for territory or power was actually a form of gigantic blackmail. As the price of an armistice, the Chinese spent two years in trying to blackmail the West into confessions of imperialist ambitions, germ warfare, disregard of Asian peoples, abandonment of

[1] *Ibid.*, p. 82.

our high moral positions. And since they did not greatly care how many Chinese lives they expended in pursuit of this astute political objective, they presented the United States and the other Western democracies with policy and military issues of extraordinary difficulty.

In such a situation the generals could give no more expert advice than anyone else on how to utilize military force in accomplishing political ends. The military are always, and necessarily, imperfect prognosticators even in their own fields. Clark himself mentions the Snipers' Ridge–Triangle Hill operation in October 1952. Intended as a minor rectification of the line which could be accomplished in two or three days by no more than two battalions with an estimated 200 casualties, it actually dragged on for weeks, sucked in vastly greater troop concentrations and ended with a casualty list of over 8,000 South Koreans and Americans, without any significant result, either military or political. Washington was perhaps well advised in not accepting Clark's "broad plan" for ending the war. But if so, it must be remembered that this was as much a military as a political decision; the Joint Chiefs consistently agreed with the White House and the State Department. If the policy was wrong it sprang, at least, from an equal bafflement all around.

When Clark arrived in Tokyo in May 1952, the war was, in a sense, already over. What might be called the "purely military" issues — that is, the issues susceptible to resolution by the normal military means of bloodshed, destruction and territorial advance — had been settled. The truce line had been marked out and accepted. Questions as to either side's freedom to reinforce and prepare for another struggle had been settled, on paper at any rate. Only one major issue remained, and this was an issue which could not be settled by force of arms. It was the political issue over the Chinese Communist prisoners of war. The Chinese insisted that all be forcibly restored to Chinese Communist control; the United States stood on the position that it would and could repatriate none who were unwilling to go. This was a "moral" issue of that rather ambiguous kind which becomes deeply involved in major questions of power policy. It is unlikely that there were many in either Peking, Moscow, Tokyo or Washington who had much emotional interest in the fate of the prisoners as human beings. They were pawns in a game for much greater stakes. If Peking could force Washington to relinquish them, America's prestige and authority throughout the Far East as the major bulwark against Communist infiltration and domination would be shattered. If Washington could force Peking to give them up, thus proving that tens of thousands of Communist citizens preferred the non-Communist to the Communist world, the prestige and authority of communism throughout the Far East, as the representative and defender of the Asian common man against Western imperialist exploitation, would likewise be shattered.

From the spring of 1952 onward, Korea was a propaganda and political rather than a military war; but the Chinese willingness to expend life on propaganda and political objectives made it no less a war. And the onset of the Presidential election made it no easier for the American governmental system to deal with the issues which the war posed. The approach of every American Presidential electoral campaign announces a period of near-paralysis in American policy. It invites all those whose interests hang upon the shifts in the American political scene to wait to see what the outcome will be. In the summer of 1952 the shrewd manipulators in Peking may well have felt it worth while to sustain the Korean operation. They had been trying without much visible result to put pressure on the Truman Administration; its successors might be more amenable or more gullible. At any rate, the interminable wrangle over the prisoners of war went on at Panmunjom through the various suspensions and recesses, varied only by the occasional limited-objective pushes across the now stabilized lines. In Clark's judgment, while the Chinese never knew when Washington might reinforce 8th Army to an offensive capability, they did know that the UN forces within Korea were too weak to mount an effective attack against their now deeply dug-in defensive system.

With this assurance the enemy was able at any time to mass enough men to dent our line . . . When the enemy made these pushes we rolled with the punch . . . Then, if the Communists had taken terrain features important to our defense line we had to counterattack to recapture them.

That is where we suffered our heaviest casualties.[1]

It was a futile, dispiriting kind of war. The very strength of the Chinese defense in depth, which rendered it immune to any serious attack, also rendered the more lightly fortified UN lines more or less immune to Chinese assaults. The Chinese artillery was dug in so deeply that it could not easily be got out and moved up in support of an infantry advance; an infantry push was thus likely to peter out when it reached the limit of its fixed artillery support. The result was a war consisting mainly of small patrols and occasional small-patrol actions, varied at rather long intervals by violent upsurges of attack and counter-attack that often cost many lives but that could have no military effect. Something of the same situation obtained in the air war fought by the MIG's and Sabrejets in "bomb alley" along the Yalu. Heroic as these encounters often were, they could have little effect upon the ground fighting some 200 miles away to the southward. The Americans had to prevent the Communists from bringing their fighter forces and airfields farther south, where they could interfere with our own air cover, but the air operations were at the most of a secondary and holding character. This was not "war" as most Americans had been taught to think of it. It was the use of military action as an instrument of politics and propaganda — an instrument of "policy" in a sense which Clausewitz could scarcely have envisaged.

DEFENSE ORGANIZATION RE-EXAMINED

It was war of a kind in which most of the intricate organs of civilian control seemed inept — as inept as the military directorate in JCS. The Congress, the White House, the civilian bureaucracy in State and Defense, the ever-helpful newspaper editors, could no more bring it to an end than could the soldiers. It was natural that many of the soldiers should have blamed the "inhibitions" imposed upon them. It was perhaps equally natural that civilians should have

---

[1] Clark, *From the Danube to the Yalu*, pp. 100-01.

begun to blame the military "system" which seemed to lead to such fruitless results. Dissatisfaction mounted. In September 1952 Vannevar Bush began making speeches and preparing articles denouncing the whole Defense structure. "Our organization is not effective. . . . This country is not in a position to do its military planning adequately and well." Bush believed that the Joint Chiefs should be relieved of their separate command functions and made into a solely planning staff. In the excitement of the Presidential campaign he may not have received much attention. But at Baltimore in the last week of September the Republican candidate, Eisenhower, made his strongest statement on military policy, the field in which he was assumed to be most competent. Like most campaign utterances, it was a promise of the best of both worlds, of "security with solvency," of more efficient defense at smaller cost.

The candidate accurately outlined the areas in which such results might be sought. There should, he said, be a more efficient utilization of military manpower, a more "realistic" weapons system, a simplification of weapons adopted. But he did not indicate with any clarity how these ends were to be achieved; and his additional recommendations for a greater degree of service unification and a greater measure of civilian control were at best somewhat beside the point. For years, the problem had not been the degree of unification, but the form it should take; for years the problem had not been the authority of the civilians (always admitted by everybody to be in final control) but their inability to exercise the responsibility which that authority placed upon them. The Baltimore speech was less than a final answer to the accumulating problems of military policy. But it left the candidate committed, by whatever means he might discover, to a reduction of military and defense costs.

In early October Clark got authority to break off the Panmunjom negotiations; the Chinese would either have to fish or cut bait. Whether by cause or effect, this development was accompanied by the heaviest Chinese offensive in more than a year. On October 7, as the negotiations were suspended, 93,000 artillery and mortar rounds fell on 8th Army, the largest volume of fire it had received in the course of the war. There were local attacks and counter-attacks; the weekly American casualty report was trebled, but there was no significant change in either the military or the political situation. If the Chinese thought that they could affect American policy by limited military offensives at the height of a Presidential election, they were badly deceived. The Korean War was swallowed in the oratory; our newspapers scarcely noticed that an offensive had been launched, and Eisenhower's famous pledge that he would "visit Korea" had far more influence over American opinion and American policy than anything actually happening in Korea itself or any military pressures the Chinese could exert.

Eisenhower was, of course, elected by an overwhelming majority. Between November and his assumption of office in January it became increasingly clear that the underlying structure of civil-military relationships would be revamped. It was not so clear what form the new relationships should take. It was obviously a "time for a change." Republican statesmen, like Senator Taft, had long been expressing their dissatisfactions. Vannevar Bush who, though a nonpolitical figure, had long served Democratic administrations, had been campaigning since September against the Defense system as it stood. Lovett, Truman's Secretary of Defense, was known to be unhappy over the situation.

After the election, Truman was concerned to insure a proper transfer of power from the Democratic to the new Republican managers, and he called upon his principal advisers for memoranda on the subject. Lovett responded with a letter severely criticizing the Defense organization. It was organized throughout on the committee principle — from the Joint Chiefs and the Armed Forces Council down through Research and Development and Munitions Board to the innumerable lesser joint boards and committees. The result everywhere, the Secretary felt, was simply inter-service log-rolling, with neither effective military plan nor effective civilian control. Lovett's principal proposal was the familiar one: separate the planning and command functions of the Joint Chiefs of Staff. JCS, he intimated, should become purely a planning staff; the chiefs should relinquish their command functions over the several services to vice chiefs or deputies. The chain of command would then run from the President through the civilian Secretaries direct to the services or, when appropriate, to the unitary theater commanders in the field. The Joint Chiefs, both as individuals and as an agency, would be retired to an advisory and staff role. Much in Lovett's argument was to reappear in the policies actually adopted by the new Administration; but its experience was in turn to indicate that the real problem was far more complex than the Lovett analysis suggested.

## NEW IMPACTS ON THE NATION

Korea had wrought other changes in the civil-military relationship with which the Eisenhower Administration would be compelled to deal. One of the more important was the revival of compulsory military service. For years the Army had been advocating universal military training, and for years Congress had remained deaf to all pleas for peacetime military conscription. Korea forced the issue. It created a sudden demand for trained military personnel, who either did not exist or were beyond the reach of the ill-designed series of compromises which passed for our reserve system. It was simple for Congress to revive the draft, but that could not yield even partially trained men for months. The immediate recourse had to be to the reserve officers and the relatively few reserve enlisted men left over from the Second War, and to the National Guard. In 1950 probably most National Guard officers and not a few of its noncommissioned officers were combat veterans. Some of its smaller, specialized units were summoned as such and thrown directly into the combat, while many Guard personnel were called back individually. But when two Guard divisions were called up, as divisions, to replace the regular forces that had been in Japan, it was found, quite naturally, that they were in an even lower state of training, equipment, numbers and discipline than the regulars had been when the Communist attack was launched. It was to take months to raise them to an efficiency with which they could serve even as garrison troops.

This was an embarrassing discovery. It meant that the National Guard and reserve system as a whole was unable promptly to field a combat force of the kind which it had been expected to produce. While its various echelons did provide the individuals requisite to fill out the regular formations, these had to come predominantly from Second World War veterans — the only available source of trained men. Many of these veterans felt, not unreasonably, that they were being subjected to a form of double jeopardy. They had done their stint in the Second War; and it was not clear to them why countless youths who had never served at all — to say nothing of their fellow veterans who had avoided reserve or National Guard duty after 1945 — should now escape the iron hills of Korea while they were summoned back to the front lines. Congress re-established the draft and laid an eight-year "military obligation" on all young American males, but these measures could not produce trained soldiers in time to affect the equities involved in the Korean service.

No good solution for the peculiar difficulties of the manpower problem was to be achieved. In effect, Congress gave the Pentagon an authority over the training and, to some extent, the education of American youth which the Pentagon did not know how to exercise effectively. Not until 1955, in the third year of the Eisenhower Administration, was a Reserve Act finally adopted, intended to regularize the whole situation. It was something less than satisfactory to begin with and was complicated by the concurrent shift of military policy and strategic plan from the concepts of total mobilization, on the First and Second War patterns, to those of nuclear deterrence and the substitution of atomic fires for manpower in even conventional war. With the establishment of the universal military obligation the power of military control over vital aspects of civilian life had been greatly extended, but there was little clarity as to how it would be used.

Korea affected the underlying civil-military relationships in other ways, generally expanding the authority of military considerations and military officers in civilian affairs without providing the officers with a fully adequate competence to exercise it. The economic effects of the huge and presumably continuing new programs of military procurement raised many issues, concerning the extension of quasi-monopoly, the survival of small business, the power of labor unions

over defense-connected production contracts, the increasing dependence of large segments of industry on government orders, with the
inevitable "infiltration" of government by both "big business" and
"big labor." The supposed requirements of military and defense
secrecy spread through all echelons of government, buttressing the
power of the civilian bureaucrats at the same time that it reduced
the power of the press and public opinion to exert a genuine civilian
or popular control over the operations of the governmental machine.
A vast system grew up for the security screening of personnel in
government employ, in the uniformed forces and in the classified
defense industries. All these and many similar developments represented critical trends in the relationship between the civil and the
military factors in our affairs, though they were seldom recorded in
high-level debate between the uniformed officers and the civilian
politicians and bureaucrats. With all of them the new Administration would have to deal in one way or another; with few of them
was it to deal clearly, concisely or with a full appreciation of all the
implications involved.

# CHAPTER 9

# The New Look

## EISENHOWER, RADFORD AND
## REORGANIZATION PLAN NO. 6

### EISENHOWER

Eisenhower, in the words of Samuel P. Huntington,[1] was to become the nation's "most effective instrument in the reduction of the armed forces. . . . As a popular military hero candidate, he helped the minority party secure control of the national government for the first time in two decades. Once in office, his military prestige aided the dominant elements in that party toward a realization of their goals of reducing expenditures, lowering taxes, and balancing the budget." Walter Lippmann has similarly suggested that it was the historic function of Eisenhower, as both a general and a Republican, to supply a bridge over which the nation could retreat from the positions of diplomatic intransigence and military threat which it had assumed under his Democratic predecessors. After the fierce assaults upon the Truman and Roosevelt Administrations for having been "soft" toward communism, only a Republican, in this view, could have taken even the modest steps toward "co-existence"

[1] *The Soldier and the State,* Harvard University Press, Cambridge, 1957, pp. 371, 372.

which have been made since 1953; while only a general clothed in the prestige of the conquest of Europe could have effected the reduction, withdrawal and redesign of our military forces which followed upon the truce in Korea.

The thesis is exaggerated; Eisenhower remained a prisoner of the "anti-Communist" campaign which helped elect him, while the military retrenchment had actually begun under Truman. But it is an ironic thesis in the light of all the argument in 1952 over the wisdom of electing a professional soldier to the Presidency. The fact is that Eisenhower, precisely because he was a professional who had spent his whole career in military service, found it at least easier than another might have done to restore non-military considerations to a greater authority in the formulation of national policy. Only one other graduate of West Point, Ulysses S. Grant, had been returned to the Presidency, and the Grant Administrations had not been happy. But those who made the comparison of the two Presidents failed to carry the analysis deep enough. The same military "habit of command" which proved unfortunate in the 1870's was to find a place in the 1950's; the military naiveté which set Grant adrift among thieves and adventurers was to serve Eisenhower well in the different political atmosphere which prevailed eighty years later. As soldiers who had spent most of their careers on modest salaries, both Grant and Eisenhower entertained an uncomplicated respect for the titans of civilian industry and politics who had filled their horizons and, until they reached high position, had ruled their destinies. Too many of those on whom Grant relied were unworthy of him; it was Eisenhower's fortune that the giants of civilian law and industry to whom he turned were in the main men of integrity and ability.

Eisenhower could influence the Joint Chiefs as a civilian, such as Adlai Stevenson, might not have been able to do; but he himself accepted the guidance of the great businessmen, bankers and lawyers — the effective leaders of our civilian society — as Stevenson might have refused to do. With a former professional soldier in the White House we were to experience a considerable diminution of the power of "purely military" factors in the control of our affairs.

It began when the President-elect, in conformity with his campaign promise, flew to Korea in early December, taking with him John Foster Dulles and Charles E. Wilson ("General Motors Wilson"), whom he had designated respectively as Secretary of State and Secretary of Defense. They were joined at Iwo Jima by Admiral Arthur W. Radford, still commanding the Pacific Fleet, as he had been at the time of the B-36 controversy two years before. The Eisenhower-Dulles-Wilson military and foreign policies were taking shape; and Radford, though he can hardly have endeared himself to Eisenhower by his conduct of the B-36 affair, now seemed well suited to assist in carrying those policies out. His strategic ideas, forcefully expressed, appeared to coincide with their own; his attitude and background recommended themselves in other ways. According to Robert J. Donovan:

> Eisenhower felt that the new chairman [of JCS] should be an officer who was in sympathy with the notion of a broadened strategy in Asia, which Radford surely was. . . . the Republicans had been charging for years that the Roosevelt and Truman administrations had concentrated too much on Europe and too little on Asia, and Eisenhower was looking for a chairman of the JCS whose record would indicate an urgent interest in the Far East.[1]

Bradley's term as chairman would not expire until August 1953 and the selection of Radford to succeed him was not to be announced until May. But the choice of the admiral during the Korean trip marked the first step toward the "politicization" of the military high command. The Republicans had complained bitterly over the way in which the Truman chiefs had tended to serve the political interests of the Administration; Eisenhower was now determined to secure a new set of chiefs who would better serve his own political purposes. Though this was later to cause much lifting of eyebrows, it was in fact an inevitable consequence of circumstances.

The basis of the new policy was, as the candidate had put it, "security with solvency." The primary requirement was a balanced budget on a lower level of expenditure; this could be achieved only by a reduction in military spending, and this in turn required some withdrawal from our world commitments. It would be necessary

[1] *Eisenhower: The Inside Story,* Harper, New York, 1956, p. 19.

to revise the original concept of a fully adequate conventional ground defense of Europe under NATO; in the East, the policy was to leave it "to the Asians," as the candidate had declared in a famous passage, "to fight Asians." But this would be impossible until the Korean War had been brought to an end, and there seemed to be but two ways of accomplishing this. One was by a massive further expenditure of life and money — which the new policy ruled out — the other was by *threats* of action sufficiently awesome to induce the Communists to grant the armistice. The nuclear arsenal provided the only means of making such a threat, just as in Europe the nuclear weapons provided the only possible substitute for the conventional manpower which was henceforth to be maintained on a scale much lower than that originally contemplated. Radford, despite his forceful arguments in 1949 against nuclear strategic war, seems readily to have lent himself to this policy of withdrawal under cover of the nuclear threats of advance. But the Joint Chiefs and much military opinion were uncertain and divided on the question. If the policy was both to succeed diplomatically and to produce the desired reduction in military spending, it would be helpful to bring the military command as a whole to a somewhat greater subservience to civil policies, and politics. It seemed desirable to enhance the power of the civilian Secretaries over the military commanders; it was desirable to find a JCS chairman in sympathy with the civilian policy and then enhance his authority over his military colleagues.

It was in these directions that the Eisenhower Administration was to move from its first days in office. It is not suggested that there was anything improper in this. Some military opinion has been inclined to speak bitterly of the Radford selection and later appointments to JCS as "political" appointments. If such they were, it was because high military command had become unavoidably political in nature. Either the Joint Chiefs had to support the policies of the civil administration or else they would have to be walled off completely from all influence over "political" and "economic" affairs, something which by this time had become quite impossible. But as the Eisenhower Administration took up in its turn the problems

of military reorganization the result was to precipitate, in the spring
of 1953, still another debate over civil-military relationships.

## ORGANIZATION PLANNING

One of the new Administration's first actions was the establishment of a committee to study the Defense Department and recommend changes in its organization in order to provide the nation with
"maximum security at minimum cost, and without danger to its
free institutions." This difficult assignment was confided to Nelson
Rockefeller (as chairman), Lovett, who had already voiced his criticisms of the existing order, Vannevar Bush, Omar Bradley, Milton
Eisenhower, David Sarnoff and Arthur S. Flemming, Director of
Defense Mobilization. While they were still deliberating, Bradley
published a statement which, to many, had a self-exculpatory tone:
"Generally . . . we [the Joint Chiefs] should confine our part to
pointing out the military implications and military capabilities . . .
Perhaps some people might feel that the Joint Chiefs of Staff should
stand up and resolutely and strongly recommend a national policy
which we would prefer, but to date I have not been convinced that
this is a proper role for a military leader."[1] Bradley, too, was ready
to accept the "politicization" of the military command; and there
was little doubt that the Rockefeller committee would recommend
to carry it further.

The President published the committee report and the accompanying "Reorganization Plan No. 6" embodying its recommendations
at the end of April 1953. In doing so he heavily underlined the
theme that "basic decisions relating to the military forces must be
made by politically accountable civilian officials. Conversely, professional military leaders must not be thrust into the political arena
to become the prey of partisan politics." Yet the committee itself
had unanimously found that it was "impossible" to make a sufficiently clear distinction within the Department of Defense between
military affairs and civilian affairs "to serve as a practicable basis for
dividing responsibility between military and civilian officers or for

---

[1] As quoted by Matthew B. Ridgway, *Soldier*, Harper, New York, 1956, p. 330.

establishing two parallel lines of command." Consequently, the military still had to be mingled with the politicians and the bureaucrats all along the line; and the political implications of the military officers' responsibility could not be disposed of as readily as General Bradley appeared to imagine.

The President stated the purposes of the reorganization in those somewhat elusive terms which political leaders in general (and perhaps Eisenhower in particular) too often use to discuss military subjects:

> One of our basic aims is to gain again for the free world the initiative in shaping international conditions under which freedom can thrive. . . . In providing the kind of military security that our country needs, we must keep our country free and our economy solvent. We must not endanger the very things we seek to defend. . . . We must remain ever mindful of three great objectives in organizing our defense.

These objectives were: a "clear and unchallenged civilian responsibility in the Defense Establishment"; "maximum effectiveness at minimum cost"; the "best possible military plans." To achieve the first the Secretary of Defense was to be put in unequivocal control — "no function in any part of the Department of Defense" should be performed "independent" of the civilian Secretary, who would, however, act "through" the three service Secretaries. JCS was to be excluded from the chain of command. They would still designate the unitary theater commanders, but they would no longer designate one of their own number to act as their executive agent for the theater, as Collins had acted in respect to the Far Eastern commanders in chief. The Secretary of Defense would now designate one of the military departments (not its Chief of Staff) as executive agent for a theater. But while this may seem to have disposed of JCS as a corporate body, it did not so easily dispose of its members as individuals. Since for "the strategic direction and operational control of forces" the Secretary of Defense was to authorize the Chief of Staff of the designated department "to act for that department in its executive agency capacity," it was not clear that this greatly altered matters.

To achieve the second objective of "maximum effectiveness at minimum cost" the plan suppressed the two principal joint agencies — the Munitions Board and the Research and Development Board — involved in military costs, and transferred their functions to two newly created Assistant Secretaries of Defense. Six new assistant-secretaryships in all were added to the three existing posts on that level. This was to provide one-man supervision over each of the various major areas — such as finance, manpower, health, Congressional relations as well as procurement and research — which were of more or less common concern to all three services. The aim was to do away with the inter-service "log-rolling" which Secretary Lovett had so severely castigated in the joint boards, as well as to strengthen the hand of the civilian Secretary of Defense. It was explained that the Assistant Secretaries were to be strictly staff helpers and advisers to the Secretary; they were not to be in the chain of command and were not to "impose" themselves between the Secretary and the service Secretaries. But since they were to operate in just those areas which were of greatest concern to the service Secretaries in administering their departments, they still seemed to leave the latter in a somewhat ambiguous position.

The third objective, the "best possible military plans," was to be achieved by severely reminding the Joint Chiefs that they "are not a command body" but purely advisers to the President and the Secretary of Defense; and by confining them, as a corporate body, to that planning function. But this again failed to dispose of them in their capacities as individual service commanders. To this end the chairman, the only member not also head of a military service, was to be given increased responsibility over the work and the personnel of the Joint Staff (the 200-odd junior officers who "staffed" the JCS papers); and was to encourage them to bring representatives of civilian agencies like State or Treasury, or qualified experts from private life, into participation in their military planning.

THE MODEL OF REORGANIZATION PLAN NO. 6

Reorganization Plan No. 6 was rather clearly modelled upon the example of the giant modern industrial corporation. The Secretary of Defense was to be the analogue of the corporation president (the position Wilson had held in General Motors). The service Secretaries represented the subordinate presidents or vice presidents in charge of operating divisions; the Assistant Secretaries were the vice presidents in charge of functional areas — such as promotion, sales, finance — with which the top management has to deal. The Joint Chiefs were to become a kind of long-range planning body, resembling the organizations which large corporations maintain for long-range economic or technical analysis.

Yet the Department of Defense was not a giant industrial corporation controlling three major subsidiary operating companies; and in several respects the analogy failed. One reason for the General Motors type of organization, in which the subsidiary producing divisions (like Cadillac or Buick or the rest) are maintained as largely separate operations, is to keep them in strong competition with each other as well as with outside producers. A major objective of the Eisenhower policy, however, was to end, or at least reduce, the competition between the three services for the taxpayer's dollar. In an industrial organization like General Motors, the parent corporation exercises only a very general supervision over the manufacturing, sales and promotion policies of the subsidiary corporations, and the subsidiary presidents have an active and urgent administrative responsibility. But the Assistant Secretaries of Defense were created for the very purpose of removing such independent responsibilities from the service Secretaries and concentrating them under the direct control of the top management. The Assistant Secretaries were not to be in the chain of command, but they were deliberately linked to it, and the roles and responsibilities of the service Secretaries were inevitably to dwindle.

Finally, industrial life offers no real analogue for military command; and despite the effort to reduce the role of the Joint Chiefs to an industrial pattern, it remained floating in the new system almost as in the old. The Rockefeller committee had grappled with the old argument between a four-headed, committee command system (represented by JCS) and a single Chief of Staff who would be the military commander of all the armed forces. The solution it found was one more of appearance than of fact. It was to confine the Joint Chiefs, as a body, to a purely planning and advisory function. The President would then approve the plans and be responsible for ordering their execution through a chain of command running by way of the Secretary of Defense to, ultimately, the individual Chief of Staff of the department having executive responsibility. But this not only failed to remove the confusion between the individual and the corporate responsibilities of the several Chiefs of Staff; it also confused the responsibilities of military command in peacetime or "cold war" conditions with those involved in the conduct of active war operations.

Under modern conditions it is impossible, even in time of active war but to a much greater extent in time of "cold war" or peace, to draw a sharp distinction between planning and command. During the Second World War, planning decisions were to a considerable extent command decisions, since they established the conditions under which field command would have to work and determined the tools it would have available to work with. With the coming of peace or cold war (whichever term one prefers), planning became an even greater element in command. Under combat conditions the field commanders necessarily make the major decisions; under noncombat conditions, the responsibility necessarily falls to the staffs. The essential questions cease to concern the best utilization of organized troops in the field; they become questions of the adoption of weapons systems, the over-all utilization of manpower, the expansion of the "readiness" of one service at the expense of the "readiness" of another. All these are staff, rather than command, decisions. They are not taken in the heat of battle, but rather in cool calculation of what battle might at some unknown future date require.

Yet they have the effect of command decisions. Those who make or endorse the plans are in effect determining the strategy both for peace and for the opening phases, at least, of a future war; they are giving the commands which really count. It was for this very reason that the old office of (military) Commander in Chief had been abolished after the Spanish-American War and the Chief of Staff of the Army had been thereafter recognized as its peacetime commander. If an unwieldy amount of minor administrative detail had accumulated in the hands of the Joint Chiefs, it was not because they were, individually, the commanders or executives of their services; it was precisely because they were, jointly, a staff, and the staff (or planning) decisions had become controlling all down the line of minor administrative decision. Under the circumstances, the attempted separation of the command from the staff or advisory function could be of little effect. The real command lay in the staff planning; that being so, it could make little difference whether the plans prepared by the Joint Chiefs were routed to the President and then back through themselves to one of them serving as executive agent, or were routed from the President back through the Secretary of Defense and the service Secretaries to the same individual.

But if the Joint Chiefs system was to remain, in essence, much what it had been before, it might be possible to simplify the structure and relieve it of some of the detail with which it had been struggling. The Joint Chiefs, as a corporate body, represented much more than four eminent flag officers. It had its own secretariat. It had its own Joint Staff, drawn equally from the three services. It had innumerable joint commissions, boards and groups and sub-groups. The Rockefeller committee found that in the previous year the Office of the Joint Chiefs had dealt with no less than seventeen hundred items. Some issues had remained in the Joint Chiefs for as long as two years without decision. Some were so trivial that it seemed absurd that they should ever have reached the highest military planning and policy agency. Rockefeller cited as an example a question of who should pay for repairing secondary roads in France torn up by heavy American military equipment. "There was nobody," he observed, "who had the authority to say, 'That is not of sufficient importance'" for the Joint Chiefs.

It was thought that a good deal of this administrative jungle might be cleared up by giving the chairman of JCS (who alone had no military service to administer) direct responsibility for and authority over the Joint Staff and its complicated planning substructure. By concentrating the "planning" function more in the hands of the chairman and leaving the "command" functions more in the hands of the service chiefs it was probably hoped that JCS could be forced to arrive at a clearer (or at any rate less expensive) resolution of the service conflicts over strategic concepts and weapons systems. If strengthening the chairman did not make JCS into an agency of decision, it could lessen its character as an agency to prevent decision. The promotion of the chairman of JCS into a larger measure of control over its planning functions seemed an obvious step toward his promotion to a unified command authority over his three service colleagues.

THE ATTACK ON THE PLAN

Despite the Administration's efforts to deny any such intention, Reorganization Plan No. 6 came under severe attack on these grounds. Finletter, who had been Truman's Secretary of the Air Forces, assailed it in articles and interviews: "This plan accentuates the tendency toward a single service and the unification of three services into one . . . I don't think it will work well." The result would be an "unwieldy" organization, a "monolithic" structure giving too much power to one man or one service interest; it would "submerge air power and the needs of the new weaponry." Finletter thought that the 1949 act, which created the office of Chairman of the Joint Chiefs, had been unwise; he now questioned whether there should be any chairman at all. A Republican businessman, Robert W. Johnson, gave even more impassioned testimony: "Few indeed are those who realize the extent of the direct and indirect power of the military in our nation today. . . . The Army General Staff has engaged in an unrelenting struggle for power." Johnson's "two great fears" were socialism and militarism — which have in fact through the past century been closely allied — and he had warned Rockefeller that several members of his committee had joined it "committed to the German system which captured civilian authority, lost two wars and ruined Germany." But others of great experience in the subject, like Ferdinand Eberstadt, were far more moderate in their doubts.

When the House Government Operations Committee held hearings in June 1953 on the plan, the questioning turned mainly on two brief clauses relating to the chairman of JCS. One made selection of officers for the Joint Staff and "their tenure" subject to the chairman's approval; the other transferred the "management" of the Joint Staff from JCS as a whole to the chairman alone. The Administration defended these provisions as no more than technical, intended to get the staff work better organized and to make possible the elimination of unsuitable or inefficient personnel; the critics here envisaged the all-powerful single Chief of Staff, controlling all the processes of staff planning and elbowing his service colleagues into subordinate status. The committee finally drafted a resolution which it hoped would have the effect of accepting Reorganization Plan No. 6 as a whole, but at the same time eliminating these two clauses. The House, however, took no action on the resolution, and the plan went into effect, under the law, as originally submitted. The fears of those who foresaw an all-powerful Chief of Staff have not materialized; nor have the hopes of those who thought that here was a complete solution for the problem of a four-headed command.

The four-headed command, and many of the questions it raised, was to remain. Radford's prestige, in relation to that of his three colleagues, was clearly to rise; and with it, probably, his power to influence (though not to overrule) them in conformity with the policies and wishes of the political Administration. This further strengthened the Secretary of Defense. But the assurances of Roger M. Kyes, then Deputy Secretary of Defense, that the intention was to "get down into the services all of what we term the 'operating functions,' . . . trying to make the military Secretaries the chief operating officers, the operating vice-presidents, so to speak," were not well borne out. At one point he put it a little oddly: "What we have done is to make certain that we are cutting the civilian Secretaries of the services into the chain [of command] so that they are not only informed, but actually know what is going on ahead of time." Cynics might feel that this was about all they did do for the civilian service Secretaries. William L. Dawson (Democratic Representative from Illinois) put it too strongly when he said that it seemed to him "you are by-passing your Secretaries of the services and reducing them to office boys, almost, men who once had Cabinet rank." But it is rather plain that the service Secretaries have undergone a diminution of prominence, power and prestige since 1953.

There was one slightly ironic note. The previous reorganization, in 1949, had sprung in part from the work of the Eberstadt task force of the first Hoover Commission. Hoover and the majority of the commission had substantially accepted the task force report, but there had been a dissent from Dean Acheson, the target of so much Republican animosity. An analysis for the House committee now showed that Reorganization Plan No. 6 followed very closely the proposals which Acheson had advanced in 1949, while departing rather widely from those which had then been accepted by the Republican former President. Hoover felt it inappropriate to appear at the hearings in 1953. And two years later, when a second Hoover Commission task force re-examined the problem, it was to find most of the old faults still apparent in the military system.

## ENDING THE KOREAN WAR: OPERATION CANDOR

The professional soldier in the White House was to introduce other changes in civil-military relations, generally tending to favor the appointed bureaucracy as against both the uniformed forces and the Congressional committees. The most significant were the expansion of the "staff system" in the White House Office, and the upgrading and reorganization of the National Security Council. During the latter years of the Truman Administration the importance of NSC and its staff structure had been growing, as more and more complex issues of practical policy had presented themselves. The Soviet atomic explosion had led to NSC 68 as an answer. Truman's *ad hoc* study of the H-bomb problem was constituted as a special committee of NSC. Korea presented urgent problems which neither State nor Defense was competent to deal with alone, and NSC provided a convenient nexus through which all the various planning bodies of the several agencies could be mobilized. In addition to its own administrative staff, NSC had developed its Senior Staff as a means of bringing together all the top planning agencies from the various departments concerned. At any given crisis in Korea, the President could summon informally his Secretaries of

State and Defense, the Joint Chiefs and those policy advisers on whom he relied; but if their advice was to be sound, a greater and greater amount of "staffing" on the lower levels had to go into it.

## BUREAUCRATIZING NSC

The National Security Council was growing in significance under Truman, but its position was still somewhat casual. One of the Eisenhower campaign promises had been to raise NSC to the status which the 1947 act had contemplated for it, to make it his chief arm for policy formulation in the areas of defense, international affairs and internal security. The new Administration proceeded here, as elsewhere, to introduce system, staff work, clear lines of responsibility and authority. As usual, it began with a study of the problem, this one carried out by Robert Cutler, the very competent Boston banker whom the President had appointed to the White House staff as Special Assistant for National Security Affairs.[1] In consonance with his report, presented in March 1953, the President in effect confined the Cabinet — the traditional agency of policy formation — to the domestic field; while Cutler elevated NSC (most of whose statutory members were also members of the Cabinet) into an organ of policy formation in the international, defense and security fields of comparable prestige and of much greater mechanical efficiency.

A fixed day and hour — Thursdays at 10 — was set for NSC meetings, and it never skipped a meeting throughout the first 115 weeks of the Eisenhower Administration. (Through the previous five years the Truman NSC had met, on an average, less than once every two weeks.) Eisenhower normally took his place as chairman, as Truman frequently had not done, and the attendance was considerably enlarged. To the five statutory members there were added the Secretary of the Treasury, the Director of the Budget Bureau and the Special Assistant on Disarmament (Harold Stassen) with membership status; the Special Assistant on National Security and his aides, the NSC Executive Secretary and Deputy, the Chairman of JCS and the Director of Central Intelligence were normally present as ad-

[1] The following account is from Robert Cutler, "The Development of the National Security Council," *Foreign Affairs,* April 1956.

visers, while other consultant or advisory officials were called in as required. There were thus some fifteen or more people usually present at 10 o'clock on Thursdays.

These would proceed on a rigidly organized agenda to consider a series of "carefully staffed" policy papers. The staff work is the most striking feature of the new system. NSC's own executive staff was continued, with the function not only of keeping track of the paper-work and coping with the incoming "flood" of policy recommendations, but also of providing — through its "think people" — a body of non-political, permanent officials capable of surveying the various fields of policy from a detached and non-partisan position. Above them, the former Senior Staff was replaced by a Policy Planning Board directly under the Special Assistant for National Security Affairs (Cutler) and composed of Assistant Secretaries from the departments and agencies whose chiefs sat on NSC itself. As political (non-civil service) appointees, they were to represent the policy of the administration in power; they also represented the various special interests of their agencies, but their task was to combine these into coordinated or unified policy recommendations. Apparently, it is in the Policy Planning Board that the real work is centered. The members may be summoned at the lift of a telephone and set to work for grinding hours or days on some special problem, undistracted by the administrative responsibilities of their superiors. They are, indeed, a kind of high-level echelon of the assistants who had long done most of the work anyway.

In later 1953 an additional staff organ, the Operations Coordinating Board (OCB), was established. According to Cutler, this "arose like a phoenix out of the ashes of the old Psychological Strategy Board." It was at least a no less surprising transformation than that of the phoenix. Psychological warfare necessitates a clear policy as ammunition; one cannot make propaganda without a "line" to propagandize. C. D. Jackson's psychological warfare command was certainly among the least fortunate of the Eisenhower Administration's ideas for rebuilding the national defense; it seems strange that it should have given rise to what was to become a major element in the new machinery of policy formation. Policy Planning originates the papers; NSC debates and tests them and submits them for Presidential approval; it is the job of OCB to see that they are carried out. Cutler has explained the process with a metaphor at once arresting and, to some, rather alarming:

> Assume that the National Security Council sits at the top of Policy Hill. On one side of this hill, policy recommendations travel upward through the Planning Board to the Council, where they are thrashed out and submitted to the President. When the President has approved a policy recommendation, it travels down the other side of Policy Hill to the departments and agencies responsible for its execution. . . . Part way down this side of the hill is the Operations Coordinating Board, to which the President refers an approved national security policy as its authority to advise with the relevant departments and agencies as to their detailed operational planning . . .

Admiration for the mechanical neatness of this arrangement cannot still a certain doubt as to whether policy — that is, really effective policy — is susceptible to this form of mass production, packaging and distribution. "The standardization of these techniques," Cutler has explained, "made it possible for the Council to transact, week in and week out, an enormously heavy load of work." On examining the record, according to Cutler, it appeared that the Truman NSC, in its five and a quarter years, had taken 699 "policy actions." In its first three years the Eisenhower NSC was to take 809 "policy actions," thus doubling the output per annum. But as to the quality or national significance of the product (normally kept secret) it is not easy to speak.

When the Eisenhower Administration took over, it found "something like a hundred national security policy statements in effect," some old, some more recent. The first task of the new NSC, and its staff, was to review all these as well as to cope with the urgent new questions which came pouring in. Through its gruelling first 115 weeks NSC ground the papers up and down "Policy Hill." Then the President went to Denver and presently suffered his heart attack. NSC meetings declined in frequency. But Cutler makes the interesting claim that as a result of its labors it had "accumulated a reservoir of basic policies and forward strategy" copious enough to carry the nation (and the Administration) safely and smoothly through the disability of its President. While this may seem to be claiming a good deal, it at least suggests the power which NSC's civilian staff men and political appointees may have established in the military and diplomatic affairs of the American people.

It is the effect of this policy-planning mechanism which remains obscure. No doubt NSC has infused a new order and system into decisions which were once more various and chaotic; no doubt it has assisted in bringing the departments together in more orderly and cooperative effort in those areas which, while their problems may be difficult enough, are of comparatively minor importance. Cutler himself grants the inability of any staff or planning organization to deal with the big "basic" problems, such as the integration of the armed services, the choice of weapons systems or the "jealousies and jurisdictional disputes" which thrive at many levels of government. The new NSC would seem to have been little more successful than other mechanisms in foreseeing and providing for large, developing international situations. Robert Donovan, studying the secret history of the Indo-China crisis in 1954, received the impression "that the problem came before the President piece by piece and not altogether at the same pace as events on the battlefield." [1] The toilers on Policy Hill seem to have left little impress on the handling of the Suez crisis. In the spring of 1953 NSC produced a new paper, reviewing the world situation and supporting the general solutions at which Eisenhower had largely arrived by the time he took office. It is believed that this formed the basis of the Eisenhower policy through 1954. Whether the policy would have been much different if the NSC review had not been made, or, indeed, if NSC and its staffs had not existed, may be questioned.

## THE KOREAN LOG JAM BEGINS TO BREAK UP

The Eisenhower reorganizations and rearrangements had to proceed, of course, in the midst of the practical problems inherited from the preceding Administration. Korea was obviously the most urgent. The famous visit to Korea had not ended the war, and the gesture

[1] Donovan, *Eisenhower,* p. 262.

(never intended, it was later maintained, as anything more) of "unleashing Chiang Kai-shek" had fizzled into what came perilously near to the ridiculous. In January 1953 the Korean War was in a condition of stalemate which had lasted for over a year; and the front lines were virtually where they had been eighteen months before, when the truce negotiations had begun. Since the end of 1951 there had been little heavy fighting. Minor rectifying operations might now and then step up the casualty lists; a few handfuls of men might be lost from time to time in night patrols, but the Communists showed no sign of making another major push into South Korea. Neither, unhappily, did they show any sign of allowing us to conclude the war and get out. Agreement had painfully been achieved on all the military issues involved; the only apparent problem remaining to be settled was the essentially political-propaganda issue over the prisoners of war. But on that no progress was being made; the talks were in a state of suspension.

The new Administration's only recourse was to step up the threat of what we would do if the Chinese did not grant us an armistice. According to Donovan,[1] as Eisenhower and Dulles were winging back over the Pacific in mid-December, they "had determined to make it clear to the Communists that to delay the truce indefinitely would be to invite the United States to enlarge the war and to strike at China not only in Korea but on two or three other fronts of its own choosing." The outlines of the celebrated "massive retaliation" policy were forming, and the hypnotic phrase "of our own choosing" appeared in the President-elect's statement on his arrival at La Guardia Field on December 14. In the spring, again according to Donovan, atomic weapons were moved into Okinawa. American intelligence officers in Korea saw evidence that the Chinese were increasing their dispersal and protective measures against atomic attack, but nothing else happened.

Meanwhile, India had contributed a new idea. At a Red Cross meeting in Geneva in December India's representative had suggested an exchange of sick and wounded prisoners of war, avoiding the

[1] *Ibid.*, p. 115.

more difficult question of the able-bodied. In February this idea was being advanced in the UN, and JCS told Clark in Tokyo to try it directly on the enemy. On February 26 Clark wrote the Chinese and North Korean negotiators through his liaison officers at Panmunjom. The result was a "dead silence for over a month."

But on March 5, 1953 Joseph Stalin died. Three weeks later, on March 28, the Communist commanders answered Clark's letter, agreeing to an exchange of the sick and wounded and proposing a reopening of the negotiations over the main prisoner problem. Two days later, the Chinese Foreign Minister, Chou En-lai, broadcast a statement agreeing to turn over to a neutral agency all able-bodied prisoners not desiring repatriation. The log jam was apparently breaking up.[1]

Why, is today unknown. Secretary Dulles has indicated his belief that it was because of the threats of atomic action by the Eisenhower Administration. Others have attributed it to Stalin's death and the convulsions which shook the whole Communist world as a result. Others have suggested that the Chinese had become convinced by March that they could squeeze no more out of the new Administration than they had been able to squeeze out of its predecessor (some, at least, of the campaign oratory might have given them the opposite idea) and that it was time to call quits. Until Chinese sources are available the actual reasons will no doubt remain obscure. But by the latter part of March there was definitely light upon the horizon.

However, as Dulles had to warn his colleagues at the Cabinet meeting on March 20, the Korean crisis was far from over. Meanwhile, Senator Taft had been thundering for budgetary retrenchment — "The one primary thing we promised the American people was reduction of expenditures" [2] — while both opposition and friendly elements in Congress were questioning the cut-backs in Air Force expenditure which the President was prepared to authorize. It was the same with Korea as it was with the budget; everybody was demanding more defense for less money, but few had practicable recommendations as to how that end was to be achieved, just as every-

[1] Mark W. Clark, *From the Danube to the Yalu*, Harper, New York, 1954, pp. 240 ff.
[2] Donovan, *Eisenhower*, p. 109.

body was demanding that the Korean struggle be concluded while none was willing to spend the life and money apparently necessary to conclude it. It was primarily from the domestic and economic rather than from the foreign and military point of view that the Administration approached this compound issue. Significantly, the March 20 Cabinet meeting had begun in a discussion of "the need for standby consumer-credit controls." But Donovan well summarizes the complexities into which this led them:

> . . . a decision to allow the Korean War to continue in stalemate could cost the administration the support of Congress, endangering the whole legislative program. On the other hand, . . . the alternative of final military victory in Korea would cost a tremendous sum, threatening new inflation and necessitating new economic controls.
>
> The President said that he would not accept these as the only alternatives. There was, he told the Cabinet, a possibility of achieving a limited victory. He said that he would never consent to a course of interminable budgetary deficits.[1]

It is not clear how a decision to "allow" the war "to continue in stalemate" would differ practically from a decision to "achieve a limited victory," unless what the President really meant was that he would accept a limited defeat. Since as matters stood the decision was really in the hands of the Chinese rather than the Administration, whether or not Eisenhower would "consent" to "interminable budgetary deficits" was somewhat irrelevant — at least until Eisenhower had discovered some means of influencing Chinese policy. Until he had done so, the statements at the March 20 Cabinet meeting could mean little more than that the Truman policy of limited war for a limited and negotiated settlement would be continued without change, because there was no visible alternative. The Administration was actually in something of a trap. Its commitments to retrenchment and a balanced budget had in effect deprived it of initiative in the Korean problem; the initiative remained with Peking. It was apparently in the latter part of March that the Chinese reached their conclusion and decided to wind up the Korean War.

[1] *Ibid.*, p. 117.

But this was a Chinese decision, not an American and even less a United Nations one.

Clark unexpectedly found the negotiations over the exchange of the sick and wounded ("Little Switch") proceeding rapidly. ". . . in March and April of 1953, to our surprise, the Communists gave in on almost every disputed issue in the talks that led to Little Switch";[1] the exchange began on April 20, and on April 26 full negotiations for a final armistice were begun. It was in these days that the many Eisenhower studies and commissions were busy revising the Defense Department, NSC, the White House staff apparatus, while the new Secretary of the Treasury and Director of the Budget were busy cutting down both current expenditure and the fiscal '54 budget inherited from Truman. In April Eisenhower approved the new NSC policy review which "veered away from a military build-up for meeting major aggression by any particular D-Day. . . . the new policy aimed at leveling out the peaks and valleys of military preparedness, . . . Based on the concept of a floating D-Day, it called for maintenance of a level of forces and material which could be paid for without staggering the economy and which could be borne for an indefinite period of years."[2]

## RETRENCHMENT AND MASSIVE RETALIATION

Thus, in effect, the Truman fiscal ceiling returned to our defense planning. Henceforth the military budgets were again to represent, as Ridgway put it, "directed verdicts." The whole new policy, in fact, represented little more than a continuation of trends already apparent under the Democrats. The "concept of a floating D-Day" was, and is, something rather difficult to grasp. However it might float through a nebulous future, it would presumably require, if it ever arrived, the same state of readiness, the same numbers of men, tanks and airplanes. In the panic atmosphere of late 1950 the Joint Chiefs had formulated their huge expansion plans on the estimate that by 1953 the Soviet Union would be reaching the peak of its military capability, and that this should consequently be taken as our

[1] Clark, *From the Danube to the Yalu*, p. 258.
[2] Donovan, *Eisenhower*, p. 52.

own target date. It is questionable whether this target date ever had much significance. In the early stages it had been a matter of getting everything possible started as quickly as it could be done; it was not Soviet capabilities but our own raw material and factory capacity which governed. Well before the end of the Truman era the diminution of the military menace and the pressures for economy had pretty well muted the "target date"; certainly, the fiscal "roll forward" to "level out the peaks and valleys" of military expenditure onto a continuing "plateau" had begun under Truman. The Eisenhower Administration was simply to push the same process further; while both its reasons and its methods closely copied those which had led to the Truman ceiling in 1947.

The invention of the "floating D-Day" really changed nothing; it would seem to have been an invention of the advertising man much more than of statesmanship. It helped the Eisenhower Administration to "sell" its defense policies, however, and at the May 1953 meeting of NATO in Paris its effects were plainly apparent. The whole emphasis was now on retrenchment. The initial hope of erecting across Western Europe an armed defense capable of turning the many tank and infantry divisions maintained by the Soviet Union and its satellites was there tacitly abandoned. Much would still be done toward rebuilding the structure of defense — toward relocating the airfields, rearranging the lines of communication, increasing the ammunition stocks and strengthening the logistic "infrastructure." But to create and flesh the defense itself would not only be politically difficult (the question of West Germany's military contribution was still unsettled); it would also clearly cost too much. Not even the United States any longer regarded 1953 as a potentially "crisis year." The work of NATO's Temporary Council Committee and its "Three Wise Men" was subject to revision, downward.

There was another thread already running, obscurely, through the Eisenhower policies — the withdrawal from the front lines in Asia, perhaps even in Europe, into the Hoover-Taft concept of a "fortress America." The new policy "placed less emphasis than before on expanding American and NATO forces to the maximum levels

authorized, but heightened the emphasis on continental defense." [1]
But the constant problem was the practical one of how to do it.
There is no doubt that the Eisenhower Administration took very seriously both halves of its pledge of "security with solvency." And there
can be little doubt as to the basic answer which it found to meet the
resultant dilemma. It was that which had been dramatically advanced by Brien McMahon two years before: the substitution, where-
ever possible, of nuclear fire-power for the politically and economically far more burdensome accoutrements of "conventional" war. But
because the probable consequences of any actual nucleonic war would
be so appallingly ruinous to ourselves and our world as well as to
our enemies, we would rely upon the threat of these weapons only,
not upon any contemplation of their actual use. We would leave it
to "Asians to fight Asians"; we would withdraw from the far frontiers and the little wars, leaving their local issues to others, while we
policed the world order with the menace of the nuclear arsenal.

The core of the policy, however, was the substitution of nuclear
fire-power for men and conventional weapons, in order, to put it
bluntly, to save money. The hope of withdrawal into a continental
fortress was much more a consequence than an object of the new
policies. The basic decision was to rest our defense, whether local or
global, whether in small wars or total ones, upon the nuclear arsenal.
This was soon to become evident — in the agreement to admit our
NATO allies into at least some knowledge of the tactical employment of nuclear weapons; in Dulles' announcement (January 1954)
of a "capacity for massive retaliation"; in the intensive study by all
our own services of the tactical as well as the strategic employment of
nuclear fire-power.

It was by far the most fundamental policy decision of the Eisenhower Administration, and from it have flowed many consequences
in diplomacy, in military plan, in organization and equipment, in
popular control of military policy and in the relations between the
people and their military shield. It was a civilian decision, in that it
was taken and has been enforced primarily from civilian (fiscal) con-

[1] *Ibid.*, pp. 52-53.

siderations and by the civilian administrators and bureaucrats. Obviously, they sought military advice in making it, but mainly from those military men who were prepared to agree. What is striking is that, although a civilian decision, it was never exposed in any meaningful way to Congressional, much less to public, debate. There was never any great discussion in the press or on the public platform to reveal all the complicated implications which might lie behind it — not all of which were by any means apparent even to the President and his appointed civilian administrators who made it. Organization, system, the mass production of "carefully staffed" policy papers, the rearrangement of the lines of policy and command — all these could correlate and expedite the work on the minor questions. But the system necessarily forced a compartmentation and fragmentation of the work on the colossal issues that really mattered. NSC, producing 809 "policy actions" in the space of three years, was hardly an organization capable of bringing into its purview all of the vast consequences of just one basic policy decision.

OPERATION CANDOR

How little the policy-making officials themselves understood of what they were doing may be illustrated by the curious history of "Operation Candor." The nuclear threats, both those which we might wield against others and those which we might be inviting against ourselves, were raised to another terrible level on November 1, 1952 (in the final stages of the electoral campaign), when the world's first successful fusion device was fired at Bikini, with staggering effect. "Mike" was not a usable weapon, but its colossal explosion — some hundreds of times as great as those produced at Hiroshima and Nagasaki, and almost immediately revealed by a fortunate *lacuna* in the Atomic Energy Commission's arrangements for censorship — seemed to justify the men who had pressed two years earlier for a crash program for the "Super." The new device was not the Super then imagined; but it was a clear sign that super-giant weapons would soon be with us.

In the spring of 1952, the AEC's General Advisory Committee, headed by Robert Oppenheimer, had submitted a report to Truman on the fantastically destructive potentialitites of the weapons then in prospect. Later, a State Department panel, also headed by Oppenheimer, submitted a long report (in the final days of the Truman Administration) recommending, among other things, a franker public approach to the problem. This was turned over by the new Administration to NSC for "staffing." Unfortunately, what emerged was not a broad policy for dealing with the dreadful vistas which had opened; it was a proposal that C. D. Jackson, then Special Assistant in charge of psychological warfare, should go to work on "a candid Presidential speech about nuclear weapons." Jackson, of course, formed a committee; he named his project "Operation Candor," and began to turn out drafts for the candid Presidential speech.[1]

What this speech was supposed to accomplish is unclear. Perhaps, since it was placed in the hands of the psychological warfare chief, it was intended to frighten our enemies and reassure our friends. If so, it would inevitably run the risk of frightening our friends and ourselves more than the enemy. Many drafts appeared, but "no one particularly liked them." They were too gruesome. ". . . the President," according to Donovan, "did not wish to be put in a position merely of horrifying the American people or of horrifying the Russian people. He wanted to tell the world of the awful consequences of nuclear warfare, but he did not want to leave the matter at that dead end."[2] It seems fair to say that the President's own purposes were obscure to him. Having based his policy directly on "the awful consequences of nuclear warfare," he did not want to horrify anybody by revealing the horrors implicit in the policy. Had the speech been driven through to completion and delivery, it might have clarified much in the minds of our own policy-makers as well as in the mind of our own public and the international world. But through another year no practicable way of being candid to the American people about the policies to which the Administration had committed them was to appear. Under Lewis Strauss as its new chairman, the Atomic

[1] Donovan, *Eisenhower,* pp. 184-85.
[2] *Ibid.*

Energy Commission was to devote itself even more earnestly than before to preventing any hint of the data essential to a rational discussion from leaking to the public.

By the summer of 1953 Operation Candor had "pretty nearly run out of steam." For many reasons, candor had become an inexpedient if not unusable instrument in the management of national security policy. But the nuclear problem was still "weighing on Eisenhower's mind."[1] And on August 12, 1953 it suddenly assumed an even greater urgency, when the Soviet Union fired a thermonuclear (or H-bomb) explosion of its own. The dread sequence which Oppenheimer and the other scientists had foreseen in late 1949 had been duly fulfilled. For all its staff machinery, the Administration had been no more able than Oppenheimer or anyone else to prepare for or provide against this consummation. But now something would have to be done.

In September 1953 the President transmitted, through Cutler, a new suggestion to Strauss and Jackson: "Suppose the United States and the Soviets were each to turn over to the United Nations for peaceful uses X kilograms of fissionable material." This was quite a new idea for the speech on which Operation Candor had been working. It was eagerly seized; it was "staffed" by NSC and passed by an *ad hoc* NSC committee; it became a Project, and at a White House breakfast on October 3 was approved by Eisenhower. Thus was born the "atoms for peace" speech delivered before the United Nations in December 1953, as well as the policy which it embodied. The name assigned to this new project (because of the breakfast conference which generated it) seems singularly unfortunate, yet curiously accurate, in its symbolism: "Operation Wheaties."[2]

The memorandum from the General Advisory Committee of AEC on the frightful gravity of the new weapons problem seems to have disappeared. In the following spring Oppenheimer himself was to be haled up and publicly disgraced as a "security risk." "Candor," the noble proposal to tell the truth (or at least seem to), had been replaced by "Wheaties," connoting nothing but an advertising

[1] *Ibid.*, pp. 185, 186.
[2] *Ibid.*, pp. 185-91.

slogan. There is obviously much of hope in the slow subsequent development of "atoms for peace," of Euratom, of the proposal (submitted to the United Nations in the winter of 1957) for confining all future production of fissionable material to industrial uses. But most of this is peripheral to the terrible problems of nuclear weapons. Where candor might have, conceivably, compelled facing of the whole problem of nucleonic warfare, "Wheaties" conveniently concealed it under an advertising man's device.

## NEW CHIEFS OF STAFF: END OF THE KOREAN WAR

The consistent, though doubtless unplanned, effect of the various Eisenhower changes and reorganizations has been to reduce the popular, the Congressional and also the professional military influence over the most critical issues of military and international policy. If it is not the military men who determine the basic structure of our military defense, neither is it the civilian public, the civilian editors, the civilians in Congress, none of whom is any longer allowed to know enough about the vital data to exert much influence on the course of policies based upon them. Behind the veils of security, censorship and military secrecy, the power resides, not in the uniformed officers, but in the civilian and political appointees of the Administration — the Secretaries of State and Defense, their numerous Assistant Secretaries and staff men, the Secretary of the Treasury and Director of the Budget, the White House Special Assistants, the Chairman of the Atomic Energy Commission, the Director of Defense Mobilization and many more.

Before this phalanx of civilian directors, the Joint Chiefs have been immobilized primarily by their own inability to agree. The organization charts and lines of authority could be drawn and redrawn; but however the charts were designed, no military directorate could make its military advice effective unless it could present a unified body of military advice. This the Joint Chiefs have never been able to do in peacetime. Both in the Second World War and in Korea they proved a reasonably effective instrument of over-all command; but the command problems of peace are more difficult, in a sense, than those of war. They concern such things as budgets, taxation and conscription, partisan politics, economic rivalries — all matters which the military professionals in JCS usually feel unauthorized to deal with. The civilian administrators have to deal with them. They have to write the budgets and win the elections. Each of the first five Secretaries of Defense from Forrestal to Wilson felt compelled at one time or another to demand agreement within the Joints Chiefs, on pain of making the military decision himself if they did not provide one. Just as the military have never ceased to complain that they cannot get clear statements of civil policy to guide them, so the civilians have never ceased to complain that they cannot get clear strategic advice from the military; and many influential civilians have continued to demand a single, all-powerful Chief of Staff on whom the single "military" responsibility could be pinned.

But such demands tend to overlook the question of whether a monolithic military power would really provide better solutions for the military issues of our times than the present "committee system." A single and responsible Chief of Staff would no doubt enable the civilian administrators to transfer many responsibilities which they now find difficult and onerous; but they would be transferring power as well. The civilians might feel more comfortable, but the nation would lose the creative values of difference, of variety and of debate. If "civilian control" is to be a reality, then the civilians must assume their share of the arduous responsibility. The Eisenhower Administration's solution for the problem was not a single Chief of Staff; it was to maintain the Joint Chiefs, but to "politicize" them. In particular, it was Admiral Radford. In the course of the Korean trip at the end of 1952 he had been selected as the man to provide a bridge between the military plan and the civilian political requirements. A single chief would have exercised too much authority over civilian policy; a purely military command committee, such as the Joint Chiefs, might have been so far divorced from the policies of the political administration as to invite chaos in major defense policy.

Radford, a forceful, highly intelligent naval officer sufficiently supple to accommodate himself to both the political and the military requirements, was an obvious answer. When his somewhat unexpected appointment as Chairman was announced, a story went the rounds in the Navy: As a destroyer commander, Radford had been convinced that the destroyer was the one weapon above all others vital to success in war; when he rose to command cruisers, he forgot the destroyer and became a zealous advocate of cruisers; when he rose to command the Pacific Fleet he had fought for the Navy as a whole as against the Air Force and the Army; elevated to the chairmanship he was likely to forget his devotion to the Navy and take a total view of the military establishment as a unit. Something like that had happened to Carl Vinson, the long-time chairman of the House Naval Affairs Committee, when he became chairman of the Armed Services Committee; and something like that was to happen to Radford. If Radford was unable to resolve the serious strategic differences between the services, and if he was not empowered to command their agreement, he was at least able to give the political administration the military advice which it wanted to support its political decisions.

It is not suggested that this was an ignoble role. It was probably a necessary one; indeed, it was the role which Eisenhower himself was fulfilling on a higher level. Radford's function, in his enhanced position as Chairman of JCS, seems to have been less that of an expert military representative to the civilians than that of an expert political representative to the military. On the one occasion when he seems most clearly to have acted as a military adviser — when he recommended naval-air action in Indo-China — his advice was not taken.

Radford's appointment (announced in May 1953, to take effect in August) was accompanied by a further shuffle in JCS. Nathan F. Twining replaced the ailing Hoyt Vandenberg as Chief of Staff of the Air Force on the latter's retirement in June. Robert B. Carney was to be brought back from the Mediterranean to replace Fechteler (a conventionally rugged sea dog who had made no great impression) as Chief of Naval Operations; and Matthew Ridgway was to be recalled from the Supreme Command in Europe to replace Collins as Army Chief of Staff. The "Truman chiefs" would give way to the "Eisenhower chiefs." This ran quite contrary to the tradition of non-political control over the professional military command. The military command, like the judicial command vested in the Supreme Court, is supposed to be above partisan considerations. But the shift accorded with political realities, just as shifts in the composition of the Supreme Court are likely to do. In this case, however, the "politicization" of JCS was to prove something less than complete.

Ridgway soon discovered that he was expected to support the "pre-planning" of late 1952, which required, among other things, the reduction of Army force levels by one third and the slash of the Army budget from over $16 billion to less than $9 billion. Ridgway did not believe that these reductions were wise; he could adduce cogent military reasons against them as well as reasons of Army sentiment, and he resisted them. The "pressure" was immediately and "strongly" applied, not only by Wilson but also by Radford. ". . . the efforts of the Secretary of Defense and the Chairman of the Joint Chiefs were directed toward securing the unanimous assent of the country's top military men to these pre-set plans." Ridgway did not assent; and when the President, in his State of the Union Message in January 1954, declared that his military proposals were "based on a new military program unanimously recommended by the Joint Chiefs of Staff," Ridgway, as he says, was "nonplused." [1] As a soldier he could not oppose the policies of his civilian superiors, but he felt an understandable sense of grievance at thus being required to take responsibility for them. When his first two-year term was over in 1955 he was not, as he might have been, reappointed. Maxwell Taylor, who had commanded 8th Army in the final days in Korea, replaced him. As he departed, *U. S. News and World Report* commented: "Hand-picked men who may be more of one mind in backing Administration concepts of U. S. defense policy are to make

[1] *Soldier*, pp. 287-89.

up the Joint Chiefs of Staff, now that President Eisenhower has completed a mid-term shake-up that he deliberately planned two years ago." But even "hand-picked" chiefs, with the complete assertion, which they implied, of the political power over military affairs, would bring no final solutions; and in 1956 the old strategic disputes, the old doubts about JCS, the old arguments over still another new "new look," were as active as ever.

END OF THE KOREAN WAR

In mid-summer of 1953, before the new chiefs had even taken office, the long agony and headache of Korea reached its end in an unexpected welter of bloodshed. It had seemed in the final days of March that the Chinese Communists were preparing to make peace. The more hopefully the United States and the United Nations looked forward to this consummation, the more alarmed did Syngman Rhee, President of Korea, become. That tough and shrewd little ancient was determined, if he could manage it, to save the whole and not merely half of a country to whose freedom he had given his long career. As he now saw armistice approaching, he flung himself into pleas, maneuvers, threats of independent action, all directed toward keeping the United States in the war. To this, the Chinese Communists, on their side, responded by increasing their activity on the long-quiescent front. By the latter part of May, American intelligence had evidence that a big Communist offensive was being prepared.

Again, matters were serious. The Administration moved in several directions. Dulles was visiting in New Delhi; and in a three-day conference with Nehru beginning on May 22 he endeavored, he later intimated, to convey to the Chinese, through the Indian leader, the idea that if the Korean stalemate continued the United States would blast the Manchurian bases, presumably with atomic weapons. On May 23 Clark in Tokyo was given new instructions. India had introduced a resolution in the UN seeking to compromise the prisoner-of-war issue; this called for the delivery of all prisoners refusing repatriation, both Chinese and North Korean, to a neutral commission which would ascertain their true wishes and determine their fate.

Clark was told to make a final offer along these lines; but if the Communists rejected it he was authorized to "break off" rather than merely recess the truce talks and "to carry on the war in new ways never yet tried in Korea." The new ways have not been described. "At this writing," Clark said in 1954, "the plans still cannot be de-disclosed." [1]

At Panmunjom progress still seemed rapid. But Rhee continued to make trouble, and the Communist offensive still seemed to impend. On June 6 Eisenhower dispatched a fatherly letter to the Korean President: "The moment has now come when we must decide whether to carry on by warfare a struggle for the unification of Korea or whether to pursue this goal by political and other methods." The trouble with this was, of course, that each man had long since made the decision, and in opposite senses. Four days later the Chinese hit the ROK IId Corps with the heaviest offensive seen for many months. The ROK's were driven back to a depth of some two miles along a seven-mile front. It was apparently intended as an object lesson both to Rhee and to the United States, designed to convince the former that he could not carry on the war alone and to convince us that we could not support Rhee's ambitions without paying heavily for it. But Rhee was devious in resource. The offensive was just dying down when, on June 18, "all hell broke loose," in Clark's expressive words. Rhee had ordered that the prison gates be opened to some 25,000 North Korean prisoners of war who were under ROK guard, and they had dissolved into the night. These were men whom the UN had, under the Indian compromise, just agreed to deliver to a neutral commission. The Chinese, after their prolonged and stubborn insistence upon the forced repatriation of all prisoners, could hardly accept this sabotage of the compromise to which they had finally consented. If Rhee could not prevent the United States and the UN from making peace, he could perhaps prevent the Chinese from doing so.

The anguish and dismay into which this threw the Eisenhower Administration were plainly perceptible. These emotions were not lessened by the Chinese response, which was to renew and step up

[1] *From the Danube to the Yalu*, p. 267.

the offensive to some of the bloodiest heights of the war. The main weight of the attacks fell again upon ROK divisions, whose lines were penetrated to a depth of seven miles, but other forces, particularly the United States 3d Division, were also involved. The artillery fires were so violent that the Americans suspected the Chinese, who were still continuing the armistice talks, of "deliberately using up all the shells they had stockpiled near the front during the two years of the talking war." Clark believed that the only reason for this strange final savagery was to "give the ROK's a 'bloody nose' " and demonstrate to Rhee that his demands to "go north" were easier made than fulfilled.[1] If it was also intended to put pressure on the United States, it was unnecessary. The Eisenhower Administration and the American public did not have to be convinced; the one overriding fear in Washington was that now the Communists would refuse to sign. Rhee's adroit (and courageous) maneuver was a failure. The Communists continued the negotiations, despite their loss of the 25,000 prospective victims. The State Department rushed Assistant Secretary Walter S. Robertson to Seoul to bring the Korean President to reason, and on July 12 he returned to Tokyo bearing Rhee's undertaking not further to obstruct the armistice.

The Korean armistice was formally signed on July 27, 1953. Thus Eisenhower had "ended the Korean War." He fortified the rather complex position in which he was left, alike as to the ethics, the policy and the military power values of the settlement, by resolving to take "very strong action," including the use of atomic weapons if necessary, should the Communists resume the fighting. The necessity was not to arise. The Chinese have since flagrantly violated many of the armistice terms; and the subsequent political settlement which it envisaged has never even been approached. But a practical decision had been returned which has since stood well enough.

## EISENHOWER'S ADMINISTRATIVE STATE

The ending of the Korean War and the reduction of the military budget are the two outstanding illustrations of the conduct of civil-

---

[1] *Ibid.*, p. 291.

military relationships under Eisenhower. A whole series of difficult episodes involving both military plan and civil policy were to follow, ranging from the international power issues of Indo-China, Formosa, Suez, through the military manpower problems which gave rise to the Reserve Act of 1955, through questions of disarmament and the weapons revolution, through the renewed disputes in 1956 over strategic plan and service unification, down to the staggering shock administered to our defense and foreign policies by the Russian satellite, placed in orbit by a military ballistic missile. The facts as to most of these episodes and issues are still hidden in the top-secret papers, however, and too little information is available to permit of much useful comment.

The Eisenhower policies, it may be said, have commanded a striking degree of popular acquiescence. Whether this has been due to superior organization, to skill or in large measure to luck may be arguable. Whether it would have been true if the Eisenhower Administration had been subjected to the bitter and corrosive criticism which assailed the Truman regime may be open to question. It is hard to doubt that the willingness to accept the soldier-President's word as final on any question involving military factors — a willingness all but universal in the press and widespread throughout the political opposition in Congress — has contributed significantly to the smooth course of his civil-military policies. That it has ensured the wisdom of the policies themselves is, however, less apparent; while it may be that the advantages of the Eisenhower system have brought countervailing disadvantages in their train. It might be maintained that there has been a dangerous reduction of both public and Congressional participation in the determination of issues of military policy which are now appalling in their magnitude and implications; it might, with perhaps equal force, be argued that these issues are of a kind which only an administrative elite can deal with, and which therefore must be entrusted to them.

THE SECOND HOOVER COMMISSION

But whatever the broader effect of the Eisenhower policies may prove to be, it can be that they have not removed the old problems and the old complaints perennial in this area of government. In the spring of 1955 a task force of the second Hoover Commission was reporting on the problem of Defense procurement in terms often indistinguishable from those which had been used by study committees and task forces through the preceeding fifteen years. It was discovering again that "there is a natural, inseparable relationship between political, economic and military planning"; that it is "a fallacy to assume that there is any such thing as 'purely military planning,'" and yet that the statutory responsibility for all planning still resided in the Joint Chiefs, who remained obdurate against "efforts to bring non-military advice into the process." Despite the Eisenhower reorganization, such efforts had proved "unfruitful."

Once more the task force was complaining of a lack of "clear, well-defined, integrated national policy" from NSC. Once more it was seeing the problem as that of converting JCS "from a trading post to an objective group in which the national interest is paramount" — not realizing, as so many of its predecessors had failed to realize, that the national interest *is* paramount with each individual chief, but that each has a different concept of what that interest may be. Once more the task force brought in the familiar remedies — more staffing, more research.

"A stronger National Security staff" under the President's Special Assistant "is needed to assist the President and the National Security Council." This enlarged staff should, of course, still be "small" (a standard prerequisite in all proposals for enlarged staffs, from the days in 1947 when the Secretary of Defense had been launched on his new duties with "not more" than three staff assistants), but it was also to be "highly competent" (another standard specification) and was to take over (standard again) a colossal job. The new staff, naturally, would not replace any of the prolific staff structures which had grown up in the Defense system. But it would "supplement" the work of "the NSC, the Planning Board, the OCB and their subordinate committees." The existing staffs "of these organizations are believed to be inadequate in size and scope of functions." So Pelion was to be piled on Ossa, without (once more standard) the new staff men "interfering with the authority of the Departmental heads" or getting themselves into the chain of command from the President.

But staffs, however multiplied, seemed not enough. The task force was aware of a larger issue: What were they all, the staffs and the administrators and everyone else, supposed to be doing? It proposed a more abstract fount of wisdom. This would be a "research activity to analyze alternate strategic policies and programs in terms of long-range implications." The phrase "research activity" is arresting and perhaps indicative of the morasses into which the faith in the staff system was leading. Not just staffing; not research into any specific problem, but a research "activity" — a stirring of the little grey cells in the hope that something might emerge. The task force gave some indication as to what it expected the research activity to be active about:

> If we are to profit by past mistakes, careful and critical analysis of the successes and failures of past programs must be instituted. Such studies might include, for example, the study of our postwar policies and programs in respect to Indo-China; a study of the Marshall Plan, its objectives, its achievements and its shortcomings; and a detailed study of the Korean truce negotiations from start to finish.

This was, perhaps, a more than usually naive statement of the faith that in "staffing" salvation lies. The future may conclude that the enlargement of the "staff system," borrowed directly from the field of combat military operations, where its utility and necessity are most apparent, was the Eisenhower Administration's most significant and fundamental contribution to the art of government. It has great strengths; it also has weaknesses. As with the electronic "brains," to which the staff system is somewhat analogous, there are some things which it can do well and some which it cannot do at all. The calculating machine uses electronic tubes; the staff system uses men and their minds, but in each the division and recombination of the work is quite similar. The machine has its "memory banks" in which experience is stored; the staff system has its separate repositories of experience, like State's Policy Planning Board or Defense's Joint Staff, to perform a similar function. It is the glory of the machine that it can, on order, extract what may be required from its memory and recombine the data into useful new patterns; it is the hope of the staff system that it can do the same. But however capacious the memory of the machine, however swift its ability to recombine the data, it will operate with effect only after it has been asked the right questions. The deepest problems of modern government are still not in getting answers; they lie in asking the right questions.

THE PROBLEM OF THE NEW WARFARE

In the first half of 1957, many of the old problems of military policy, many of the old, well-worn issues of civil-military relations, were more and more clearly coalescing into one large problem — vague in outline, elusive in its innumerable implications, yet absolutely basic to the history of our times. One might give it many names; the simplest is the "problem of the new warfare." The new weapons, new tactics and new strategies which in the late 1940's were still in the realm of prophecy were ten years later becoming the actualities of the international world. The varying solutions which the prophets had confidently offered were beginning to meet the hard tests of fact; it was not apparent that any of them were really applicable. It was even less apparent that either the shibboleths of tradition or the calculations of the staffs were generating answers that would apply to this shapeless problem of our times.

On May 15, 1957 the British tested their first thermonuclear bomb at Christmas Island (a name odd in its symbolism) in the mid-Pacific. Three great states now possessed "megaton" weapons. The mere testing of such devices, to say nothing of their use in war, already presented perils to humanity at least real enough to give rise to acute controversy throughout the world. Their military and diplomatic potentials were already leading to a profound, yet unanalyzable, transformation in military institutions and international military relationships which had remained fundamentally unaltered since the rise of the armed nation-state. In April Great Britain had already announced her intention to reduce, if not to eviscerate, her conventional military forces and to fall back upon the thermonuclear "deterrent" as the one practicable bulwark of the national security. Since, if the deterrent failed to deter a major attack, there seemed to be no really practicable defense, any forces not directly connected with thermonuclear war would be maintained only for local police purposes. The mass armies and huge mobilization schemes of the First and Second World War periods would be scrapped.

In mid-1957 the United States, under a heavy budget squeeze applied for fiscal rather than military reasons, was visibly moving in a similar direction. Then in August the Soviet Union announced the achievement of an accurate intercontinental ballistic missile, and backed the claim in October by its spectacular success in being the first to place an artificial earth satellite in orbit. To American policy the shock was almost as profound as that of the first Soviet atomic explosion in 1949. With the appearance of a practicable long-range ballistic missile capable of carrying a thermonuclear warhead, the problems of nuclear warfare, already unmanageable enough, were enormously aggravated. The Russian satellite itself may have been of small military importance, but the situation which it dramatized raised appalling issues of policy — as to the basis and course of our diplomacy, as to disarmament, as to fiscal and budgetary policy, as to the utilization and training of military manpower, as to military organization and the state of our scientific and technical progress. There were frantic demands for "leadership" from the Eisenhower Administration raised by many of its most devoted supporters. But despite the high perfection of its staff work, despite its installation of civilian business management in the Department of Defense, despite its initial promise to provide "the best possible military plans" while at the same time restoring "civilian control" over the military forces, there still seemed no way in which to sum the multiple factors of the national security problem into equations which would yield a workable guide to national action.

To discuss issues of this kind in conventional terms of the civil-military relationship seems irrelevant. The civil and military elements in our society have become so deeply intermeshed that neither the uniformed officers nor the administrative bureaucracy nor the representative legislature speak from any firm, independent position of principle or policy. There are no adequate standards by which either the military officer demanding greater defense efforts or the congressman resisting these demands in the interests of tax reduction can gauge the real effect of either position on the national security. The civil administration, supposed to be the regulator standing between the two, and today holding the real power of the purse which ultimately controls, is likewise without adequate standards by which to discharge its mission. It is this situation which presents the true problem of civil-military relations in the mid-twentieth century. It is not greatly affected by such matters as the relative ascendancy of the civilian Secretary of Defense or the military directorate of JCS. It is not greatly affected by the relative predominance of military or civilian officials on the lower levels of staff planning. These things may have their importance in administration, but cannot help much in meeting the central civil-military problem of our times — the problem of adequately relating the popular impulses, the "civilian" interest, to the ineluctable facts of international life and power policy.

How well the Eisenhower Administration has met this problem is, patently, a matter of opinion. Some will feel that it has made significant reassertions of "civilian control" and in so doing has driven a fair middle line between the demands of economy and of preparedness. To others it will seem that the Administration has evaded rather than faced most of the basic issues of military policy — that at most it has put only a new and somewhat propagandist gloss upon methods, ideas and approaches differing in no essential from those of its predecessors. There one must leave the argument.

NEW LOCUS OF POWER

What remains is the conclusion that the late-eighteenth-century disputes over the proper locus of the civilian and the military power in the state have largely lost their force. The modern democratic state is more or less inescapably a monolithic structure. It is devoted, as the Constitution declares, to the twin objects of providing for the common defense and promoting the general welfare. In the long international isolation of the nineteenth century it was possible to separate the two and largely to forget the common defense in the pursuit of the general welfare. It is possible no longer; today the common defense has taken on an immediacy and urgency which it had not possessed since the early days of the Republic. If the institutions involving, or expressing, the military and the non-military factors in the national life are to be brought into a proper relationship, it will have to be done in terms other than those which seemed appropriate to the past.

# Notes on Sources

The basic sources in government files and Congressional hearings, for official records of the events noticed in Chapters 1, 2 and 3, are so voluminous as to be beyond the grasp of one who attempts a summary and selective account like this. I have necessarily relied on the siftings of others, chiefly of five sorts.

First, the military departments have made official provision for the history of their manifold activities. In the massive series *United States Army in World War II* (G.P.O., Washington) under the general direction of Kent Roberts Greenfield, the volumes by Mark S. Watson, *Chief of Staff: Prewar Plans and Preparations* (1950), by Maurice Matloff and Edwin M. Snell, *Strategic Planning for Coalition Warfare, 1941-1942* (1953), by Ray S. Cline, *Washington Command Post: The Operations Division* (1951), and by Richard M. Leighton and Robert W. Coakley, *Global Logistics and Strategy, 1940-1943* (1955), have been most useful. The Navy furnished access to sources and other assistance for Samuel Eliot Morison's ten-volume series *History of U. S. Naval Operations in World War II* (Little, Brown, Boston, 1947-56), without adopting the result as officially its own. As its title implies, it concentrates on the narrative of naval engagements and so is less pointed to the concerns of the present work. The Air Force established its own Historical Office, which produced, under the editorship of W. F. Craven and J. L. Cate, the six-volume series *The Army Air Forces in World War II* (University of Chicago Press, Chicago, 1948-55); the first volume, *Plans and Early Operations,* contains much to the point. An extraordinary item belonging in this category is the report on the Manhattan District project, H. D. Smyth, *A General Account of the Development of Methods of Using Atomic Energy for Military Purposes . . . 1940-1945* (G.P.O., Washington, 1945).

Second, under the original sponsorship of the Committee on Records of War Administration, of which Pendleton Herring was chairman, and with Presidential blessings, all the civilian war agencies were encouraged in 1942 to provide or procure histories of their activities. Until after the close of hostilities not much was accomplished to carry out this purpose except in the War Production Board, where a professional staff under James W. Fesler was engaged. By the middle of 1947 enough had been done to assure official publication of the Budget Bureau's over-all account, *The United States at War* (G.P.O., Washington, 1946); the first of three WPB volumes, *Industrial Mobilization for War* (G.P.O., Washington, 1947); and *A Short History of OPA* (G.P.O., Washington, 1948), along with a number of supplementary OPA volumes, paperbound. At that juncture a combination of Congressional hostility (in the person of John Taber, newly become chairman of the House Appropriations Committee) and misunderstanding or indifference in the Executive Office put an end to most of the official efforts. A number of partially completed manuscripts went to the Budget Bureau's library or to the National Archives. A few were finished and published under private auspices, among them: H. M. Somers, *Presidential Agency: OWMR* (Harvard University Press, Cambridge, 1950); S. McKee Rosen, *The Combined Boards of the Second World War* (Columbia University Press, New York, 1951); W. W. Wilcox, *The Farmer in the Second World War* (Iowa State College Press, Ames, 1947); James P. Baxter 3d, *Scientists Against Time* (Little, Brown, Boston, 1946), dealing with the OSRD; and Frederic C. Lane, *Ships for Victory* (Johns Hopkins Press, Baltimore, 1951), covering the Maritime Commission but not the War Shipping Administration. A UN trusteeship sheltered the three-volume report prepared under the direction of George Woodbridge, *UNRRA: The History of the United Nations Relief and Rehabilitation Administration* (Columbia University Press, New York, 1950). Histories of the War Labor Board and of the Office of War Information never saw the light of day. The Office of Censorship left behind an uninformative fifty-page pamphlet. The Office of Strategic Services has remained largely the province of personal reminiscence of romance and derring-do.

Third, the memoirs of leading participants are major sources, with all their advantages and pitfalls of contemporaneity and personal recollection. Among the great number of these the most useful to my purpose were Robert E. Sherwood, *Roosevelt and Hopkins* (Harper, New York, 1948 and rev. ed., 1951); Winston Churchill's six volumes, *The Second World War* (Houghton Mifflin, Boston, 1948-53); Henry L. Stimson and McGeorge Bundy, *On Active Service in Peace and War* (Harper, New York, 1948); *The Memoirs of Cordell Hull* (Macmillan, New York, 1948, 2 vols.); Dwight D. Eisenhower, *Crusade in Europe* (Doubleday, Garden City, 1948); Harry C. Butcher, *My Three Years with Eisenhower* (Simon and Schuster, New York, 1946); and Ernest J. King and Walter M. Whitehill, *Fleet Admiral King* (Norton, New York, 1952).

Fourth, professional historians in the post-war years have already made notable contributions to the endless task of recital, clarification and interpretation, of analysis and synthesis of the events of World War II, and their antecedents and consequences. Among such works, acknowledgment should be made here to William L. Langer and S. Everett Gleason, *The Challenge to Isolation, 1937-1940* and *The Undeclared War: 1940-1941* (Harper, New York, 1952 and 1953); William L. Langer, *Our Vichy Gamble* (Knopf, New York, 1947) and the review of it by Louis Gottschalk in *Journal of Modern History*, March 1948, pp. 47-57; Herbert Feis, *The Road to Pearl Harbor* and *The China Tangle* and *Churchill, Roosevelt, Stalin* (Princeton University Press, Princeton, 1950, 1953, 1957), and the review of *The China Tangle* by Harold Stein in *World Politics*, April 1954, pp. 378-93; and for a British viewpoint, Chester Wilmot, *The Struggle for Europe* (Collins, London, 1952).

Fifth, a number of the case studies prepared in connection with this project relate to pre-war and wartime episodes and focus on concerns of my chapters. These studies are: Michael D. Reagan, "The Far Eastern Crisis of 1931-32: Hoover, Stimson and the Services" and "The Helium Controversy"; Arthur S. Olick, "Conference

for the Reduction and Limitation of Armaments — Geneva, 1932";
Albert A. Blum, "Birth and Death of the M-Day Plan"; Robert J.
Quinlan, "Home Base for the Fleet: Diplomacy, Strategy and the Al-
location of Ships" and "The Italian Armistice"; Marvin D. Bernstein
and Francis Loewenheim, "Aid to Russia: The First Year"; and
Paul Y. Hammond, "Directives for the Occupation of Germany:
The Washington Controversy."

In writing the first three chapters I have used freely a shorter preliminary draft prepared earlier by Harold Stein. I have also had
the great benefit of critical readings and comments on the manu-
script by Louis Morton and his associates in the Office of the Chief
of Military History, Department of the Army, and by Professor
Richard D. Challener, of the Department of History at Princeton.

HARVEY C. MANSFIELD

## PART II

The sources for Part II were of four kinds: conversations and
correspondence with leading participants in the events described;
official documents — mainly hearings and reports of Congressional
committees and of other official inquiries, such as those of the Hoover
Commissions, the Finletter Commission, the Oppenheimer hearings
and so on; current newspaper and magazine material and the relevant published memoirs, histories and studies; finally, the mono-
graphs, as yet unpublished, prepared as "case histories" of salient
episodes by the colleagues with whom I have been associated in this
project.

My debt to Harold Stein, as project director, editor and critic,
is very great. Others to whom I also owe much for supplying me
with information or for reading and criticizing my drafts I will not
name as I do not wish to involve them in responsibility for the results. I have had the use of the following case studies, and am grateful to their authors: Paul Y. Hammond, "Super-Carriers and B-36
Bombers: Appropriations, Strategy and Politics"; Martin Lichter-

man, "To the Yalu and Back"; Laurence W. Martin, "The American Decision to Rearm Germany"; and Michael D. Reagan, "Demobilization and Post-war Military Planning."

Among published sources the most important are, of course, the two volumes of President Truman's *Memoirs* (Doubleday, Garden City, 1955 and 1956). Robert J. Donovan's *Eisenhower: The Inside Story* (Harper, New York, 1956) is so far the best available continuation of the Presidential narrative. Other memoirs I have used are those of Henry L. Stimson (*On Active Service in Peace and War*, with McGeorge Bundy, Harper, New York, 1948), *The Forrestal Diaries* (Viking, New York, 1951), Mark W. Clark's *From the Danube to the Yalu* (Harper, New York, 1954) and Matthew B. Ridgway's *Soldier* (Harper, New York, 1956).

On MacArthur, I have used Courtney Whitney's *MacArthur, His Rendezvous with History* (Knopf, New York, 1956), which seems the nearest thing to an authorized biography, and *The General and the President and the Future of American Foreign Policy,* by Richard H. Rovere and Arthur M. Schlesinger, Jr. (Farrar, Straus & Young, New York, 1951), the most perceptive of the critical studies. I should also acknowledge my debt, on other aspects of the subject, to Eric F. Goldman's *The Crucial Decade: 1945-1955* (Knopf, New York, 1956); Elias Huzar's *The Purse and the Sword* (Cornell University Press, Ithaca, 1950); S. L. A. Marshall's two studies of the Korean fighting, *The River and the Gauntlet* and *Pork Chop Hill* (Morrow, New York, 1953 and 1956); Leland M. Goodrich's *Korea: A Study of United States Policy in the United Nations* (Council on Foreign Relations, New York, 1956); Ralph E. Lapp's *Atoms and People* (Harper, New York, 1956); and Robert Cutler's article in the April 1956 issue of *Foreign Affairs* entitled "Development of the National Security Council." Frequent use was made of the files of the *New York Times.*

The bulk of the material, however, has been drawn from the official hearings and reports. The earlier post-war planning is recorded in numerous hearings and reports of the Senate and House Committees on Military and Naval Affairs and the House Appropriations military subcommittee. The most important source for the earlier course of Far Eastern policy is the "White Paper" released under the title *United States Relations with China,* Department of State Publication 3573, August 1949. The "B-36 controversy" is recorded in Hearings, House Committee on the Armed Services, 81st Congress, 1st session, on H. R. 234 and on *Unification and Strategy.* The chief source for American policy after the Soviet atomic bomb explosion is the record *In the Matter of J. Robert Oppenheimer,* Atomic Energy Commission, 1954. The discussion of the Korean War rests, of course, primarily on the MacArthur hearings, *The Military Situation in the Far East,* Hearings by the Senate Armed Services and Foreign Relations Committees, 82d Congress, 1st session. The hearings by the same two committees on *Assignment of Ground Forces of the United States to Duty in the European Area,* S. Con. R. 8, 82d Congress, 1st session, supply much of the information on American policy toward NATO and rearmament on the Continent. The principal source for the Eisenhower reorganization of the Defense Department is *Reorganization Plan No. 6 of 1953,* Hearings of the House Committee on Government Operations, H. J. Res. 264, 83d Congress, 1st session.

This does not exhaust the official sources which have been consulted, but these are the leading documents.

WALTER MILLIS

# Index

## A

AAFCE (Allied Air Forces Central Europe), 359

ABC-1 and 2, 51, 97

A-bomb, *see* Atomic bomb

Acheson, Dean G.: appointed Secretary of State, 231-32; and civil-military relations, 358-59; Congressional opposition to, 231-32, 235, 341, 345; and H-bomb program, 253, 254; and Johnson, 235, 281; and Korean War, 260, 261, 277, 279, 287, 292, 328; and Marshall, 282; and Marshall Plan, 202; and military reorganization, 170, 387; and National Security Council, 203; and NATO, 237, 335-36, 343; and post-war China, 194, 225, 341; and rearmament of West Germany, 336, 337, 338; and relief of MacArthur, 319; and sharing atomic secrets, 159; witness at MacArthur Hearings, 325, 328

Acheson-Lilienthal plan, 166, 176

Act of Havana, 46

Adams, Henry, cited, 4

AEC, *see* Atomic Energy Commission

Africa, *see* North Africa

Agricultural draft deferments, 72, 77

Air Corps, Army: naval aviation and, 25, 174

Air Force: size of, Korean War period, 342, 354; size of, post-war, 147-48, 198, 200, 207, 215, 217, 239-40; *see also* Navy–Air Force disputes

Air Force, Department of the: establishment of, 174, 175, 176, 179

Air Forces, Army: autonomy of in World War II, 82, 107, 144; establishment of, 109

Air power: Korean War and, 201; post-war strategy and, 148, 200-01, 240; pre-war policy and, 25, 32, 35; World War II

and, 149; *see also* Finletter Commission on Air Policy; Navy–Air Force disputes; Nuclear weapons, and post-war strategy

Air Transport Command, 67

Airlines: World War II, 67

Alvarez, L. W., 251

America Firsters, 18

Anderson, Clinton P., 159, 193, 195

Anglo-American-Canadian cooperation: and atomic energy control, 155, 163; pre-war, 34, 58; World War II, 98, 101; *see also* Anglo-American cooperation; Canada

Anglo-American cooperation: and atomic weapons, 209, 225; pre-war, 29, 30, 32-33, 36, 41, 42, 51; World War II, 92, 98-101; *see also* Anglo-American-Canadian cooperation; ARCADIA; ARGENTIA; Churchill; *and various entries under* Combined

ANMB, *see* Army-Navy Munitions Board

Anti-Comintern Pact, 30, 32

ARCADIA, 80, 85, 97-102, 103, 105, 106, 108

ARGENTIA, 42, 98

Armaments limitation agreements: Japan's refusal to renew, 29, 32; pre-war attempts at, 15, 29

Armaments race, post-war, *see under* Nuclear weapons

Armed forces: peacetime uses of, 21-23; post-war size of, 208, 214, 217, 334; size of, Korean War period, 334, 342, 354-55; unification of, *see* Collins Plan; Eberstadt Plan; Military Establishment; Thomas bill; wartime relations of with civilians, 66; *see also names of individual armed services*

Arms embargo, 17, 28, 30, 31; *see also* Economic sanctions; Neutrality Act

Army: size of, post-war, 147

Army Air Forces, *see* Air Forces, Army

Army Ground Forces, 109

Army-Navy Joint Board, *see* Joint Board

Army-Navy Munitions Board (ANMB), 44, 52, 54, 82, 83, 84; *see also* Munitions Board

Army Post Office, 67

Army Service Forces (ASF), 81, 87, 109, 126

Army Services of Supply (SOS), 81, 109

Arnold, H. H., 97, 107, 109, 111, 151, 153

ASF, *see* Army Service Forces

Atcheson, George, Jr., 190

Atlantic Charter, 42

421

Atomic bomb: project for development of, 41; and spies, 257; *see also* Atomic energy; Hiroshima; Nagasaki; Nuclear energy; Nuclear weapons

Atomic energy: post-war issues of use and control of, 143, 155-69; Smyth, H. D., report on, 70, 415-16; *see also* Atomic bomb; May-Johnson bill; McMahon bill; Nuclear energy; Nuclear weapons

Atomic Energy, National Committee for Civilian Control of, 169

Atomic Energy, Senate Special Committee on, 161, 164-66, 167

Atomic Energy Act, 178, 209; *see also* May-Johnson bill; McMahon bill

Atomic Energy Commission (AEC), 243; appropriations for, 342; composition of, 166, 168, 169; and H-bomb, 251, 253; secrecy of, 399-400

*Atomic Scientists, Bulletin of the,* 71

"Atoms for peace," *see* Nuclear energy, proposals for international peaceful uses of

Attlee, Clement R., 155, 163, 298, 299, 300

Attlee-Truman conference, 1950, 343, 345

Austin-Wadsworth "work-or-fight" bill, 74

Austria: occupation policies in, 143

Austrian peace treaty: attempts at agreement on, 205

Avery, Sewell L., 76

Axis regimes: crushing of as war aim, 91; *see also* Italy; Japan; Nazi Germany; Nazis

## B

Badoglio, Pietro, 121, 122

Baldwin, Hanson W., 219

Baruch, Bernard, 17, 52, 82, 176

Baruch-Hancock report on manpower, 74

Bases: Soviet unwillingness to permit U. S. use of, 102; *see also* Destroyers-for-bases deal; Naval bases

Batt, William L., 100

Baxter, James P., cited, 416

*Béarn,* the, 39

Beaverbrook (William Maxwell Aitken), 100

Berlin airlift, 224, 244

Berlin blockade, 132, 221-22

Berlin corridor, 128, 131-32

Bernstein, Marvin D., cited, 418

Bevin, Ernest, 212

Bikini, 209, 226, 398

Black markets, World War II, 76

Blum, Albert A., cited, 418

Board of Economic Warfare, 124, 126

Bohlen, Charles E. ("Chip"), 228

BOLERO, *see* Cross-Channel invasion

Bonus marchers, 22

Borah, William E., 38

Bradley, Omar N., 140, 228, 241, 249, 253, 333-34, 377, 379; on influence of the military, 362, 380; and Korean War, 281, 291, 308, 319, 320, 325, 328; and rearmament of West Germany, 336

Bretton Woods, 147

Bridges, Styles, 327

Britain, Battle of, 37

British Merchant Shipping Mission, 101

British Supply Council, 45, 58

Bruening, Heinrich, 14

Brussels Pact, 212, 221, 237, 333

B-36 controversy; *see under* Navy–Air Force disputes

B-29: dispatch of to Europe, 226-27

Budd, Ralph, 55

Bulge, Battle of the, 90, 123

Bullitt, William C., 35

Bundy, McGeorge: cited, 417, 419; *see also* Stimson, memoirs quoted

Burke, Arleigh A., 240

Burma, *see* China-Burma-India theater

Burns, James H., 41, 45, 58

Bush, Vannevar, 41, 70, 202, 369, 370, 379

Butcher, Harry C., cited, 417

Byelorussia, 135

Byrd, Harry F., 349

Byrnes, James F., 65, 74, 78, 89, 90, 134, 155, 170, 189, 194, 195, 196

## C

Cabinet: function of under Eisenhower, 388

CAD, *see* Civil Affairs Division, War Department

Cairo conference, 1943, 104, 110, 111, 130

Canada: and Monroe Doctrine, 34; *see also* Anglo-American-Canadian cooperation

Cannon, Clarence, 240

Carney, Robert B., 359, 403

Casablanca, 121, 125, 188

Cate, J. L., cited, 415

CCAC, *see* Combined Civil Affairs Committee

CCS, *see* Combined Chiefs of Staff

Censorship, World War II, 67, 68-69, 110

Central Intelligence Agency (CIA), 171, 178, 184-85, 213, 221, 222; and Korean War, 284

Challener, Richard D., cited, 418

Charlottesville, Virginia: Roosevelt's speech at, 37, 40

Chennault, Claire L., 104

Chiang Kai-shek: and allied coalition, 103, 104, 110, 133; characterization of government of, 192, 211; and Chinese civil war, 190-96; offer of troops in Korean War, 267, 269, 295; retreat to Formosa, 236; and Stilwell, 104, 190; "unleashing" of, 392; U. S. pre-war support of, 26, 39; see also China; Chinese Nationalists; Formosa

*Chicago Tribune,* 68

China: aid to, World War II, 26, 39, 117; and allied coalition, 98, 99, 103-04, 110, 133; civil war in, 103, 176, 190-96, 204-05, 236; and lend-lease, 49; State Department "White Paper" on, cited, 196, 236, 244, 420; wartime isolation of Foreign Service in, 95; and Yalta conference, 134; see also Chiang Kai-shek; Chinese Communists; Chinese Nationalists; Formosa

China-Burma-India theater, 104, 110, 112

"China lobby," 196

Chinese Communists: declared aggressors by UN, 315; Koje Island revolt of, 365; threat of "massive retaliation" against, 392; U. S. aim to avoid war with, 303-04; U. S. reaction to Korean offensive of, 342-43; U. S. threats of war with, 298-99, 299-300, 303, 304-05; use of American weapons by, 39; in World War II, 104, 190, 191; see also China, civil war in; *and various entries under* Korean War

Chinese Nationalists: collapse of, 222, 223, 224-25, 258; government of characterized, 192, 211; proposed use of in Korean War, 264, 267-68, 295, 299, 308, 318, 322; and threat of attack on mainland, 268-70, 302, 304-05, 322; U. S. support of, 39, 190, 191, 193, 194-95; see also China, civil war in; Chiang Kai-shek; Formosa

Chongchon River, 284, 285, 286, 289, 293, 322, 342

Chosin Reservoir, 285, 289, 296

Chou En-lai, 273, 275, 393

Christmas Island, 411

Churchill, Winston S.: cited, 417; and cross-Channel invasion, 118-19; Fulton, Mo., speech of, 176; and German zonal boundaries, 130-31; and landing craft shortage, 86; quoted, 97; rallying of British people by, 37, 39-40; and Roosevelt, 37, 39-40, 95, 119; and Soviet Union, 119; wartime power of, 64; see also ARCADIA; ARGENTIA; Cairo conference, 1943; Yalta

CIA, see Central Intelligence Agency

CINCFE, Commander in Chief Far East, see Clark, Mark W.; MacArthur, Douglas; Ridgway, Matthew B.

Civil Affairs Division, War Department (CAD), 96, 122, 123, 126-28, 129, 130, 131, 188

Civil Affairs Section, AFHQ, 125

Civil Defense, 54-55

Civilian Conservation Corps (CCC), 23

Clark, Grenville, 42

Clark, Mark W.: as CINCFE, 364; cited, 364, 365, 367-68, 395, 406, 407, 419; and Darlan, 120; and Italian campaign, 118; and Korean truce negotiations, 393, 395, 405-06, 407; plan for ending Korean War, 364-65, 366; quoted, 364, 365, 368, 393, 395, 406, 407

Clark, Tom C., 159

Clausewitz, 324, 368

Clay, Lucius D., 23, 126, 128, 210, 211, 213, 221, 223, 229

Clayton, Will, 97

Cline, Ray S.: cited, 415; quoted, 87, 88, 96, 129

Coakley, Robert W., cited, 415

Coalition warfare: Anglo-American, 98-101; see also ARCADIA; ARGENTIA; Cairo conference, 1943; Yalta

"Co-existence": and Eisenhower, 375-76

Cold war, 5, 176, 187-229; problem of military planning in, 383; see also Berlin blockade; Marshall Plan; Military appropriations, and cold war strategy; Nuclear weapons, and U. S. post-war strategy; Soviet Union, and post-war tensions; Truman Doctrine

Collective security, 15, 16, 17

Collins, J. Lawton, 153, 262, 272, 282, 295, 298, 301, 313, 349, 404

Collins Plan, 153-55, 170, 176

Combined Chiefs of Staff (CCS), 99-100, 105, 106, 107, 126, 129

Combined Civil Affairs Committee (CCAC), 126, 128, 188; Supply Subcommittee of [CCAC(S)], 126

Combined Committee for North Africa (CCNA), 125

Combined Food Board, 101

Combined Production and Resources Board, 101

Combined Raw Materials Board, 100

Combined Shipping Adjustment Board (CSAB), 101

Combined Staff Planners (CPS), 107

Communism: domestic threat of in U. S., 257-58; effects of on U. S. global policies, 202, 242-44, 333-36; MacArthur's call for action against in Asia, 271; see also China, civil war in; Chinese Communists; Czechoslovakia, Communist coup in; Greece, civil war in; Marshall Plan; Truman Doctrine

Conant, James B., 41

Condon, Edward U., 165

Congress of Vienna, 3

Connally, Tom, 161, 346-47

Consolidated-Vultee, 241, 242

"Containment," policy of, 202, 242-43

Controlled materials plan (CMP), 84

Coolidge, Calvin, 21, 24

Coral Sea, battle of, 85

Corregidor, 64

Coulter, John B., 293

Council of Foreign Ministers, see Foreign Ministers, conferences of

Council of National Defense, 19; Advisory Commission to (NDAC), 44, 53, 54, 55, 56

Coy, Wayne, 113

Cox, Oscar, 113

Craven, W. F., cited, 415

Crommelin, John G., Jr., 245, 249

Cross-Channel invasion (OVERLORD), 96, 122, 130; decision for, 86; demand of Soviet Union for, 102; disagreement with British re, 110; political considerations re, 118-19; preparations for (BOLERO), 112

Cutler, Robert, cited, 388, 389, 390, 391, 400, 419

Czechoslovakia, 18, 36; Communist coup in, 210, 212; see also Munich settlement

D

Darlan, Jean Louis, 120-21

Darling, Jay, 152

Davis, Chester C., 55, 56

Davis, Elmer, 69

Davis, Norman H., 15, 30

Dawson, William L., 386

D-Day, 127

Dean, Gordon, 253, 254, 255

Declaration of Panama, 46

Defense, Department of: confusion in role of, 359-61; established, 233-34; interdepartmental relationships of, 8; reorganization of, 379-87; see also Defense, Secretary of; Military Establishment

Defense, Secretary of: development in role of, 177, 180-81, 233-34, 380-81, 386

Defense Aid Reports, Division of, 49

Defense expenditures, post-war: see Military appropriations

Defense planning, pre-war, 24-27

Defense reorganization, see Military reorganizations

de Gaulle, Charles, 121, 123

Denfeld, Louis E., 241, 249

Destroyers-for-bases deal, 42, 46

Dewey, Thomas E., 222

Dill, John Greer, 96, 99

Disarmament conferences, pre-war, 15, 29

Distant Early Warning network, 34

Doctors, in World War II, 70

Dodd, Francis T., 365

Dondero Committee, 65

Donovan, Robert J.: cited, 419; quoted, 377, 391, 392, 394, 399

Douglas, Lewis, 101, 105, 110, 112-13, 226

Douglas, Paul H., 353

Douglas, William O., quoted, 361-62

Draft, see Selective Service System; Universal military training

Dulles, John Foster, 260, 377, 393, 405

Dumbarton Oaks, 147

"Dumbbell theory," 237-38

Dunkirk, 37

E

EAC, see European Advisory Commission

East Germany: build-up of "police" in, 337; see also Germany, occupation zones in

Eastern Europe: Yalta agreement on, 133; Churchill's aim to forestall Soviet advances in, 118-19; Soviet demand for recognition of gains in, 102

Eastman, Joseph, 105

Eberstadt, Ferdinand, 82, 84, 171, 173, 177, 385, 387; and Defense reorganization, 1949, 233

Eberstadt Plan, 145, 150, 151-52, 154, 176

Economic controls: Korean War period, 339, 343

Economic Cooperation Administration (ECA), 49

Economic mobilization: Axis, British, U. S. concepts compared, 79-80; pre-war, 52-59, 92; World War II, 79-90

Economic sanctions, 16, 17, 28; *see also* Arms embargo; Export Embargo Act; Neutrality Act

*Economist,* quoted, 176

EDC, *see* European Defense Community

Eden, Anthony, 30

Edison, Charles, 34, 53

Eighth Army: in Korean War, 274, 275, 277, 283, 284, 285, 292-301 *passim,* 306, 308, 313, 314, 363, 367

Einstein, Albert, 41

Eisenhower, Dwight D., 140; cited, 417; commander in Europe, World War II, 97, 111; and de Gaulle recognition, 123; and German rearmament, 348; and Grant, Ulysses S., compared, 376; and Italian armistice, 121-22; and Italian campaign, 118; and Korean War, 377, 391, 394; as military elder statesman, 241; Military Governor in Germany, 188; as NATO Supreme Commander (SCAPE), 237, 343, 348, 357, 359; New Year's message, 1944, 78; 1952 Presidential campaign of, 369, 370; and North African occupation, 96, 120-21, 125; and OPD, 106, 108; and political factors in World War II, 115; postpone-ment of North African landings by, 116; and "security with solvency," 375-79, 380, 394-98; and Syngman Rhee, 406; and unification of armed services, 146; and United Nations, 3

Eisenhower, Milton, 379

Elliott, Harriet W., 55

Embick, Stanley D., 25, 33

Emergency Price Control Act, 63, 68; *see also* Price control

England: as possible enemy, 16, 25-26; *see also* Anglo-American cooperation; Great Britain

Eniwetok, 209, 226, 254

Ethiopia, 18

Euratom, 401

European Advisory Commission (EAC), 96, 128-30, 131

European Defense Community (EDC), 356, 357

Executive Office of the President: establish-ment of, 43

Export controls, pre-war, 92; *see also* Arms embargo; Export Embargo Act

Export Embargo Act, 47

## F

Fair Employment Practices, Committee on, 71

Far Eastern Commission, 189

Far Eastern policy: and Eisenhower, 378, 396, 397; post-war Foreign Ministers agreement on, 155; *see also* China; For-mosa; Japan; Korea; Manchuria; Philip-pines

Farley, James A., 22

Farm labor problems, World War II, 77; *see also* Agricultural draft deferments

Farm production, World War II, 77

Fascists: infiltration of Latin America by, 19

FEA, *see* Foreign Economic Administration

"Feasibility" dispute, 83-88

Fechteler, William M., 403-04

Federal Bureau of Investigation (FBI), 168

*Federal Register,* 66

Feis, Herbert: cited, 417; quoted, 104-05, 112

Fesler, James W., cited, 416

Finletter, Thomas K., 385

Finletter Commission on Air Policy, 203, 205-08, 209, 215, 229

First War Powers Act, 63, 108

Fleet Marine Force, 147, 172, 176; *see also* Marine Corps

Flemming, Arthur S., 379

"Floating D-Day," 395, 396

Food supply, World War II, 76-79

*Foreign Affairs,* cited, 129, 202, 419

Foreign aid, post-war, 49; appropriations for, 334; *see also* Economic Cooperation Administration (ECA); Foreign Eco-nomic Administration (FEA); Marshall Plan; Mutual Defense Assistance Pro-gram (MDAP); Truman Doctrine; United Nations Relief and Rehabilitation Administration (UNRRA)

Foreign Economic Administration (FEA), 126, 127

Foreign Ministers, conferences of: Big Three, September 1950, 338; on German and Austrian peace treaties, 205; Mos-cow, 1943, 96, 128; Moscow, 1945, 155

Foreign Service: characterized, 6; isolation of in China, World War II, 95

Formosa: MacArthur's visit to, 268-70; U. S. attempt to neutralize, 268, 269; U. S. defense of, 225, 236, 260, 261, 272, 408; *see also* Chiang Kai-shek; Chinese Nationalists

Forrestal, James: and "MacArthur problem," 267; resignation of as Secretary of Defense, 232; as Secretary of Defense, 173, 197, 203, 204, 214-17, 220, 221, 226-27, 232, 233; as Secretary of Navy, 146, 149, 150, 151-52, 153, 154, 165, 166, 170, 171, 173, 174, 177, 194, 201, 202; as Under Secretary of Navy, World War II, 68, 82, 84, 109

*Forrestal Diaries:* cited, 419; quoted, 150, 171, 173, 192, 194, 208, 210, 211, 212, 216, 218, 220, 226-27, 228, 237

France: occupation of, 120, 123-24; prewar aid to, 39, 41; rejection of German rearmament by, 338; surrender to Hitler, 39; *see also* Vichy, France; Free French

Franco, Francisco, 18

Franco-British Economic Coordination Commission, 45

Frankfurter, Felix, 65

Free French: in North Africa, 121

Fuchs, Klaus, 257

Fulbright, J. W., 329, 330

G

Garner, John Nance, 38

Gauss, Clarence, 95

General Appropriation for Relief in Occupied Areas (GARIOA), 124

George III, 140

Gerhardt, H. A., 337

Germany: attempts at agreement on peace treaty with, 205; occupation policies in, 127-28, 143, 187-88, 257; occupation zones in, 128-32; *see also* East Germany; Nazi Germany; West Germany

Gerow, Leonard J., 106, 108

Giraud, Henri, 120, 121, 125

Gleason, S. Everett, cited, 417

Goering, Hermann, 35, 39

Goldman, Eric F., cited, 419

Good Neighbor policy, 19, 21-22, 124

Goodrich, Leland M.: cited, 419; quoted, 262, 263, 299

Gottschalk, Louis, cited, 417

Gouzenko, Igor, 257

Grant, Ulysses S., 376

Great Britain: dispatch of B-29's to, 226-27; and lend-lease, 42, 49, 57, 103; pre-war aid to, 41, 42; testing of thermonuclear bomb by, 411; *see also* Anglo-American cooperation; Churchill, Winston; England

Greece: acceptance of in NATO, 357; civil war in, 200, 210; post-war aid to, 176, 177, 199, 202, 204, 205, 210, 244

Greenfield, Kent Roberts, cited, 415

Griffin, Robert M., 113

Gross, Mervin E., 112

Groves, Leslie R., 161, 163

Gruenther, Alfred M., 208

Guadalcanal invasion, 86

Guam, 24, 29, 124

GYMNAST, 98; *see also* North Africa

H

Halsey, William F., 146, 150, 245

Hammond, Paul Y., cited, 128*n*, 418

Hancock, John M., *see* Baruch-Hancock report on manpower

Handy, Thomas T., 106

Hannegan, Robert E., 159

Harriman, Averell, 95, 134, 269, 319, 356

Hatch Act, 31

H-bomb, *see* Hydrogen bomb

Helium: for Nazi zeppelin, 23

Helium Act of 1937, 28

Hemisphere defense, 18-20, 24, 25, 33-34

Henderson, Leon, 45, 55, 56, 57, 58, 68, 116

Hepburn Board, 29

Herring, Pendleton, cited, 416

Hill, Lister, 151

Hilldring, John H., 96, 126

Hillman, Sidney, 55, 56, 73

Hiroshima, 4, 5, 143, 156

Hiss, Alger, 257

Hitler, Adolf, 18, 25, 30, 31, 36, 37, 38, 39, 45, 47, 61; *see also* Nazi Germany

Holifield, Chet, 162

Hoover, Herbert, 15, 16, 20, 21-22, 346

Hoover Commissions: first, 232-33, 387; second, 387, 408-11

Hopkins, Harry L.: adviser to Roosevelt, 35, 40, 45, 94, 95, 134; and ARCADIA, 97; and JCS, 88; and Joint Board, 92; and lend-lease, 58, 88, 95, 111; and MAB, 99-100; and Marshall, 111, 115; negotiations with Iceland, 51; and Nelson, 81, 84; and post-war occupation policies, 128; and pre-war economic mobilization, 57, 58, 59; and WSA, 112-13

Hull, Cordell: and ARCADIA, 97; cited, 417; and Congress, 38; and de Gaulle recognition, 121; and German zonal boundaries, 130; and Ingersoll mission, 33; and Japanese negotiations, 47, 93; memoirs, quoted, 93; and military planning, 49-52; and Munich settlement, 31; and occupation policies, 120, 128; and pre-war foreign policy, 15, 26, 28, 45-52; and Roosevelt, 94; and Standing Liaison Committee, 19; and United Nations, 98; as wartime Secretary of State, 94-95; and Sumner Welles, 48

Huntington, Samuel P., quoted, 266, 375

Hurley, Patrick J., 20, 155, 191, 193, 194, 196, 325

Huzar, Elias: cited, 419; quoted, 199

Hydrogen bomb: possession of by Soviet Union, 400; program for development of, 250-55, 333, 350; testing of, 254, 255, 398, 400, 411; see also Nuclear weapons

I

Iceland: U. S. garrisoning of, 51

Ickes, Harold L., 23

IMP, see Industrial Mobilization Plan

Inchon, 267, 272, 274, 275, 280, 281, 303, 340

India, 276, 301, 392, 405

Indo-China, 244, 391, 403, 408

Industrial Mobilization Plan (IMP), 53

Ingersoll, Royal E., 32-33

Intercontinental ballistic missile: possession of by Soviet Union, 412

Interim Committee (on atomic energy), 156, 160

Iolanthe, 174

Ismay, Hastings Lionel, Lord, 357

Isolationism, 15, 16-18, 28; decline of, 35-43

Italy: allied landing in, 122; armistice with, 121-22; invasion of, and Churchill, 118; occupation problems in, 120, 128; U. S. declaration of war against, 63; see also Fascists; Mussolini

Iwo Jima, 176

J

Jackson, C. D., 389, 399, 400

Jackson, Robert H., 65

Japan: and Anti-Comintern Pact, 30; attack on Pearl Harbor, 61; occupation of, 143, 189, 257; post-war constitution of, 17; and pre-war armaments limitation, 29, 32; pre-war expansionist policy of, 14, 16, 18, 20, 23, 26; U. S. declaration of war against, 63; and U. S. pre-war defense plans, 23, 24, 25-27, 31-33; U. S. pre-war negotiations with, 47, 51-52, 93

Japanese-American relocation centers, 65

JCS, see Joint Chiefs of Staff

Jenner, William E., 341

Johnson, Edwin C., 226

Johnson, Louis: as Assistant Secretary of War, 34, 53, 54; and Defense budgets, 240, 243; as Defense Secretary, 184, 232, 234-36, 240, 241, 353; and hydrogen bomb, 253, 254; and Korean War, 263, 273, 325, 334; and rearmament of West Germany, 337-38; resignation of as Secretary of Defense, 273, 281, 339; and State Department, 235-36, 337

Johnson, Robert W., 385

Joint Army-Navy Basic War Plans: BOLERO, 118; DOG, 50; GYMNAST, 98; ORANGE, 26, 27, 33, 34; OVERLORD, 122, 130; RAINBOW series, 27, 36; RED, 16; TORCH, 98

Joint Board, 24, 44, 58, 92, 106, 174; see also Army-Navy Munitions Board

Joint Chiefs of Staff (JCS): composition of, 1949, 232, 234; emergence of as permanent body, 105-13, 144; estimates of manpower needs, World War II, 74; and "feasibility" dispute, 84, 87; and Hopkins, 88; and hydrogen bomb, 251; Joint Post-War Committee of, 96; Key West conference of, 210-13, 240-41; and Korean War, 262, 264, 265, 271, 272, 274, 275, 281-82, 291, 292-94, 295-96, 302, 308-14, 318, 319, 320, 322-23, 334, 335; and Lovett, 352-53, 370-71; and National Security Act, 179-80, 182-84; Newport conference of, 227-28; and 1949 evacuation of South Korea, 236; and occupation policies, 126, 129; and rearmament of West Germany, 337; and redefinition of roles and missions, 175; role of under Eisenhower, 377-87, 401-05, 409; and Roosevelt, 44, 105, 109, 110-13, 133; and second Hoover Commission, 409

Joint Committee on Atomic Energy, 8

Joint Post-war Committee, see under Joint Chiefs of Staff

Joint Staff Planners (JPS), 87, 107

Joint Strategic Survey Committee (JSSC), 107

Joint War Plans Committee (JWPC), 87, 107

Jones, Jesse, 126

JPS, see Joint Staff Planners

JWPC, see Joint War Plans Committee

K

Kellogg-Briand Pact, 17

Kem resolution, 345

Kennan, George F., 202, 242-43, 279

Kennedy, Joseph P., 95
Kersten, Charles J., 212
Keynes, John Maynard, quoted, 3
Kimball, Dan A., 241
Kimmel, Husband E., 106
King, Ernest J., 87, 109, 110, 111, 147; cited, 417
King, William Lyon Mackenzie, 155, 163
Knox, Frank, 40, 43, 45, 47, 97, 109
Knudsen, William S., 55, 56, 58
Koje Island prisoner-of-war revolt, 365
Korea: Eisenhower's visit to, 377, 391; occupation of, 143, 189
Korean War, 259-332; and air power, 201; Eisenhower's' plan for ending, 378; evacuation of UN troops considered, 303-04, 329; manpower problem in, 371-72; objectives in, 273, 274, 275-77, 314, 327, 328, 331; ROK troops in, 276, 277, 278, 283, 284, 285, 294; stalemate in, 357, 363-68, 369-70, 392, 394; threat of nuclear warfare in, 298, 378, 392, 393, 405; Truman promise of limitation of, 335; see also Chinese Communists; Chinese Nationalists; Mac-Arthur, Douglas; South Korea; Syngman Rhee; Truman-MacArthur clash
—armistice negotiations in, 290, 292, 300, 301, 314, 331, 349-50, 350-51, 365-66, 369-70; concluded, 407; and exchange of sick and wounded prisoners, 392-93, 395; and prisoner-of-war issue, 366-67, 392, 405-06
—Chinese Communists and, 278, 283-85, 294, 296, 303; threats of intervention, 268, 273-75, 276, 277, 279, 291-92; UN charges aggression, 315
Krug, Julius A., 90
Kyes, Roger M., 386

**L**

Labor disputes, World War II, 75-76
Labor turnover, wartime rate, 74
Land, Emory Scott, 113
Landing craft, shortage of, 86, 112
Lane, Frederic C., cited, 416
Langer, William L., cited, 417
Lapp, Ralph E., cited, 419
Latin America: Nazi-Fascist infiltration of, 19; see also Good Neighbor policy; Hemisphere defense; Monroe Doctrine
Lawrence, Ernest Orlando, 251
League of Nations, 16, 28
Leahy, William D., 23, 46, 95, 96, 107, 232
Leighton, Richard M., cited, 415

Lend-lease, 42, 58, 76, 86, 126; and Hopkins, 58, 88, 95, 111; and post-war policies, 49, 127; and Soviet Union, 42, 45, 49, 57, 102, 103
Lend-Lease Act, 47
Lend-Lease Administration, 41, 49, 57, 113, 124
Leva, Marx, 202
Liberated areas: food supply for, 77-79; see also Occupation policies
Lichterman, Martin, cited, 418-19
Lie, Trygve, 273
Lilienthal, David E., 251, 253; see also Acheson-Lilienthal plan
Lima, Declaration of, 1938, 34
Lincoln, G. A., 237
Lindbergh, Charles A., 35
Lippmann, Walter, 16, 375
Livestock production, World War II, 78
Lodge, Henry Cabot, Jr., 340
Loewenheim, Francis, cited, 418
Long, Huey, 22
Look, cited, 361, 362
Lovett, Robert A., 184, 201, 221, 228, 232, 287, 352-53, 355, 370, 379, 381
Loyalty and security programs, 5, 8, 178, 373
Lucas, Scott, 341
Luce, Clare Boothe, 168
Ludlow resolution, 17, 33
Luftwaffe, the, 35
Lund, Wendell L., 73

**M**

MAB, see Munitions Assignments Board
MacArthur, Arthur, 188
MacArthur, Douglas: attitude in Philippines and Korea, compared, 310; and bonus marchers, 22; characterization of, 266-67; as Chief of Staff, 80; concept of war, 113-14; evacuation from Corregidor, 64; and Japanese constitution, 17; and Japanese occupation, 188, 189; and 1949 evacuation of South Korea, 236; as Pacific commander, World War II, 97, 111; and pre-war Far Eastern policy, 20; and retaking of Philippines, 117; Roosevelt's opinion of, 22; and unification, 146, 151-52; see also Chinese Nationalists, proposed use of in Korean War; MacArthur Hearings; Truman-MacArthur clash; Whitney, Courtney
—and Korean War: address to Congress re, 321-24; cease-fire proposals, 301-02, 317; and Chinese intervention, 285-87, 294-302; directives to, 261, 262, 264,

273-75, 276, 278, 279, 288, 289, 293, 295, 300, 303-04, 309, 312, 314, 316; and JCS, 292-94, 295-96, 318, 319, 320, 322-23; message to VFW, 270-72; predictions of victory, 279, 293; and relief of command, 317-20; and risk of war with China, 297-99, 302, 304-05, 307, 308; surrender demands to North Korea, 277, 278; UN Supreme Commander in, 262, 264, 265; and visit to Formosa, 268-70; and Wake Island meeting of with Truman, 279-80

MacArthur Hearings, 324-31, 347, 349; cited, 420

MacLeish, Archibald, 69

Macmillan, Harold, 122

Mahan, Alfred Thayer, 15

Malik, Jacob, 331

Manchuria: evacuation of Japanese forces from, 192, 193, 195; Japanese invasion of, 14, 16, 18, 32; and Korean War, 268, 284, 286, 287, 288, 295, 308, 322, 323; proposed trusteeship of, 204

"Manhattan Engineer District," 161; see also Atomic bomb, project for development of

Manpower policies: in World War II, 69-75; see also Selective Service System

Mao Tse-tung, 191, 196, 205, 224

Marbury, William L., 156

Marine Corps: in China, 192, 193, 194; in Korean War, 270, 281, 296, 340; and post-war military organization, 172, 173, 176; post-war, size of, 211

Marshall, George Catlett: appointed Secretary of Defense, 339, 340-41; and ARCADIA, 97, 106; as Chief of Staff, 23, 50, 58, 70, 84, 86, 88, 106, 107, 108; and MacArthur, 318, 319, 320, 325; mission to China, 176, 194-97, 224, 341; and political-military issues, 115, 117, 140, 348-49, 358-59; resignation of as Secretary of Defense, 352; resignation of as Secretary of State, 231; and Roosevelt, 111; and second front, 110, 119; as Secretary of Defense, 281-82, 302; as Secretary of State, 197, 201, 213, 218, 226, 228; and unification, 151; and universal military training, 147; see also Marshall Plan

Marshall, S. L. A.: cited, 419; quoted, 284, 285

Marshall Plan, 49, 202, 205, 213, 214

Martin, Glenn L., 241

Martin, Joseph W., Jr., 318

Martin, Laurence W., cited, 419

Masaryk, Jan, 212

Masland, John W., quoted, 141

"Massive retaliation" policy, 392, 397-99

Matloff, Maurice, cited, 415

May, Alan Nunn, 257

May, Andrew Jackson, 62, 167; see also May-Johnson bill

May, Stacy, 58

May Committee, see May-Johnson bill

May-Johnson bill, 160-66, 167

McCarran, Patrick A., 341

McCarthy, Joseph R., 257, 347

McCarthyism, 103

McCloy, John J., 58, 96, 97, 113, 125, 126, 337

McCormick, Lynde D., 356, 359

McCoy, Frank, 188

McMahon, Brien, 155-56, 161, 164-66, 326, 353-54, 397; see also McMahon bill

McMahon bill, 165, 166-69

McNair, Lesley J., 108, 109

McNeil, Wilfred J., 202, 218, 355

McNutt, Paul V., 72, 73, 74

MDAP, see Mutual Defense Assistance Program

Megaton weapon, see Hydrogen bomb

Mellett, Lowell, 69

Merchant marine, 73

Merchant Marine Act of 1936, 27

Mexican oil expropriations, 22

Midway, battle of, 85

Military appropriations: and cold war strategy, 197-201, 213-20; under Eisenhower, 404 (see also Eisenhower, and "security with solvency"); Korean War period, 334, 335, 339, 342, 343-45, 353, 354-55; in 1930, 21; and Truman's budgetary ceilings, 171, 198, 238-39, 243; World War II, 63

Military budgets, post-war: responsibility for preparation of, 180-81, 183-84

Military Establishment: and foreign policy, 204; under Forrestal, 203-04, 220; organization of, 174, 179-81; replaced by Department of Defense, 233-34

Military government: in occupied areas, World War II, 124-28; see also Civil Affairs Division, War Department; Occupation policies

"Military mind," 140-41

Military procurement, World War II, 80-88; see also Army-Navy Munitions Board; Army Services of Supply; Army Service Forces; "Feasibility'" dispute; Somervell, Brehon B.

Military reorganizations, post-war, 144, 145-55, 169-78, 232-34, 379-87; and civil-military coordination, 142-43, 144, 151-52, 153, 177, 178-79; roles and missions and, 148, 149, 172-73, 174-76, 210; *see also* Hoover Commissions; National Security Act; Navy–Air Force disputes; Rockefeller, Nelson

Military service: characterized, 5-6

Military Transport Service, 112

*Minneapolis Tribune,* cited, 236

Molotov, Vyacheslav M., 102

Monnet, Jean, 45, 58, 356

Monroe Doctrine, 18, 24, 34, 115

Montgomery, Bernard Law, 237

Montgomery Ward, 76

Morgan, Frederick E., 130, 131

Morgan, J. P. & Co., 53

Morgenthau, Henry, Jr., 35, 39, 41

Morison, Samuel Eliot, cited, 415

Morse, Wayne L., 211, 326

Morton, Louis, cited, 418

Mosely, Philip E., 129

Munich settlement, 27, 31, 36; *see also* Czechoslovakia

Munitions Assignments Board (MAB), 99, 111

Munitions Board, 180, 184, 381; *see also* Army-Navy Munitions Board; Munitions Assignments Board

Murphy, Robert D., 120, 121, 122, 125

Mussolini, Benito, 18

Mutual Defense Assistance Program (MDAP): appropriations for, 334, 335, 336; and German rearmament, 337

### N

Nagasaki, 4, 143, 156

Nathan, Robert R., 84, 87

*Nation,* cited, 16

National Association for the Advancement of Colored People (NAACP), 8

National Defense Act of 1920, 24, 52

National Defense Management Commission, 243

National Defense Research Committee (NDRC), 41-42

National Guard: and Korean War, 371-72

National Security Act, 187, 195, 201, 203, 210, 222, 250; amendment of for Marshall appointment, 339, 340-41; amendment of in 1949, 232-34; civil-military coordination and, 176-81

National Security Council (NSC), 33, 151, 171, 174, 178, 180, 184, 202, 203, 204, 223, 226, 354; composition of, 1949, 234; under Eisenhower, 388-91, 398, 409-10; and H-bomb, 253; and Korean War, 273-74, 281-82, 291-92, 339; review of national policy by (NSC 68), 256-57, 333, 334, 387; and second Hoover Commission, 409-10; under Truman, 181-82, 387, 388, 390

National Security Resources Board, 171, 178, 179, 184

Nationalist China, *see* Chiang Kai-shek; Chinese Nationalists; Formosa

Naval Air Transport Service, 67

Naval bases: pre-war plans for, 29; *see also* Destroyers-for-bases deal

Navy: pre-war expansion of, 23, 26-27, 29, 31-33; size of, post-war, 147

Navy Department: independent procurement policy of, World War II, 82; reorganization of, World War II, 109

Navy–Air Force disputes: B-36 and the super carrier, 239-42, 244-45, 247-49, 377, 420; control of atomic weapons, 207, 209, 211-12, 227-28; jurisdiction over air-sea operations, 25, 107, 147, 149-50, 153-54, 172, 173, 174

Nazi Germany: conquest of Poland by, 36, 37, 54; declaration of war on U. S., 61; invasion of Low Countries by, 37, 45; invasion of Soviet Union by, 42, 102; landing of saboteurs in U. S. by, 65; rearmament of, 18, 25; U. S. declaration of war against, 63; and U. S. pre-war foreign policy, 36-43; *see also* Hitler, Adolf; Nazis

Nazi-Soviet Pact, 36

Nazis: infiltration of Latin America by, 19; Nuremberg trials of, 155

NDAC, *see* Council of National Defense, Advisory Commission to

NDRC, *see* National Defense Research Committee

Nehru, Jawaharlal, 299, 405; *see also* India

Nelson, Donald M., 81, 82, 83, 84, 85, 86, 87, 90

Neutrality Act, 17, 28, 38, 41; cash-and-carry amendment to, 47

New Deal, 41, 53, 57; and the military, 22-23

*New York Times:* cited, 276-77, 344, 419; quoted, 315, 319, 342

Newman, James R., 165

Newmann, John von, 251

Newport conference, 227

Nimitz, Chester W., 146, 150, 171, 174

Nitze, Paul H., 202, 236, 238

Nixon, Richard M., 212

Normandy landings, *see* Cross-Channel invasion

Norstad, Lauris, 170, 203-04, 359

North Africa: decision on invasion of, 85-86, 97-98, 110, 111; occupation policies in, 96, 119, 120-21, 124-25; political considerations re invasion of, 115, 119; postponement of landings in, 116; preparation for landings in, 46, 112

North African Economic Board, 125

North Atlantic Treaty, 224, 244; signing of, 238

North Atlantic Treaty Organization (NATO): American contributions to, 336, 337, 340, 346-47, 349 [*see also* Mutual Defense Assistance Program (MDAP)]; and civil-military relations, 223, 355-60; and Eisenhower, 378, 396; formation of, 237-38; hearings on, cited, 420; and integrated defense plans, 343, 355-58; precursors of, 212-13, 221, 222, 333; rejection of West German rearmament, 338

NSC, *see* National Security Council

NSC 68, 256-57, 333, 334, 387

Nuclear energy: proposals for international peaceful uses of, 160, 163, 400, 401; *see also* Atomic bomb; Atomic energy; Hydrogen bomb; Nuclear weapons

Nuclear weapons: AEC vs. Air Force custody of, 227; Anglo-American agreements on, 155, 163, 209, 225; possession of by Soviet Union, 200, 207, 245-47, 249, 250, 255, 333, 335, 400; and postwar armaments race, 164, 252, 353-54; testing of, 209, 226, 250, 254, 255, 398, 400, 411; U. S. advances in, 252, 352; and U. S. post-war strategy, 200, 205-10, 222, 223, 225-29, 239-40, 243, 245-56, 397-99, 411-13; use of in Korean War considered, 298, 378, 392, 393, 405; *see also* Atomic bomb; Hydrogen bomb; Navy–Air Force disputes

Nuremberg trials, 155

Nye Committee, 17

O

OCB, *see* Operations Coordinating Board

Occupation policies: World War II and post-war, 119-29, 143, 178, 187-89, 257; *see also* Liberated areas; *and specific countries and areas*

Odlum, Floyd B., 242

O'Donnell, Emmett, Jr. ("Rosie"), 327

OEM, *see* Office for Emergency Management

OES, *see* Office of Economic Stabilization

Office of Censorship, 68

Office of Defense Mobilization (ODM), 184, 343

Office of Defense Transportation (ODT), 67, 105

Office of Economic Stabilization (OES), 65, 89

Office for Emergency Management (OEM), 43, 56

Office of Foreign Relief and Rehabilitation Operations, 124

Office of Price Administration (OPA), 68; enforcement of regulations of, 66

Office of Price Administration and Civilian Supply (OPACS), 57

Office of Procurement and Material (OP&M), 87, 88

Office of Production Management (OPM), 56, 57, 58, 80, 105

Office of Scientific Research and Development (OSRD), 42, 70

Office of War Information (OWI), 69, 105

Office of War Mobilization (OWM), 74, 89

Office of War Mobilization and Reconversion (OWMR), 78

Ofstie, R. A., 248-49

Olick, Arthur S., cited, 417

OLLA, *see* Lend-Lease Administration

OPA, *see* Office of Price Administration

OP&M, *see* Office of Procurement and Material

OPD, *see* Operations Division, War Department

"Open Door" policy, 26

"Operation Candor," 398-400

"Operation Wheaties," 400-01

Operations Coordinating Board (OCB), 389, 390, 409

Operations Division, War Department, 84, 87, 96, 97, 106, 108, 126

OPM, *see* Office of Production Management

Oppenheimer, J. Robert, 162, 251, 253, 255, 399, 400; *see also* Oppenheimer hearings

Oppenheimer hearings, 247, 420

OSRD, *see* Office of Scientific Research and Development

OVERLORD, *see* Cross-Channel invasion

OWI, *see* Office of War Information

OWM, *see* Office of War Mobilization

## P

Pace, Frank, Jr., 232, 263, 264, 320, 343
Pacific operations, World War II, 103, 117; allocation of resources to, 111-12
Palestine, 221
Pan American Union, 33
*Panay* incident, 22, 26
Papen, Franz von, 14
Patterson, Robert P., 58, 68, 81, 82, 84, 109, 151, 161, 165, 166, 171, 172, 173, 174, 177, 201, 203
Patton, George S., Jr., 288
Peace Conference of 1919, 3
Peace efforts of U. S., pre-war, 28-29, 47
Pearl Harbor, 61, 63, 75, 80, 97; investigations of, 64, 65, 107, 155, 166
Pearson, Lester B., 299, 314
Perkins, Frances, 23
Permanent Joint Board on Defense Canada–United States, 34
Pétain, Henri, 46; *see also* Vichy, France
Philippines: fortification of, 24, 29; independence of, 26, 29, 124; and Japanese expansion, 20; MacArthur's proposal to evacuate, 310; as Pacific base, 27; and pre-war defense plans, 24, 25, 26, 27; retaking of, 117
"Phony war," 37, 54
Pike, Sumner Tucker, 253
Plowden, Edwin, 356
Poland: German invasion of, 36, 37, 54
Policy Planning Board of NSC, 389, 390, 409
Policy Planning Staff, State Department, 202, 410
Pratt, John Lockwood, 20
President's Committee on Administrative Management, 43
Price, Byron, 68
Price control, 39, 65, 116; *see also* Emergency Price Control Act; Office of Price Administration; Office of Price Administration and Civilian Supply
Priorities, administration of, World War II, 84
Production goals, World War II, 80
Progressives, 16
Propaganda, official use of, 90, 116
Protective Mobilization Plan, 27
Psychological Strategy Board, 389
Public Works Administration (PWA), 23
Purvis, Arthur B., 58
Pusan, 267, 270, 274, 298, 306
Pyongyang, 283, 286, 301

## Q

Quebec conference, 1943, 130
Quezon, Manuel, 117, 310
Quinlan, Robert J., cited, 418

## R

Radford, Arthur W., 170, 247, 248, 249, 377, 378, 386, 402-03, 404
Radway, Lawrence I., 141
Rationing, 64, 65, 77
Reagan, Michael D., cited, 417, 419
Reciprocal trade agreements, 15, 28
Rent control: constitutionality of, 65
Reorganization Act, 1939, 43
Reorganization Plan No. 6, 379-87; Hearings on, cited, 420
Reorganizations, *see* Military reorganizations, post-war; National Security Act; *and in World War II under* War Department, Navy Department
Republic of Korea, *see* South Korea
Research and Development Board, 180, 184, 381
Reserve Act of 1955, 372, 408
Reynaud, Paul, 39
Richardson, James O., 33, 146-47, 149, 150; *see also* Richardson Committee
Richardson Committee, 146, 152
Ridgway, Matthew B., 306, 309, 404; as CINCFE, 357; cited, 419; 8th Army commander in Korea, 302, 306, 313; and Korean Armistice negotiations, 331, 350, 351; quoted, 306, 313, 364, 404; as SACEUR, 364
Roberts, Owen J., 65; *see also* Roberts Commission
Roberts Commission, 107
Robertson, Walter S., 407
Robinson, Samuel M., 82, 87, 88
Rockefeller, Nelson A., 358, 379; *see also* Reorganization Plan No. 6
ROK (Republic of Korea), *see* South Korea
Roles and missions, *see under* Military reorganizations, post-war
Rommel, Erwin, 63, 115
Roosevelt, Franklin D.: characterization of as President, 133; Charlottesville speech of, 37, 40; and Churchill, 37, 39-40, 95, 119; and cross-Channel invasion, 118; and Darlan, 120-21; and de Gaulle recognition, 121, 123; and Eastern Europe, 119; and German zonal boundaries, 130-31; and Hopkins, 35, 40, 45, 94, 95, 134; and Hull, 94; and Japanese and

Nazi threat, 23, 32; and the Joint Board, 92; and Joint Chiefs of Staff, 45, 105, 109, 110-13; and MacArthur, 22, 267; and Marshall, 111; and the military, 22-24 (*see also* and Joint Chiefs of Staff, *above*); and military government, 124; and Munich settlement, 31; and Philippines, 117; and pre-war economic mobilization, 53-57; and pre-war foreign policy, 15, 17, 28, 37-43; "quarantine" speech of, 17, 19; responsibility of for strategic direction of war, 100; seven-point stabilization program of, 88-89; and Soviet Union, 102-03; and Spanish civil war, 30-31; and Standing Liaison Committee, 19; and third term, 40; and United Nations, 3; and war production, 88; and War Shipping Administration, 113; working habits of, 44-45, 92-93; and Yalta, 133-35

Roosevelt, Theodore, 27, 197

Root, Elihu, 185, 188

Rosen, S. McKee: cited, 416; quoted, 100

Rovere, Richard H., cited, 345, 419

Royal Air Force (RAF), 107

Royall, Kenneth C., 156

Rusk, Dean, 302, 303

Russell, Richard B., 326

Russia, *see* Soviet Union

Russo-Japanese War, 27

## S

SACEUR (Supreme Allied Command in Europe), 356-57; *see also* Eisenhower, Dwight D.; Ridgway, Matthew B.

Sachs, Alexander, 41

SACLANT (Supreme Allied Command for sea warfare), 356, 359

Salerno, *see* Italy, allied landing in

Salter, James Arthur, 101

Saltonstall, Leverett, 341

Santayana, George, quoted, 3, 8

Sarnoff, David, 379

Schlesinger, Arthur M., Jr., cited, 345, 419

Schuman, Robert, 338

Scientists: and May-Johnson bill, 161-62; in World War II, 70-71

Second front, *see* Cross-Channel invasion

Second War Powers Act, 64

Selective Service System, 38-39, 92; age limits under, 63; deferments under, 71-72, 77; monthly draft by, World War II, 74; post-war proposals re, 212, 213, 214, 215, 219, 220; renewal of, 1941, 63; *see also* Reserve Act of 1955; Selec-

tive Training and Service Act, 1940; Universal military training

Selective Training and Service Act, 1940, 42, 43

Seoul, 274, 283, 301, 306, 316, 340

Services of Supply, *see* Army Services of Supply

Seventh Fleet: and Formosa Strait, 261, 262, 263, 268

Sherman, Forrest, 262, 272, 299, 311, 312, 343

Sherwood, Robert E: cited, 8, 39, 69, 417; and OWI, 69; quoted, 95, 115

Shipping problems, World War II, 78-79, 101, 112-13; *see also* War Shipping Administration

Short, Dewey, 168

Short, Walter Campbell, 106

Sinuiju, 287, 289, 290

SLC, *see* Standing Liaison Committee

Smith, Adam, 15

Smith, Frederic Harrison, Jr., 148*n*

Smith, Harold, 43, 113

Smith Committee, 64-65

Smyth, Henry DeWolf, 70, 253; cited, 416

Snell, Edwin M., cited, 415

Snipers' Ridge–Triangle Hill, 366

Snyder, John W., 271

Somers, H. M., cited, 416

Somervell, Brehon B., 23, 81, 82, 83, 84, 87, 109, 113, 116 126

SOS, *see* Army Services of Supply

South Korea: attack on, 260, 261; evacuation of occupation troops from, 1949, 236, 244, 260; order of U. S. military aid to, 262-63; strikes in, 1948, 210; troops of in Korean War, 276, 277, 278, 283, 284, 285, 294; UN call for assistance to, 263; UN cease-fire order in, 261; *see also* Korea; Korean War; Syngman Rhee

Soviet Union: and China, 191, 192, 193, 194, 292; denounced by Truman, 213-14; and Eastern Europe, 102, 118-19, 133; exclusion of from Anglo-American coalition, 98, 99, 102-03; and Far Eastern claims, 133; German invasion of, 37, 42, 102; and German zonal boundaries, 128-32; goals of, World War II, 92; and Japan, 133; and Korean War, 271, 273, 305, 307, 330, 350; launching of satellite by, 408, 412; and lend-lease, 42, 45, 49, 57, 102, 103; military aggression by, 333; military capabilities of, 1953, 395-96; position of after World

Soviet Union (*continued*)
War II, 4; possession of intercontinental ballistic missile, 412; possession of nuclear weapons by, 200, 207, 245-47, 249, 250, 252, 255, 333, 335, 400; and postwar tensions, 187, 192, 193, 194, 199, 200, 202, 204, 205, 210, 221-22, 223-24, 280, 333 (*see also* Berlin blockade; Cold war); and U. S. atomic monopoly, 157-60, 163-64

Spaatz, Carl H. ("Tooey"), 148, 215, 227

SPAB, *see* Supply Priorities and Allocations Board

Spanish civil war, 17, 18, 30-31, 35; *see also* Neutrality Act

Spofford, Charles Milton, 335, 342, 357

Stabilization Act, 1942, 89

Stalin, Joseph V., 111, 135, 191, 194, 221, 393

Stalingrad, 102

Standing Liaison Committee (SLC), 19, 33, 34, 43, 47, 97

Stark, Harold R., 38, 50, 97, 106, 107, 109

Stassen, Harold E., 388

State Department: and German zonal boundaries, 129-32; and Japanese negotiations, 51-52; and JCS in Korean War period, 302; and Latin American solidarity, 45-46; and lend-lease, 49; and McCarthy, 257, 258; and NATO, 335; and occupation policies, 125, 126, 127, 128, 129; Policy Planning Staff of, 202, 410; post-war inter-departmental relationships of, 7-8; pre-war role of, 28-30, 45-52; and Vichy, France, 46, 95; wartime role of, 92-97; "White Paper" on China, 196, 236, 244, 420; and Yalta, 134

State-War-Navy Coordinating Committee (SWNCC), 96, 97, 133

Stein, Harold, cited, 417

Stettinius, Edward R., Jr., 53, 55, 56, 94, 97, 134

Stevenson, Adlai E., 376

Stilwell, Joseph Warren ("Vinegar Joe"), 103-04, 117, 190

Stimson, Henry L., 8, 70, 111, 197; and A-bomb, 41, 156, 157-60; appointment of as Secretary of War, 40; and AR-CADIA, 97; cited, 417; and Japanese expansion, 16, 20; memoirs, quoted, 93-94, 146, 157, 158, 185, 188, 190; and National Security Act, 185; and occupation policies, 124, 126, 187-88, 190; and Philippines, 117; and pre-war foreign policy, 28, 38; resignation of as Secretary of War, 159; and Roosevelt, 45, 94, 109; and Stilwell, 117; and unification, 146, 150; and War Shipping Administration, 113

Strasbourg, 123

Strategic Air Command, 201, 214, 240, 248

Strategic bombing, *see* Air power, post-war strategy and; Finletter Commission on Air Policy; "Massive retaliation" policy

Stratemeyer, George E., 287

Strauss, Lewis L., 251, 253, 399, 400

Stresemann, Gustav, 14

Suez crisis, 391, 408

Sullivan, John L., 241

"Super," *see* Hydrogen bomb

Supply Priorities and Allocations Board (SPAB), 57, 58, 80, 105

Supreme Court: wartime role of, 65

Supreme Court–packing controversy, 31

Surplus farm commodities, wartime use of, 77

Swanson, Claude A., 34, 44

SWNCC, *see* State-War-Navy Coordinating Committee

Swope, Herbert Bayard, 176

Symington, W. Stuart, 215

Syngman Rhee, 264, 306, 405; release of Communist prisoners by, 406-07

Szilard, Leo, 161

**T**

Taber, John, 198, 416

Taegu, 270

Taft, Robert A., 40, 221, 340-41, 346, 370, 393

Taft, William Howard, 27

Taylor, Maxwell D., 404

Teheran, 104

Teller, Edward, 251, 255

Temporary Council Committee (TCC), 355, 356, 357, 396

Tenth Corps: in Korean War, 274, 275, 283, 289-301 *passim*, 306

Thermonuclear energy, *see* Hydrogen bomb; Nuclear energy; Nuclear weapons

Thirty-eighth Parallel: as basis for ceasefire negotiations, 300, 329; issue of in Korean War, 263, 272-77, 316, 339; Ridgway's drive to, 313

Thomas, Elbert D., 155, 169-70

Thomas, J. Parnell, 168

Thomas bill, 170

Thomas Committee, 170

"Three Wise Men," *see* Temporary Council Committee
TORCH, 98; *see also* North Africa
Towers, John H., 227
Trieste, 203
Truman, Harry S.: and atomic bomb custody, 227; and atomic energy control, 155, 159, 160, 161, 163, 165, 166, 167; and budgetary ceilings, 171, 198, 238-39; and Chiang Kai-shek, 196; cited, 419; and Congress in Korean War period, 339-50; and H-bomb, 5, 254; and Marshall, 197; memoirs quoted, 148, 154, 155, 158-59, 161, 164-65, 166-67, 254, 261-62, 263, 273, 279, 289, 292, 294-95, 298, 300, 317, 319, 320; and military reorganization, postwar, 154, 171, 173; and military support for South Korea, 261-64; and National Security Council, 182; 1948 election of, 231; and post-war China, 195; and post-war military requirements, 148; as President, World War II, 135; and rearmament of West Germany, 336; Soviet Union denounced by, 213-14; and United Nations, 3; and universal military training, 155, 209, 213, 214, 219
Truman-Attlee conference, 1950, 343, 345
Truman Committee, 64, 82
Truman Doctrine, 176, 199
Truman-MacArthur clash: and civil-military issue, 142, 259-60, 289, 320, 325, 328, 333; and Formosa, 268-70; and Lincoln-McClellan differences, compared, 267, 317; and relief of MacArthur, 299, 317-20; VFW message, 270-72; Wake Island meeting, 279-80; *see also* Chinese Nationalists, proposed use of in Korean War; MacArthur, Douglas, and Korean War; MacArthur Hearings; Whitney, Courtney
Tugwell, Rexford G., cited, 22
Turkey: acceptance of in NATO, 357; U. S. aid to, 176, 177, 199, 202, 205
"Twelve Apostles," *see* Temporary Council Committee
Twining, Nathan F., 403
Tydings amendment, Selective Service Act, 72

## U

Ukraine, 135
UMT, *see* Universal military training
United Nations (UN), 103, 115, 133, 155, 187, 204; and atomic energy, 159, 163;

Charter of, 135, 222; Declaration of, 98; and Korean War, 261, 262, 263, 273, 274, 275-77; 286, 287-88, 301, 314, 315, 316
United Nations Relief and Rehabilitation Administration (UNRRA), 79, 123
United States Employment Service (USES), 72, 74
Universal military training: adoption of, 371, 372; post-war proposals for, 155, 178, 203, 209, 211, 212, 213, 214, 215, 219; *see also* Reserve Act of 1955; Selective Service System
UNRRA, *see* United Nations Relief and Rehabilitation Administration
Uranium Committee, 41
Urey, Harold C., 162
USES, *see* United States Employment Service
*U. S. News and World Report*: cited, 271; quoted, 404-05
*U.S.S. United States,* 240, 243

## V

Vandenberg, Arthur H., 160-61, 236; *see also* Vandenberg resolution
Vandenberg, Hoyt, 241, 251, 262, 327, 403
Vandenberg resolution, 222, 224, 237, 347
Van Fleet, James A., 351, 363-64
Van Zandt, James E., 242, 244
VE-Day, 78, 90, 133, 135
Veterans of Foreign Wars: MacArthur message to, 270-72
VFW, *see* Veterans of Foreign Wars
Vichy, France, 46, 95, 120
Victory Program, 58, 80
Vinson, Carl, 26, 239, 242, 244, 245, 249, 403
Vinson, Fred M., 89, 158
VJ-Day, 157
Von Newmann, *see* Newmann, John von
Von Papen, *see* Papen, Franz von

## W

Wages-and-hours act, 31
Wake Island, Truman-McArthur meeting on, 279-80
Walker, Walton, 284, 285, 291, 293, 294, 298, 302
Wallace, Henry A., 57, 126, 159
Walsh, David I., 63, 150, 170-71
War Council, 43, 180, 184
War criminals: post-war trials of, 65, 155

War Department: peacetime and wartime roles compared, 93; reorganization of, World War II, 108-09

War Food Administration, 101

War Labor Board (WLB), 75, 76

War Manpower Commission (WMC), 72-75, 90, 105

War Plans, see Joint Army-Navy Basic War Plans

War Plans Division, War Department (WPD), 106, 108

War Production Board (WPB), 73, 74, 77, 80-87, 89, 90, 101, 105

War, pure: military doctrine of, 113-16

War Resources Administration (WRA), 54, 55

War Resources Board (WRB), 53, 54, 55

War Shipping Administration (WSA), 73, 78, 101, 105, 110, 112, 113, 127

Watson, Mark S., cited, 51, 415

Webb, James E., 232

Wedemeyer, Albert C., 25, 104, 188, 191-92, 193, 195, 203, 204, 329-30

Welles, Sumner, 19, 34, 45, 47, 48, 51, 94

West Germany: and EDC, 356; plan for including troops of in NATO forces, 343; rearmament of, 336-39, 341-42, 396; see also Germany, occupation zones in

Western Hemisphere, see Good Neighbor policy; Hemisphere defense; Latin America; Monroe Doctrine

Wheeler (Burton K.) "father-draft bill," 72

Wherry, Kenneth S., 337, 346

White, William Allen, 42

Whitehill, Walter M., cited, 417

"White Paper" on China, 196, 236, 244, 420

Whitney, Courtney: cited, 419; quoted, 189, 268, 270-71, 271-72, 280, 286, 290, 293, 303-04, 309, 314

Wilcox, W. W., cited, 416

Willkie, Wendell L., 40

Wilmot, Chester, cited, 417

Wilson, Charles Edward (General Electric), 85, 343

Wilson, Charles Erwin (General Motors), 377, 382, 404

Wilson, Woodrow, 3

Winant, John G., 95, 128, 129, 130, 131

WLB, see War Labor Board

WMC, see War Manpower Commission

Wonsan, 275, 278, 283

Wood, Leonard, 188

Woodbridge, George, cited, 416

Woodring, Harry H., 34, 41, 44

Woodrum, Clifton A., 146

Woodrum Committee, 146

Working Security Committee (WSC), 96, 129, 131

Works Progress Administration (WPA), 23

World War II, 61-136; allied basic strategy in, 50, 85, 110, 111-12, 135; divergent political aims of allies in, 105; surrenders of enemy powers in, 120, 121-22, 129-30; U. S. entry into, 61-62; U. S. goal in, 91

Worth, Cedric R., 241-42, 244

WPB, see War Production Board

WPD, see War Plans Division, War Department

WRA, see War Resources Administration

WRB, see War Resources Board

WSA, see War Shipping Administration

WSC, see Working Security Committee

# Y

Yalta conference, 104, 133-35

Yalu River, 275, 276, 278, 279, 283-95 passim, 305, 368